Astragalus purshii var. *tinctus,*
Woollypod Milkvetch

Spine: Sierra Primrose • Julie S. Carville
Front Cover: Arroyo Lupine • Chet Blackburn
   The South Yuba River from the Buttermilk Bend Trail • Karen Callahan
Back Cover: Mountain Meadow at Tahoe; Alpine Lily • Julie S. Carville
   Davy's Gumweed; Sierra Nevada Pea; Rigid Hedge Nettle;
   Foothill Penstemon • Karen Callahan
Half-Title Page: Indian Warrior • Karen Callahan
Title Page: Paper Onion, Hartweg's Sidalcea, and Pratten's Buckwheat
   at Hell's Half Acre • Cindy Rubin
Page v, above: Woollypod Milkvetch • Richard Hanes
Pages vi–vii: Sweet Trillium at Bear Valley; Low Phacelia • Julie S. Carville
Page viii: Springtime • Richard Hanes
Pages 66–67: Mountain Mule Ears and lupine at Barker Peak at Tahoe • Julie S. Carville
Page 374: Mountain Pride at Grouse Ridge • Julie S. Carville

Caution:
All participants in the recreational activities suggested by this book must assume
responsibility for their own actions and safety.

Disclaimer:
We discourage the gathering of native plants for a variety of reasons: It is against the
law without a permit; many plants have become rare or extinct due to excessive
gathering; and wild foods used internally or externally, based solely on book write-ups,
can be misidentified or incorrectly prepared, which can cause illness or death
through allergic reactions or poisoning. Neither the authors nor the publisher can be
held responsible for claims arising from the ingestion or use of plants as described
in this book.

The publisher has made every effort to ensure the accuracy and currency of the
information contained in this book. Please feel free to let us know if you find
information in this book that needs to be corrected or updated.
Your comments and suggestions are always welcome.

Wildflowers

of Nevada and Placer Counties, California

Wildflowers

of Nevada and Placer Counties, California

Redbud Chapter
California Native Plant Society

In association with
CNPS Press • Sacramento

Redbud Chapter
California Native Plant Society

Text: © 2007 Redbud Chapter,
California Native Plant Society
Photographs: © by the respective photographers

The Checklist, along with a Common Names list, are available on the Redbud Chapter's Web site: *www.redbud-cnps.org.*

Library of Congress Cataloging-in-Publication Data

Wildflowers of Nevada and Placer counties, California / Redbud Chapter, California Native Plant Society ; in association with CNPS Press.
    p. cm.
  Summary: "Describes and illustrates with color photos 520 species of wildflowers found in Nevada and Placer Counties, California. Also provides a physical description of the area, places to see wildflowers, Native American uses, and a complete plant checklist, which includes thirty-eight percent of the plants known to grow wild in California"—Provided by publisher.
  Includes bibliographical references and index.
  ISBN 978-0-943460-48-2
  1. Wild flowers—California—Nevada County—Guidebooks. 2. Wild flowers—California—Placer County—Guidebooks. 3. Wild flowers—California—Nevada County—Identification. 4. Wild flowers—California—Placer County—Identification. 5. Nevada County (Calif.)—Guidebooks. 6. Placer County (Calif.)—Guidebooks.
  I. California Native Plant Society. Redbud Chapter. II. CNPS Press.
  QK149.W55 2007
  582.1309794'37—dc22   2007025110

Book Committee Chairman: Chet Blackburn
Copyeditor: Anna Reynolds Trabucco, Edify Editing
Publication Design and Production: Cindy Rubin, Harmony Works
Photo Production and Illustrations: Richard Hanes and Bill Wilson
Published in association with CNPS Press, Sacramento, California
Printed in Hong Kong through Global Interprint, Santa Rosa, California
Printed on 100% recycled paper with soy inks

$\mathcal{T}$able of Contents

Phacelia humilis,
Low Phacelia

*D*edication

This book is dedicated to the "environmental whackos" of the world whose vision extends beyond the limited horizon of financial gain. These are the people who are able to wander off into woodlands and waysides with a sense of wonder, an appreciation for natural beauty, and a tolerance for other forms of life that share our planet, and who work diligently to provide future generations with that same opportunity.

Two members of the Redbud Chapter who had those qualities and deserve special mention are no longer with us.

Lillian Mott loved California's wildflowers and had such an intimate knowledge of Nevada County and its flora that she was inevitably sought out by visiting botanists, including such notables as Gordon True and J. Thomas Howell. Lillian, her husband Doc, and Gordon True spent many hours roaming the Nevada County landscape compiling plant lists for specific locations. From 1963 through 1968 Lillian wrote a series of weekly articles on wildflowers that appeared in the *Sacramento Bee* weekend gardening section and she was a regular contributor to the Grass Valley *Union* during the same period. She led numerous field trips for the Redbud Chapter, introduced many people to the wildflowers of the county, including some of the authors of this book, and was one of the strongest advocates for preserving Nevada County's environment. In 1995 Lillian was honored with a California Native Plant Society fellowship in recognition of her many years of disseminating knowledge of our native flora and her efforts to preserve it.

Kate McBride was one of the original members of the committee established to produce this book and was scheduled to write some of the text, but passed away suddenly before having the chance to do so. She was a nursery owner at Tahoe before retiring and moving to Grass Valley. She was known for her pleasant personality, enthusiasm,

2

NANCY BASCOM

Kate McBride being her usual
enthusiastic and fun-loving self.

and her omnipresence in Redbud
Chapter activities. She was the
type of friend and member that
every chapter covets. Whenever a
call would go out for volunteers,
Kate almost had to be physically
restrained; such was her enthusiasm to advance the cause of pro-
tecting our native plants.

This book is dedicated to them
and to the many others like them,
past, present, and future, who
work hard to preserve the quality
of life and experiences all too
rapidly disappearing from today's
world.

MOTT FAMILY

Lillian Mott immersed in the beauty of lupines on Grouse Ridge, a place that was
very close to her heart.

$\mathcal{I}$ntroduction

More than 2,000 species, subspecies, and varieties of native and non-native vascular plants are known to occur within Nevada and Placer Counties. We have selected over 500 of the wildflower species most likely to be seen, due either to their conspicuous nature or to their abundance. Also covered are a few plants that may not be commonly found but are distinguished by some unique feature or by their rarity. This book covers the annual and perennial herbaceous flowering plants and a few of the smaller shrub (subshrub) species.

This is the first of two books on the native plants in our two counties. The second book will describe the trees, shrubs, ferns, grasses, rushes, and sedges.

This book is a project of the Redbud Chapter of the California Native Plant Society and was undertaken on a voluntary basis by participating members. Any income derived from the book will be used in support of the chapter's mission and goals. The Redbud Chapter is fortunate in having within its membership a number of knowledgeable botanists, both amateur and professional, as well as a number of accomplished photographers, writers, and individuals with publishing and computer technical skills. This book is a natural outcome of such a happy circumstance.

The Editorial Committee was established in April 1999 and potential authors and photographers contacted. The book was originally intended to be a two-year project involving seven members, but the scope of the book, the number of people participating in its preparation, and the length of time required to produce the book have all expanded beyond original expectations. The book, although published later than anticipated, is the better for it. The Editorial Committee, authors, and photographers involved in this project follow.

Chet Blackburn
Chet served as the book project coordinator. He has been a Redbud Chapter president, vice president, field trip coordinator, publications chair, and treasurer. With varied interests in natural history, he was also editor of an international botanical journal, the *Journal of the Bromeliad Society,* for seven years, has been a director at large for the California Native Plant Society, and served on the board of directors of the Placer Nature Center.

Karen Callahan
Karen is an accomplished photographer and experienced botanist. She has spent many hours in the backcountry of the northern Sierra Nevada assembling an impressive collection of wildflower photos. Her images of Sierra landscapes and plant life have been published in several regional books and magazines. She has served as Redbud Chapter president and as newsletter editor and rare plant coordinator.

Julie Carville
Local naturalist and author of *Hiking Tahoe's Wildflower Trails,* Julie has led wildflower hikes in Nevada and Placer Counties for over 25 years. She has written and photographed for numerous publications and was a contributing author of *California's Wild Gardens.* A cofounder and past president of the Tahoe Chapter of CNPS, she is presently the publications chair of the Redbud Chapter.

Carolyn Chainey-Davis
Carolyn is a botanical consultant and environmental advocate specializing in restoration projects. She has worked for several environmental consulting firms and has served as president, conservation chair, field trip coordinator, and rare plant coordinator for the Redbud Chapter. She has played a major role in helping to preserve several biologically important locations in Nevada County.

Monica Finn
Monica is a biologist employed by Caltrans, specializing in erosion control and revegetation projects. Monica has served as the Placer County vice president of the Redbud Chapter, has served on the chapter's board of directors, and has been a frequent volunteer involved in organizing the chapter's plant sales.

Richard Hanes
Richard is a retired soil scientist from the US Forest Service and has been photographing Nevada County wildflowers for many years. His knowledge of plants is extensive, as is his collection of plant photos. He has

served as president, rare plant coordinator, and membership chair of the Redbud Chapter.

Vicki Lake

Vicki is a staff environmental scientist for the California Department of Fish and Game, a former member of the Redbud Chapter board of directors, and a frequent volunteer at the chapter's plant sales.

Shawna Martinez

Shawna is a biology instructor at Sierra College in Rocklin, and a two-term president of the Redbud Chapter, including serving as the chapter's founding president.

Roger McGehee

Roger is a former naturalist for the National Park Service and for the Yosemite Institute in Yosemite, and a retired high school biology teacher. He has served as president, field trip coordinator, and newsletter editor of the Redbud Chapter of the California Native Plant Society.

Cindy Rubin

Cindy is a professional electronic prepress production artist, specializing in page layout and typography. She holds a BS in Design from UC Davis. She has a lifelong love of nature and has been an amateur nature photographer for several years. She did the layout for this book and currently does the page layout for the Redbud Chapter newsletter.

Kathy Van Zuuk

Kathy is a Tahoe National Forest botanist and has been the noxious weed coordinator for over ten years. She is currently the district ecologist/botanist for the Yuba River Ranger District.

Bobbi Navickis Wilkes

Bobbi, a physiologist, is a former field trip coordinator, newsletter editor, membership chair, and publications chair for the Redbud Chapter. She is making extensive use of native plants in her landscaping and is one of the original seven members of the Editorial Committee for this book.

Bill Wilson

Bill is a retired Computer Sciences instructor at Modesto Junior College. He has a BA and MA in Biological Sciences and has lived or vacationed in the Sierra all of his life. He is the current Redbud Chapter Web site editor and the source of much of the technical advice required in the preparation of this book.

Although the people mentioned above were the largest contributors to this book, the quality of the publication has been enhanced by the contributions of many others.

Both Gordon True and Lillian Mott passed away before this project was even conceived, but their influence is present in a number of ways. Gordon True's fascination with the flora of Nevada County resulted in his assembling a checklist of Nevada County plants that became the starting point for this book. Lillian Mott, the local "guru" for Nevada County native plant enthusiasts for many years, was responsible for originally introducing some of our authors and photographers to the many special places and plants in Nevada County.

Some photographs used in the book were taken by the late, accomplished photographer Prentiss Ferguson, whose daughter, Karen Anderson, graciously provided them for our use. Other photographs were provided by Gordon J. Harrington, an amateur photographer with a large collection of photos of non-native species typically found in the Sacramento Valley. The following people also granted use of one or more of their photographs: Carol Witham, Michael Graf, Don Jacobson, Steve Matson, Virginia Moran, Brad Carter, Janell Hillman, Barry Rice, the Mott family, Nancy Bascom, and Lee Hayes.

Kate McBride, one of the original seven members of the Editorial Committee, helped define the book's content and approach.

Many thanks go to Anna Reynolds Trabucco, who took on the Herculean task of editing the text before its release for review. It was

KAREN CALLAHAN

A Redbud Chapter field trip group pauses to enjoy a view of the western Sierra foothills from Wolf Mountain.

certainly not a small job, considering the number of authors and their different styles. Thanks also go to Jean Blackburn and Diane Wilson for logistical support (food and refreshments) during our long editing and review sessions and to John Button and Chuck Godfrey for technical assistance.

We would like to thank the following individuals for reviewing the book before publication and for the suggestions they subsequently provided: Dr. Lee Kavaljian and Dr. Michael Baad, botany instructors at California State University, Sacramento; Joe Medeiros, biology instructor at Sierra College; John Krogsrud, a lifelong resident of Placer County with a deep interest in its natural history; Kathi Keville, ethnobotany teacher and president of the American Herb Association; Holly Forbes and Steve Hartman of the California Native Plant Society Publications Committee; Brad Carter, an expert on the Lily family in California, who contributed to the descriptions in that section; and Julie Becker, who provided a perspective from a novice's point of view.

And finally, we would especially like to thank the members of the Redbud Chapter of the California Native Plant Society who have volunteered at the numerous plant sales sponsored by the chapter over the years. Without them, the financing needed for this book would not have been available.

Chet Blackburn

Members of the Editorial Committee from left to right: Julie Carville, Cindy Rubin, Karen Callahan, Roger McGehee, Chet Blackburn, Richard Hanes, and Bill Wilson.

LEE HAYES

State of California

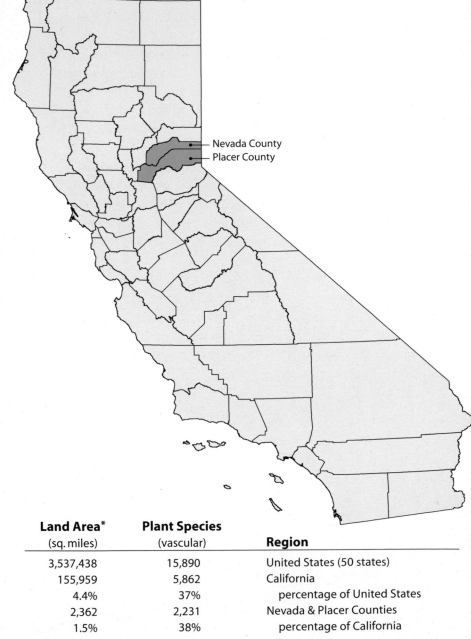

— Nevada County
— Placer County

Land Area* (sq. miles)	Plant Species (vascular)	Region
3,537,438	15,890	United States (50 states)
155,959	5,862	California
4.4%	37%	percentage of United States
2,362	2,231	Nevada & Placer Counties
1.5%	38%	percentage of California

* does not include water area

*D*escription of the Area Covered by This Book

Richard Hanes and Chet Blackburn

Nevada and Placer Counties are located in Northern California northeast of Sacramento in the northern Sierra Nevada. Their western edges lie in the valley grasslands and lower foothills along the eastern side of the Sacramento Valley. The counties then extend eastward, over the crest of the Sierra to the Nevada state line, which forms the eastern boundary.

Much of the northern boundary of Nevada County is formed by the Middle Yuba River, and the southern boundary of Placer County by the Middle Fork of the American River and the Rubicon River.

The smaller and northernmost of the two counties is Nevada County, an area occupying 974 square miles. The shape of the county resembles that of the small pistol known as the Derringer, a popular icon of the fictional old West. The population of Nevada County in 2000 was slightly more than 92,000 people.

Placer County lies south of Nevada County and covers an area of 1,504 square miles. The population of Placer County in 2000 was just under 250,000, most of which was concentrated in the populous western edge of the county in the cities of Roseville and Rocklin, to which continuous subdivisions from Sacramento now extend. The western edge of Placer County is one of the fastest growing areas in the state.

The Sierra Nevada is the dominant feature of the area but the two counties are much more diverse than that situation might imply. Elevations range from under 40 feet in Placer County at the juncture where the Placer, Sacramento, and Sutter County boundaries converge, to 9,143 feet at Mt. Lola in Nevada County and 9,006 feet at Granite Chief in Placer County.

The Sierra Nevada began forming approximately 210 million years ago when molten magma beneath what was then a shallow sea floor began to slowly cool to form a huge granite batholith. In the process

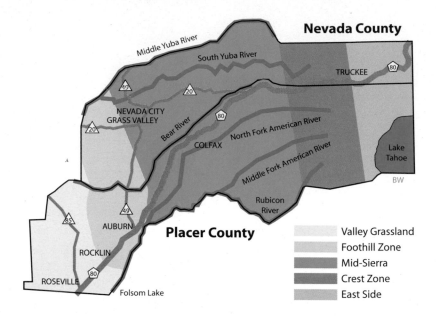

it began lifting the sedimentary rock forming the sea floor. The old rock layers were lifted as a block and tilted upward, resembling a partially open trap door with the western slope gradually ascending eastward to the summit, then dropping sharply on the eastern side.

Although the gradient of the eastern slope is steep, it is not as steep as it is in most parts of the southern Sierra because in our area the descent is into the high Tahoe and Truckee basins that lie between the Sierra and the Carson Range in Nevada. The elevation at the surface of Lake Tahoe is 6,225 feet, while that of Truckee is just under 6,000 feet.

The western slope is heavily dissected by numerous fast-flowing streams that have carved narrow ridges and deep canyons into the older rock formations. This process has resulted in the formation of some of the most rugged country to be found anywhere in the state. The largest watercourses are the North and Middle Forks of the American River, the Rubicon River, the Bear River, and the Yuba River, but there are numerous other permanent and intermittent streams feeding into them.

The headwaters of the major drainages, most of which are fed by melting snow, start in the glaciated crest zone. The headwaters for the South Yuba River, the North and Middle Forks of the American

River, the Bear River, Rubicon River, and Truckee River all start in our area. The Middle Yuba River headwaters are just to the north in Sierra County.

There are numerous natural and man-made lakes in this part of the Sierra. Our area includes a portion of Lake Tahoe, as well as Donner Lake, Fordyce Lake, French Lake, and many smaller lakes created by both glaciations and human beings. Some of the major reservoirs are Boca, Prosser, Independence, French Meadows, Bowman, Spaulding, Ralston, Rollins, and a portion of Folsom Lake.

Much of the area covered in this book is within the Tahoe and El Dorado National Forests, although there are many parcels in private ownership that form a checkerboard pattern throughout the National Forest lands.

All three of the major categories of rock (igneous, sedimentary, and metamorphic) are found within the two counties and each is found in abundance, including but not limited to such different kinds of rock as granite, andesite, diorite, sandstone, shale, limestone, slate, greenstone, various schists, serpentine, gabbro, and others. The geology is so diverse and complex that in some areas, such as the American River Canyon outside of Auburn, all three major types occur within short distances of each other.

As would be expected, the various soils derived from weathering of the many different types of rock are themselves unique.

The serpentine and gabbro soils in particular represent a special situation. They are high in heavy metal content such as chromium and nickel and deficient in the calcium, nitrogen, and phosphorus required for plant growth; hence they tend to be toxic or hostile to

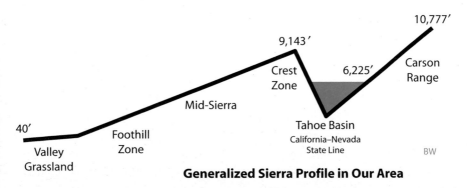

10,777'

9,143'

Carson Range

6,225'

Crest Zone

Mid-Sierra

40'

Foothill Zone

Valley Grassland

Tahoe Basin
California–Nevada State Line

BW

Generalized Sierra Profile in Our Area

the growth of many plant species. As a result they have developed a unique flora capable of withstanding those conditions better than other plants.

Valley Grassland

The western edge of our area once consisted primarily of valley grassland, often interspersed with numerous vernal pools. Now, however, much of it consists of subdivisions and shopping malls. The remaining unpopulated areas are devoted mostly to agriculture but remnants of the once abundant wildflower populations, although rapidly decreasing, still remain. Besides grasses and wildflowers, occasional large graceful Valley Oaks with their extensive branches sweeping nearly to the ground give the eastern edge of the grass-lands a parklike appearance. Meandering streams lined with willows and cottonwoods snake their way through the relatively flat landscape.

This western grassland area is characterized by hot dry summers and relatively mild but wet and often foggy winters. An average of 75 days each year have temperatures above 90°F, while minimum win-ter temperatures normally don't fall below the high 20s. Snowfall is very rare. Rainfall averages around 18 inches per year, with the aver-age rainfall amounts increasing as the elevation increases eastward, and the grasslands eventually give way to the lower foothills.

Foothill Zone

The foothills consist of gently sloping to moderately steep hills that have few conspicuous peaks. Elevation ranges from about 300 to 2,000 feet and the mean annual precipitation ranges between 18 and 45 inches. The foothill area is primarily vegetated with Blue Oak and Gray Pine woodlands but also includes vegetation associated with the numerous streams, as well as extensive areas of chaparral, and serpentine/gabbro chaparral. The summers are hot and dry, the winters wet and mild but usually free of the valley tule fog, allowing for more frequent light frosts. Snowfall is not common but does occur in some years. The foothill area is blessed in being one of the few places in the world where apples and oranges can be grown side by side. The growing season is long, the temperatures moderate,

JULIE S. CARVILLE

Tickseed and lupine bloom among oak woodlands in April along Ponderosa Way.

and there is just enough winter chill required for dormancy by most deciduous fruit trees without being so cold as to damage the more tender oranges and lemons. At an elevation around 1,300 feet, Auburn averages 36 inches of annual rainfall, twice as much as Roseville in the valley grasslands only 20 miles away.

Mid-Sierra

Eastward from the foothills, the western slope of the Sierra Nevada ascends relatively gently toward the crest. However, this mid-Sierra area is dominated by deeply incised canyons separated by long narrow ridges. Drainages are generally toward the west and southwest, with stream channels cutting through and across the various geologic formations. Precipitation typically ranges from 45 to 60 inches annually, with higher totals at some locations. Snowfall occurs every year but over most of the area it does not persist on the ground throughout the winter as it does at higher elevations. Grass Valley, at approximately 2,500 feet elevation at the western edge of this zone, averages 55 inches of annual precipitation, while Blue Canyon at

JULIE S. CARVILLE

Bigleaf Maples shelter a
mossy creek garden near
the Bear River.

5,300 feet averages 68 inches of precipitation. This zone is rich in
vegetation consisting mostly of species found in mixed conifer forests.

Crest Zone

The crest zone, or High Sierra, generally occurs above 6,000 feet
and has a mean annual precipitation of 60 to 70 inches, most of it in
the form of snow. The snow persists as a thick snowpack well into
the spring and early summer. Glaciers were once active from the crest
down to about 4,800 feet. Glaciation sculptured the present-day
crest zone, exposing large areas of glaciated granitic rock. Glacial till
and outwash material were deposited in basins and along drainages
at the margin of the crest glaciation. Vegetation ranges from primarily

JULIE S. CARVILLE

View of Sierra crest from Donner Peak near Donner Summit.

coniferous forests to low, windswept shrubbery and includes other plants associated with rock outcroppings, streams, and meadows.

East Side of the Sierra

On the other side of the crest, the area north and east of Truckee, locally referred to as the "east side," is a glacial plain dominated by sagebrush and pine. It is drier because of the rain-shadow effect of the crest. The mean annual precipitation ranges from 25 to 40 inches. The average annual precipitation at Truckee and Lake Tahoe is 32 inches.

Most of our weather moves in from the west and travels eastward over the Sierra, but sometimes a continental cold air front from the continental interior moves in a westward or southwestward direction. On those occasions, the Sierra actually serves as a barrier to keep California warmer. Winter temperatures on the east side of the Sierra tend to be considerably colder than those at the same elevations on the west side. For example, the coldest temperature ever recorded in California (–34°F) was recorded at Boca in Nevada County, and

Truckee is consistently among the coldest spots in nightly recorded temperatures in the contiguous United States.

An example of the sharp climatic differences due to elevation can be seen in the contrast between Rocklin and Blue Canyon, only 50 miles to the east. Rocklin, at an elevation of 250 feet, averages 75 days a year above 90°F and 16 days below freezing, while Blue Canyon, at 5,300 feet, averages less than 1 day a year above 90°F and 96 days below freezing.

Such incredible diversity in elevation, topography, climate, geology, and soils is responsible for the rich flora to be found here. Of the 5,862 species of plants listed in the 1993 edition of *The Jepson Manual: Higher Plants of California,* more than 2,000 of them can be found in our two-county area. Although the combined area of Nevada and Placer Counties occupies only 1.5 percent of California's 163,707 square miles, 38 percent of the plant species that are found within California can be found growing here.

RICHARD HANES

Native American grinding rock located near oak trees and the water of Clover Creek in Placer County. This area is planned for development.

*T*hreats To Native Plants

Vicki Lake, Cindy Rubin, Roger McGehee, and Chet Blackburn

There have been drastic changes in the natural environment from intensive use for agriculture, mining, timber harvesting, and land clearing for housing, business, and infrastructure. Our discussion highlights some of the most important threats to native flora related to the ongoing increase in human impact.

Development

Some of the threats to native plants, such as the loss of habitat through development, are so obvious that discussing them here is unnecessary, other than to point out that the effects of development always extend beyond the immediate piece of land being developed. Adjacent lands, even those that have been "preserved," are also changed forever. Drainage patterns are altered, runoff is accelerated, chemicals are introduced into the runoff, the introduction of pets alters the fauna and consequently the balance of life, migratory patterns are disrupted, and non-native animals and plants are inevitably introduced.

Non-native Invasive Plants

Non-native invasive plant species encroachment in particular is one of the gravest threats facing native ecosystems today. Invasive species decrease the biological diversity of native ecosystems by outcompeting and displacing native species. They can also reduce habitat quality for dependent native plant, fish, and wildlife species; reduce water quality and availability; poison wildlife and livestock; increase the risk of fire hazard; alter nutrient cycles; and contribute to soil erosion.

Native plants are species that historically occurred in a particular ecosystem, and are found growing within their natural range. They evolved over millions of years to fill unique ecological niches. They are kept in check in their native environment by insects, diseases, and competition with other species.

Non-native (also called *introduced* or *alien*) plants are native to other ecosystems, but are now found growing beyond their natural range. Whether intentionally or unintentionally, non-native plants escaped or were released or disseminated as a result of human activity. Early European settlers in North America, for instance, inadvertently brought non-native seeds with them in hay, grain, and ship ballasts. Activities such as clearing the land opened up niches for these non-native species to grow. Settlers also purposely brought plants from their home countries for food, fiber, medicinal, and ornamental uses. Non-native plant introductions in recent times are facilitated by extensive global trade and modern transportation systems. Many plants are introduced for erosion control, forage, and ornamental uses. Without the natural checks and balances of their native ecosystem, some introduced plants become invasive, reducing the diversity and abundance of native plants.

Invasive plant species (also called *pest plants, weeds,* or *noxious plants*) are non-native plants whose introduction causes significant changes in native species composition or abundance, community structure, or ecosystem function. Common characteristics of invasive plants include high reproductive output, good dispersal mechanisms, rapid growth rates, and the ability to adapt readily to different environmental conditions. Disturbed areas are generally more susceptible to invasion than undisturbed areas.

JULES, CARVILLE

Hillsides of once beautiful wildflowers have been smothered by English Ivy, which over the years has aggressively spread to cover large areas along the meandering road down into Edward's Crossing by the South Yuba River.

Here, Klamath Weed has
taken over land once
used for pasture.

KAREN CALLAHAN

Nevada and Placer Counties, endowed with expansive natural areas,
are increasingly being subjected to invasions by non-native plants. In
particular, invasive plant species take advantage of open niches presented after disturbance, such as along roadsides, in pastures, and
along riparian corridors. Their ability to disperse and reproduce
rapidly and abundantly lends them a competitive advantage during
establishment. Locally, invasive subcanopy trees and shrubs include
Tree of Heaven, Scotch Broom, and Himalayan Blackberry. Invasive
herbaceous plants include Yellow Star Thistle, English Ivy, Johnson
Grass, Klamath Weed/St. John's Wort, Hedge Parsley, Periwinkle, and
Woolly Mullein. Some species, such as Giant Reed, Salt Cedar, and
Pampas Grass, are more troublesome in other parts of the state but
are known in our area, though presently in limited distribution and
abundance.

As individuals and organized groups we can collectively minimize
the spread of invasive plant species and control existing stands.
Prevention is the most effective means of weed control. By familiar-
izing ourselves with the identification of invasive plants, we can
refrain from transplanting them to our properties and ensure that
we do not purchase them from nurseries. Several invasive species
are quite attractive, such as Scotch Broom, English Ivy, Tree of
Heaven, Giant Reed, and Pampas Grass. Being aware of changes in
our local environment is also crucial. New spot occurrences should
be targeted for control before further spread can occur. Subsequent
control efforts should be focused on larger populations.

Controlling invasive species is crucial to preserving native plant and wildlife populations. Control means to eradicate, suppress, reduce, or manage invasive species populations. Control prevents the spread of invasive species from areas where they are present, and involves steps such as restoration of native species and habitats to prevent further invasions.

Control efforts can be physical, biological, or chemical. Numerous resources are available to determine the best control method for a particular site. The publication entitled *Invasive Plants of California's Wildlands* (Bossard *et al.,* 2000) is a good starting point, as is contacting organizations focused on invasive plant species control. Effective control is generally realistic, although often permanent eradication cannot be achieved and ongoing monitoring and maintenance is required.

Common invasives in our area include:
- Scotch Broom (*Cytisus scoparius*)
- Himalayan Blackberry (*Rubus discolor*)
- Yellow Star Thistle (*Centaurea solstitialis*)
- Tree of Heaven (*Ailanthus altissima*)
- Johnson Grass (*Sorghum halepense*)
- English Ivy (*Hedera helix*)
- Klamath Weed/St. John's Wort (*Hypericum perforatum*)
- Hedge Parsley (*Torilis arvensis*)
- Periwinkle (*Vinca major*)
- Woolly Mullein (*Verbascum thapsus*)

Wildfires and Fire Suppression

The effects of fire and fire management policies are both complex and controversial topics. A lengthy discussion of either is beyond the scope of this book, but a brief discussion of some of the issues involved is relevant. Interested readers who wish to pursue the topic will find references in the bibliography.

In our Mediterranean climate, almost all rain and snowfall comes during the cool season. Our summers are hot and dry with rain rarely occurring, except for an occasional summer thunderstorm, especially in the mountains. Over the centuries, native plants have adapted to this situation. Some allow their above-ground parts to die off completely during this period, others drop many of their leaves and produce smaller, less lush leaves, and still others simply reduce moisture content in existing leaves. All of these adaptations increase the potential for fire.

Lightning-caused fires are not uncommon. Therefore, the plants that live in our counties, and the ecosystems that include them, have long adapted to a cycle of periodic fires. Some plants need fire in order for their seeds to germinate. Some are even known as "fire followers," appearing in great numbers immediately after a fire. Others need fire to keep them from overpopulating. Still others indirectly need fire to keep competitors in balance. Chaparral in particular is adapted to fire and most chaparral shrubs have the capability of resprouting rapidly from rootstock.

In the Lower Conifer Forest, prior to the advent of fire suppression, lightning fires would sweep through an area on an average of every 5–16 years. Grasslands and Foothill Woodlands burned on an average of every 2–8 years, and Upper Conifer Forests on an average of 16–26 years. Because only a few years' accumulation of litter and smaller undergrowth covered the ground, the natural fires were low and "cool." These cool fires removed the litter, thinned small trees and shrubs, and burned the lower limbs on the larger trees, but seldom killed the large trees.

The natural forests were a complex patchwork of smaller areas in various stages of succession. Early explorers to the Sierra Nevada

A fire devastated hillsides along the Stevens Trail a few years ago. Lupine seeds had lain dormant in the soil for many years, but with the fire's stratification and nurturing rains, a profusion of lush grasses and lupines appeared in the spring.

JULIE S. CARVILLE

commented that in some places the trees were large and widely spaced, without lower limbs, producing forests that were parklike, diverse, and with an abundance of wildflowers. Hot wildfires, which kill all the trees, probably occurred only rarely. With the exception of fires deliberately set around permanent sites occupied by Native Americans, fires were due entirely to natural causes.

That all changed with the coming of settlers. They built homes in areas that were naturally prone to frequent fires. They began leaving slash behind on the forest floor after lumbering. Vehicles, tools and other equipment, railroads, power lines, cigarettes, campfires, chimney sparks, and green waste burning all increased the potential for sparking wildfires. The newcomers instituted policies of fire suppression and "managing" forests.

Over the decades, the result of these policies and practices has been a major buildup of fuels in the wildlands. In many areas, the fuels are continuous from the litter on the ground, up through thick shrubbery, through dense understory trees, and up into the forest canopy (fuel ladders). This has resulted in "hotter" fires that reach into the crowns of the trees, burning all the above-ground vegetation. It should be emphasized that the vast majority of fires these days are caused by human activity and, therefore, should be preventable.

Although there is universal agreement that fire presents a problem that must be addressed in today's world, controversy surrounds the means to be employed. There are widely divergent opinions, a paucity of scientific research, and many unanswered questions. Solutions include controlled burning, thinning forests by logging, chemical control, and mechanical brush removal. How-

JULIE S. CARVILLE

Leafy stems resprout from the stumps of fire-blackened oaks.

ever, the natural cycle of periodic fires that existed prior to the arrival of settlers is a necessary component of the long-term existence
of all our fire-adapted ecosystems as they had evolved over the centuries. Thus, fires occurring too seldom, too frequently, or at the
wrong time of year, along with the specific methods of fire suppression, all impact our native plants and alter their ecosystems. The
impacts, immediate and long term, of any proposed solution must be
considered carefully.

Plant Collecting

Who hasn't lusted after a favorite wildflower, shrub, or tree upon
seeing it in its magnificent glory in the wild? The temptation to dig
one up and bring it home is a strong one, but one that is best
resisted.

There are many reasons not to collect plants from the wild, especially entire plants, but cuttings and seed should not be collected
either. An obvious reason is that it is against the law. Get caught and
you will find yourself facing stiff fines that will be many times the
cost of simply purchasing the plant from a native plant nursery. Most
of the desirable native plants are available from nurseries, and your
chance of being successful with one grown in cultivation is far
greater than it would be for one dug from the wild.

Keep in mind that if the plant is not available at a native plant
nursery, there is probably a very good reason for it. If professionals
are unable to grow it, what chance does a novice have? There are

A happy customer leaves the Redbud Chapter spring plant sale with a wheelbarrow full of native plants for her home garden.

KAREN CALLAHAN

many factors that reduce the chance of success in relocating wild plants. With our Mediterranean climate, a significant number of our native plants are either semi-parasites attached to nearby deeper rooted plants or are connected to mycorrhizal networks in the soil. Some grow in specialized circumstances that are difficult to recreate in the garden. Others are virtually impossible to remove without damaging them because their roots extend to a great depth or are lodged in crevices.

The temptation to collect is strongest when seeing a specimen in flower. Experienced gardeners know that the worst time to move any plant is while it is in bloom. The plant has put most of its energy into the flowering and fruiting process and usually has little reserve to help it recover from the trauma resulting from inevitable root damage suffered while being removed.

Most people who attempt to collect wild plants do it on the spur of the moment from a roadside, a campground, or some other area associated with humans. These are the same areas most frequently occupied by non-native plants, and the space left behind by native plant removal will most likely be filled by a non-native.

In the northern Sierra region, wild populations of showy and desirable native plants such as lewisias, orchids, lilies, and succulents have declined from illegal horticultural collecting.

The use of native plants for gardens and landscaping should be encouraged for a variety of reasons, but removing them from the wild is illegal, irresponsible, and destructive.

Global Warming

Global warming is another controversial topic beyond the scope of this book, but one that needs comment regarding its impact on plant life. The distribution of plant species is highly dependent on climate. Any significant changes in temperature or precipitation jeopardize not only the range of a plant species, but in some cases, even its very existence, as well as that of the animal life that has evolved in association.

Nearly a third of the plant species growing wild in the United States are found in California. California also supports the greatest number of endemic (found nowhere else) plants of any state. One-third of the plants in California are identified as rare, endangered, or threatened.

The California flora is the richest of any state in the country and is also one of the most threatened. Once a species is gone, it is gone forever.

Monkeyflowers and Fireweed once bloomed in this lush seep garden along Highway 89 near Tahoe City. Unfortunately, a road-widening project diverted the spring, destroyed the garden, and replaced it with a hillside of nothing but boulders.

JULIE S. CARVILLE

KAREN CALLAHAN

From a rocky bluff above the steep canyon of the North Fork of the American River, this is a view looking east toward the Sierra crest in Placer County.

*P*laces To See Wildflowers in Nevada and Placer Counties

Karen Callahan

Wildflowers spring up along country roads, in forgotten woodlands, in open fields, and even in our own backyards. But though wildflowers may be encountered throughout most of the undeveloped areas of Nevada and Placer Counties during the right seasons, easy access is not always a given. Luckily there are a number of excellent wildflower-laden trails to explore. The following places were selected for mention because of their exceptional diversity of plants within a moderate walking distance.

Azalea Lake Trail
Donner Pass, Nevada and Placer Counties

Azalea Lake Trail is a four-mile section of the Pacific Crest Trail between I-80 and Old Highway 40, with thrilling views of Castle Peak, Donner Lake, and Mount Rose. The trail passes small lakes, windswept Sierra Junipers, and giant granite boulders. Flowers to look for from June to August are Mountain Pride, Azure Penstemon, Sulfur Buckwheat, Mountain Pennyroyal, Lobb's Buckwheat, Wright's Buckwheat, Mountain Spiraea, Creambush, California Fuchsia, and Mountain Heather. This trail is beautiful in late summer when the golden flowers of Rabbitbrush decorate the hillsides.

Distant view of Donner Lake from a high ridge on Azalea Lake Trail. Many small plants grow in sheltered gardens of sand and gravel between the granite boulders along the trail. Look for King's Sandwort, Mountain Jewelflower, and Steer's Head in these gardens.

Hiking here is moderately difficult, with some steep climbs and rocky portions. The Glacier Meadow Loop is a short interpretive trail near the Boreal trailhead parking area. Azalea Lake Trail ends at the north side of Old Highway 40, but hikers may want to continue south for an additional half mile to the Mt. Judah trail. For detailed descriptions of the Mt. Judah area and beyond, read the "The Ridge Route" chapter of Julie Carville's book, *Lingering in Tahoe's Wild Gardens,* later released as *Hiking Tahoe's Wildflower Trails.*

To Get There: From eastbound I-80 take the Boreal Ridge exit (Exit 176). Go south one block and follow the signs to the Pacific Crest trailhead parking.

Elevation: 6,500' to 7,200'
Habitats: UC, SA, RO, AQ, RP
Land Manager: Tahoe National Forest
Facilities: Restroom, drinking water, picnic tables
Quad: Norden
GPS Coordinates: N39° 20.385' W120° 20.692'

Buttermilk Bend Trail
Bridgeport, South Yuba River State Park, Nevada County

From the Buttermilk Bend Trail you'll enjoy spectacular views of the South Yuba River and a profusion of spring wildflowers and butterflies. The grassy hillsides are covered with neon orange annual Tufted Poppy, and along the sunny trail look for Bush Lupine, Sky Lupine, Spider Lupine, Blue Dicks, Common Fiddleneck, Ground Iris, Zigzag Larkspur, Foothill Penstemon, Birds-eye Gilia, Canyon Dudleya, Pipevine, and Fairy Lanterns. Shrubs include Mock Orange, Western Redbud, California Buckeye, Bush Monkeyflower, and Spicebush. The Buttermilk Bend Trail is mostly level and about 3 miles round trip. An alternative to the Buttermilk Bend Trail would be a leisurely

An early April profusion of Tufted Poppies along the Buttermilk Bend Trail. Lupines, gilias, madias, penstemons, and other treasures brighten the grassy hillsides from March through May in this wooded chaparral environment.

JULIE S. CARVILLE

walk from the visitors' center following the river downstream. There you can see Snowdrop Bush, California Bay Tree, Bigleaf Maple, California Wild Grape, Buttonwillow, Blue Elderberry, and four different species of native oaks. Information on other scenic trails at Bridgeport is available at the visitors' center. Park docents lead wildflower and bird walks, usually from March through April.

To Get There: Take Highway 20 west from Grass Valley, turn right onto Pleasant Valley Road near Penn Valley, and go 8 miles to South Yuba River State Park. Parking for the visitors' center and historic covered bridge is just before the South Yuba River. Continue across the bridge for the Buttermilk Bend Trail parking area on the right.

Elevation: 560'
Habitats: FW, RO, RP
Land Manager: South Yuba River State Park
Facilities: Restroom, picnic tables, information center, no drinking water
Quad: French Corral
GPS Coordinates: Trailhead: N39° 17.597′ W121° 11.551′

Codfish Falls
North Fork of the American River, Placer County

This 1.5-mile, mostly level trail meanders along the North Fork of the American River before turning to follow Codfish Creek upstream to a cascade of cool, shady waterfalls. Along the path Tufted Poppy blooms with Spider Lupine, Cream Cups, Kellogg's Monkeyflower, Twining Brodiaea, Snowdrop Bush, Fairy Lanterns, Purple Milkweed, and the unusual Evening Snow. The best viewing is from late March to early May in this historic mining area. There are some rocky and narrow places along the trail. Depending on spring weather conditions, the drive down to the river can be a thrill for flower lovers, with hillsides of Blue Dicks, Common Madia, Popcorn Flower, Tomcat Clover, Bush Lupine,

JULIE S. CARVILLE

Lovely Codfish Falls welcomes hikers
at the trail's end.

KAREN CALLAHAN

Tufted Poppy and Stillman's Tickseed
bloom along Ponderosa Way.

Yellow Pincushion, Stillman's Tickseed, Tufted Poppy, and fiddlenecks.

To Get There: From I-80 north of Auburn, take the Weimar Cross Road exit, and turn right onto Ponderosa Way. Take Ponderosa Way about 5 miles to the North Fork bridge. Ponderosa Way is unpaved for the last several miles. Park at the bridge and begin your walk down river on the north side.

Elevation: 900'
Habitats: FW, RO, RP
Land Manager: Auburn State Recreation Area, Placer Land Trust
Facilities: None
Quad: Colfax, Greenwood
GPS Coordinates: Falls area: N38° 59.834' W120° 57.389'

Drum Powerhouse Road
Near Dutch Flat, Placer County

Overlooking the forested Bear River canyon, the Drum Powerhouse Road is exceptional for its plant diversity. Along the road are numerous seeps, rock gardens, and large serpentine outcrops to explore. Brewer's Rock Cress, Wild Bleeding Heart, Milk Maids, Woolly Morning Glory, Grand Hound's Tongue, Draperia, Shelton's Violet, Wild Heliotrope, White Meadow Foam, Western Wallflower, Brown Bells, Pacific Sedum, Mountain Pink Currant, and larkspurs are just some of the species flowering in April and May, depending on the spring weather conditions. A few weeks later, you may find pink-flowered California Thistle, Leopard Lily, Mock Orange, Bush Poppy, Gay Penstemon, and several phacelia species amid the mix of Sierra foothills shrubs and trees. The paved 6-mile-long road ends at the Powerhouse and usually has little traffic. Park at one of the turnouts and walk on the mostly level road to view the plants along the steep roadcuts.

To Get There: Take the Monte Vista-Dutch Flat exit from I-80 and go north of the freeway on Ridge Road. At the sign to Dutch Flat, go left onto Sacramento Street, cross the railroad tracks, and continue through the charming village of Dutch Flat. Go right onto Main Street and onward several miles to Nary Red Road on the left. Look for the Drum Powerhouse

Pink-flowered Wild Bleeding Heart covers a shaded slope above Drum Powerhouse Road.

KAREN CALLAHAN

Road turnoff on the left. Once on Drum Powerhouse Road, travel a few miles past the homes to the beginning of the open area.

Elevation: 3,500'   **Habitats:** LC, RO, SG, RP
Land Manager: Pacific Gas and Electric, Tahoe National Forest
Facilities: None
Quad: Dutch Flat
GPS Coordinates: Intersection of Drum Powerhouse and Main Street: N39° 12.581' W120° 49.106'

Empire Mine State Historic Park
Grass Valley, Nevada County

Empire Mine State Historic Park includes over 700 acres with 12 miles of wide hiking and biking trails. The trails wind through a pretty forest of Canyon Live Oak and Black Oaks, Ponderosa and Sugar Pines, Douglas-fir, Pacific Madrone, and Incense Cedar. The forest understory has an interesting mix of Kit-kit-dizzy, Hairy Honeysuckle, Whiteleaf Manzanita, Indian Manzanita, Sierra Coffeeberry, Lemmon's Ceanothus, Sierra Plum, Poison Oak, and Deerbrush. From April to July is the best season for wildflowers along the trails. Look for Gold Wire, Humboldt Lily, Whitestem Swertia, Sierra Iris, Pine Lupine, Tongue Clarkia, Gay Penstemon, and Creeping Sage. Though the park's unpaved trails vary in difficulty, most are easy, with some elevation change. The best trails for wildflowers are the Union Hill-area trails and the Osborn Hill Loop.

To Get There: Take the Highway 20 exit from northbound Highway 49 in Grass Valley. Turn right on Empire Street and continue past the Empire Mine Park Visitors Center to the intersection of Empire Street and Highway 174. Turn left on Highway 174 and shortly thereafter, turn right on Silver Way. Go about a block on Silver Way and turn right on Gold Hill Drive. At

Along the trails at Empire Mine State Historic Park in early July, Humboldt Lilies flower in open sunny places. During the dry season trees, shrubs, and vines produce seeds to feed a wide variety of birds and other animals found at the park.

KAREN CALLAHAN

the end of Gold Hill Drive parking is available at the Union Hill Trail entrance (no fee). Maps of the trails are available at the visitors center on Empire Street and at the trailhead. For another no-fee access trail, start at the Penn Gate parking area on Empire Street.

Elevation: 2,500′
Habitats: LC, RP
Land Manager: California State Park
Facilities: None except at visitors' center
Quad: Grass Valley
GPS Coordinates: N39° 12.748′ W121° 2.698′

Fairy Falls Trail
Spenceville Wildlife Area, Nevada and Yuba Counties

Covering 11,000 acres, Spenceville is one of the largest remaining oak woodland reserves in the Sierra foothills. Over 160 bird species have been recorded here, including several rare ones. Spenceville features serene vistas of grassy rolling hills with majestic Blue Oak, Interior Live Oak, and Valley Oak. Spring wildflowers include Fairy Lanterns, Royal Larkspur, Douglas' Violet, Harvest Brodiaea, Red Maids, Grass Nut, Winecup Clarkia, Blue Dicks, Caterpillar Phacelia, Gold Nuggets, Woolly Sunflower, Tufted Poppy, and popcorn flowers. The 5-mile round trip, on a gently hilly trail to Fairy Falls, starts at the parking area near the old bridge across Dry Creek. Because the trails are not signed at Spenceville, your first visits should be with a person familiar with the trails. There are some restrictions by the California Department of Fish & Game on groups of hikers during the hunting season. Friends of Spenceville publishes an illustrated map and natural history guide to the reserve. For detailed descriptions of several trails at Spenceville, read Hank Meals' book *Yuba Trails 2.*

Dry Creek meanders through a dense Riparian habitat in Spenceville, until it cascades over the rugged rock face as Fairy Falls. Dry Creek and the Spenceville area support hillsides of wildflowers from April through May and provide habitat for 80 known nesting species of birds.

JULIE S. CARVILLE

To Get There: From the intersection of Highway 49 and Highway 20 in Grass Valley, take Highway 20 west for 12.5 miles. When you see a sign that says "Beale Air Force Base" turn left onto the Smartville-Hammonton Road. Drive about a mile to an intersection and take Smartville Road on the left. Continuing 5 miles on Smartville Road, turn left onto Waldo Road. Drive another 5 miles to the end of Waldo Road, where you can park at the old Spenceville townsite and the bridge across Dry Creek.

Elevation: 600'
Habitats: GR, FW, RO, RP
Land Manager: California Department of Fish & Game
Facilities: None
Quads: Smartville and Camp Far West
GPS Coordinates: End of Waldo Road: N39° 6.652' W121° 18.481'

KAREN CALLAHAN

Thousands of colorful spring flowers at Hell's Half Acre in early May easily elicit that sense of wonder to which this book is dedicated. White Meadow Foam, Ramm's Madia, and Sky Lupine thrive in the shallow volcanic soil that inhibits most non-native plants.

Hell's Half Acre
West of Grass Valley, Nevada County

Hell's Half Acre's distinctive landscape is formed by an ancient volcanic mud flow. From April through May the bare ground between lichen-covered rocks, twisted manzanitas, and Gray Pine trees is covered with a dazzling display of wildflowers. Over 100 species have been identified on the 25+ acres that the Redbud Chapter is working to preserve as a special botanical area. Early May brings White Meadow Foam, Miniature Lupine and Sky Lupine, Ramm's Madia, Johnny Tuck, Pansy Monkeyflower, and Cowbag Clover. In late May look for Graceful Clarkia, Hartweg's Sidalcea, Paper Onion, White Brodiaea, Purple Milkweed, and Pratten's Buckwheat. By mid-July, most of the plants are drying in the heat, but Sanborn's Onion and a forest of Soap Plant will be flowering. The paths are mostly level and easy. The property owners of the former Kenny Ranch have cooperated with the Nevada County Land Trust and CNPS to allow several guided field trips to the site every year.

JULIE S. CARVILLE

Hell's Half Acre blooms with Hartweg's Sidalcea and Paper Onions in early June, while only a few feet away other meadows bloom with lupines, monkeyflowers, and madias to delight the soul with a rainbow of color—a botanist's and photographer's paradise!

To Get There: Located about two miles west of Grass Valley, at the intersection of Rough & Ready Highway and Ridge Road.

Elevation: 2,600'
Habitats: CH, LC
Land Manager: Private
Facilities: None
Quad: Grass Valley
GPS Coordinates: N39° 13.687' W121° 5.201'

Independence Trail
South Yuba River Canyon, Nevada County

Independence Trail follows a Gold Rush-era canal bed for about a mile to the waterfalls of Rush Creek. The native trees, shrubs, and flowers are typical of the South Yuba River Canyon, making this an interesting hiking area throughout the year. At least ten species of ferns grow along the shaded banks with lichens, liverworts, mosses, and fungi. Along the mostly level trail from April through July, you will see Sierra Onion, Pipevine, Brown Bells, Humboldt Lily, Indian Pink, Sierra Sedum, Yellow Cat's Ear, Indian Warrior, Showy Phlox, Twining Brodiaea, Spicebush, and penstemons. Independence Trail is unpaved, but is nonetheless designed to be accessible for wheelchairs, including ramps to view the creek and falls.

To Get There: Take Highway 49 toward Downieville northwest of Nevada City for 5.5 miles. Look for the trail parking area on the right before the bridge over the Yuba River. Walk through the underpass for the trail toward Rush Creek. Another portion of the Independence Trail goes north from the parking area and continues for about a mile.

ROGER MCGEHEE

Elevation: 1,500'
Habitats: LC, RO, RP
Land Manager: South Yuba River State Park
Facilities: Restroom, picnic tables, disabled accessible
Quad: Nevada City
GPS Coordinates:
N39° 17.539' W121° 5.829'

Black Oak leaves cover the gently sloping, former canal bed trail in fall.

Limestone Quarry Road Trail
East of Auburn, El Dorado County

This wide and mostly level trail follows an old historic railway roadbed just above the American River on the El Dorado County side of the river. It offers inspiring views of the river canyon plus a wide variety of trees, shrubs, and spring wildflowers. Look for White Globe Lily, Sierra Sedum, Waterfall Buttercup, Woolly Sunflower, Giant Blazing Star, Blue Dicks, Bilobed Clarkia, Wally Basket, Chaparral Honeysuckle, Clematis, Western Redbud, and several species of ferns. The trail continues for several miles along the river.

To Get There: Take Highway 49 from Auburn south toward Cool for about 3.5 miles. Shortly after Highway 49 crosses the American River, there is a left turn to the parking lot for the trailhead.

Elevation: 750'
Habitats: CH, FW, RO, RP
Land Manager: Auburn State Recreation Area
Facilities: Restroom, picnic tables
Quad: Auburn
GPS Coordinates: Parking and trailhead: N39° 14.385' W121° 12.329'

View of the Middle Fork of the American River from the trailhead of the Limestone Quarry Trail. The left side of the river is Placer County and the right side is El Dorado County, showing various densities of Foothill Woodland Chaparral.

Loney Meadow
Grouse Ridge, Nevada County

An easy, mostly level trail goes about 1.5 miles around the edge of scenic Loney Meadow, crossing creeks and winding through dry open forest. Soon after the snow melts (usually early June), look for Alpine Shooting Star, Plainleaf Fawn Lily, Western Centaur, Wild Bleeding Heart, Macloskey's Violet, and Western Dog Violet on the meadow's edges. The meadow is

filled with wildflowers from mid-June through July, including Common
Camas Lily, Alpine Lily, Bog Orchid, Giant Red Paintbrush, Cow Parsnip,
Blue-eyed Grass, Western Bistort, Alpine Aster, Whorled Penstemon, Meadow
Rue, Tower Butterweed, and Mountain Spiraea. In drier habitats you'll see
Bitter Dogbane, Silverleaf Phacelia, Bridge's Gilia, Mountain Mule Ears,
Tahoe Lupine, King's Sandwort, and Dwarf Lousewort.

To Get There: From Nevada City drive east 23 miles on Highway 20. Turn
left onto Bowman Lake Road (USFS road #18) toward Sierra Discovery Trail.
From the Highway 20 intersection, drive 10.5 miles on Bowman Road. Just
past the end of the paved road, look for a sign on the right to Loney
Meadow. From the turn, the gravel access road is rough in spots. Keep to
the left at the forks for about 2 miles (passing Aspen groves) to the
trailhead parking.

Elevation: 6,000'
Habitats: UC, MM, RO, RP
Land Manager: Tahoe National Forest
Facilities: None
Quad: Graniteville
GPS Coordinates: On site: N39° 25.575' W120° 39.309'

Texas Creek meanders through Loney Meadow. Melting snow from the surrounding
high peaks feeds the creek and waters this large, flower-filled wetland.

JULIE S. CARVILLE

The Maidu Center's interpretive trail takes visitors to the sandstone rock outcroppings that are carved with petroglyphs seemingly of animals, fertility symbols, and the tree of life. One of the petroglyphs points to the North Star.

Maidu Interpretive Center
Roseville, Placer County

The Maidu Interpretive Center is a 35-acre preserve within the Maidu Regional Park. The park's land includes a tributary of Linda Creek and Strap Ravine. Walk the easy loop trail to view ancient petroglyphs and bedrock mortars. The museum exhibits feature local Native American culture. There are guided walks and nature activities sponsored by the museum throughout the year. Plants of the preserve's vernal pools include Folded Downingia, Coyote Thistle, California Goldfields, Tidy Tips, Quillwort, and White Meadow Foam. Late March and April are the best times for wildflowers. In the surrounding regional park you may also see Stinkbells, Indian Milkweed, Frying Pans, Valley Tassels, and popcorn flowers growing with grasses, oaks, willows, and alders.

To Get There: The Maidu Interpretive Center is located at 1960 Johnson Ranch Drive east of I-80 near Roseville. For detailed information, hours, and visitor fee call 916-774-5934.

Elevation: 100'   **Habitats:** VP, GR, RP
Land Manager: City of Roseville
Facilities: Restroom, drinking water, picnic tables, information center
Quad: Roseville
GPS Coordinates: N38° 44.285' W121° 14.81'

The Narrows Recreation Area
Lake Englebright, Nevada County

Pretty displays of spring wildflowers grow along the entrance road, including the magenta-flowered Peninsular Onion and Chinese Houses, plus Fairy Lanterns, Prettyface, and paintbrushes. Several short walks are possible from the parking area, such as the Fishermen's Trail that follows the lake edge. Bring bug repellent! More roadside wildflower hunting is available along the unpaved section of Mooney Flat Road that ends at Pleasant Valley Road next to Lake Wildwood.

To Get There: Take Highway 20 west of Grass Valley toward Marysville, then take Mooney Flat Road to The Narrows entrance.

Elevation: 500'
Habitats: GR, FW, AQ, RP
Land Manager: US Army Corps of Engineers
Facilities: Restroom, picnic tables, information center
Quad: Smartville
GPS Coordinates: End of Mooney Flat Road: N39° 14.411' W121° 15.937'

KAREN CALLAHAN

Chinese Houses and Prettyface grow near Lake Englebright.

Placer Big Trees Grove
Southeast of Foresthill, Placer County

This is the northernmost grove of Big Trees, *Sequoiadendron giganteum*, in the Sierra Nevada. Tahoe National Forest maintains a 160-acre Special Botanical Area for the grove of six Giant Sequoias, some estimated to be a thousand years old. Several species of conifers are growing with the Sequoias and form an old-growth forest habitat. A short and easy half-mile trail with

A fallen giant at the Placer Grove of Big Trees. Limited to the western side of the Sierra Nevada, this is the northernmost grove of the Giant Sequoias.

CHET BLACKBURN

interpretive features circles through the grove. Along the trail can be found exceptional specimens of Douglas-fir and Sugar Pine, as well as White Fir, Western Azalea, Greenleaf Manzanita, Deerbrush, and Mountain Whitethorn. Among the herbaceous plants are Sierra Iris, Pine Violet, Bracken Fern, Starflower, White-veined Wintergreen, One-sided Wintergreen, Fawn Lily, and False Solomon's Seal.

To Get There: From the Foresthill exit off I-80, take Foresthill Road 16 miles to Foresthill. At Foresthill, turn right on Mosquito Ridge Road and go 27 miles to Road 16. Mosquito Ridge Road is a scenic, paved, winding road. Turn at the sign leading to the Placer Big Trees. The trailhead is 0.5 mile from that point.

Elevation: 5,500'   **Habitat:** UC
Land Manager: Tahoe National Forest
Facilities: Restroom, drinking water, picnic tables, camping
Quad: Greek Store
GPS Coordinates: Parking and trailhead: N39° 3.556' W120° 34.297'

Placer Nature Center
Christian Valley, near Auburn, Placer County

Originally a ranch used to grow food for the California Conservation Corps, the Placer Nature Center is now a nonprofit educational venture. A small intermittent stream flows through the woodland and early spring wildflowers bloom along the self-guided nature trail. Look for Superb Mariposa Lily, Twining Brodiaea, Woodland Star, Valley Tassels, Pipevine, Woolly Sunflower, Narrowleaf Mule Ears, and Hartweg's Doll Lily.

To Get There: From I-80 east of Auburn, take the Dry Creek Road exit and proceed west. Turn right on Christian Valley Road. The Nature Center is located approximately 5 miles down Christian Valley Road where the road

JULIE S. CARVILLE

A level trail winds its way through woodland gardens and golden meadows at the Placer Nature Center. Colorful wildflowers decorate the meadows in spring, offering a fun place to take children, with hand lenses, to experience nature's beauty up close.

ends. It is located within the California Conservation Corps compound called the Placer Energy Center. Turn left immediately after entering the CCC site. The address is 3700 Christian Valley Road. The Nature Center is open to the public only for designated tours and monthly open houses. For more information, see the Nature Center's Web site at *www.placernaturecenter.org.*

Elevation: 1,600'   **Habitats:** CH, FW
Land Manager: Placer Nature Center
Facilities: Restroom, drinking water, picnic tables, information center
Quad: Auburn
GPS Coordinates: Visitors' center: N38° 59.476' W121° 4.424'

Rock Creek Nature Trail
Washington Ridge, Nevada County

Rock Creek Nature Trail meanders along Rock Creek among diverse riparian and forest plant life. Just under 1 mile in length, the trail is unique for the number of orchid species to be found there. Look for Phantom Orchid, Spotted Coralroot Orchid, Striped Coralroot Orchid, Rattlesnake Plantain, Twinflower, Lady Fern, Creeping Snowberry, Pine Rose, Sweet Trillium, Brookfoam, Elk Clover, Fringe Cups, Brewer's Bishop's Cap, and Hooker's Fairybell. The mostly level path is shaded by large specimens of Pacific Yew, Douglas-fir, and Madrone, along with California Hazelnut and three species of dogwood.

To Get There: Drive Highway 20 east from Nevada City for 6 miles. Make a left turn at the "Forestry Conservation Camp" sign and follow the paved road for about a mile. Look for the "Rock Creek Nature Trail" sign at the left turn. Drive about 1.5 miles of unpaved road to the trailhead parking.

Elevation: 3,000'
Habitats: LC, RP
Land Manager:
Tahoe National Forest
Facilities: Restroom, picnic tables
Quad: North Bloomfield
GPS Coordinates:
Parking and trailhead:
N39° 18.033' W120° 55.559'

JULIE S. CARVILLE

Rock Creek's level trail offers streamside delights for children.

Sagehen Creek
Highway 89, north of Truckee, Nevada County

A mostly level 2-mile trail (4 miles round trip) following Sagehen Creek from Highway 89 to Stampede Reservoir offers its best wildflower viewing from May to July. The Sagehen Trail has a wonderful array of wildflowers representing a transition zone between the rich floras of the Sierra Nevada and the Great Basin. You'll see many typical plants of the east side meadows, including masses of blue Common Camas Lily, Western Peony, Meadow Penstemon, Hairy Paintbrush, Marsh Marigold, Plumas Ivesia, California Valerian, Low Phacelia, Wood Rose, Sierra Lewisia, sedges, sagebrush, arnicas, and asters. Sagehen Creek is also an excellent area for animal and bird watching. See Julie Carville's books, *Hiking Tahoe's Wildflower Trails* or *Lingering in Tahoe's Wild Gardens,* for a detailed description of the flowers along this trail as well as for many other wildflower hikes of the Tahoe area.

To Get There: From Truckee, take the Highway 89 exit from I-80 north toward Quincy. The trailhead is 7.5 miles north of Truckee. A parking area is just past the Sagehen Creek bridge on the right, or eastern, side of the road.

Elevation: 6,000′
Habitats: MM, SP, AQ, RP

JULIE S. CARVILLE

Camas Lilies form a sea of blue-purple in early June at Sagehen Meadow. The lilies were gathered by the Washoes and roasted in earthen ovens.

Land Manager: Tahoe National Forest
Facilities: None
Quad: Truckee
GPS Coordinates: Parking and trailhead: N39° 26.039' W120° 12.305'

Sierra Discovery Trail
Bear Valley, Nevada and Placer Counties

The Sierra Discovery Trail's easy, mostly level 1-mile loop follows the Bear River through wetlands and mixed conifer forest. Along the trail there's Western False Solomon's Seal, Sweet Trillium, Pine Violet, Western Blue Flax, Sierra Gooseberry, and California Harebell. In early July the meadows have a beautiful display of Lemmon's Ginger, Leopard Lily, Swamp Onion, Corn Lily, Bog Orchid, Meadow Lupine, Nettleleaf Horsemint, Goldenrod, and Alpine Knotweed. Colorful autumn leaves of Black Oak, Mountain Dogwood, and Bigleaf Maple make Bear Valley a wonderful place to visit in October. About a mile farther on Bowman Lake Road past the Discovery Trail there's a scenic view of the South Yuba River at Lang's Crossing.

To Get There: Take Highway 20 east 23 miles from Nevada City. Turn left onto Bowman Lake Road (USFS road #18) toward Sierra Discovery Trail. Go a short distance on the paved road to the well-marked parking area for the trail.

Elevation: 4,500'
Habitats: LC, MM, RP
Land Manager:
Pacific Gas and Electric Co.
Facilities: Restroom, drinking water, picnic tables, information center
Quad: Blue Canyon
GPS Coordinates: Parking lot: N39° 18.543' W120° 39.957'

The Bear River flows through a woodland garden along the Sierra Discovery Trail.

JULIE S. CARVILLE

South Yuba River Trail
Relief Hill Trailhead, Nevada County

For the first mile the trail follows Poorman Creek. Where the creek joins the South Yuba, the trail turns and follows the river downstream, eventually to a shaded forest ravine along McKilligan Creek. There are beautiful views of the river along this part of the canyon and plenty of wildflowers on the rock outcrops. Flowers to look for include Harlequin Lupine, Mountain Jewelflower, Indian Pink, Grand Hound's Tongue, Sierra Fawn Lily, Milk Maids, Wood Strawberry, Seepspring Monkeyflower, and Rabbitbrush. The trail has some rocky, narrow places and is moderately difficult, with some elevation change. The South Yuba trail continues for several miles farther to the Missouri Bar campground. As you drive to the trail on Washington Road and Relief Hill Road you will pass extensive serpentine outcrops. Take time to stop and look at the distinctive plants on the rocky barrens.

To Get There: Take Highway 20 for 12 miles east of Nevada City, and turn left onto Washington Road. Pass through the town of Washington, go over the South Yuba River bridge, and take the first left turn to continue on Washington Road. Drive 0.5 mile and bear left onto Relief Hill Road (unpaved) and continue about 1.5 miles to the clearly marked trailhead parking.

Elevation: 2,600'
Habitats: LC, RO, SG, RP
Land Manager: Tahoe National Forest
Facilities: Restroom
Quad: Washington
GPS Coordinates: Start of Relief Hill Road: N39° 21.81' W120° 47.467'

ROGER MCGEHEE

Hiking the narrow trail offers many impressive views of the South Yuba River. Late summer views such as this reveal the rocky river channel, but in spring and early summer the river covers the rocks as it cascades and roars through the canyon.

Stevens Trail
Colfax, Placer County

The historic Stevens trail follows a road that went from Colfax to Iowa Hill. The North Fork of the American River is about 4 miles from the trailhead parking area. Some portions of this moderately strenuous trail are rocky, narrow, and steep. The long uphill grade coming out is shaded by the mixed conifer forest for half of the distance. The rewards for your climbing effort will be dramatic views of the river canyon and a fantastic array of wildflowers, shrubs, trees, and ferns all along the trail. Waterfall Buttercup, Bush Lupine, Silver Lotus, Baby Blue-eyes, Kellogg's Monkeyflower, Wild Mock Orange, Sticky Chinese Houses, and Tufted Poppy are just a few of the botanical treats. The best time to see flowers is late March through May.

Dramatic view of the American River and its canyon from Stevens Trail.

JULIE S. CARVILLE

To Get There: Take the Colfax exit from eastbound I-80. On the off-ramp go straight to the stop sign, then across the street (the eastbound freeway entrance will be on your left) toward the gas station, where you'll turn left and then right onto Canyon Court and then a quick left onto North Canyon Way (which parallels the freeway) by the "Not a Through Road" sign. Go less than a mile to the parking near the trailhead sign. It is a popular trail in the spring, and if the parking lot is full, park carefully along the road so that you do not block private driveways and, please, do not leave any trash.

Elevation: 1,500′
Habitats: CH, LC, RO, RP
Land Manager: Bureau of Land Management
Facilities: None
Quad: Colfax
GPS Coordinates: Parking lot and trailhead: N39° 6.330′ W120° 56.830′

Yankee Jim's Road
Near Colfax, Placer County

This is not a trail but a lightly traveled, unpaved road running from Canyon Way below Colfax and Foresthill. Although lightly traveled, one should never stop in the roadway. For much of its length it is a narrow one-lane

KAREN CALLAHAN

Though a quiet back road today, Yankee Jim's Road led to a busy gold mining camp on the North Fork of the American River in the 1850s.

road but there are a few pullouts that can be used to park and reconnoiter. The 4 miles from the intersection of Yankee Jim's Road and Canyon Way to the old suspension bridge that crosses the North Fork of the American River is a veritable rock garden of flowers in the early spring. Rather than drive the whole 15-mile length of the road, the best bet is to park by the suspension bridge and head off on foot in either direction for whatever distance one feels comfortable with. Heading in the Colfax direction you'll come across Tufted Poppy, Canyon Dudleya, Fairy Lanterns, Kellogg's Monkeyflower, Caterpillar Phacelia, and lots of other rock-loving, sun-loving flowers. Heading in the Foresthill direction, you'll come across more shade-tolerant plants such as Crevice Heuchera, California Saxifrage, Waterfall Buttercup, and California Maidenhair Fern. There are waterfalls in both directions. The best flowering time is late March through May.

Silver Lupine and Tufted Poppies flowering along Yankee Jim's Road.

To Get There: From eastbound I-80 take the Canyon Way exit and turn right at the stop sign on Canyon Way. Turn left on Yankee Jim's Road, which is a short distance down Canyon Way.

Elevation: 2,200'
Habitats: CH, FW, RO, RP
Land Manager: Auburn State Recreation Area
Facilities: None
Quad: Colfax
GPS Coordinates: Intersection of Canyon Way and Yankee Jim's Road: N39° 4.115' W120° 57.356'

CHET BLACKBURN

A waterfall on Deadman's Creek in Hidden Falls Regional Park.

Addendum: Hidden Falls Regional Park preserves a fine example of the lower Foothill Woodland habitat. Public access was granted to this important new regional park shortly before this book was ready to go to press.

Hidden Falls Regional Park
Near Auburn, Placer County

By late 2008, this park will cover over 1,180 acres, making it one of the largest regional parks in the state. The first phase, consisting of 220 acres, opened in late 2006. Two large adjacent ranches were acquired under the Placer Legacy Open Space and Agricultural Conservation Program that was established to preserve some of the county's remaining open space for wilderness recreation and habitat protection. The park preserves a type of flora that was once typically found in the lower Foothill Woodlands. Hidden Falls Park is traversed by a 3-mile stretch of Coon Creek and a smaller permanent stream known as Deadman's Creek. Several waterfalls occur on the site. The annual wildflower display begins with the emergence of Blue Dicks in February and is soon followed by many species of wild bulbs. Among the other wildflowers are several species of lupines, poppies, and clarkias, as well as typical foothill trees and shrubs such as Toyon, Coffeeberry, Whiteleaf Manzanita, Buckbrush, California Buckeye, Blue Oak, Interior Live Oak, and Gray Pine.

CHET BLACKBURN

To Get There: Take Atwood Road west from Highway 49. Atwood Road merges with Mt. Vernon Road and continues on as Mt. Vernon Road. Turn right on Mears Road, about 3.5 miles from Highway 49, and follow it to Mears Place and the park entrance. There are signs on both Mt. Vernon Road and Mears Road pointing to the park.

Elevation: Ranges from 600′ to approximately 1,100′
Habitats: FW, CH, RP
Land Manager: Placer County
Quad: Gold Hill
GPS Coordinates:
N38° 57.388′ W121° 9.871′

A picturesque rock formation on Deadman's Creek.

A bench along the Buttermilk Bend Trail offers a resting place to soak up the sunshine and enjoy a view of Bush Lupine and the South Yuba River.

$\mathcal{U}$sing This Book
Richard Hanes and Chet Blackburn

The objectives of this book are to expand appreciation and knowledge of the flora of Nevada and Placer Counties and to stimulate interest in preserving it. We started with the assumption that most people buying the book would have a general interest in the outdoors, but perhaps little or no botanical training. We have therefore tried to make the book more useful to novices by keeping the usage of botanical terms to a minimum. For example, instead of using terms such as "sagittate" we use the term "arrow-shaped."

On the other hand, we recognize that the book will be a "must" for more knowledgeable wildflower enthusiasts interested in the plants of Nevada and Placer Counties. Though these readers may be fewer in number, they are likely to be the heaviest long-term users of the book.

The book, therefore, attempts to provide a balance between these two primary audiences. The format is designed to make the book as easy as possible for a novice to use, while not frustrating more experienced readers by placing plants in artificial groupings. Whereas it can be argued that presenting plants by flower color would be easier for novices, it can also be misleading because there are various color

A budding young botanist examines White Meadow Foam and Ramm's Madia at Hell's Half Acre. The colorful palette includes Sky Lupine, Blue Dicks, and Wild Carnations all mixed in a green meadow of Paper Onion foliage masquerading as grass (until you catch its scent).

JULIE S. CARVILLE

forms for some species and some species simply do not fall easily into white-yellow-pink-red-blue-purple groupings. It would be impractical to reproduce the same species descriptions for every color variation that might be found.

Novices usually attempt identification of a particular plant by thumbing through the pictures looking for photos that resemble the plant. Arranging them by color only reduces the number of pages they would need to thumb through, while making the book less user friendly to more experienced users. Another goal of the book is to be an educational tool and introduce botanical newcomers to the concept of plant families, which in turn will enhance their enjoyment of "wildflower watching."

Here are a few tips that will help in identifying plants by using this book.

- Learn to identify plant families. An efficient way to learn the families is to start by learning to identify the three most common plant families. The Sunflower family (Asteraceae), Pea family (Fabaceae), and Lily family (Liliaceae) all have characteristics that make them easy to recognize; 140 of the more than 500 plants described in this book are included within just those three families. If you add the Mint family (Lamiaceae) and the Figwort family (Scrophulariaceae) to the list of families you can identify on sight, you will be able to recognize the families in which nearly half the plants in the book are found.

- Use blooming time, elevation, and habitat codes shown in the book to help in identification or confirmation of the identity of a plant.

- Check the Comments sections for tips that could aid in determining or confirming species identification.

The plants are grouped by botanical family, and the families are presented in alphabetical order. A brief description of each family is provided, with the most important characteristics that identify that family shown in boldface italic.

Within the family, individual plants are listed in alphabetical order by genus and then within each genus by species. The format used to describe each species in the book is illustrated below:

Primula suffrutescens	Native perennial
Sierra Primrose	Jul–Sep

Description: Plant 6–12″. Creeping stems from a woody base form a low mat. The spoon-shaped leaves are less than 2″, and toothed on the margins. The flowers are less than 1″ in diameter, with 5 magenta petals with a yellow center.

Habitat: 8,000–13,500′. Rocky places. UC, SA, RO.

Comments: Only hikers to the high country will have the opportunity to see California's only native *Primula*. Uncommon, it grows in isolated colonies near melting snowbanks in rock crevices. The colonies, however, may be large and, in good years, spectacular. The growing season is short, so the plant must rush to manufacture the food it needs, flower, and set seed. The Sierra Primrose does not adapt to lower elevation gardens. Look for it in rocky slopes near Sagehen Creek, Castle Peak, and Grouse Ridge.

Botanical Name: The first entry for each plant is the botanical name. The scientific community has given every class of living creatures with common attributes a standard two-part name that is unique and is used in every part of the world and in all languages. This is true for both plants and animals. The first of the two parts is the genus name; it is always capitalized. The second part is never capitalized and together both form the species name. Botanical names are italicized. The botanical name for the Leopard Lily, for example, is *Lilium pardalinum*. In some cases, a species may be divided further into subspecies or variety (e.g., *Lilium pardalinum* ssp. *pardalinum*). This happens when a species has special characteristics that have occurred over time because of its particular environment. We have used subspecies or variety names where it will help in identifying a plant in the field. For further reference, a Checklist of Plants by Family of Nevada and Placer Counties is included in the back portion of our book. It includes the complete botanical name of all the plants known to occur in our area.

The botanical names used in this book conform to the 1993 edition of *The Jepson Manual: Higher Plants of California*, which at the time of our publication is the most widely accepted authority on California plant taxonomy.

Growth Habit: The growth habit is shown to the right of the botanical name and indicates whether that plant is native or non-native and whether it is an annual, biennial, or perennial.

Common Name: A plant may be known by many different common names, and conversely, the same common name is often applied to different plants. This makes usage of the common name impractical for arranging plants in any reasonable order. We have provided one or more common names for each plant. The common names used are those that are either the ones shown in the *Jepson Manual* or the ones most frequently used for that species in California. The Checklist of Plants in the back portion of our book includes common names.

Blooming Period: The blooming period is shown to the right of the common name. This indicates the months in which the plant being described would be expected to be in flower. Keep in mind that if a particular species is found at different elevations, it is not likely that it would be blooming at the same time at all elevations. For example, the blooming period for Blue Dicks, *Dichelostemma capitatum,* is given as late February through May, but those growing at higher elevations will not yet be blooming in late February, while those in lower elevations may have already flowered and gone to seed by May. The influence of weather should also be kept in mind. Flowering may be delayed by a cool spring or accelerated by a warm one.

Description: The physical description of the plant is arranged in a specific order in most cases, beginning with the plant's size. After the size is, in order, the plant habit (erect, trailing, etc.), information about the roots, then the foliage, followed by the inflorescence description, then the flower parts, and finally details of fruit and seed structure. Not all of these factors are shown for every plant.

Habitat: The habitat description consists of three parts:

The first part shows the elevations at which the plant is likely to be found. Note that although elevation in our two-county area ranges from about 40 feet to 9,143 feet, we have used elevations from sea level to 14,000 feet. This is in recognition that the book's usefulness extends beyond Nevada and Placer Counties.

The second part of the habitat description describes some of the local environmental situations where the plant is typically found, e.g., gravelly streambeds, grassy slopes, etc.

The third part is a series of two-character codes defining specific habitats with which the plants are usually associated. We have categorized the various habitats in the two counties into 13 general types that are defined and arranged primarily from low to high elevation. The abbreviations, along with elevation, are used to help locate the described plant species. Remember that nature does not always follow our definitions and there could be considerable variations. Remember also that there is transition rather than clear demarcation between adjacent habitats, and pockets of one type of habitat may occur within another. The habitat descriptions are provided as a guide and an additional step in helping to identify a plant.

GR   **Grasslands:** This habitat occurs in the Sacramento Valley and into the foothills (Foothill Woodland habitat) and is composed of a sea of grass that may have scattered individual trees or islands of trees. Prior to settlement the grasses were dominated by native perennial bunchgrasses. Within the last century these have been replaced by such non-native annual species as Wild Oat, Soft Cheatgrass, Smooth Brome, Ripgut Grass, and Foxtail Fescue. Annuals sprout each year from seeds produced the previous year. Growth is rapid and by early summer most annuals have died. Some of the more common wildflowers include Baby Blue-eyes, Purple Owl's Clover, Common Madia, California Goldfields, Prettyface, meadow foams, popcorn flowers, fiddlenecks, butter-cups, poppies, paintbrushes, and lupines.

Large graceful Valley Oaks favor areas of moisture and deeper soils within the Grasslands habitat.

KAREN CALLAHAN

FW   **Foothill Woodland:** This habitat is between the Valley Grasslands and the Lower Conifer Forest habitats. Blue Oak is the most common foothill tree and has the characteristic white bark of the deciduous "white oak" group. It is commonly associated with the blue-green-needled Gray Pine and Interior Live Oak. The stately Valley Oak mostly occurs on low, fairly moist grassland sites, such as near the town of Penn Valley. The understories of these open stands of oaks consist largely of grasses and forbs typical of the

Ancient Blue Oaks growing on a Foothill Woodland hillside above the South Yuba River near Bridgeport. Found only in California, their numbers continue to be drastically reduced by development.

Grasslands habitat, along with such shrubs as Buckbrush, Whiteleaf Manzanita, Poison Oak, and coffeeberries. Some of the more common wildflowers are Indian Pink, Miner's Lettuce, Yarrow, brodiaeas, larkspurs, mustards, shooting stars, lupines, mariposa lilies, and irises.

CH   Chaparral: This habitat occurs in the areas of Foothill Woodland, Lower Conifer Forest, Upper Conifer Forest, and Subalpine/Alpine habitats. It is composed of dense, often impenetrable thickets of shrubs. At the lower elevations, Whiteleaf Manzanita, Buckbrush, Toyon, and Redbud may dominate this shrub community. Scrub Oak and a shrubby form of Interior Live Oak may dominate other stands. In the conifer forests this habitat is primarily associated with burned or disturbed areas. Natural areas do occur that are related to a combination of soil characteristics and climate (e.g., shallow soils, a south aspect, or limited moisture). The more common

Chaparral covers lower elevation foothill slopes.

Subalpine Chaparral on Donner Peak softens the rocky hillsides.

JULIE S. CARVILLE

shrubs are Deerbrush, Bittercherry, Tobacco Bush, Huckleberry Oak, Bush Chinquapin, Mountain Whitethorn, and manzanitas.

SG   Serpentine/Gabbro: Abrupt transitions from woodland to chaparral on otherwise uniform slopes may indicate the boundary of a serpentine or gabbro habitat.

Serpentine is California's state rock and has a distinctive waxy greenish gray appearance. It often contains white streaks of minerals known as asbestos. Soils developed from serpentine are unusually high in magnesium, as well as some heavy metals such as chromium, colbalt, iron, lead, and nickel. Many essential plant nutrients are unavailable or have limited availability to plants, especially calcium, nitrogen, phosphorus, and potassium.

Gabbro rock contains high amounts of the heavy metals magnesium and iron. It is relatively rich in calcium and sodium. It is dark in color and is relatively heavy compared with same-sized samples

Bright yellow Woolly Sunflowers and purple California Brodiaea thrive in the sun-heated rocks and gravel of the Serpentine habitat.

KAREN CALLAHAN

KAREN CALLAHAN

Bolander's Mule Ears flourishes on rocky Gabbro habitat soils.

of other rocks. Common minerals include olivine, pyroxene, amphibole, biotite mica, and the plagioclase feldspars.

These soils can be toxic or hostile to plant growth. Plants tend to be very slow growing and smaller in size than the same species would be on "normal" soils. The density of plant growth is very low on soils developed from serpentine and slightly better on gabbro soils. Gray Pine may inhabit these areas, along with McNab Cypress, Whiteleaf Manzanita, Leather Oak, Chaparral Pea, and Buckbrush. Because of the unusual soil chemistry, these habitats may contain unique or rare plants.

Small areas of very shallow soils developed from slightly weathered hard volcanic rock may also exhibit the same plant growth and density as described above. Hell's Half Acre is an example.

VP   **Vernal Pools:** A special type of wetlands occurring in only a few places in the world, vernal pools are shallow depressions underlain by an impermeable layer that fill with water in the winter and dry up in the spring. These seasonal pools foster unique flora and fauna, many of which are rare, that have adapted to a cycle of

JULIE S. CARVILLE

Vernal Pool in early spring before evaporation has occurred.

Wildflowers form rings of color as Vernal Pools dry.

JULIE S. CARVILLE

several months of living in pools of standing water that later dry to hard, sun-baked depressions. Plants tend to be fast growing. Colorful annuals appear in concentric rings around the pool as it slowly evaporates. A few common plants are navarretias, downingias, meadow foams, and monkeyflowers. Vernal pools may range in size from several feet to hundreds of yards across. While they primarily occur in the Valley Grasslands, they do occasionally occur in some of the other broad habitats.

LC   Lower Conifer Forest:
This habitat occurs above the Foothill Woodlands at an approximate elevation of 2,000 feet and transitions into the Upper Conifer Forest at 6,000 feet. Ponderosa Pine and White Fir dominate most conifer stands, but as many as five different conifers may be found in the same stand. Incense Cedar, Sugar Pine, Douglas-fir, and Jeffrey Pine are important associates. Some tree stands may be dominated by a single species.

KAREN CALLAHAN

View of Lower Conifer Forest near Scotts Flat Lake, Nevada County.

California Black Oak is the most common of the more than two dozen broadleaf trees and treelike shrubs in this habitat. Also common are Madrone, Tanbark Oak, Mountain Dogwood, Bigleaf Maple, Quaking Aspen, and Mountain Alder. The more common understory shrubs are Whiteleaf Manzanita, Buckbrush, Deerbrush, Bittercherry, Kit-kit-dizzy, Western Azalea, roses, snowberries, willows, gooseberries, and currants.

Wildflowers are numerous. A few of the more conspicuous are Indian Pink, Snow Plant, Western False Solomon's Seal, Sierra Iris, Checkerbloom, violets, penstemons, paintbrushes, lupines, asters, and onions.

AQ   **Aquatic:** This habitat consists of standing or slowly moving, more or less permanent bodies of water such as ponds, lakes, marshes, bogs, fens, and reservoirs. Included are fully aquatic and emergent plants. It may occur in any of the other broad habitats, at any elevation. Common plants in this environment are pond lilies, cattails, rushes, sedges, and pond weeds.

Pond lilies float on a high mountain pond at Tahoe—a picturesque example of one of a variety of types of Aquatic habitat.

MM   **Mountain Meadows:** This habitat ranges in size from a few yards across to large open flats associated with lakes, streams, and moist open areas. It occurs in the Lower Conifer Forest, Upper Conifer Forest, Subalpine/Alpine, and Sagebrush/Pine habitats. Species will vary because of climate and elevation. Although sedges dominate most meadows, rushes and grasses are common associates and in some cases locally dominate. Numerous broad-leaved herbs and a few shrubs complete the meadow flora. From May to September, meadow wildflowers provide the most spectacular displays of

Penstemons bloom purple in Loney Meadow, a large Mountain Meadow habitat, at Grouse Ridge.

JULIE S. CARVILLE

massed color found in the Sierra. These bright displays include asters, paintbrushes, irises, shooting stars, elephant heads, gentians, saxifrages, lilies, lupines, buttercups, and cinquefoils.

RP   Riparian: This habitat is associated with water sources such as stream banks, lake shores, springs, meadow edges, or Aquatic habitats. Riparian plant species require a source of moisture and may occur along these areas without visible water on the surface. The botanical diversity is high compared with surrounding dry habitats. Riparian habitats transect all other habitats and are usually recognized by the change in species from the surrounding drier habitats. For example, while walking through a conifer forest you may encounter Quaking Aspen, dogwoods, alders, or maples. In other areas the shrubbery changes from manzanitas to willows along with more grasses and sedges and wildflowers.

The Bear River marks the boundary between Nevada and Placer Counties. Growing in the Riparian habitat along the river below Rollins Reservoir are willows, alders, rushes, California Ash, and California Wild Grape.

KAREN CALLAHAN

Red Firs with yellow-green lichen above the average winter snow level in Upper Conifer Forest.

Rocky Subalpine habitat with Mountain Pride and buckwheat.

UC   Upper Conifer Forest: This habitat occurs above the Lower Conifer Forest habitat at elevations of about 6,000 to 8,000 feet. Lower summer temperatures, harsh winters, and frequent long-lasting snowfall typify this habitat. Mature stands of Red Fir form such a dense canopy that other conifers, understory shrubs, and forbs are often shaded out; they are mainly found in forest openings. Lodgepole Pine is the most common associate of Red Fir. Other conifers associated with Red Fir are Jeffrey Pine, Mountain Hemlock, Western White Pine, and Sierra Juniper on exposed rocky sites. Shrubs are Bush Chinquapin, Huckleberry Oak, Tobacco Bush, manzanitas, currants, and snowberries.

SA   Subalpine/Alpine: Winter comes early to this habitat that is mostly above 7,500 feet. It is covered with snow throughout the winter and into late spring. This habitat is scarcely represented north of Lake Tahoe. The forest community consists of small groves and scattered individual trees of Lodgepole Pine, Mountain Hemlock, Whitebark Pine, Western White Pine, and Sierra Juniper. Wildflowers adapted to this environment may start growing before snow melt, grow fast, and flower and set seed rapidly. The flowering period may be only one month.

RO   Rock Outcrops: This habitat may occur in any of the other habitats. It primarily consists of outcroppings of various types of rock (rock that is exposed above the surface of the surrounding soil). The soils associated with the fractures in the rocks and the areas surrounding are normally coarse and relatively infertile. Yet plants, some of which are unique or rare, have adapted to this environment. Rock outcrops are usually

Rock Outcrops shelter cascades of California Fuchsia and Eupatorium.

warmer and drier than the surrounding habitats. Ironically, wetter environment plants are found growing around the bases of boulders because they receive more moisture due to runoff from the boulders that maintain the moisture longer.

SP   Sagebrush/Pine: Locally known as the "east side," this habitat is in the area east and north of Truckee, on the east side of the Sierra crest. The overstory is primarily open stands of Jeffrey Pine,

On the "east side" of the crest, sagebrush, Deltoid Balsamroot, and paintbrush, with an overstory of Jeffrey Pine and Western Juniper, define the Sagebrush/Pine habitat.

KAREN CALLAHAN

Kyburz Flat is one of the largest meadows north of Truckee in the Tahoe National Forest. A dry forest of Jeffrey Pine and small shrubs such as Antelope Bush, Western Peony, and sagebrush surround the wetlands.

Incense Cedar, and Western Juniper. The understory is Antelope Bush, Huckleberry Oak, sagebrush, manzanitas, and wild roses, along with Mountain Mule Ears, balsamroots, violets, shooting stars, and paintbrushes. Riparian and meadow habitats contain many species unique to this drier habitat.

Comments: The comments section provides general information about the plant, including such things as how to tell it from closely related species, toxicity if relevant, ethnobotanical uses, and other facts of interest relating to the plant. Information about culinary, medicinal, and other uses of plants is included for historical and educational purposes only—to add to the appreciation of the plants and the people who used them.

Since its beginning in 1965, the California Native Plant Society (CNPS) has collected science-based information on rare plants throughout California, using a ranking or rating system with codes and numbers to describe the degree of rarity of a particular species. Instead of using the CNPS system for uncommon plants, we've chosen to use general terms such as "uncommon" or "rare" in our plant descriptions. For more detailed information, the *Inventory of Rare and Endangered Plants of California,* published by CNPS, is the basic reference book about rare California plant species. An online version of the *Inventory* is available on the CNPS Web site, *www.cnps.org.* CNPS also shares research and field information with the California Department of Fish and Game.

Chaparral shrubbery with scattered Gray Pines in the Foothill Woodland habitat generally indicates an area of serpentine, gabbro, or shallow volcanic soil.

The distinctive shape of Castle Peak, one of the highest peaks in Nevada County (7,808') and a potential wilderness area, is created by an extrusion of andesitic lava.

Plant Descriptions

$\mathscr{P}$lant Descriptions

Plant Families Described

In winter, fog often covers our lower foothills, as in this mid-winter view of Dry Creek in the Spenceville Wildlife Area not long before our wildflower season begins.

Alismataceae
WATER PLANTAIN FAMILY
Chet Blackburn

Freshwater marsh or aquatic herbs with long, smooth-edged, basal leaves arising from a corm, tuber, stolon, or rhizome. There are often two types of foliage. The submersed leaves tend to be grasslike or have narrow flat blades, while the emergent or floating leaves tend to be oval-shaped or arrow-shaped. There are ***3 persistent sepals, 3 deciduous petals, and 6 or more stamens. The fruit is a group of achenes mounted on a headlike structure.*** There are 12 genera and 75–100 species worldwide, mostly in the Northern Hemisphere. There are 4 genera and 10 species in California, of which 4 genera and 7 species have been recorded in Nevada and Placer Counties.

Alisma plantago-aquatica   Native perennial
Common Water Plantain   Jun–Aug

Description: Plant 2–6′ in flower. Leaves generally lance-shaped to ovate with a truncate base. The much-branched erect inflorescence is 2 to 6 times taller than the leaves. The flowers are less than ½″ across with 3 white smooth-edged petals.

Habitat: Below 4,500′. Wet places, shallow water, muddy shores of ditches, marshes, and slow-moving streams. AQ, RP.

Comments: The similar non-native *Alisma lanceolatum* usually has pink flowers and leaves that taper at the base. Both species grow in our counties and are variable enough to make identification difficult. The tuberous roots of Water Plantain are much relished by wildlife, especially ducks.

CINDY RUBIN • CINDY RUBIN

Common Water Plantain

Fringed Water Plantain

Damasonium californicum   Native perennial
Fringed Water Plantain   Apr–Jul

Description: 6–18″. Leaves of two types. As plants emerge in the spring, they are often under water and produce narrow floating lance-shaped leaves on petioles reaching to the surface. Out of water, the new leaves are basal, the blades elliptic and with a sheathing petiole. Flowers may appear both in the water and out of it. They consist of 3-toothed or incised (fringed) white petals with a yellowish base. The fruit structure is a starlike cluster of achenes.

Habitat: Below 5,000′. Wet places in shallow water and receding waterlines. AQ, VP, RP.

Comments: An uncommon plant that in our area was once occasionally seen in the vernal pools and intermittent streams around Roseville. It is rapidly disappearing in that area as a result of development.

Broadleaf Arrowhead

Sagittaria latifolia   Native perennial
Broadleaf Arrowhead   Jul–Sep

Description: 1–4′. The leaves are shaped like an arrowhead, rising from the plant base. The 3-petaled flowers are arranged in whorls of 3 along a leafless flower stem. There are two types of flowers; those in the upper whorls are stamen bearing (male) and those in lower whorls are pistil bearing (female).

Habitat: Below 5,000′. Year round in wet places. Marshes, bogs, edges of lakes and ponds. AQ, RP.

Comments: An extremely variable species in leaf shape. Arrow lobes may be thick or slender, longer than broad or broader than long. The tubers are relished by wildlife and Native Americans. It is the most common species at lower elevations. At higher elevations, especially snow lakes, the common species is *Sagittaria cuneata*.

Apiaceae
CARROT FAMILY
Carolyn Chainey-Davis

This family is the source of many important herbs and spices (parsley, fennel, dill, coriander) and vegetable crops (carrots, parsnips, celery). Some species are very poisonous. Make sure of identity before tasting. *They have umbrella-like clusters (umbels) of many tiny 5-petaled flowers* and *fruits of 2 one-seeded halves that separate when mature.* Seeds are often the diagnostic characteristic. Each flower has *5 stamens, sepals, petals, and a single inferior ovary with a swollen base with 2 styles* that attract beneficial insects. This family includes annuals, biennials, and perennials, with dissected leaves sheathed around mostly hollow stems. They are generally taprooted or have tuberous roots. Many of the members of this family found locally are introduced non-native species. There are roughly 300 genera and 3,000 species worldwide, mostly from the Northern Hemisphere.

Conium maculatum Non-native perennial
Poison Hemlock Apr–Sep

Poison Hemlock

Description: 6–10′ tall branching, coarse biennial with a stout hollow stem covered with purple blotches and streaks. The inflorescence of white flowers is much branched.

Habitat: Generally below 3,500′. Usually in shady to semi-shady disturbed places on wet ground. MM, RP.

Comments: Native to Europe. All parts are highly poisonous. The plant supposedly was used to poison Socrates. The foliage often has a disagreeable mouselike odor. Often confused with an equally poisonous plant, *Cicuta douglasii,* Western Water Hemlock, but *C. maculatum* has a long white taproot, while *C. douglasii* has a branched, Dahlia-like root system. The veins of *C. maculatum* run to the tip of the leaf teeth, but in *C. douglasii* they run between the teeth.

RICHARD HANES

Queen Anne's Lace

Daucus carota   Non-native biennial
Queen Anne's Lace, Wild Carrot   May–Sep

Description: A 2–5′ tall plant with carrot-scented taproots. Flat-topped, compound umbels of upright and converging flowers forming a somewhat dense nestlike flower head that is 3–6″ wide. Mature ⅛″ fruits conspicuously barbed and bristly, unlike the similar, but poisonous, *Conium* and *Cicuta.* The pinnately dissected leaves have very narrow segments. The leaf margins, veins, and stems are short hairy.

Habitat: Below 3,500′. Roadsides, disturbed areas, many plant communities. GR, CH, FW, LC.

Comments: Introduced from the Old World. It is a common roadside weed at mid to low elevations and in meadows and pastures. Roots sometimes were stored or steamed and boiled for food.

Great Valley Button Celery

Eryngium castrense   Native biennial
Great Valley Button Celery   Jun–Aug

Description: An erect plant, 6–20″ tall. Main stem branches profusely from 1–5″ above the basal rosette of deeply and sharply pinnately lobed leaves. Small flowers, greenish white to faintly blue, are in dense, rounded heads surrounded by spiny bracts.

Habitat: Below 2,400′. Vernally wet depressions, drying streambeds. VP, RP.

Comments: Also known as Coyote Thistle. The roots have been used as a powerful diuretic, stimulant, and expectorant. Juvenile leaves, developed when submerged in vernal pools, are linear and segmented and very different from the coarse spiny adult leaves that form when the pools dry. These juvenile leaves are adapted to submerged conditions by special oxygen-transporting "snorkel" cells.

Foeniculum vulgare   Non-native perennial
Fennel   May–Sep

Description: 2–6′ tall. An anise- or licorice-scented erect perennial. The flower head is 2–3″ wide, with flat-topped compound umbels without bracts or bractlets. The flowers are yellow and without sepals. The petioles are sheathing and conspicuous. The leaves are finely dissected with threadlike segments.

Habitat: Below 3,000′. Roadsides and disturbed places. GR, CH, FW, RP.

Comments: An abundant and invasive introduction from southern Europe. One of several host plants for the Anise Swallowtail butterfly. The seeds are served with meals and eaten for flavor in India and other countries. Easily identified by crushing or tasting the foliage, which has a strong licorice taste and smell.

CHET BLACKBURN

Fennel

Heracleum lanatum   Native perennial
Cow Parsnip   Apr–Jul

Description: 3–10′ tall. Strong-scented and robust. The hollow stems are stout, hairy, and grooved. The huge maplelike leaves are palmately lobed and 8–20″ wide. The petals are white, yellowish, or rosy. Fruits are very flattened, unlike the cylindrical fruits in Angelica.

Habitat: Below 9,000′. Wooded or open moist places, at mid to high elevations in our counties, but at sea level on the coast. MM, RP.

Comments: Sometimes used as an ornamental. The young raw shoots were peeled and eaten like celery by Native Americans. The dried hollow stems were used as toy blowguns to shoot berries and pebbles, and were also used to carry water. *Heracleum* is from the Latin *Hercules,* referring to its robust stature.

RICHARD HANES

Cow Parsnip

Gray's Lovage

Ligusticum grayi   Native perennial
Gray's Lovage   Jun–Sep

Description: 1–2′ tall. Stem erect. Taprooted, the roots are not licorice-scented as in *Osmorhiza.* The base is conspicuously fibrous. Nearly all leaves are basal, pinnate, with narrow leaf segments with 2–3 points. The compound umbels have no bracts at the base. Flowers are white or pinkish.

Habitat: 4,000–10,500′. Mid to high elevations in situations of wet soils. UC, MM.

Comments: The tender leaves were soaked in water, cooked, and used for food by Native Americans, who needed to be wary because of its close resemblance to Western Water Hemlock, *Cicuta douglasii.* The roots were also pulverized and used for poisoning fish and as a cold and cough remedy, analgesic, and for children's stomachaches.

Foothill Lomatium

Lomatium utriculatum   Native perennial
Foothill Lomatium   Feb–May

Description: 4–20″ tall with leafy stems from a slender taproot. The leaves are dissected with many long, threadlike segments. The ovary has many tiny hairs. The fruit is smooth with broad wings that are of equal or greater width than the fruit, and broader than *L. triternatum* and *L. dissectum.* It can be distinguished from *L. macrocarpum* by the presence of a stem.

Habitat: 150–5,000′. Grassy slopes and flats. GR, FW, LC, SG.

Comments: Leaves, sometimes with flowers, were fried in grease and salt or eaten raw by Native Americans. The roots were also chewed for headaches and stomachaches. One of several host plants of the Anise Swallowtail butterfly. It is one of our earliest blooming wildflowers. It is tolerant of many soil types.

Osmorhiza chilensis   Native perennial
Mountain Sweet Cicely   Apr–Jul

Description: 1–4′ tall. An erect plant with a hairy stem. A few compound leaves with long petioles rise from its base bearing 3 sharply serrated or lobed leaflets. Thick, clustered licorice-scented roots. Loose umbels of tiny flowers followed by caraway-like fruits with bristly tails. The tailed fruits and hairy stems distinguish it from the similar *O. occidentalis.*

Habitat: 300–8,400′. Dry wooded areas. FW, LC, UC.

Comments: Easily overlooked because of its delicate nature and tiny flowers. Native Americans used the roots as a stimulant "to bring one around," and also as a cold remedy. The whole plant was fed to mares during the winter to condition them for foaling. Seeds stick tightly to clothing

Mountain Sweet Cicely

Perideridia bolanderi ssp. *bolanderi*
     Native perennial
Bolander's Yampah   Jun–Aug

Description: Stems 8–16″ tall. Short, plump, tuberous roots resembling radishes distinguish it from other *Perideridia* species. The white, flat-topped flowers are on graceful stems.

Habitat: 3,000–6,500′. Drier habitats than other yampahs, often on slopes surrounding meadows. LC, UC, SP.

Comments: This is one of five *Perideridia* species in our area. All are called Yampahs. The tuberous roots of Yampahs, especially Kellogg's Yampah, were an important food source of Miwok and other Native Americans. They were said to have a sweet, nutty flavor. The stored, dried roots were also pounded and made into bread or soup. Yampah roots served as a substitute for acorns.

Bolander's Yampah

Poison Sanicle

Sanicula bipinnata   Native perennial
Poison Sanicle   Mar–May

Description: 1–2′ tall. Leaves twice pinnate; each leaflet is slightly enlarged with rounded marginal teeth. The whole plant is rough to the touch. The flowering branches are almost leafless. The flowers are yellow and inconspicuous.

Habitat: 100–1,500′. Grassy places, especially Blue Oak woodlands. GR, FW, CH.

Comments: The crushed leaves have a pungent odor that is very reminiscent of cilantro, which is the easiest way to identify the plant and distinguish it from other sanicles. The plant is poisonous to livestock but is rarely eaten. It can be found in sun or shade, often under Blue Oaks, but is frequently overlooked because of its wispy nature. Most, if not all, sanicles contain saponins that are poisonous, especially to fish.

Purple Sanicle

Sanicula bipinnatifida   Native perennial
Purple Sanicle, Shoe Buttons   Mar–May

Description: 6–24″ tall. Distinguished from other Apiaceae by having its flowers in simple, dense, rounded (not compound) umbels. The flowers are usually purple-red with conspicuous stamens, but a yellow form also exists. The stamens are longer than in most sanicles. The pinnately divided leaves separate it from *S. crassicaulis,* which has palmate leaves, and its sturdy leaves with a broad serrated margin distinguish it from *S. bipinnata,* which bears little resemblance to it anyway.

Habitat: 60–3,500′. Locally common in open to partly shaded areas. GR, FW, LC, SG.

Comments: The Miwok used an infusion from the leaves to apply to snakebites. A root extract was taken as a cure-all. *Sanicula* is a derivative of the Latin word *sanare,* meaning "to heal."

Sanicula crassicaulis   Native perennial
Gamble Weed, Pacific Sanicle   Mar–May

Description: 1–3′ tall. Distinguished from other Apiaceae by having its flowers in simple, dense umbels, not compound umbels. It has palmately lobed or segmented toothed leaves, and the petioles are not winged, unlike *S. bipinnatifida*. Tiny yellowish flowers are clustered in umbels at the top of the branching stems.

Habitat: Below 3,000′. Open slopes, ravines, and woodlands. GR, CH, FW, LC.

Comments: Locally common at mid to low elevations, usually in the shade or partial shade of oak woodlands. Native Americans made a poultice of leaves for rattlesnake bites and other wounds. The roots were chewed and rubbed on the body for good luck in gambling.

Gamble Weed

Sanicula tuberosa   Native perennial
Tuberous Sanicle, Turkey Pea   Mar–Jul

Description: 4–32″ tall. The plant emerges in the spring from a small, rounded tuber. A slender simple or branched stem with pinnately divided leaves develops rapidly. The basal leaves are fernlike and crinkly. The small, bright yellow flowers are in branched, somewhat rounded umbels. The fruits have rounded bumps, not hooks such as are found in *S. bipinnatifida* and *S. crassicaulis*.

Habitat: 500–8,000′. Open to wooded slopes, gravelly meadows, including serpentine. Widespread in California and fairly common. CH, FW, LC, UC, SG.

Comments: Native Americans ate the tuberous roots raw, roasted, or boiled. The presence of the tuber distinguishes it from the other sanicles, which have taproots.

Tuberous Sanicle

Ranger's Buttons

Sphenosciadium capitellatum
Native perennial
Ranger's Buttons, White Heads   Jul–Aug

Description: 2–5′ tall. A robust wetland plant with a stout erect stem. The leaves are once or twice pinnate, 4–12″ long with sheathing petioles that are swollen at the base. The inflorescence contains several dense ball-like, 2–3″ wide flower clusters containing dense matted hairs. Petals are white or with a purplish tinge.

Habitat: 2,700–9,000′. Swampy places, streamsides, and lake shores. AQ, MM, RP.

Comments: Toxic to livestock but rarely eaten. Native Americans used an infusion of roots as an insecticide for lice. A conspicuous plant in damp spots at higher elevations. Look for it at Sagehen Creek and at various locations around Lake Tahoe and other high-elevation lakes and streams, and in wet meadows.

Hartweg's Tauschia

Tauschia hartwegii   Non-native perennial
Hartweg's Tauschia   Mar–May

Description: Robust plant 3–4′ tall. Large, uniquely serrated compound leaves up to 1′ in length. The terminal leaflet is 3-lobed, while the rest of the leaflets are often a combination of egg-shaped and lobed leaflets. The flowering stem is stout and leafless, culminating in a loose umbel of greenish yellow flowering heads.

Habitat: 300–2,500′. Generally in moist areas on shaded to partly shaded wooded or brushy slopes and canyons. CH, FW, LC, SG.

Comments: The long stalks of the greenish yellow flower heads in the outer ring of the umbel cause them to appear to be orbiting around those in the center. It is an attractive plant, yet its succulent appearance and unusual leaves make it appear to be out of place in its surroundings.

Torilis arvensis   Non-native annual
Hedge Parsley   Apr–Jun

Description: 1–3′ tall. Taprooted, erect, branched, and with slender stems. Loose, open umbels of tiny white flowers. There are no leaflike bracts as in *Daucus*. The small oblong fruits have many barbed prickles. The leaves are 2–3″, pinnately divided, hairy, and somewhat fernlike in appearance.

Habitat: 120–4,800′. Disturbed places, open to shaded hills. GR, CH, FW, LC.

Comments: A relatively new but now common weed of grasslands, woodlands, and disturbed places. It was introduced from Eurasia, especially the Mediterranean region, and continues to spread and proliferate in our area. Its seed dispersal is by means of barbed fruits that stick tightly to clothing and fur. This is perhaps the plant most often responsible for "sock burs."

JULIE S. CARVILLE

Hedge Parsley

CINDY RUBIN • KAREN CALLAHAN

Both native and introduced species of the Carrot family are host plants for the caterpillars of the Anise Swallowtail butterfly, shown in three different life stages.

Apocynaceae
DOGBANE FAMILY
Chet Blackburn

A large, mostly tropical family consisting of plants with simple, entire, opposite leaves *usually containing latex or a milky juice.* The flowers are in parts of 5 except for the pistils, of which there are 2. A few species have only 4 sepals, but most have 5. *Corolla is urnlike.* There are 150–200 genera and about 2,000 species worldwide. Most members of the family are poisonous. The family could most easily be confused with Asclepiadaceae, the Milkweed family, to which it is closely related. The family is not well represented in California, where there are only 6 species, 1 of which was introduced. There are only 3 species in our area, 2 in the genus *Apocynum* and 1 in *Vinca*.

KAREN CALLAHAN

Bitter Dogbane

Apocynum androsaemifolium

Native perennial

**Bitter Dogbane,
Spreading Dogbane**

Jun–Sep

Description: 1–3′ tall, erect or spreading with a forking, reddish stem. Opposite drooping egg-shaped to round leaves on short petioles. The flowers are pinkish white, ¼–½″ across, and scented. The long seedpods (2–8″) are out of proportion to the small flowers, contain cottony seeds, and appear in August–September.

Habitat: 600–7,000′. Dry, semi-open areas in forests and edges of thickets. CH, LC, UC.

Comments: The flowers make an excellent grade of honey. Native Americans used stems collected after the first frost for string. They can cause poisoning in cattle, sheep, and horses, but are usually avoided because of the bitter sap. The milky sap may cause a rash in some individuals.

Vinca major   Non-native perennial
Periwinkle   Mar–Sep

Description: 1' tall. An evergreen sprawling plant with green, lancelike opposite leaves containing a milky sap. The sterile (nonflowering) stems are trailing and rooting as they touch ground. The flowering stems are erect, bearing 1–1¼" broad blue flowers in every other leaf axil.

Habitat: Under 3,000'. Locally common to rampant along streams and in moist canyons. FW, LC, RP.

Comments: Its native range is from Switzerland to Portugal and North Africa, but now it is an almost worldwide nuisance, albeit an attractive one. It is hard to get rid of once established. It is a shade-loving species that chokes out native growth and is a tough, durable, and invasive plant. Responsible plant nurseries no longer carry it but carry a smaller, less invasive form.

RICHARD HANES

Periwinkle

KAREN CALLAHAN • KAREN CALLAHAN

A Pipevine Swallowtail butterfly is shown taking nectar from Canyon Dudleya flowers. Its caterpillars (inset) depend on the leaves of the Pipevine for food.

Araliaceae
GINSENG FAMILY
Chet Blackburn

Herbs, vines, shrubs, or trees. Stems solid, sometimes prickly. The leaves are usually alternate and either palmately or pinnately compound. *The small greenish white flowers grow in round umbels. The calyx is small and sometimes absent. When the calyx is present, it is composed of 5 sepals, the corolla of usually 5 petals but in a few species 4 or 10 petals.* It has 5 *stamens that alternate with the petals.* The fruit is a fleshy berry. There are 60–70 genera and about 700 species worldwide, mostly in the Indo-Malaysian region and South America. There is 1 native species and 1 introduced species found in California, both of them occurring in our area. The non-native species is English Ivy, *Hedera helix.*

Elk Clover

Aralia californica　　　Native perennial
Elk Clover, California Spikenard　　Jun–Aug

Description: 3–10′ giant herb from a thick aromatic rootstock. The stems are fleshy, bearing 1–3′ compound serrated leaves with oval leaflets 4–8″ long. The leaves turn yellow in the fall. It has ball-like umbels of small greenish yellow flowers that eventually become black berries.

Habitat: Below 5,000′. Moist shaded canyons and streamsides. LC, RP.

Comments: Winter dormant. Stalks can shoot up to 10′ in a single season. A good plant for attracting berry-eating birds, it is on the Audubon Society's recommended plant list for backyard habitats in the western United States. One of its common names, Elk Clover, illustrates how puzzling common names can be. It is a deer-resistant plant, so presumably is also elk resistant and certainly bears no resemblance to clover.

Aristolochiaceae
PIPEVINE FAMILY
Chet Blackburn

Vines, twining shrubs, or low herbs with mostly alternate, heart-shaped leaves. The flowers are *without petals but the calyx is prominent and petal-like, usually of some purplish color, and usually flaring out to form an inflated flower.* 6 or 12 stamens, styles usually 6. The *ovary is embedded in the tubular end of the flower stalk.* This largely tropical family includes 10 genera and 600 species worldwide, some of them highly ornamental. There are 2 genera and 5 species in California, with both of the genera and 3 of the species found within our area.

Aristolochia californica   Native perennial
Pipevine, Dutchman's Pipe   Jan–Apr

Description: Twining to 12′. Alternate, heart-shaped, somewhat fuzzy leaves on sparingly branched stems. Semi-deciduous. The 2–4″ greenish veined flowers are streaked with purple. There are no petals; the "flower" is the fused calyx that is conspicuous and curved to form a structure shaped like the bowl of a smoking pipe. Fruit a large leathery pod to 2″.

Habitat: 100–1,600′. Low wooded hills and thickets. FW, CH, RP.

Comments: One of our earliest and most unusual spring flowers. It scrambles over banks and through shrubbery, and climbs into trees. It is the host plant of the beautiful blue-black Pipevine Swallowtail butterfly. It is deer resistant and drought resistant, but thrives with summer water.

JULIE S. CARVILLE

Pipevine

Hartweg's Ginger

Asarum hartwegii   Native perennial
Hartweg's Ginger   Apr–Jun

Description: 2–6″ trailing evergreen from a stout rootstock. The foliage is roughly heart-shaped, green, 2–3″ long, and usually with pale mottling along the veins. The undersides are hairy, the upper surface not. Long hairy petioles. The flowers are dark purple but appear grayish because of the numerous soft hairs, and are usually hidden by the leaves.

Habitat: 500–7,500′. Shaded floors of coniferous forests, often growing together with Rattlesnake Plantain, *Goodyera oblongifolia.* LC, UC.

Comments: The plant has a spicy odor when crushed. This plant is pollinated by flies attracted to the fetid odor of the flowers. It grows in drier habitats than *A. lemmonii.* Of California's 3 native gingers, this is the only one with mottling in its leaves.

Lemmon's Ginger

Asarum lemmonii   Native perennial
Lemmon's Ginger   May–Jul

Description: 6–10″ with bright green heart-shaped leaves from a stolonlike aromatic root-stock. The leaves are somewhat rounded at the apex and semi-evergreen. The brown flowers lack tails and are usually hidden among the leaves.

Habitat: 3,500–6,000′. Uncommon in moist shaded thickets and coniferous forests near streams and boggy places. RP, LC, UC.

Comments: The least common of California native gingers, it is endemic to the Sierra Nevada. A population can be seen in a boggy area along the Sierra Discovery Trail near Bear Valley (Nevada County). Out of bloom it closely resembles the Common Wild Ginger, *Asarum caudatum,* which does not occur in our area but is easily distinguished from it by the lack of the tail on the flower.

Asclepiadaceae
MILKWEED FAMILY
Chet Blackburn

Perennial herbs with opposite or whorled leaves containing a *milky sap.* The family is known for its *ornate and complex pollination mechanism in which stamens and style are fused, but filaments of stamens are enlarged into nectar-bearing cups, sometimes bearing "horns" which probably act as a tongue guide for pollinators. Another part of the stamen forms a ball of pollen attached to a thread with a sticky end. When a pollinator's leg comes in contact, the sticky end attaches itself to the pollinator along with the pollen ball.* The larvae of Monarch Butterflies depend on milkweed as a food source. The flower structure is unique, with 5 swept-back petals and a curving hornlike structure on a central column. Many species are toxic to livestock. It is primarily a tropical family of up to 250 genera and 3,000 species. There are 5 genera and 20 species in California.

Asclepias cordifolia　　　Native perennial
Purple Milkweed　　　Apr–Jul

Description: 1–3′ stem with broad clasping leaves to 6″ wide. The stem and leaves are waxy blue to purplish and contain a milky juice. The leaves are mostly opposite, rarely in 3s, sometimes tinged with purple. The flowers are crimson with pale pinkish hoods, giving a checkered effect. The fruit is elongate and tightly packed with flat circular seeds bearing long silky appendages.

Habitat: 200–6,300′. Scattered in brushy rocky places and semi-open slopes to forested flats. FW, CH, LC.

Comments: Slightly fragrant. Monarch Butterfly caterpillars obtain alkaloids from milkweed plants that make them unpalatable to predators. Usually not a colony-forming species, the plant is more often seen as scattered individual plants.

KAREN CALLAHAN

Purple Milkweed

Narrow-leaf Milkweed

CHET BLACKBURN

Asclepias fascicularis　　　Native perennial
Narrow-leaf Milkweed　　　Jun–Oct

Description: 2–4′ tall. An upright clumping plant from a creeping rootstock. The linear leaves are in whorls of 3–6. The blades are 2–5″ long on short petioles, generally hairless and folded upward. Numerous white to greenish, sometimes purple-tinted, flowers appear on long stalks.

Habitat: 100–5,000′. Locally common in both dry and moist locations such as roadsides, ditches, railway embankments, gravel beds, and slopes. Always in full sunlight. GR, FW, CH, LC, SG, RP.

Comments: Native Americans made chewing gum from its milky sap combined with salmon fat or deer grease. Poisonous to livestock, particularly sheep, but shunned by livestock unless the area is overgrazed. Formerly known as *A. mexicana.*

Showy Milkweed

KAREN CALLAHAN

Asclepias speciosa　　　Native perennial
Showy Milkweed　　　May–Jul

Description: 1–4′ tall plant that is leafy to the top. Soft white-hairy stems. Oval to oblong woolly leaves 3–8″ long, grayish green, that are mostly soft hairy except for the upper surfaces of older leaves. Rosy to purplish flowers in round terminal clusters. Fragrant. Fruit oblong, woolly, and soft spiny.

Habitat: 100–6,000′. Dry or moist open places, especially gravelly or sandy places such as along streams. RP, GR, LC.

Comments: Tough fibers extracted from the stem of this species and *A. eriocarpa* were used by Native Americans in making cords and ropes and weaving a coarse cloth. They also used pulverized seeds as a cleansing or healing agent for sores, cuts, and even rattlesnake bites.

Asteraceae
SUNFLOWER FAMILY
Vicki Lake

The flowers are aggregated into heads that mimic single flowers, the bracts (phyllaries) at the base of the inflorescence head forming a pseudo-calyx. The flowers form a pseudo-corolla. Ray flowers on the perimeter of the inflorescence are often strap-shaped (ligulate) and unisexual (female). The *inner disk flowers are usually tubular* and *bisexual.* Some genera have only ray flowers (e.g., dandelions); some only disk flowers (e.g., thistles), and some have both (e.g., daisies). The receptacle of the inflorescence is flat to conical, sometimes with bracts (chaff) between the flowers. The *calyx is reduced to a pappus of awns, scales, or bristles* (or is sometimes absent). Stamens are usually 5; anthers are united into a tube around the style. It is the largest family of plants in the world and in California, and is represented by 87 genera and 270 species in our area.

Achillea millefolium	Native perennial
Yarrow	Jun–Aug

Description: Stems to 3′ tall. White to pink flowers occur in a flat-topped cluster. Soft, finely divided fernlike leaves, with the upper ones clasping the stem. Aromatic.

Habitat: Below 11,600′. Meadows and damp places. GR, FW, LC, MM, RP.

Comments: Common in the foothills. Nice in gardens and attracts beneficial insects, but has a tendency to spread by both runners and seed. It has been hybridized to produce some fine cultivars. Native Americans drank a tea to encourage sweating and reduce fever, colds, flu, and stomachache. A tincture of Yarrow has been described as a "sauna in a bottle" because it is diaphoretic, which is a technical way of saying that it makes men sweat and women perspire. Also can be used externally to treat bleeding.

KAREN CALLAHAN • JULIE S. CARVILLE

Yarrow

Pathfinder

KAREN CALLAHAN

Adenocaulon bicolor   Native perennial
Pathfinder, Trail Plant   Jun–Aug

Description: 1–3' high. Plant erect and openly branched with single, slender leaves that are triangular and primarily basal. The leaf margins are shallowly lobed. The leaves are white-woolly below and green-hairless above. The flower heads are small with 6–14 whitish disk flowers.

Habitat: Below 6,600'. Shaded woodland and forest floors. FW, LC, UC.

Comments: The common name is derived from the underside of the leaves. When overturned as people walk through, the leaves briefly mark their path with their white undersides. It is a common plant at the Rock Creek Nature Trail, which has an abundance of acidic, humus-rich soil that the plant prefers. The small seeds have clinging hairs that stick to pant legs and socks in the fall.

Western Eupatorium

JULIE S. CARVILLE

Ageratina occidentalis   Native perennial
Western Eupatorium,
Western Snakeroot   Jul–Sep

Description: Plants 1–2½' tall, woody at the base, with a green or purple short, hairy stem. The leaves are generally alternate, the blades triangular with toothed edges. The flower heads are white to blue, densely clustered at the tips of stems and branches, and appear late in the year.

Habitat: 6,900–12,000'. Moist soils, especially among rocks in sun to light shade. CH, UC, SA, RO.

Comments: Native Americans used it externally for rheumatism and swelling. The plant was formerly known as *Eupatorium occidentale,* a name that can still be found in some references. It resembles a common eastern wildflower, Joe Pye Weed, to which it is related. In cultivation, it produces colonies from underground rhizomes. It is a good butterfly plant.

Agoseris grandiflora   Native perennial
Large-flower Agoseris,
California Dandelion   May–Jul

Description: 6–24″ tall with a leafless stem. Bracts subtending a lemon yellow inflorescence that is often red-tinged and soft hairy. The long lower leaves are smooth to lobed. The plant has a milky sap and a strong taproot.

Habitat: Below 6,600′. Dry areas to mountain meadows. GR, CH, FW, LC.

Comments: The large fluffy, almost cottonlike seedball heads are about 2″ wide and superficially resemble the Common Dandelion, hence its other name, California Dandelion. Another common *Agoseris* from our area is called Annual Agoseris, *Agoseris heterophylla,* and is a smaller annual plant of open areas, especially flats and around vernal pools. Its narrow hairy leaves are different from its perennial relative.

STEVE MATSON • STEVE MATSON

Large-flower Agoseris

Agoseris retrorsa   Native perennial
Spearleaf Agoseris   May–Aug

Description: 6–12″ tall in flower. A basal rosette of deeply lobed leaves with the lobes pointing backwards like barbs on a fishhook. The leafless flower stalk bears yellow dandelion-like flowers followed by dandelion-like puffy seed heads.

Habitat: Below 6,600′. Around rock outcrops and semi-open places. GR, CH, FW, LC, RO.

Comments: In limited cultivation as a rock garden plant. The seeds are sold by specialty nurseries. Some men can identify with the leaves of this plant, which start out hairy but tend to lose most of their hair with age. The leaves were boiled and eaten by Native Americans.

KAREN CALLAHAN

Spearleaf Agoseris

KAREN CALLAHAN

Pearly Everlasting

Anaphalis margaritacea   Native perennial
Pearly Everlasting   Jun–Aug

Description: 8–48″ tall. An erect white-woolly plant with leafy stems. The flower clusters are approximately 2″ wide and comprised of tight pearly white heads made of papery bracts. The leaves are alternate, curled under, greener above than below, and aromatic.

Habitat: Below 10,600′. Woods, roadsides, and disturbed places. GR, CH, FW, LC, UC, RO.

Comments: *Margaritaceus* means "of pearls," referring to the appearance of the flower heads. The plant has been used as a tobacco substitute. The leaves were chewed, smoked, or made into a tea for colds, asthma, coughs, and tuberculosis. The dried flower heads are sometimes used in flower arrangements. It is one of the host plants of the Painted Lady butterfly.

JULIE S. CARVILLE

Rosy Pussytoes

Antennaria rosea   Native perennial
Rosy Pussytoes   Jun–Aug

Description: Stems to 1′ tall. Plants form dense, low woolly mats. Each inflorescence is comprised of 3–16 flower heads. Variable in color. Typically, only female flowers are present. The lower leaves are spoon-shaped.

Habitat: 4,000–12,200′. Wooded places, meadow edges, rock barrens, and dry ridges. UC, SA, MM, RO.

Comments: To distinguish this species from other local pussytoes, all of the following characteristics must exist: (1) inflorescence of more than 3 flower heads, (2) plants forming dense mats, and (3) bracts below flower heads (phyllaries) white to rose or light brown, and without a dark spot at the base. The genus name *Antennaria* refers to the supposed resemblance of the male flowers to insect antennae.

Arnica cordifolia　　　Native perennial
Heart-leaf Arnica　　　May–Aug

Description: To 20″ tall. Stems generally
unbranched, one to several per plant. Pairs of
heart-shaped leaves with long petioles occur low
on the plant but become smaller and with short
or no petioles higher along the flower stem. The
leaves are fragrant and usually shallowly
toothed.

Habitat: 4,000–9,900′. Dry to moist areas;
often open woodlands and mountain meadows.
LC, UC, MM.

Comments: In addition to having heart-shaped
leaves, the white bristles stemming from near the
base of each disk flower (found in the central
portion of the inflorescence) distinguish this
species from Soft Arnica, which has yellow-brown
bristles. *A. cordifolia* is toxic. It may be seen at
Sagehen Creek.

MICHAEL GRAFF

Heart-leaf Arnica

Arnica mollis　　　Native perennial
Soft Arnica, Hairy Arnica　　　Jul–Sep

Description: To 2′ tall. One to several little-
branched resinous stems. The 12–18 ray flowers
form the outer margin of the inflorescence head.
The opposite leaves are fragrant and downy-soft,
with leaf edges smooth to toothed. The lowest
leaves are generally the largest.

Habitat: 8,300–11,600′. Moist places such as
meadows and stream banks. SA, MM, RP.

Comments: Source of a topical tincture used
for bruises, sprains, and injuries that increases
blood flow to an area without a warming effect.
A variable species that makes identification even
more difficult by hybridizing freely with other
Arnica species. When bruised, the foliage gives
off an odor that smells like a combination of
lemon, lavender, and turpentine.

JULIE S. CARVILLE

Soft Arnica

California Mugwort

Artemisia douglasiana   Native perennial
California Mugwort   Jun–Oct

Description: 1–8′ tall, but most often around 3′, with many erect gray-green to brown stems. The tiny inconspicuous flower heads grow in compact clusters along the top of the stem. The stongly fragrant leaves are often 3–5-lobed near the tip, though typically just the lower leaves. The undersurfaces of the leaves are densely matted with soft hairs and lighter in color than the top, sometimes almost silvery.

Habitat: Below 7,300′. Open to shady places, often in drainages. GR, CH, FW, LC, RP.

Comments: A poultice can be used as remedy for poison oak rashes or the fresh leaves rubbed directly onto the rash. Native Americans used the plant for ceremonial incense in sweat lodges. The leaves are also used to repel insects in clothing and grains. Birds like the seeds.

Alpine Aster

Aster alpigenus var. *andersonii*
                                         Native perennial
Alpine Aster   Jun–Sep

Description: Plant 4–16″ high, with branches arching upward or erect. The almost leafless stems support solitary flower heads. The linear leaves occur in a clump at the base of the plant. The stem, leaves, and leafy receptacles holding the flower heads are covered with white woolly hairs. The flower heads consist of light blue or violet to lavender ray flowers, the predominant color, but with yellow to orange central disk flowers. The plant has a fleshy taproot.

Habitat: 5,000–12,200′. Moist or boggy meadows. UC, SA, MM.

Comments: It can be seen growing in Castle Valley below Castle Peak. This colorful species is frequently sold at native plant sales, although it is not always happy in low-elevation gardens.

Aster chilensis
Common Aster

Native perennial
Jun–Dec

Description: 6–36″ high. A slender sprawling plant with blue, white, or violet ray flowers (the predominant color) and yellow central disk flowers. The flowers are relatively small. The stem leaves are short and sessile. The few large basal leaves soon wither.

Habitat: 100–2,000′. Common in various habitats from dry open sunny slopes to partly shaded seeps and stream, ditch, pond, and lake edges. GR, FW, LC, CH, RP.

Comments: The species name *chilensis* means "from Chile," but this is a misnomer resulting from a mix-up. The original collector, Thaddeus Haenke, passed away in 1817 but the plant from his collection was not named until 1932 by Nees von Esenbeck, who misinterpreted Haenke's locality notation, which was written in Spanish.

KAREN CALLAHAN

Common Aster

Aster eatonii
Eaton's Aster

Native perennial
Jun–Oct

Description: 1–3′ tall. Minutely hairy stems rise from a creeping rhizome. The leaves are linear to lance-shaped. The inflorescence is tall and leafy, with white or pink ray flowers and yellow central disk flowers.

Habitat: 200–5,000′. Widespread in wet soil and open areas along streams. FW, LC, CH, RP.

Comments: This is only one of ten *Aster* species found in our area, many of which are similar in appearance. To add to the confusion, the similar genus *Erigeron* is also frequently confused with *Aster.* In general, species of the genus *Erigeron* are spring bloomers and species of the genus *Aster* bloom in late summer to fall, but there are exceptions to both.

CHET BLACKBURN

Eaton's Aster

Deltoid Balsamroot

RICHARD HANES

Balsamorhiza deltoidea   Native perennial
Deltoid Balsamroot   Apr–Jun

Description: Stem 8–36″ tall. The flower heads are one to few. The outer ray flowers are approximately 1″ long. The leaves are widely triangular, sparsely hairy, opposite or alternate, smooth-edged or shallowly toothed, and much smaller along the stem than at the plant base.

Habitat: 1,000–7,900′. Grassy slopes, open forests, and shrubby areas on deep sandy soils. GR, FW, LC, UC, SG.

Comments: Distinguished from Arrow-leaf Balsamroot, *Balsamorhiza sagittata,* by its leaves being green on both surfaces and by being only sparsely hairy, whereas Arrow-leaf Balsamroot leaves are densely hairy, at least when young. Roots, stems, leaves, and seeds are all edible. Balsamroots are so called because of the sticky sap of the plant's taproot.

Common Blennosperma

JULIE S. CARVILLE

Blennosperma nanum   Native annual
Common Blennosperma,
Stickyseed   Feb–Apr

Description: 2–8″ tall with a succulent well-branched stem. The flower heads are yellow and borne in cymes. The pollen appears as white dots interspersed among the inner (disk) flowers. The outer ray flowers are purplish underneath. The leaves are narrow, pinnately divided, ½–2½″ long.

Habitat: Below 5,300′. Wet open areas, woods, vernal pool edges, and grasslands. VP, GR, FW, LC.

Comments: This is a species that may be dependent on a specific pollinator (in this case the specialty bee *Andrena blennosperma*) rather than general pollinators. Hence, trying to relocate *Blennosperma* from existing vernal pools to new locations may be ineffective without its pollinators present.

Calycadenia spicata   Native annual
Spiked Rosinweed   May–Sep

Description: 8–24″ tall. Densely hairy and glandular. The leaves are longest at the midstem. There are one to several white flower heads per node. The inflorescence is glandular.

Habitat: Below 1,500′. Dry soils in sunny places such as open hillsides, rocky ridges, and talus slopes. GR, FW, CH, LC, RO, SG.

Comments: The genus name *Calycadenia* is derived from Greek *kalux*, meaning cup, and *adenos*, meaning gland, in reference to its inflorescence glands. The plant has a pungent smell. This is the common species in our area. *C. multiglandulosa* is a similar species but the lobes of the ligules are distinctly unequal, whereas the ligule lobes in this species are about equal. The other two rosinweeds in our area, *C. truncata* and *C. mollis,* have yellow flower heads.

KAREN CALLAHAN

Spiked Rosinweed

Carduus pycnocephalus
     Non-native annual/biennial
Italian Thistle   May–Jul

Description: 1–6′ tall. The erect stems are more or less woolly. The inflorescence heads are 2–5 per cluster, the flowers pink-purple. The spiny leaves are deeply cut into 2–5 pairs of lobes, becoming smaller up the stem.

Habitat: Below 3,300′. Invasive weed along roadsides and in pastures and disturbed areas. GR,CH, FW, LC.

Comments: Native to the Mediterranean region of southern Europe. It has become a significant problem weed locally since arriving in the 1930s. Grows in full sun to shade but seems to be more abundant in bright shade under oaks, where it creates a natural ladder for flames from grass fires to climb into the trees.

CINDY RUBIN

Italian Thistle

Yellow Star Thistle

RICHARD HANES

Centaurea solstitialis   Non-native annual
Yellow Star Thistle   May–Oct

Description: 4–36″ tall. A branched, rounded, grayish, short hairy plant. The inflorescence head has palmately arranged spines. Leaves are bristly, the lower ones 2–6″ long and 1–2-lobed. Leaves are generally absent at the time of flowering.

Habitat: Below 4,300′. Pastures, roadsides, and disturbed grassland and woodland. GR, CH, FW, LC, SG.

Comments: Invasive weed, especially in disturbed areas such as pastures. Cumulatively toxic to horses. It causes "Chewing Disease" in which the horse is unable to swallow. Goldfinches love the seed and beekeepers seek it out, but the plant's negative attributes far outweigh its positives. Sicilian Star Thistle, *Centaurea sulphurea,* is a closely related species similar in appearance that is also found in our area.

Dusty Maidens

JULIE S. CARVILLE

Chaenactis douglasii   Native perennial
Dusty Maidens   May–Jul

Description: Plant less than 20″ high, erect to spreading. The upper parts of the stems are branched and thinly cobwebby woolly. The flowers are white to pinkish. The inflorescence head is comprised entirely of disk flowers, the outer flowers enlarged. The leaves are alternate, pinnately lobed, and cobwebby. The leaf lobes are near the middle with their tips curled under.

Habitat: 3,300–11,600′. Dry, open, rocky areas. CH, LC, UC, RO, SG.

Comments: Native Americans rubbed the mashed plant on limbs for soreness or aching and put an infusion of young leaves on hair for headaches. The ray flowers age to white seeds, expanding as they dry and forming a spherical seed head that is even more conspicuous than the original flowers.

Chamomilla suaveolens   Non-native annual
Pineapple Weed   May–Aug

Description: Plant less than 1′ high, and usually much less. The stems are branched from the base and sweet smelling. The inflorescence heads are cone-shaped, $\frac{1}{16}$–$\frac{1}{3}$″ high with many yellowish green disk flowers. No ray flowers.

Habitat: Below 2,600′. Disturbed areas, sand bars, riverbanks, footpaths, roadsides, and grazed land. GR, CH, FW, LC, RP.

Comments: A common weed in disturbed places throughout most of California. The seed may sprout at any time of the year. Late-sprouting seed overwinters as small leafy rosettes. In Latin, *suaveolens* means sweet smelling. Formerly known as *Matricaria matricarioides,* a name that is still in wide use. The leaves smell like pineapple when crushed.

Pineapple Weed

Chondrilla juncea
    Non-native biennial/perennial
Skeleton Weed   Jul–Oct

Description: Plant 1–4′ tall with much-branched stems and milky sap. The juvenile leaves form a rosette but soon wither as the flower stem develops. The stem leaves are inconspicuous, narrow, and smooth margined. The inflorescence heads are scattered on the branches with 7–15 yellow strap-shaped ray flowers.

Habitat: Below 2,000′. Well-drained, light-textured soils in disturbed areas, along roadsides, and in pastures and agricultural fields. GR, FW.

Comments: A noxious weed native to Europe. Extensive, deep root system makes control difficult. The flowering stalk appears to be leafless and wiry, hence the common name. Distribution is mainly by seed, but it can also be spread by roots being scattered by deep cultivation.

Skeleton Weed

Chicory

Cichorium intybus   Non-native perennial
Chicory   Jun–Oct

Description: Stems 1–6′ tall with spreading branches and milky sap. A deep, woody taproot. The flowering heads are borne 1–3 together in the axils of the upper leaves. Only ray flowers are present and they are usually blue, but occasionally purple or white and up to 1½″ across. The leaves are rough, in a basal rosette, toothed and pinnately lobed, oblong to elliptic in outline, and 2–10″ long. The upper leaves are much reduced.

Habitat: Below 5,000′. Widespread along roadsides and disturbed sites. GR, FW, LC, RP.

Comments: Native to the Mediterranean region. It has been planted for use as salad greens and a coffee substitute (root) as well as an ornamental for its bright, sky blue flowers. Native Americans used a root infusion as a tonic for nerves.

Anderson's Thistle

Cirsium andersonii   Native perennial/biennial
Anderson's Thistle, Rose Thistle   Jun–Oct

Description: Plant 1–2½′ tall, with one to several stems. The leaves are 4–8″ long, green above, gray-hairy below, with a spiny-winged petiole. The red to reddish purple flowers are in one to a few heads.

Habitat: 4,000–10,500′. Dry, open places in woodlands and forests. LC, UC, SA.

Comments: The peeled stems may be cooked as greens. Young leaves are edible raw. In this species, the phyllaries (the stiff spiny structures on the cup just below the red flowers) are not spread out to right angles or recurved downward, and are not cobwebby like they are in our other red-flowering species, *Cirsium occidentale*. *Cirsium andersonii* is also a smaller plant and more confined to higher elevations.

Cirsium occidentale var. *californicum*
Native biennial
California Thistle   Apr–Jul

Description: 4–10′ tall. Typically consisting of
1 stem, branched above and soft short hairy. The
plant may be either erect or low and moundlike.
The flowers are white to purple or rose. Phyllaries
(tightly held bracts at the base of the inflorescence head) many, graduated in several series,
the outer ones spine-tipped. The lower leaves
are 4–16″ long with spiny-winged petioles and
widely triangular lobes. The upper leaves become
gradually smaller.

Habitat: Below 7,600′. Often in disturbed
places in woodland and open forest. FW, LC, UC.

Comments: Native Americans ate the fresh
spring stalks extensively. Roots were eaten raw,
boiled, or roasted. Its cobwebby flower buds
help distinguish it from the previous species.

California Thistle

Cirsium vulgare   Non-native biennial
Bull Thistle   Jun–Sep

Description: 2–5′ tall. The erect stem is spiny
winged with spreading branches above the
middle. The inflorescence heads are round to
bell-shaped, 1½–2″ wide, clustered at the ends
of branches. Phyllaries numerous, narrow, and
graduated in several series, with the outer ones
spine-tipped. The leaves are lobed, with surfaces
harshly bristly on the upper surface, cottony with
prominently raised veins below.

Habitat: Below 7,600′. Pastures, fields, roadsides,
and other disturbed areas. GR, FW, LC, UC, RP.

Comments: Young flowering stalks and roots
are delicious when boiled 20 minutes and
seasoned with salt and butter. Sometimes confused with Milk Thistle, *Silybum marianum,* but
lacks the heavy spines at the base of the flower
head of Milk Thistle.

Bull Thistle

Canadian Horseweed

Conyza canadensis   Native annual
Canadian Horseweed   Apr–Dec

Description: 1 to 8′ tall. Stems erect, un-branched below, may be branched above. The leaves are alternate, many, short-petioled, and hairy. They are coarse and rough. The inflorescence is branched and bears an abundance of small creamy white or yellow flowers.

Habitat: Common in disturbed places below 3,000′. GR, FW, LC.

Comments: Native to North American grasslands, it has spread widely around the world. It contains a terpene that is irritating to the nostrils of horses. South American Horseweed, also known as Hairy Fleabane, *Conyza bonariensis,* is a smaller relative (1–3′) that is also common in our area. Unlike *C. canadensis,* the whole stem is branched, bearing very leafy branchlets covered with rough hairy leaves.

GORDON J. HARRINGTON

Coulter's Daisy

Erigeron coulteri   Native perennial
Coulter's Daisy   Jul–Aug

Description: Stems 8–28″ tall, sparsely hairy. Stem leaves 2½–5″ long, smooth edged or with 2–6 pairs of shallow teeth. They are widest above the middle, have a clasping stem, and are not much smaller up the stem. The inflorescence heads are 1–4 per flowering stem. Both ray and disk flowers are present. Approximately 50–100 ray flowers, each approximately ½–1″ long.

Habitat: 6,300–11,200′. Stream banks, wet meadows, coniferous forest. UC, MM, RP.

Comments: *Erigeron* is derived from Greek *eri,* early, and *geron,* old man. It refers to the early flowering and the white downy hairs, characteristic of some species in this genus. It tends to grow widely scattered in open woods but forms masses in sunlight.

PRENTISS FERGUSON

Erigeron foliosus var. *hartwegii*
                                    Native perennial
Foothill Daisy Fleabane   May–Jul

Description: Stems 8–40″ high, arching upward, branched above. Inflorescence heads are
flat-topped, one to several per flowering stem,
consisting of both ray and disk flowers. There are
15–60 blue to lavender ray flowers, ¼–½″ long,
weakly coiled. Disk flowers are numerous and
golden yellow. Phyllaries strongly graded in 3–5
series. Leaves less than 2″ long, narrow, well
distributed around stem, evenly sized and spaced.

Habitat: 330–2,000′. Rocky riverbanks, oak
woodlands. FW, RP.

Comments: It can be observed along the Middle
and South Yuba Rivers and the various trails in
the American River Canyon. *Erigeron foliosus* is
widespread in California and five distinct varieties
are recognized.

KAREN CALLAHAN

Foothill Daisy Fleabane

Erigeron miser   Native perennial
Starved Daisy   Jul–Aug

Description: Plant 2–10″ tall with long spreading hairs. Numerous relatively unbranched stems
arch upward from a woody base. The inflorescence heads are one to few in close cymes at the
stem tips. Only disk flowers are present, with
phyllaries strongly graded in 3–5 series. The
leaves are evenly spaced and sized along the
stem, narrow, and less than ¾″ long.

Habitat: 6,000–7,600′. Granite cliffs and
similar rocky areas in red fir forest. UC, RO.

Comments: A rare plant found growing in only
a few locations at upper elevations in Nevada and
Placer Counties in the Tahoe National Forest.
The genus *Erigeron* is a large one in California;
51 species occur within the state, some of them
with a number of varieties. At least 13 species
are found in Nevada and Placer Counties.

RICHARD HANES

Starved Daisy

Woolly Sunflower

RICHARD HANES

Eriophyllum lanatum
                    Native annual/biennial/perennial
Woolly Sunflower   Apr–Aug

Description: Stems 4–40″ high, unbranched or few-branched, erect or arching upward from a woody base. It often occurs as a subshrub with white-woolly herbage. The flowers are bright yellow with 8–13 ray petals, their tips turning pale with age, solitary or in loose clusters at the top of stems. The leaves are gray-green on top, white-woolly below, deeply lobed, and fragrant.

Habitat: Below 12,000′. Widespread with at least 4 varieties locally in open, dry, often rocky, places. CH, FW, LC, RO, SG.

Comments: A hardy garden plant, good for rock gardens and front borders. It requires full sun and well-drained soil. Native Americans used it medicinally as a poultice for aching parts of the body. Size variable.

White Everlasting

KAREN CALLAHAN

Gnaphalium canescens ssp. *beneolens*
                    Native biennial/perennial
White Everlasting,
Feltleaf Everlasting   Jul–Oct

Description: 10–28″ tall, a white-woolly herb with a maplelike scent. The stems are loosely branched. The inflorescence is panicle-like with many white heads. The phyllaries are white papery, graded in several series and enclosing disk flowers, the outer soft short hairy. The 1–2″-long leaves are alternate, entire, narrow, and widest above the middle.

Habitat: Below 4,000′. Dry, open areas. GR, CH, FW, LC, RO, SG.

Comments: Endemic to California. Pyrrolizidine alkaloids render this plant potentially toxic. Native Americans are recorded as inhaling ground-up flowers for head colds. This soft, furry-looking plant is common in dry areas.

Grindelia hirsutula var. *davyi*

Davy's Gumweed

Native perennial
May–Oct

Description: 1–5′ tall. An erect herb, few-branched above; the stems are often reddish. The leaves are 1–2½″ long, shiny, and entire. The rounded flower heads have hooked phyllary tips with a white gummy resin between them.

Habitat: Below 5,000′. Sandy bottomlands, dry banks, rocky areas, fields, and roadsides, including serpentine areas. GR, CH, SG, FW, RP, RO.

Comments: Resins from some *Grindelias* have been patented for use in adhesives, rubber, coatings, textiles, and polymers. A similar species, *G. camporum,* is common in our area at lower elevations. It is much-branched from the base, the stems have the appearance of a white varnish covering, and the foliage has sawtooth margins.

KAREN CALLAHAN

Davy's Gumweed

Helenium bigelovii
Bigelow's Sneezeweed

Native perennial
Jun–Aug

Description: Stems 1–3′ high, few-branched on the upper plant. The leaves are alternate, oval, and smooth margined, with the upper ones becoming gradually smaller. Stem leaf bases clasp the stem. Solitary globe-shaped flower heads occur on long flower stems. There are 14–20 yellow ray flowers and many disk flowers with yellow throats and lobes ranging from yellow to red, brown, or purple.

Habitat: Below 10,000′. Moist places such as wet meadows, marshes, and bogs. MM.

Comments: Used medicinally by Native Americans for a variety of uses, including fever, swellings, and headaches. The dried flowers were also used as snuff to induce sneezing (hence the common name). The plant is in cultivation and a number of cultivars have been developed.

RICHARD HANES

Bigelow's Sneezeweed

GORDON J. HARRINGTON

Rosilla

Helenium puberulum
Native annual/short-lived perennial
Rosilla   Jun–Nov

Description: 1–5′. The main stem has conspicuous wings. The plant branches in a gangly way. The leaves are alternate, entire, and soft to the touch. The upper leaves are sessile (without petioles). Ray flowers are tiny and inconspicuous. The numerous disk flowers are yellow with a brownish tinge.

Habitat: Up to 3,000′. Streamsides, marshes, and other wetlands. FW, LC, CH, RP.

Comments: The tiny yellow ray flowers are almost completely obscured by the numerous yellow disk flowers. This results in a flower that is an almost perfectly rounded yellow ball. It is attractive to butterflies. Because it often grows on floodplains, it tends to come and go depending on the severity of the previous season's floods.

KAREN CALLAHAN

California Helianthella

Helianthella californica var. *nevadensis*
Native perennial
California Helianthella   May–Sep

Description: To 2′ tall. Stems one to several, slender. Leaves entire, 3-veined, lancelike (less than 1½″ wide), on long petioles. The inflorescence heads are generally solitary on long flower stalks. The anthers of the disk flowers are yellow to purple.

Habitat: 800–8,600′. Grassy sites and dry openings in woodland and forest. GR, FW, CH, LC, UC.

Comments: The flowers were cooked and eaten by Native Americans. *Helianthella* is closely related to the sunflower, which it resembles, only on a much smaller scale. The seeds look like miniature sunflower seeds and although too small for human consumption they are an important food source for birds and rodents.

Hemizonia fitchii   Native annual
Fitch's Tarweed, Fitch's Spikeweed Jun–Nov

Description: 6–36″ high. Stem branched, leaves green, glandular, covered with long hairs. Flowers yellow with characteristic black anthers.

Habitat: 100–3,000′. Common on dry grassy flats and open woodlands from the Great Central Valley up to the foothills. GR, FW, LC, CH.

Comments: By late summer the open flats that were covered with colorful wildflowers in the spring have turned dusty and golden as they lie sweltering in the summer heat, no longer a destination for eager wildflower enthusiasts. That's unfortunate, because this is the time of the year when the interesting tarweeds, with their sticky, pungently scented foliage and bright little flowers, reign supreme. This is perhaps the most common of the three species with yellow flowers in our area.

KAREN CALLAHAN

Fitch's Tarweed

Hieracium albiflorum   Native perennial
White Hawkweed   Jun–Aug

Description: Stems 1–2′ tall in flower. The leaves are mostly at the plant base, entire or few-toothed, and bear long hairs. A few narrow leaves occur on the tall flowering stem, but get progressively smaller up the stem. Open heads of small white flowers occur on upright stems. The inflorescence heads are ray flowered, in open cymes or panicles, each head comprised of 15–30 ligules. The sap is milky.

Habitat: 1,500–9,600′. Summer dry forests and open woodlands. FW, LC, UC.

Comments: The genus name is derived from *hierax*, Greek for hawk, because the ancients believed that hawks used the sap to sharpen their eyesight. It can be seen on the road to Edward's Crossing, at Rock Creek, and a number of other wooded places in our area.

KAREN CALLAHAN

White Hawkweed

Smooth Cat's Ear

JULIE S. CARVILLE

Hypochaeris glabra   Non-native annual
Smooth Cat's Ear   Mar–Jun

Description: Stems 4–16" high, smooth without hairs. Flower heads of ray flowers only, which are short and inconspicuous. The leaves are at the base of the plant, and are entire to shallowly lobed. The sap is milky.

Habitat: Below 4,000'. A weed of disturbed places. GR, FW, LC, CH, RP.

Comments: Naturalized from Europe. It has spread widely, and is one of the most abundant plants at lower elevations. The Rough Cat's Ear, *Hypochaeris radicata,* is also an introduced species, is equally abundant, and grows in the same places. The leaves are basal in both species, but Smooth Cat's Ear leaves are hairless and shiny green, while Rough Cat's Ear leaves are larger, coarser, and rough to the touch. Both form carpets of dandelion-like flowers.

Prickly Lettuce

CINDY RUBIN

Lactuca serriola   Non-native annual
Prickly Lettuce   May–Sep

Description: Plant 2–5' tall. Stems prickly-bristled. The inflorescence is open, with branches widely spreading and with ray flowers only. The small flower heads open during the morning hours. The leaves are coarsely lobed, clasping the stem, and prickly-bristled on the midvein, but especially on the bottom of the vein. Milky sap in all parts of the plant.

Habitat: Below 7,300'. Disturbed places. GR, FW, LC, UC.

Comments: A widespread weed native to Europe. Another introduced species, Tall Blue Lettuce, *Lactuca biennis,* is sometimes confused with this one but is taller and has white to bluish flowers, whereas Prickly Lettuce has yellow to creamy yellow flowers. Tall Blue Lettuce is also less common and confined to lower elevations.

Lasthenia californica
California Goldfields

Native annual
Mar–May

Description: Plant less than 16″ high. Stem simple or freely branched, and hairy. Leaves opposite, entire, hairy. Inflorescence head with 6–13 ray flowers and many disk flowers.

Habitat: Below 5,000′. Heavy soils, vernal pools, low alkaline fields, hillsides. VP, GR, FW.

Comments: Forms familiar sheets of gold across open wet ground in early spring. Native Americans ground parched seeds into flour to make porridge. Many species of the genus *Lasthenia* are lumped together under the common name of "Goldfields," but this is the most common and widest ranging species in our area. Another species, *Lasthenia fremontii*, which is more or less confined to the Great Central Valley, also extends into our area in western Placer County. It is found in vernal pools around Roseville and Lincoln.

California Goldfields

Layia fremontii
Tidy Tips

Native annual
Mar–May

Description: Plant less than 16″ tall. Inflorescence head consists of 3–15 yellow ray flowers with white tips, and 4–100 disk flowers with purple anthers. The leaves are narrow and pinnately lobed, appearing ladderlike.

Habitat: Below 2,000′. Grassy slopes with heavy soil. GR, FW, RP.

Comments: The "Tidy Tips" sold in seed packets for home gardens and included in most native wildflower seed packets is a closely related species, *L. platyglossa,* which is not found naturally in our area but is frequently planted. The inflorescence and foliage of *L. platyglossa* contain small, blackish glands that make them somewhat sticky, while our local species, *L. fremontii,* lacks those glands, but the two otherwise look very similar.

Tidy Tips

Ox-eye Daisy

JULIE S. CARVILLE

Leucanthemum vulgare   Non-native perennial
Ox-eye Daisy   Jun–Aug

Description: Plant 8–20″ tall, from creeping rootstock. Sparingly branched. The leaves are pinnately lobed or toothed, the lower spoon-shaped, becoming smaller up the stem. The flower heads are solitary at the ends of the branches. Each head has approximately 22 ray flowers, ½–¾″ long, and many disk flowers, together ½–¾″ across.

Habitat: Below 6,600′. Escaped from gardens, now naturalized in pastures, disturbed mountain meadows, roadsides, and fields. GR, MM, RP.

Comments: A European native, it is sometimes planted as an ornamental and is common in wildflower seed mixes. It can be confused with the Shasta Daisy. Native Americans used the plant to make eyewash, tonic, and a wash for chapped hands.

Hoary Aster

PRENTISS FERGUSON

Machaeranthera canescens
                                     Native annual/perennial
Hoary Aster   Jul–Aug

Description: Plant less than 4′ tall. Taprooted. Stems one to several, branched above, and bushy. Leaves simple, alternate, 1–4″ long. Phyllaries (bracts subtending inflorescence) in 3–10 series. Many ray and disk flowers.

Habitat: 5,000–11,200′. Dry wooded or open slopes. LC, UC, SA, SP.

Comments: Native Americans used it in various forms for different purposes, including dried and pulverized as snuff for the nose, and throat troubles. First collected by Lewis and Clark, it was subsequently named by the German botanist Frederick Pursh in 1814. The genus name *Machaeranthera* is a combination of two Greek words, *machaira* (sword) and *anthera* (anther), and refers to the swordlike anthers.

Madia elegans   Native annual
Common Madia   Jun–Aug

Description: Plant 4–48″ tall. Stems simple or
branched. Lower stems leafy and soft hairy, the
upper with yellow to black glands. The leaves
are linear to narrowly lance-shaped. The heads
are in open cymes with 5–21 deeply lobed ray
flowers, the bases of which are generally maroon
spotted. The ray flowers are generally longer
than ¼″. There are about 25 yellow or maroon
disk flowers with yellow or black anthers.

Habitat: Below 11,000′. Dry slopes and
meadow edges. GR, CH, FW, LC, UC.

Comments: The foliage is strongly scented. The
flower appears after the grasses have turned
brown. The Miwok roasted seeds with hot coals
and pounded or rolled them into flour that was
eaten dry. Many members of the genus *Madia*
are glandular and aromatic.

Common Madia

Madia rammii   Native annual
Ramm's Madia   May–Jul

Description: Plant 4–24″ high. The lower stems
are moderately leafy and softly hairy, the upper
with golden glands. The inflorescence heads are
in open cymes with 15–20 ray flowers that are
sometimes lined purple or brown. The ray flowers
are generally less than ¼″, and not lobed. There
are 20–65 disk flowers with black anthers.

Habitat: 1,300–5,300′. Sunny, grassy places.
GR, CH, FW, LC, SG.

Comments: Nevada City is the type locality for
Ramm's Madia. It is found in abundance at Hell's
Half Acre near Grass Valley. The heads open at
midday, while flower heads of *M. elegans* close
at midday. The genus name *Madia* comes from
the Chilean common name for another species
of this genus that was once grown there for the
oil extracted from its seeds.

Ramm's Madia

Woolly Malacothrix

Malacothrix floccifera   Native annual
Woolly Malacothrix   Apr–Jun

Description: Plant 2–18″ high. The leaves are alternate, pinnately lobed, smaller upward, and generally with white hairy patches at the base of lobes. The heads are comprised only of ray flowers, the outer ones exserted. Corollas usually white, sometimes yellowish. Sap milky.

Habitat: Below 6,600′. Open burns, slides, and roadcuts with loose soil. FW, CH, LC, UC, SG.

Comments: The genus name *Malacothrix* is derived from the Greek word for "soft hair." There are 14 species of *Malacothrix* in California, some of which have recognized subspecies. The common name for the genus as a whole is Desert Dandelion, which is an apt description for the dry environment in which most of them are found. The two species in our area have a preference for loose, open soils.

Slender Cottonweed

Micropus californicus var. *californicus*
Native annual
Slender Cottonweed, Q-Tips   Apr–Jun

Description: Under 6″ high. A small, slender, erect, gray-woolly plant with one to several erect stems. The leaves are alternate, linear, narrow, and smooth edged. The flower heads form small, dense clusters and are disklike and woolly.

Habitat: Below 5,600′. Dry or moist, bare or grassy places, often sandy soils and decomposed granite. GR, CH, FW, LC.

Comments: *Micropus* is Greek for "small foot," perhaps referring to its likeness to a miniature lion's paw. Because of its small size, this tiny grayish plant is easily overlooked. Both common names provide good mental images of the plant's appearance, but "Q-tips" is more whimsical. Look for it along the nature trail in open rocky areas at the Placer Nature Center in Christian Valley.

Microseris nutans   Native perennial
Nodding Microseris   Jun–Aug

Description: Plant 4–24″ high. Leaves 2–12″ long, occurring at the base, straplike with 2–4 pairs of sharp teeth near the center. Sap is milky. The inflorescence head is flat topped and comprised of 13–50 ray flowers, usually nodding in bud. The bracts subtending the head are somewhat mealy and black-hairy. There are flat brown bristles on the seeds.

Habitat: 3,300–9,900′. Moist, rocky meadows, open coniferous woodlands, sagebrush scrub. LC, UC, SP, MM.

Comments: The slender roots are edible raw. This is one of those plants that botanists refer to as "DYCs" (damn yellow composites!) because so many of them look so much alike to both the trained and untrained eye. The common name gives a clue to identifying this species.

Nodding Microseris

Psilocarphus brevissimus   Native annual
Dwarf Woolly-heads   Mar–Jun

Description: Several stems under 8″ tall spreading from the base. Plants cobwebby-hairy.

Habitat: Below 7,500′. Vernal pools and wet depressions. VP, GR.

Comments: Common and widespread. The common name is an apt one for this hairy little plant. The small flowers are rarely noticed because they are mostly hidden by the furry foliage. Another species, *P. tenellus,* may also be found in vernal pools but is more often seen in drier habitats such as dry flats and places with shallow soils.

Dwarf Woolly-heads

Silky Raillardella

Raillardella argentea   Native perennial
Silky Raillardella, Silvermat   Jul–Aug

Description: Plant less than 6" tall, stems reddish. Leaves tufted at plant base, narrow, entire, and silky-hairy. The inflorescence head is comprised of 7–26 disk flowers.

Habitat: 7,300–13,000'. Dry, open gravelly sites. SA, RO.

Comments: Its low stature and hairy leaves are adaptations to the strong sunlight, harsh winds, and cold temperatures typical of the environment in which it grows. An attractive plant forming silvery mats. The flowers are conspicuous for their size, as they rise well above the nearly prostrate mats. The yellow head provides a nice contrast to the silvery foliage. The seed heads are puffy white. The plant is in cultivation, but only in high-elevation rock gardens and alpine glasshouses.

JULIE S. CARVILLE

Western Coneflower

Rudbeckia occidentalis var. *occidentalis*
    Native perennial
Western Coneflower   Jun–Aug

Description: Plant to 5' tall. Stems several, erect, and few branched. The leaves are alternate, 4–12" long, elliptic, and toothed to entire. The one to few inflorescence heads appear as large oblong cones. The heads are comprised of disk flowers only.

Habitat: 4,000–6,100'. Wet ground in woods, meadows, and seeps. LC, UC, MM.

Comments: A weird-looking plant with a flower head that almost looks like a black cone. A ring of conspicuous green bracts at the base of the cone helps to draw attention to it. A ring of pollen begins at the base of the cone and as the days pass, the pollen ring works its way up the cone as the old pollen below dies back and turns brown. In cultivation.

KAREN CALLAHAN

Senecio integerrimus var. *major*
                              Native biennial/perennial
Single-stem Butterweed   May–Aug

Description: Plant 8–28″ tall, soft hairy. Stout, single, towerlike stem bearing many spoon-shaped leaves at the base and few small lancelike leaves on the upper stem. Numerous flower heads occur in a congested cluster with the central head often the largest. The flower head bracts are long, linear, and green or black tipped.

Habitat: 500–12,000′. Wooded areas. FW, LC, UC.

Comments: *Senecio* is one of the largest genera of flowering plants worldwide, with species ranging from small annuals to treelike perennials. The genus is so large and diverse that botanists can almost make a career of renaming and moving the various species around in their taxonomic treatments. We have at least 8 species in our two counties.

Single-stem Butterweed

Senecio triangularis   Native perennial
Arrowhead Butterweed   May–Aug

Description: Plant 1–4′ high. Lush and numerous arrowhead-shaped leaves along the stem. Flower heads 1 to numerous, usually 8 ray flowers and fewer than 40 disk flowers. The flower head bracts are black tipped.

Habitat: 3,300–11,600′. Wet meadows, stream banks, and wet openings in coniferous forests. LC, UC, MM, RP.

Comments: Native Americans took an infusion of leaves or roots as a sedative for lung pains. The Cinnabar Moth, *Tyria jacobaeae,* was introduced as a biological control for the noxious weed Tansy Ragwort, *Senecio jacobaeae,* and has proven quite effective in stripping its foliage. However, it has also been found to attack related native species in Oregon, the impact of which is yet to be discovered.

Arrowhead Butterweed

JULIE S. CARVILLE

Common Groundsel

Senecio vulgaris   Non-native annual
Common Groundsel,
Old Man of Spring   Most months

Description: Plant 4–24″ tall. Stems leafy the entire length. Leaves pinnate. Flower heads in clusters, comprised of disk flowers only. The flower head bracts are black tipped. The sap is milky.

Habitat: Below 5,000′. Gardens, farmlands, and other disturbed sites. GR, CH, FW, LC, RP.

Comments: A common introduced weed from Europe and one of the earliest of spring-blooming flowers. The plant is so common that anyone with a yard or a garden is certain to have seen it. Poisonous to livestock if taken in quantity. The name "Old Man of the Spring" comes from the resemblance of the seed head to a shock of gray hair on an elderly man.

CAROL WITHAM

Milk Thistle

Silybum marianum
    Non-native annual/biennial
Milk Thistle   May–Jul

Description: Stout erect stem 1–10′ high. Broad, spiny, shiny green leaves with white veins and spots, clasping the stem with earlike lobes. The flower head is thistlelike, with leathery, spine-tipped bracts.

Habitat: Below 1,700′. A common weed in pastures and disturbed areas. GR, FW, CH, RP.

Comments: Widely used in herbal medicines but is very invasive. An extract, Silymarin, is a powerful antioxidant used in treating liver problems. The plant is sometimes confused with Bull Thistle, *Cirsium vulgare,* that grows in the same situations, but Milk Thistle has large, leathery, spike-tipped bracts in the flower head and Bull Thistle does not. The name "Milk Thistle" refers to the white mottling on the basal leaves.

Solidago canadensis ssp. *elongata*
                          Native perennial
Canada Goldenrod   May–Sep

Description: Plant 1–5′ tall. The stem is densely leafy and thinly hairy for the entire length. The middle stem leaves are largest, in contrast to other species of this genus in the Sierra Nevada in which lower leaves are the largest. The leaves are lancelike, 3-veined, and toothed. The flower heads are panicle-like, together widely diamond-shaped in outline. 8–15 ray flowers per head, nearly the same length as the disk flowers.

Habitat: Below 9,200′. Meadows, thickets, and moist openings in woods. FW, LC, UC, MM, RP.

Comments: Native Americans used an infusion of roots and flowers for side pains. Because they are not wind pollinated, they do not contribute to hay fever as some believe—they just happen to grow where many wind-pollinated plants grow.

Canada Goldenrod

Sonchus oleraceus   Non-native annual
Common Sow Thistle   Most months

Description: Plant 1–6′ high. Stems smooth, well branched from below the middle of the plant. The lobed, spatula-shaped leaves have prickly margins and clasp the stem. The flower heads are small, sometimes subtended by cottony hairs. Sap milky.

Habitat: Below 5,000′. A common weed in disturbed places, gardens, and along roadsides. GR, CH, FW, LC.

Comments: Originally from Europe. Prickly Sow Thistle, *Sonchus asper,* is a closely related and very similar species. They can be differentiated by looking at the base of a leaf where it attaches to the stem. The leaf of both is lobed at the base. In *S. oleraceus,* the lobes are rounded, while in *S. asper,* the lobes taper to a point.

Common Sow Thistle

KAREN CALLAHAN

Largeflower Stephanomeria

Stephanomeria lactucina   Native perennial
Largeflower Stephanomeria   Jul–Aug

Description: 4–12″ high. Stems slender, single, often branched near the base. Leaves linear, up to 3″ long, the lower ones with a few teeth. Ray flowers 7–10 per inflorescence, bright pink to purple. The sap is milky.

Habitat: 3,000–8,000′. Dry forests, typically on flats and ridges. LC, UC, CH.

Comments: Species description originally authored by Asa Gray (1810–1888), Harvard botany professor and preeminent American systematist. Common along roads and trails in the right habitats, but often overlooked and usually omitted from field guides and wildflower books. Perhaps this is because its flowering period is short and it blooms in late summer when less attention is given to wildflowers. Deer certainly don't ignore it.

RICHARD HANES

Purple Salsify

Tragopogon porrifolius   Non-native biennial
Purple Salsify, Oyster Plant   Apr–Jun

Description: Plant to 3′ in height, taprooted. The stem is few branched. The leaves and stem are waxy blue. The leaves are alternate, linear, and with grasslike veins. The inflorescence heads are solitary, with only ray flowers, and phyllaries in 1 row. The flower head becomes a brown ball of parachute-like seeds in midsummer. The sap is milky.

Habitat: Below 5,600′. Common weed in disturbed places. GR, CH, FW, LC.

Comments: Native to Europe. Cultivated for its long edible root, which is supposedly oysterlike in flavor. A similar introduced species, *T. dubius,* with yellow flowers and long phyllaries, occurs in the same range.

Whitneya dealbata   Native perennial
Whitneya, Mock Leopardbane   Jun–Aug

Description: Plant 6–18″ high, densely covered with short curly hairs. Leaves light blue-gray, few, opposite, and the upper ones narrower. The 1 or 2 erect, unbranched stems have one to a few large flower heads, each head with 5–12 ray flowers and many disk flowers.

Habitat: 4,000–7,900′. Uncommon, in forest openings and on open slopes. LC, UC.

Comments: Named after California geologist J. D. Whitney (1819–1896). Some botanists refer to it as *Arnica dealbata*. The plant has a sagelike odor. The name "Leopardbane" points out another one of the vagaries of common names. Plants in at least 3 genera are called Leopardbane, none of which grow where leopards occur. It's anyone's guess which Leopardbane this plant is supposed to be mocking.

KAREN CALLAHAN

Whitneya

Wyethia angustifolia   Native perennial
Narrowleaf Mule Ears,
California Compass Plant   Apr–Jul

Description: 6–24″ high with long, narrow, hairy tapering leaves. 8–21 yellow ray flowers, and numerous disk flowers, form a combined flower head to 3″ across.

Habitat: 100–3,500′. Seasonally moist meadows, rocky or brushy places, and forest openings. GR, CH, FW, LC.

Comments: Native Americans cooked the seeds for use in pinole, utilized the raw stem for food, made a poultice from the pounded root, which was used to draw blisters, and made a yellow dye from the flowers. The new leaves and flowers of the plant are relished by cattle and sheep, so they seldom survive or have the ability to reproduce where livestock habitually graze. The seeds are relished by wildlife. It is in cultivation.

JULIE S. CARVILLE • JULIE S. CARVILLE

Narrowleaf Mule Ears

Bolander's Mule Ears

Wyethia bolanderi   Native perennial
Bolander's Mule Ears   Mar–May

Description: 6–12″ tall with decumbent stems and dark green, shiny, ovate leaves. Flower head with more than 20 ray flowers.

Habitat: 900–3,500′. Open places in the foothills. GR, CH, FW, SG.

Comments: Restricted to serpentine and gabbro soils, primarily in a narrow band running along the western slope of the northern and central Sierra foothills. The underground stems are well adapted to survive the frequent brush fires that occur in the areas where it grows. Grayish skeletonized remnants of the previous year's leaves surround the base of the plant's new leaves, sometimes persisting through the growing season. Common along Wolf Mountain Road in Nevada County. Listed as *Balsamorhiza bolanderi* in some references.

White Mule Ears

Wyethia helenioides   Native perennial
White Mule Ears,
Silver Mule Ears   May–Jul

Description: Plants 1–2′ high. The new growth is densely hairy but becomes almost hairless later in the season. Leaves are 10–18″ long, elliptic, and short petioled.

Habitat: Below 6,000′. Open grasslands, shrublands, and woodland borders. GR, CH, FW, LC, UC.

Comments: The Miwok used green leaves as a top layer over hot stones in an earthen oven. The seeds are edible. It can be distinguished from other Mule Ears by the very large oval bracts on the flower head. The seeds, as with other Mule Ear species, are relished by birds and rodents. Homeopathic medicine practitioners advocate use of the plant as a remedy for allergies.

Wyethia mollis   Native perennial
Mountain Mule Ears,
Woolly Mule Ears   May–Aug

Description: Plant 1–2′ tall, densely white-hairy, becoming less hairy with age. The leaves are oblong with rounded tips and bases, the basal leaves the largest. The large flower heads are supported by leafy flower stalks. There are 5–11 ray flowers and many disk flowers.

Habitat: 4,000–11,200′. Dry rocky slopes and wooded openings. CH, LC, UC.

Comments: The seeds are edible. When you come across a *Wyethia* at higher elevations (above 6,000′), it will be this species. A fifth, very rare species, *W. reticulata,* is found only in El Dorado County.

Mountain Mule Ears

Xanthium strumarium   Native annual
Common Cocklebur   Jun–Oct

Description: 2–4′ tall with stout stems that are branched, ridged, spotted, and very rough. The leaves are alternate, long petioled, triangular, and rough to the touch. The small flower heads are followed by 1″ woody fruit with hooked prickles and 2 curved spines at the tip.

Habitat: 100–2,500′. Common in disturbed moist areas. GR, CH, FW, LC, RP.

Comments: The seed and seedlings are toxic to livestock. The burs were the inspiration for the invention of Velcro. Spiny Cocklebur, *Xanthium spinosum,* is a related species that also produces burs. The leaves in Spiny Cocklebur are white-hairy below and possess 3 sharp spines in their axis. The Common Cocklebur leaves are green below and lack spines.

Common Cocklebur

Boraginaceae
BORAGE FAMILY
Monica Finn

Herbs and shrubs with stiff hairs and generally simple, alternating leaves, often with hispid hairs. The stems are round. The leaves usually are simple and entire. *Coiled, cymose inflorescence, with 5-merous flowers, petals alternating with stamens.* Fruit with 4 hard nutlets. There are approximately 100 genera and 2,000 species worldwide, with 22 genera native to the United States, most of them in California. There are 18 genera and 158 species in California, 10 genera and 48 species in Nevada and Placer Counties. Many are toxic from alkaloids or accumulated nitrates.

Common Fiddleneck

Amsinckia menziesii var. *intermedia*

Native annual

Common Fiddleneck   Apr–Jun

Description: 6–36" tall with rough, hairy foliage. Many small trumpet-shaped flowers in a dense scorpioid cyme. The expanded portion of the petal has 5 red-orange marks.

Habitat: Below 5,000'. Open, grassy, and disturbed places. GR, FW, LC.

Comments: Common, occurring in dense stands and creating vivid color displays. *A. menziesii* var. *menziesii* lacks red marks on the petals. Many variants can be found together. The plant contains alkaloids that cause liver damage to horses, cattle, and pigs. The dried mature plants with seeds intact will sometimes be found in hay bales. The origin of the name fiddleneck becomes obvious upon examining the inflorescence.

Cryptantha affinis   Native annual
Side-grooved Cryptantha   May–Aug

Description: 2–15″ tall. Hairy stems; leaves narrow and oblong to lance-shaped with short, bristly hairs. Its small, white, 5-petaled flowers have a tiny corona (like a crown) in the center. Sepals are bristly; fruit is 4 nutlets, shiny and black.

Habitat: 2,200–8,700′. Dryish, gravelly, sandy openings in chaparral and forests. CH, LC, UC, SA.

Comments: Several annual species of the genera of *Cryptantha* and *Plagiobothrys* carry similar-looking flowers that are commonly called Popcorn Flower. Differentiating the two genera is difficult, but can be done best by viewing the seeds under a microscope. The nutlets of *Cryptantha* carry a groove, the nutlets of the *Plagiobothrys* an elevated "scar." In addition, the flowers of *Cryptantha* tend to be smaller than those of the *Plagiobothrys*.

MICHAEL GRAFF

Side-grooved Cryptantha

Cynoglossum grande   Native perennial
Grand Hound's Tongue   Feb–May

Description: 1–3′ tall. An erect herb from a thick base or taproot. Leaves basal, emerging from the lower stem, are elliptic-ovate, 1.2–3.1″ wide, 3–6″ long. The petiole is as long as the leaf. The stems lack hairs. The inflorescence is on stalks held above the leaves on a scorpioid cyme. Blue flowers with a narrow violet tube, spreading petals, and an inner row of white teeth.

Habitat: Below 7,000′. Dry, shady openings in woods. CH, FW, LC.

Comments: The common name is derived from the shape of its broad leaves. It goes dormant and disappears during the summer months, only to revive with the first heavy rains. A related species, *C. occidentale*, also grows in our area.

RICHARD HANES

Grand Hound's Tongue

RICHARD HANES

Velvety Stickseed

Hackelia velutina   Native perennial
Velvety Stickseed   Jun–Jul

Description: 16–32″ high. An erect plant, the leaves have soft hairs. The basal leaves are petioled, the upper stem-leaves sessile. The inflorescence is a cyme, coiled at the tips. The bright blue flowers have an appendage or projection near the base of each petal lobe. The nutlets have prickles over most of the surface.

Habitat: 4,000–10,000′. Dry, open slopes. LC, UC.

Comments: There are 3 similar species. *H. nervosa* is very similar, but the corolla limb is shorter, and the stems less hairy. *H. californica* has white flowers. In *H. floribunda,* a species from wet habitats, the nutlet prickles are fused in a wing. The appendages at the base of the petals rise above the petals and have the appearance of being another flower (white) within a flower (blue).

KAREN CALLAHAN · CHET BLACKBURN

California Stoneseed

Lithospermum californicum Native perennial
California Stoneseed,
California Puccoon   Mar–Jun

Description: 6–18″ tall. One to several stems, and a few scattered broad linear hairy leaves. The yellow funnel-like flowers are in a cluster.

Habitat: 1,800–5,500′. Open pine forests, montane chaparral, and rocky outcrops, including serpentine. CH, LC, UC, RO.

Comments: *Lithospermum* is a combination of two Greek words, *litho* (stone) and *spermum* (seed), and refers to the bony hard nutlets that members of this genus produce. Puccoon is a Native American name. The plant is nowhere abundant but can be seen along the trails at the Empire Mine State Park in Grass Valley. The Western Gromwell, *L. ruderale,* is the only other stoneseed found in our area but is less common.

Plagiobothrys nothofulvus   Native perennial
Popcorn Flower   Mar–May

Description: 6–24″ tall. An erect plant with
rough spreading hairs on the stem and pale
yellow hairs adorning the leaves. The inflorescence consists of a branching raceme coiled at
the tips.

Habitat: Below 2,500′. Common in grassy
areas, hillsides, roadways. GR, FW.

Comments: The Kawaiisu from Southern
California painted their faces with reddish juice
from the base of the stem of this and other
species. There are 14 additional species in
Placer and Nevada Counties, all difficult to
distinguish from one another. The common
Spanish name for the closely related genus
Cryptantha is *Nievitas,* which means "little
snowflakes." This refers to the way they look in
large carpets of mixed flowers.

KAREN CALLAHAN · KAREN CALLAHAN

Popcorn Flower

KAREN CALLAHAN

Popcorn Flower, Blue Dicks, Spider Lupine, and Tufted Poppy bloom along the sunny
trail at Bridgeport in the South Yuba River State Park.

Brassicaceae
MUSTARD FAMILY
Monica Finn

Annual and perennial herbs, with dense branching and often elongate inflorescence of many flowers. The leaves are usually alternate and simple, with simple forked or starlike hairs. The flowers are generally with *4 free petals, many clawed, spreading to form a cross. Stamens 6, with 4 long and 2 short. Most are early spring flowers. The seedpods are long, thin siliques or short, stout silicles.* The family was formerly known as Cruciferae. This is a large family and important to humankind. It includes many food plants (cabbage, cauliflower, turnips, horseradish), but also a number of weedy plants. There are approximately 375 genera and 3,200 species worldwide, mostly in the temperate regions of the Northern Hemisphere. California contains 63 genera, 366 species, with 32 genera, 85 species in Nevada and Placer Counties.

Brewer's Rock Cress

Arabis breweri — Native perennial
Brewer's Rock Cress — Apr–Jul

Description: 2–8″ high with a woody caudex and many branched stems. Densely hairy on the lower stems. The basal leaves are spatula-shaped, green to silvery, and hairy. Stem leaves sessile, less than 1″ in length. Petals spoon-shaped, purple.

Habitat: 1,500–7,500′. Uncommon. Rocky exposed slopes and cliffs. LC, UC, RO.

Comments: The beautiful pink to purple flowers later turn into curved seedpods. A delightful little plant with an attractively hairy lower stem area. It grows in crevices in rocky places. The plant is in cultivation but not easy to find and is difficult to grow unless kept in an alpine greenhouse. The variety *breweri* has an erect inflorescence, while the variety *austiniae* usually has a sprawling inflorescence and is sometimes a slightly larger plant.

KAREN CALLAHAN

Barbarea orthoceras Native biennial/perennial
American Wintercress,
Yellow Rocket   May–Sep

Description: 4–24″ tall with erect, stout,
succulent stems. The leaves are pinnately lobed.
The basal leaves have 2–3 pairs of lateral lobes
and a larger, round terminal lobe. Stem leaves are
smaller and generally clasping the stem. Dense
clusters of bright yellow flowers. The fruit is 1–2″
long, erect to curved upward toward the stem.

Habitat: 2,000–11,000′. Damp to wet habitats,
creek sides, floodplains, and seeps. LC, UC,
MM, RP.

Comments: Native Americans ate the leaves
after boiling them to remove the bitter taste.
Another wintercress, Common Wintercress,
B. vulgaris, is a non-native species with brighter
yellow flowers. It is found below 3,000′ and
characteristically occurs on disturbed sites.

American Wintercress

Brassica nigra   Non-native annual
Black Mustard   Mar–Jul

Description: 2–8′ tall. Plant erect, branching
and open. The basal and lower leaves are lobed,
but the upper ones are entire.

Habitat: Under 5,000′. A common weed in
disturbed areas. GR, FW, LC.

Comments: Black Mustard is one of the species
used as a source of commercial prepared
mustard. It can be confused with Field Mustard,
Brassica rapa, which is even more common and
is one of the earliest harbingers of spring,
blooming as early as December. Black Mustard
leaves have a short petiole and are more hairy.
These characteristics and the later blooming
time distinguish it from Field Mustard with less
hairy leaves that clasp the stem.

Black Mustard

Shepherd's Purse

Capsella bursa-pastoris   Non-native annual
Shepherd's Purse   Feb–Sep

Description: 4–20″ tall. An erect forb characterized by flat, heart-shaped seedpods. Flowers small and many, petals clawed. The basal leaves are lobed or dissected.

Habitat: Below 7,500′. Common on disturbed sites, especially grasslands. GR, CH, FW, LC.

Comments: Herbalists find many uses for the plant, including remedies for poor eyesight, urinary tract problems, bleeding disorders, and menstrual difficulties. It has been discovered recently that the seeds may be carnivorous. When wet, they attract protozoan-sized creatures, trap them by adhesion, and secrete proteases (digestive enzymes) that absorb nutrients from their victims. If true, this would be the first potentially carnivorous seed discovery.

Milk Maids

Cardamine californica   Native perennial
Milk Maids, Toothwort   Mar–Jun

Description: 8–28″ tall. Erect plant. The upper stem leaves are pinnate, often with 3–5 leaflets and toothed. The leaves arise from the rhizome, are simple to pinnately trifoliate, and round in outline. Stem leaves few, alternate. The lower leaves are long petioled, the upper leaves short petioled to sessile. The leaflets are round to oblong, margins smooth to toothed. Petals rose-white, $^2/_5$–$^3/_5$″ long.

Habitat: Below 4,000′. Shady woods, canyons, and stream banks. CH, FW, LC, RP, SG.

Comments: The name "toothwort" refers to toothlike bulges on the tuberous rootstock. The tiny tubers, which are said to taste like pepper, send up foliage shortly after the first rains, followed by early-blooming fragrant flowers. They die back to the ground during the summer.

Draba verna   Native annual
Whitlow Grass   Feb–Apr

Description: 1–3″ tall. The flowering stalk can sometimes be up to 6″. The plant forms a small basal rosette of 1–2″ hairy leaves. The flower stalk is leafless, and bears a raceme of tiny white flowers. The four petals are deeply divided, almost to the point of looking like 8 petals. These are followed by small football-shaped seeds.

Habitat: Under 2,000′. Open or disturbed areas. GR, CH, FW, LC, UC, RP.

Comments: It is odd that this plant is called "Whitlow Grass" because it is not a grass and does not resemble grass. It is a California native but is not restricted to California. It has almost cosmopolitan distribution. Individual plants are inconspicuous. In some parts of the country it is called Shad Flower.

Whitlow Grass

Erysimum capitatum
                        Native biennial/perennial
Western Wallflower   Apr–Aug

Description: 6–40″ tall. An erect plant characterized by a dense terminal cluster of showy yellow-orange flowers. The raceme is rounded rather than elongated. The individual flowers are up to 1½″. The leaves are linear to spoon-shaped; the edges are smooth to toothed and have branched hairs.

Habitat: Below 13,000′. Common on open, dry slopes. GR, FW, CH, LC, UC, SA.

Comments: Variable. Several subspecies intergrade. Fragrant. A very conspicuous plant in bloom; the yellow-orange color of the flower is about the same color as in California Poppies. The plant stands out among the brushy vegetation of the dry slopes where it is normally found. Grows in both full sun and partial shade.

Western Wallflower

Short-Pod Mustard

CHET BLACKBURN

Hirschfeldia incana   Non-native biennial
Short-pod Mustard,
Summer Mustard   May–Oct

Description: 8–40″ tall. Erect, branching. The basal leaves are in a rosette. Individual leaves have a large terminal lobe and many small lateral lobes. Stem leaves are sessile, tiny, and do not clasp the stem. The plant bears short, linear seedpods, ¼″ long, that are pressed to the stem.

Habitat: Below 5,000′. Common weed in roadsides, drainages, and disturbed areas. GR, CH, FW, LC.

Comments: A smaller, coarser plant than the common mustard. This one blooms throughout the summer after the others have already gone to seed. It is also less conspicuous. The seedpods are substantially shorter than other mustard seedpods. These and the late blooming period are identifying characteristics.

Dagger Pod

JULIE S. CARVILLE

Phoenicaulis cheiranthoides
     Native perennial
Dagger Pod   May–Jul

Description: 2–8″ high. A low-growing herb to subshrub, with a thick stem and taproot. The stem base is covered with old leaf bases. The leaves are simple, the edges smooth, gray-whitish, and with dense multibranched hairs. Basal leaves, 2–8″ long, in a rosette. Dense, terminal clusters of small pink-purplish flowers. Seedpods ½–3″ long, broad, and lance-shaped.

Habitat: 5,000–10,500′. Basalt outcrops, clay soils, slopes. UC, SA, RO, SP.

Comments: The conspicuous seedpods bear a resemblance to daggers. The plant is native to much of the West that lies east of the Cascades from Washington and Idaho south to California and Nevada. In our area it is found only in the easternmost portion of our two counties.

Raphanus sativus   Non-native annual/biennial
Wild Radish   Feb–Jul

Description: 1–4′ tall. An erect plant with a deep
taproot. The leaves are basal and pinnately lobed.
The showy purple flowers have dark venation.
The petals are clawed and the fruit is beaked.

Habitat: Below 3,000′. Common weed of
disturbed places, fields, and roadsides. GR, CH,
FW, LC.

Comments: Our cultivated radishes were derived
from this plant from the Mediterranean region.
Two species of plants in our area are often called
Wild Radish. The seedpods of the true Wild
Radish contain only 3 seeds or fewer. It has
purple flowers with dark veins. The other species,
more correctly known as Jointed Charlock, has
up to 12 seeds in the pods and the flowers are
yellow fading to whitish, but occasionally purple-
flowered plants can also be found.

GORDON J. HARRINGTON

Wild Radish

Rorippa nasturtium-aquaticum
                              Native perennial
Water Cress   Apr–Oct

Description: 1–2′ tall. Plant sprawling and
rooting at the nodes. The succulent stems are
hollow and bear pinnate leaves. The small white
flowers are in a terminal cluster.

Habitat: Below 9,000′. Wet areas along streams,
lakes, springs, and marshes. AQ, MM, RP.

Comments: Cultivated for edible greens, it can
be separated from other species of *Rorippa* by
the flower color and its perennial habit. Its use
in salads and water cress sandwiches is well
known, but it is also sought by herbalists for a
variety of uses. Care should be taken in harvesting Water Cress, as our waterways have become
increasingly polluted. The Liver Fluke, *Fasciola
heptacia,* sometimes lays its tiny eggs among
the foliage.

KAREN CALLAHAN

Water Cress

Milkwort Jewelflower

Streptanthus polygaloides　　　Native annual
Milkwort Jewelflower　　　　　　Apr–Jul

Description: 1–3′ tall. The leaves are linear. The urn-shaped calyx is yellowish to purplish. The petals are yellow-green to white.

Habitat: 600–4,000′. A plant of rocky serpentine outcrops. FW, LC, CH, RO, SG.

Comments: A serpentine endemic. This is one of the plants that create their own systemic insecticides through a process known as hyperaccumulation. Nickel is one element found in serpentine, and the plant has the ability to absorb such high amounts of nickel as to discourage chewing insects from feeding on it. There are 24 species of *Streptanthus* found in the state, but only two of them occur in Nevada or Placer Counties.

Mountain Jewelflower

Streptanthus tortuosus
　　　　　　　Native annual/short-lived perennial
Mountain Jewelflower　　　　　May–Aug

Description: 6–36″ tall. Characterized by round or heart-shaped middle stem leaves that clasp the stem. The flower is urn-shaped. Fruit 2–6″ long, curving downward.

Habitat: 700–11,000′. Common. Dry, rocky slopes. FW, CH, LC, UC, SG.

Comments: This is a widespread and variable species; three recognized varieties of Mountain Jewelflower are found in the Sierra Nevada. Flowers may be shades of yellow or violet. When viewing the flowers with a hand lens, look for the 4 curved petals and 3 pairs of stamens that emerge from the urn-shaped calyx. Drum Powerhouse Road and the South Yuba River Trail are good places to see Mountain Jewelflowers.

Thysanocarpus curvipes   Native annual
Fringepod, Lacepod   Mar–May

Description: 6–36″ tall. A slender, erect herb. The basal leaves are toothed and in a rosette, the stem leaves smooth edged. Inconspicuous white flowers. The fruit is round, winged, and often wavy or perforated, ¼–½″ long, and appears papery with distinct center and edges tinged pink-purple.

Habitat: Below 6,000′. Common in open areas, washes, and meadows. GR, CH, FW, LC, UC.

Comments: The seedpods are conspicuous. The flowers are not. A similar species, Spokepod or Ribbed Fringepod, *T. radians,* occurs in the western part of our area. Unlike *T. curvipes,* it does not have a hairy base and the seedpod looks more like the spokes of a wagon wheel radiating out from the center.

JULIE S. CARVILLE

Fringepod

KAREN CALLAHAN

One of the earliest flowers of spring, Milk Maids often grows on rocky outcrops along trails in the American and Yuba River Canyons.

Campanulaceae
BLUEBELL FAMILY
Chet Blackburn

Mostly perennial herbs with a few shrubs and trees. The leaves are generally alternate and simple. Sepals 5, and there are 5 petals united to form a bowl-like or tubelike structure. ***Stamens 5, fused into a prominent baseball bat–shaped structure.*** The ovary is inferior. The fruit is generally a capsule. The family is sometimes divided into two families, with the second family known as Lobeliaceae. The family includes some important horticultural plants, especially from the genera *Campanula* (Bluebells), *Platycodon* (Balloon Flowers), and *Lobelia.* There are about 70 genera and 2,000 species worldwide, of which 12 genera are found in the United States. Of the 10 genera and 49 species found in California, 7 genera and 14 species occur in the area covered by this book.

California Harebell

Campanula prenanthoides   Native perennial
California Harebell   Jun–Sep

Description: 1–2′ tall. Taprooted with a reclining to erect hairless stem. The narrow green leaves are 1–1½″ long with toothed margins and are arranged alternately up the stem. The flowers are in a loose inflorescence, arranged in clusters of 2 to 5. The petals are pale blue, narrow, and curve downward toward the tip. The style is blue, longer than the petals, and conspicuous.

Habitat: 1,500–6,000′. Uncommon, dry shaded floors of coniferous forests, wooded slopes, and roadcuts. CH, LC, UC, SG.

Comments: It also occurs on serpentine. Delicate in appearance, it is easily recognized by its recurved petals and the long blue style, which extends well beyond the petals. In good years, it is abundant along the road to the Rock Creek Nature Trail from late June to early July.

Downningia bicornuta   Native annual
Horned Downingia   Apr–Jul

Description: 2–6″ tall. A tiny plant with petals arranged in a two-lip form. The lower lip is 3-lobed, but indentations between the lobes are slight. The upper lip is 2-lobed, and deeply divided. The flowers are blue; the lower lobe has a large white center with butter yellow markings inside.

Habitat: 100–500′. Drying edges of vernal pools and small, seasonal, slow-moving streams. VP, RP.

Comments: Once abundant around Roseville, *Downingias* have developed a unique relationship with certain kinds of pollen flies, which are their major pollinators. The flies build burrows in higher ground between the pools and time the arrival of their young to take advantage of *Downingia* pollen, their only source of food.

KAREN CALLAHAN

Horned Downingia

Githopsis specularioides   Native annual
Bluecup   May–Jun

Description: 2–8″ tall with erect stems bearing small bright blue flowers with a whitish center. The foliage is rough pubescent.

Habitat: 100–4,200′. Drainage depressions or on open vernally moist rocky slopes. VP, GR, FW, LC, SG.

Comments: Most common after a fire, but still not a common plant. It is a tiny plant that is easily overlooked, even when occurring in relatively large numbers. Plants are often found around vernal pools, but not in them. This is one of the miniature species botanists refer to as "belly plants" because one must lie on his or her belly to either examine them or photograph them. It occurs sparingly at Hell's Half Acre but the existence of masses of other flowers at that site tends to render these even less visible.

KAREN CALLAHAN

Bluecup

JULIE S. CARVILLE

Porterella

Porterella carnosula   Native annual
Porterella   Jun–Aug

Description: 1–12″ tall. A branching plant bearing slightly fragrant blue flowers with yellow and whitish markings. The submersed leaves are triangular, the emerged leaves oval. The two top lobes of the flowers are blue, the bottom three lobes are about half blue with the other half occupied first by a white, then a yellow band on them as they approach the attachment point.

Habitat: 5,000–6,500′. Wet places on margins of drying high-elevation bodies of water, snow lakes, temporary streams, etc. VP, UC, MM.

Comments: The flower superficially resembles a *Downingia* but differs by having flowers on short pedicels instead of attaching directly to the stalk.

KAREN CALLAHAN

The delicate, bluish flowers of Toothed Downingia, *Downingia cuspidata,* appear in masses in drying meadows and vernal pools of the Great Valley and Sierra foothills.

Caprifoliaceae
HONEYSUCKLE FAMILY
Chet Blackburn

Mostly shrubs and vines, rarely herbs. Leaves opposite, simple (except for *Sambucus,* which has compound leaves). *The calyx tube is fused to the ovary, and is small.* The ovary is inferior. *The petals are fused together to form long, funnel-shaped flowers that terminate in 5 (sometimes 4) lobes. The flowers are in pairs* (although in some genera such as *Sambucus,* the pairs of flowers are densely packed to superficially resemble flower heads). The fruits are berries, drupes, or nutlets. Many members of the family are important garden plants such as abelias, Beauty Bush, elderberries, honeysuckles, viburnums, and weigelas. There are 12 genera and 450 species worldwide, with 5 genera and 19 species in California. All 5 genera occur in our area, and out of the 13 species, all but one are shrubs or woody vines.

Linnaea borealis ssp. *longiflora*

Native perennial

Twinflower — Jun–Sep

Description: 2–6″ tall. A creeping groundcover forming dense blankets of shiny evergreen leaves. The leaf margins are serrate midway to the tip. Twin pairs of nodding flowers at the end of a leafless stem rise above the blanket of evergreen foliage.

Habitat: 3,500–4,200′. Moist shady woods and thickets. LC, UC, RP.

Comments: The plant is named after Linnaeus, whose portraits sometimes show him holding or wearing this plant. It is more common farther north in Oregon and Washington than in our area. The small, waxy-looking, pink flowers have a delicate vanilla scent. It can be seen growing along the Rock Creek Nature Trail, where it forms mounds as it scrambles across fallen limbs.

KAREN CALLAHAN

Twinflower

Caryophyllaceae
PINK FAMILY
Chet Blackburn

Herbs with mostly simple, entire, opposite leaves. The **stem joints are characteristically swollen.** Sepals 4–5, free or united. **Petals 4–5, often notched or deeply divided.** Stamens 10 or fewer. The family is important horticulturally, including such common garden inhabitants as *Gypsophila* (Baby's Breath), Carnation, *Saponaria* (Bouncing Bet), *Silene* (Pinks), *Dianthus,* and *Lychnis* (Campion, Bladder Campion). Of the 85 genera and 2,400 species worldwide, there are 28 genera and 108 species in California, and 17 genera with 45 species in our area.

Ballhead Sandwort

Arenaria congesta　　　　Native perennial
Ballhead Sandwort　　　　Jun–Aug

Description: A 4–10″ tall plant. Many simple slender flowering stems rise from a close cluster of a matted crown. The flowers are in a headlike structure.

Habitat: 5,000–6,500′. Locally common on outcrops and gravelly slopes and flats of volcanic origin. UC, RO, SP.

Comments: Out of flower, the plant resembles a small sedge or grass clump. Flower stalks are taller than most arenarias. Native Americans used arenarias for eyewash and tea (not concurrently, of course). Prickly Sandwort, *A. aculeata,* also grows in Nevada and Placer Counties, but it can be distinguished from *A. congesta* because *A. aculeata's* flowers don't cluster together in compact heads.

Arenaria kingii var. *glabrescens*

Native perennial

King's Sandwort   Jun–Sep

Description: 2–8" high. Tufted growth, stems glandular-hairy, leaves are needlelike and sharp-pointed. Its small, white flowers bloom in open clusters; each flower has 10 very noticeable bright red anthers.

Habitat: 6,000–12,000'. Dry sandy flats in full sun. CH, LC, UC, SA, RO.

Comments: Looks somewhat like the Baby's Breath that is used in floral bouquets. Petals of the sandworts are unlobed, which differentiates them from the lobed petals of most members of the Pink family. King's Sandwort is very common in sandy soils at Tahoe. *Arenaria* is derived from Latin for "sand," which describes its common habitat.

King's Sandwort

Cerastium glomeratum   Non-native annual

Mouse-ear Chickweed   Feb–Jun

Description: 4–12" tall plant with paired oval leaves attached directly to the stem. The flowers are white in clusters at the tip of the hairy stem. The petals are deeply notched, often shorter than the sepals that are sharply pointed and extremely hairy.

Habitat: Below 5,000'. A widespread weed of grassy flats, sandbars, and disturbed places from the Valley floor to coniferous forests. GR, FW, CH, LC, RP.

Comments: The very hairy stems, leaves, and calyx and the elongate (not oval) seed capsules separate this from the equally abundant Common Chickweed, *Stellaria media;* both of these are frequent weeds of containerized plants. Native to Europe.

Mouse-ear Chickweed

Douglas' Sandwort

Minuartia douglasii   Native annual
Douglas' Sandwort   Apr–Jun

Description: A 2–8″ tall plant with a delicate, threadlike, much-branched stem and needlelike leaves. It has a loose inflorescence of white flowers with yellow centers on long slender stalks. The flowers are relatively large for the size of the plant.

Habitat: 100–4,000′. Locally abundant on thin sterile soils on flats and rocky hillsides, often on granite sands. GR, FW, CH, LC, SG.

Comments: Douglas' Sandwort can be distinguished from the other *Minuartia* in our area, California Sandwort, *Minuartia californica*, by having longer leaves (from 0.2″ to 1.5″ as compared to less than 0.2″) and by its slightly sticky inflorescence. Look for this small, fragile-looking plant on sparse shallow sandy or coarse soils where it does not face competition.

Wild Carnation

Petrorhagia dubia   Non-native annual
Wild Carnation   Apr–Jul

Description: 4–20″ tall on a coarse, wiry stem. Leaves opposite, few, linear to oblong. The bright rose-colored flowers are in compact terminal clusters, usually with only one flower open at a time. The cluster is covered by papery overlapping bracts. The seeds are black.

Habitat: 100–2,800′. Common on grassy flats, open shrublands, and disturbed areas. GR, FW, CH, LC.

Comments: Introduced in the 1920s, it has spread throughout the state at low elevations. The small but conspicuous bright rose-colored flowers that strongly resemble miniature carnations always attract attention, and participants in our field trips are often surprised that it is not a native. Some references still refer to the plant by its old generic name, *Tunica dubia.*

Silene californica   Native perennial
Indian Pink   Mar–Jul

Description: 6–12″ tall from a stout taproot. It forms a low compact leafy plant with sticky dark green, paired, fuzzy, ovate leaves and 1″ crimson flowers. The petals are deeply 4-lobed.

Habitat: 300–4,000′. Brushy or wooded slopes. CH, FW, LC.

Comments: The "Pink" in the common name does not refer to the flower color but instead to the Pink family to which it belongs. The striking flowers are attractive to hummingbirds as well as people. While a close relative from Southern California, *S. laciniata,* is easy to cultivate, *S. californica* is both difficult to find in nurseries and difficult to grow. This is a pity because it is one of our most attractive wildflowers. The leaves are sticky to touch and were used by Native Americans to make a tea for aches and pains.

Indian Pink

Silene douglasii   Native perennial
Douglas' Catchfly   Jun–Aug

Description: 4–15″ tall. The leaves are chiefly basal and tapering at both ends. Each stem is few flowered (1–3) and bears creamy white petals that are barely bilobed. They emerge from a conspicuously ribbed calyx tube.

Habitat: 5,500–7,000′. Rocky and brushy places, rocky slopes in coniferous forest. Especially abundant in subalpine volcanic soils. UC, SA, RO.

Comments: It has a fused, ribbed, and often inflated calyx and lobed petals. The name "Catchfly" is in reference to the sticky glandular hairs that cover the foliage in which gnats often become entangled. Sticky foliage is beneficial to plants for several reasons, including moisture retention and protection from insect predation.

Douglas' Catchfly

Windmill Pink

Silene gallica   Non-native annual
Windmill Pink   Feb–Jul

Description: 4–20″ tall with dull green, narrowly spoon-shaped, hairy, sticky opposite leaves. The 5 white to pink petals are slightly twisted. There are 10 stamens. Each petal tip is rounded, with 2 inner toothlike appendages. The calyx tube has purplish ribs. The flowers are mostly all on one side of the stem.

Habitat: 100–2,600′. Common weed on grassy slopes and flats, especially on disturbed ground. GR, CH, FW, LC, RP.

Comments: The common name "Windmill Pink" comes from the way the petals twist, resembling the paper windmills that children used to make. It is considered a noxious weed in grain fields but is seldom a serious pest.

Lemmon's Catchfly

Silene lemmonii   Native perennial
Lemmon's Catchfly   Apr–Aug

Description: 6–20″ tall with slender stems that are glandular in the upper parts. The flowers are mostly nodding, and are white or tinted yellowish to pink. The petals are recurving, divided into 4 linear lobes with 4 short linear teeth. The styles and stamens are strongly exserted.

Habitat: 1,500–6,500′. Open woods, brushy slopes in coniferous forests. GR, LC, UC.

Comments: The foliage is not as sticky as most Catchflies. In her book, *Hiking Tahoe's Wildflower Trails,* Julie Carville describes the flower in a colorful way, stating that "each blossom looks like a many legged ballerina in a tutu with tiny yellow dancing slippers." The plant can be seen dancing at Sagehen Creek, among other places. Four other white-flowered species of *Silene* are also found in our area.

Spergularia rubra   Non-native annual
Ruby Sand Spurry   Apr–Sep

Description: 4–9″ sprawling plants forming
mats of small fleshy leaves and fibrous roots and
sending out clusters of pale pink to lavender
flowers. The petals are concave and shiny, ¼″
in diameter.

Habitat: 100–7,000′. Common in parking lots,
dredge tailings, unpaved roads, footpaths, and
other disturbed areas. GR, CH, FW, LC, UC, RP.

Comments: Usually found in sandy, gravelly, or
other loose, nonhumus soils. It is also a common weed in irrigated cultivated fields but not a
problematic one. Another spurry in a different
genus, Corn Spurry, *Spergula arvensis,* is also
an introduced European species and is a very
common component of grassy places, including
even the best-kept lawns.

JULIE S. CARVILLE

Ruby Sand Spurry

Stellaria longipes var. *longipes*
      Native perennial
Long-stalked Sandwort   May–Aug

Description: 3–12″ tall. A dainty-looking plant
with a slender running rootstock bearing erect
hairless stems and linear to lancelike leaves that
are strongly keeled. The 5 deeply lobed white
petals resemble a 10-pointed star.

Habitat: 3,500–6,000′. Moist meadows,
streamsides, lake margins, and other wet places.
MM, RP.

Comments: *Stellaria* means star-shaped.
Circumboreal in distribution. It can reproduce
from bulbils or fragmentation of the stems. The
red anthers provide a nice contrast to the white
petals. As might be expected with such a widespread and variable species, there is not uniform
agreement as to whether the complex is one
species or as many as ten species.

MICHAEL GRAFF

Long-stalked Sandwort

Common Chickweed

Stellaria media   Non-native annual
Common Chickweed   Feb–Sep

Description: 6–12″ plant with slender, weak, trailing stems and opposite smooth-edged oval leaves. The ¼″ flowers have 2-parted petals and emerge from the leaf axils. The sepals are slightly longer than the petals.

Habitat: 100–2,800′. Common and widespread from the Valley to the foothills in both sunny and shady locations in grasslands, cultivated fields, and brushy or rocky areas. GR, CH, FW, LC, RP.

Comments: It blooms throughout the winter in mild climates, but quickly dries at the onset of summer heat. There is a single line of hairs running along only one side of the stem, which helps identify the plant. The leaves are shiny and hairless; this distinguishes it from the Mouse-ear Chickweed, *Cerastium glomeratum,* which is equally common and grows in similar situations.

Indian Pink blooms bright red among the grasses along the Stevens Trail.

Convolvulaceae
MORNING GLORY FAMILY
Monica Finn

Plants are generally twining or trailing, with alternate leaves. The flowers are generally showy, radial, bell-shaped, pleated and twisted in the bud, untwisting as the flower opens. Sepals and stamens 5, stamens attached to corolla tube. Fruit generally a capsule. Some members of the family, such as some species in the genera *Dichondra, Quamoclit,* and *Ipomaea,* are cultivated as ornamentals. The Sweet Potato is also a member of this family. Worldwide there are about 50 genera and 1,600 species, mostly in the tropics. There are 5 genera and 23 species in California, with 2 of those genera and 4 species occurring in Nevada and Placer Counties. This includes 1 rare species that has been recorded only from a few sites in Nevada and El Dorado Counties.

Calystegia malacophylla   Native perennial
Woolly Morning Glory,
Sierra Morning Glory   Jun–Sep

Description: Trailing stems to 40″. Leaves triangular, 1–2″ long, densely hairy, and soft to the touch. The white funnel-shaped flowers are night blooming. A pair of conspicuous bracts beneath the flowers almost covers the calyx.

Habitat: 1,000–7,500′. Dry slopes, forest floors. FW, CH, LC, UC.

Comments: The Latin name *malacophylla* means "soft leaves." Coming across a mature plant in bloom on an early-morning hike is always a delight, as the plant is usually heavily laden with white flowers. The seeds are eaten by a variety of birds and mammals.

KAREN CALLAHAN

Woolly Morning Glory

Western Morning Glory

Calystegia occidentalis ssp. *occidentalis*
Native perennial
Western Morning Glory   May–Jun

Description: Stems over 40″ long. Low-growing, sprawling, or strongly climbing plant from a woody caudex. Leaves are arrowhead-shaped, with sharp, pointed lobes. The basal lobes have two points. Sepals are unequal. Flowers are funnel-shaped, solitary, white to creamy yellow.

Habitat: 1,000–9,000′. Dry, open slopes. GR, FW, LC, UC.

Comments: It is sometimes confused with the introduced nuisance, Bindweed, *Convolvulus arvensis,* but differs in the lobing of the leaf and a larger flower size. Western Morning Glory is more likely to be found growing in brush and open woodlands, while Bindweed is more prevalent in disturbed areas and cultivated orchards and fields.

Stebbins' Morning Glory

Calystegia stebbinsii   Native perennial
Stebbins' Morning Glory   Apr–Jul

Description: To 40″. Stems trailing to climbing. The leaves have 7–9 deep lobes, are palmate, with the middle lobe the longest. The leaf margin is generally rolled under. Bractlets are similar to the leaves and placed well below the calyx. Corolla white to creamy yellow and tinged pink.

Habitat: 600–2,400′. Open areas in red clay, gabbro, serpentine soils. GR, CH, SG.

Comments: Its distribution is limited to gabbro/serpentine soils in Nevada County and on the Pine Hill formation in El Dorado County. A state and federally listed endangered species. The aboveground portion dies to the ground in the winter, and the plant survives as an underground rhizome.

Convolvulus arvensis   Non-native perennial
Bindweed   Apr–Oct

Description: Trailing stems, and a deep, persistent taproot. The arrowhead-shaped leaves have sharp, pointed lobes. The flowers are funnel-shaped, white or pink tinted.

Habitat: Below 5,000'. An abundant weed of orchards, gardens, roadsides, and disturbed places. GR, CH, FW, LC.

Comments: A noxious weed. An invasive, deep-rooted species, it is difficult to eradicate because of its adaptability to a variety of conditions and its deep taproot, extending down to as much as 10', and its ability to produce numerous lateral roots from which new plants arise. Although many of the lateral roots die each winter, some survive to produce new plants in favorable niches. The seeds can remain viable for 50 years.

Bindweed

Tufted Poppy and Birds-eye Gilia cascade over serpentine rocks, softening the rocks with vibrant color.

148

Crassulaceae
STONECROP FAMILY
Monica Finn

*Succulent herbs and subshrubs, with fleshy, simple leaves.
The leaves generally form a basal rosette* and are reduced in size on
the stem. When occurring on the stem they may be either alternate
or opposite. *Tubular flowers in branched clusters,* sepals and petals
3–5, stamens equal to or 2 times the number of petals. There are 35
genera and about 1,500 species worldwide, with 4 genera and 10
species in Placer and Nevada Counties.

Canyon Dudleya

Dudleya cymosa Native perennial
Canyon Dudleya Apr–Jun

Description: Under 1′ in flower. It forms a
basal rosette of succulent, pointed, 2–6″ long,
spoon-shaped leaves that wither in summer. The
2–4 flower stems arise from the rosette. The
inflorescence consists of bright red-yellow
flowers. The petals have flared ends.

Habitat: 200–9,000′. Dry, rocky outcrops and
talus slopes. GR, CH, FW, LC, UC, RO.

Comments: Also called Canyon Live Forever and
Rock Lettuce. Sparse to common on canyon
slopes. The thick succulent leaves present
during the rainy season shrivel and shrink as the
hot summer progresses. Unfortunately, their
oddity and beauty too often make these slow-
growing plants targets of illegal plant collecting
along roads and trails. Hummingbirds work the
flowers.

Parvisedum pumilum   Native annual
Sierra Stonecrop   Mar–May

Description: Forms mats 1–10″ wide. Stems succulent. The leaves are simple and densely packed on the stem. The inflorescence is a branched cyme of starlike flowers. Each flower has 5 tiny petals and 10 stamens. The flower color ranges from bright yellow to yellow-reddish brown.

Habitat: 200–4,000′. Rock outcrops, clay soils. VP, FW, LC, RO.

Comments: *Parvisedum* means "little Sedum" and *pumilum* means "dwarf," hence "dwarf little Sedum." That might sound redundant but it is an apt description. It grows in places that are wet in the winter and bone dry in the summer, such as the edges of vernal pools, especially those with shallow soils, and depressions in rocks.

Sierra Stonecrop

Sedum obtusatum   Native perennial
Sierra Sedum   Jun–Jul

Description: 1–9″ tall. A low-growing succulent, with erect stems from a basal rosette of spoon-shaped leaves. The stem leaves are reduced, obtuse, or truncate. The inflorescence consists of 8 to 60 generally flat-topped flowers. The yellow to brownish yellow flowers fade to a pinkish color with age. The petals are united at the base. Fruit erect.

Habitat: 4,000–12,000′. Rocky ridges and slopes. LC, UC, SA, RO.

Comments: This is a denizen of rocky soils, especially those of decomposing granite, and boulder crevices at high elevations. The yellow flowers and reddish stems make an attractive display in the rocky places in which they are found. The foliage often turns red at the onset of winter. The plant is in cultivation.

Sierra Sedum

King's Crown

Sedum roseum ssp. *integrifolium*
Native perennial
King's Crown, Rose Sedum   May–Jul

Description: Less than 12″ tall. A low-growing succulent, with a short, thick, fleshy stem and a fleshy aromatic root. The leaves are dense along the stem, not in a rosette. Inflorescence with 7 to 50 maroon flowers, each with flaring petal tips.

Habitat: 7,500–12,500′. Moist, rocky places, cliffs, talus slopes, and alpine ridges. SA, RO.

Comments: Another high-elevation species that can be found even above the timberline, where it thrives under harsh conditions. It is widespread in the colder parts of the Northern Hemisphere. Known as *Rhodiola integrifolia* in some references. The seedpods are also a colorful red. It is not likely to be confused with anything else, with its bluish green leaves and maroon-red flowers.

JULIE S. CARVILLE

Pacific Sedum

Sedum spathulifolium   Native perennial
Pacific Sedum   Jun–Jul

Description: 2–9″ tall. A low-growing, succulent, spreading plant. The spatula-shaped leaves occur in flat rosettes. The stem leaves are reduced and elliptic in shape. The inflorescence has 5–48 flowers. The flowers are yellow, the petals free and widely spreading. The fruit is erect at maturity and widely spreading.

Habitat: 1,000–8,200′. Rocky habitats, especially mossy outcrops, often in shade. LC, UC, RO.

Comments: Visible on winter wet, mossy rock outcrops on Independence Trail, Edward's Crossing, and Iowa Hill Road. The foliage is very brittle, breaking off easily when handled. It is in cultivation, and a cultivar known as *S. spathulifolium* 'Cape Blanco' is a particularly popular form.

RICHARD HANES

Cucurbitaceae
CUCUMBER FAMILY
Monica Finn

Annual and perennial vines, with small *gourdlike fruits. Simple, lobed, alternate leaves with 1 tendril per node, the tendrils usually spirally coiled.* The flower consists of 5 united petals forming a funnel-like floral tube. The ovary is inferior. In California, *male and female flowers are separate, but on the same stem.* The fruit is a berry (called a pepo) with a leather cap. It is an economically important family, including such food plants as watermelon, cucumbers, squash, and various other melons. There are about 100 genera and 850 species worldwide. The family contains 6 genera and 12 species in California. *Marah* is the only native genus in Placer and Nevada Counties.

Marah fabaceus   Native perennial
Common Manroot   Feb–Apr

Description: Vines 6–20′ long. The leaves are round in outline, but with 5–7 lobes. The flowers are white to yellow-green. It dies back to a large underground tuberous root in the dry season. The conspicuous fruit is globe-shaped with sparse to dense unhooked soft spines.

Habitat: Below 5,000′. Common foothill plant. GR, CH, FW, LC, RP.

Comments: Called Manroot because the root can reach the size and more or less the shape of a man. It is similar to *M. watsonii,* also called Manroot and also growing in our area, but the two can be distinguished by the fact that *M. fabaceus* has flattened saucerlike or wheel-shaped flowers, while *M. watsonii*'s flowers are more cuplike or bell-like. The fruit of *M. fabaceus* is almost twice as large as those of *M. watsonii.*

JULIE S. CARVILLE

Common Manroot

Cuscutaceae
DODDER FAMILY
Chet Blackburn

Leafless and rootless parasitic vinelike herbs that are almost totally lacking in chlorophyll. Annual parasitic vines with orange to yellow threadlike stems twining throughout the branches of host plants. Several kinds of non-native Dodders are agricultural pests. The leaves are none or reduced to tiny scales. Flowers are small, mostly white, clustered on spikes or in heads. Some authors include them in the Morning Glory family, Convolvulaceae. Worldwide, 1 genus and 150 species exist, mostly in the American tropics. There are 4 California species, 4 of which occur in our area.

California Dodder

Cuscuta californica   Native annual
California Dodder   May–Nov

Description: A leafless plant with waxy, orange-colored stems lacking chlorophyll and coiling around and twining through the host plant. The flowers are small, white, and in short clusters.

Habitat: 100–6,700′. Occasional to locally abundant, Valley floor into coniferous forests. Many hosts from herbs to shrubs. GR, CH, FW, LC, SG.

Comments: This is a parasitic plant. Soon after the seed germinates, a wandering stem attaches to the nearest host and anchors onto it, penetrating it and clambering up through it. It is difficult to remove because of the many branches attached to many points on the host. Branches can continue to grow independently when broken off. It usually looks like orange twine caught up in the host plant.

RICHARD HANES · CINDY RUBIN

Droseraceae
SUNDEW FAMILY
Chet Blackburn

Insectivorous herbs. Leaves simple, arranged as a basal rosette. Leaf surface covered with stalked, sticky, club-shaped glands. Sepals 4 or 5 fused together, petals 5, free. The flowering stems are leafless and threadlike. There are 4 genera and 100 species worldwide. They occur on every continent except Antarctica and in many different habitats, but most are bog plants. About half the species are found only in Australia. The Venus Flytrap, *Dioanae muscipula,* is included in this family but is placed into a separate family by some taxonomists. In California, 1 genus (*Drosera*) and 2 species exist, both occurring in the area covered by this book.

Drosera rotundifolia   Native perennial
Round-leaved Sundew   Jul–Sep

Description: Forms a 2–8″ rosette. Small, round leaves appear at the end of long slender stalks. The leaves are prostrate, or nearly so, and covered with (usually reddish) sticky tentacles that trap and hold small insects. White to pinkish flowers open on threadlike stalks.

Habitat: Below 6,500′. An uncommon plant of cold, wet, boggy habitats, often in thick moss. LC, UC, MM, RP, AQ.

Comments: A circumpolar species. Tiny prey such as gnats are trapped and digested by enzymes secreted by the leaves. Long-leaved Sundew, *Drosera anglica,* also occurs in our area. Rare here, it is more common to the north. It can be distinguished from *D. rotundifolia* by its ascending (not prostrate) leaves, the ends of which are lance-shaped, not round.

RICHARD HANES

Round-leaved Sundew

154

Ericaceae
HEATH FAMILY
Shawna Martinez

Family includes trees, shrubs, and woody and herbaceous perennials. *Bark sometimes peeling distinctively in shrub members.* The leaves are simple and alternate (rarely opposite or whorled), and often leathery. *Some members of this family are mycotrophic (they form symbiotic associations with fungi).* The flowers are perfect, regular, or irregular. Sepals 5, but sometimes absent. Petals 5. *The corolla is often urn-shaped.* Stamens 10. A nectary disk is usually present. Style 1, undivided. The fruit is a capsule, berry, or drupe. Some botanists break out the mycotrophic members of this family and place them in separate families called Pyrolaceae and Monotropaceae. There are 26 genera and 98 species in California, with 17 genera and 25 species found in Nevada and Placer Counties. Twelve of the genera in our area are perennial wildflowers.

Sugar Stick

Allotropa virgata　　　　Native perennial
Sugar Stick　　　　　　　Jun–Aug

Description: 6–24" tall. Leaves reduced to scales, making the plant appear leafless. The small white flowers are urn-shaped and bear red stamens.

Habitat: 250–9,000'. Oak woodlands to coniferous forests. CH, FW, LC, UC, SA.

Comments: Also called Candy Cane in reference to the resemblance of the stalk to a peppermint candy cane. When pushing up through the deep humus in the spring, the plant first looks like a pinkish stalk of asparagus, but as the stalk elongates the distinctive red stripes appear. The stalks turn brown after flowering and may persist for several years. Parasitic on mycelia of fungi. Consider yourself lucky if you come across this rare and striking wildflower.

KAREN CALLAHAN

Cassiope mertensiana   Native perennial
White Heather   Jul–Aug

Description: To 1′ tall. Small, creeping, or prostrate alpine perennials. The leaves are persistent and needlelike in rows of 4 along the branch. The white flowers are bell-shaped, solitary with 4–5 lobes. They hang from a 1″ stem. Its sepals are bright red and there are 10 stamens.

Habitat: 6,000–11,500′. Subalpine rocks in areas of late snow. SA, RO.

Comments: In Greek mythology, Cassiope was the mother of Andromeda. These are low-growing plants with scaly leaves pressed tightly against the stem so as to somewhat resemble a club moss when out of flower. Found on rocky ridges and ledges near timberline. It is the host plant of the Cassiope Blue butterfly, *Agriodes cassiope*.

JULIE S. CARVILLE

White Heather

Chimaphila umbellata   Native perennial
Prince's Pine, Pipsissiwa   Jun–Aug

Description: 4–12″. A low, evergreen perennial with running underground rootstock. The shiny, waxy, toothed leaves are clustered at the base in groups of 3 to 8. The delicate pink 5-petaled flowers are nodding.

Habitat: 1,000–9,500′. Common in dry coniferous forest. LC, UC, SA.

Comments: Out of bloom, the plant might be mistaken for a seedling shrub. It tends to grow in groups in forest detritus. The leaves were chewed for medicinal purposes to induce vomiting by Native Americans and were also chewed into a poultice to combat pain and inflammation. The most common use of the plant in more recent times was as an additive to old-time root beer. The foliage tastes like wintergreen.

JULIE S. CARVILLE

Prince's Pine

One-sided Wintergreen

Mountain Heather

Orthilia secunda   Native perennial
One-sided Wintergreen, Sidebells   Jul–Sep

Description: Plants small, less than 1′ tall. The basal leaves are shiny and smooth to round-toothed. The greenish to cream-white flowers are arranged along one side of the flowering stem. Petals 5, free, with 2 basal tubercles on the upper surface. Styles protruding and prominent.

Habitat: 1,000–9,500′. Common in dry, shaded conifer forests. LC, UC, SA.

Comments: Potentially toxic. Both common names refer to the way the flowers are all attached to one side of the flowering stem. The flowering stem starts out erect initially but the increasing weight of the developing flowers eventually causes it to arch downward. It is often found in the company of the Rattlesnake Plantain, *Goodyera oblongifolia,* growing in thick layers of conifer needles in woodland habitats.

CINDY RUBIN

Phyllodoce breweri   Native perennial
Mountain Heather   Jul–Aug

Description: Low evergreen plants under 1′ that are much branched and Heath-like. The leaves are small, linear, and needlelike. The flowers are in umbel-like arrangements. Individual flowers are cup-shaped, petals 5, sepals 5, and are pink to rose-purple.

Habitat: 6,000–12,000′. Moist rocky slopes, meadows, subalpine, usually in highly acid soils. SA, MM, RO.

Comments: The leaves resemble pine needles but are actually linear leaves with margins rolled down and tightly attached to the undersurface. Honey derived from this plant (and some other members of the Heath family) contains a substance known as grayanotoxin and can cause a condition known as honey intoxication or rhododendron poisoning.

JULIE S. CARVILLE

Pleuricospora fimbriolata   Native perennial
Fringed Pinesap   Apr–Aug

Description: 3–6″ stems covered with close clusters of cream-colored bracts from which cream-colored flowers emerge. Sepals 4, petals 4 (sometimes 5), margins jagged, stamens 8.

Habitat: 3,300–6,500′. Occasional in conifer forests. LC, UC.

Comments: A mysterious and uncommon plant that looks more like a fungus than a flowering plant. Closer examination reveals the cream-colored flowers peeking out above the matching bracts. It is most often found on thick patches of dry decaying pine needles in areas relatively free of other vegetation in shady coniferous forests. Consider yourself lucky to come across a group of them. They appear suddenly, flower, and disappear almost as suddenly. They have been observed on the Rock Creek Nature Trail.

KAREN CALLAHAN

Fringed Pinesap

Pterospora andromedea   Native perennial
Pinedrops   Jun–Aug

Description: Stem tall, up to 4′ at maturity. Stems are red and covered with scurfy hair. The leaves are reduced to scattered elongated scales along the stem, making the plant appear to be a nongreen, leafless perennial. The flowers are urn-shaped, cream to yellowish, and arranged singly along a raceme. Best identified by the tall, brown, leafless dry stalk in late summer.

Habitat: 2,600–8,500′. Dry shady coniferous forests in deep humus. LC, UC.

Comments: Once thought to be saprophytic, it is now recognized that this and similar plants derive their nutrients by forming specialized roots that attach to mycorrhizal networks that are in turn attached to other species such as tree roots, especially pines. The stems are characteristically sticky.

JULIE S. CARVILLE

Pinedrops

White-veined Wintergreen

Pyrola picta   Native perennial
White-veined Wintergreen   Jun–Aug

Description: 4–8″ tall. A low herb with an underground rootstock. The evergreen leaves are in a basal cluster. The veins are white bordered and the leaves purple below. Leaves are sometimes absent. The flowers are in a simple raceme. Petals 5, greenish, cream-white, or pink, drooping. Styles downwardly curved, exserted.

Habitat: 3,000–9,500′. Common in dry ponderosa pine or mixed conifer forests. LC, UC.

Comments: Easily identifiable out of flower by its white mottled leaves. Potentially toxic. Bog Wintergreen, *Pyrola asarifolia,* is a related species in our area that grows in wet places and lacks the white veining on the leaves. The Rock Creek Nature Trail (above the parking lot) is a good place to see them.

Snow Plant

Sarcodes sanguinea   Native perennial
Snow Plant   May–Jul

Description: 4–12″ high. A red fleshy plant, nongreen, nonphotosynthetic. The waxy-appearing flowering stalks are simple, solitary, or in clusters. The leaves are scalelike, small, and crowded along the flowering stalk. Bright red urn-shaped flowers emerge from the stem.

Habitat: 4,000–8,000′. Thick humus of coniferous forests after snow recedes. LC, UC.

Comments: Few plants attract the attention of visitors to our coniferous forests as much as the fabled snow plant does. Can anyone with a camera resist taking a photo? It is usually a denizen of red fir forests. This species is a root parasite. It has specialized roots that invade other species through associated mycorrhizal fungi and obtains its nutrients from them.

Euphorbiaceae
SPURGE FAMILY
Chet Blackburn

Shrubs, trees, and herbs. Many are xerophytic and succulent. *Flowers consist of colored bracts that resemble petals, a central cluster of stamens and glands, and a 3-lobed ovary adjacent to stamens and hanging to one side.* Plants usually have *thick, milky sap.* It is an important commercial family that is responsible for such products as rubber, castor oil, tung oil, tapioca, and cassava, as well as hundreds of horticultural collector plants. There are 300 genera and 7,500 species worldwide but the family is especially well represented in tropical Africa and Latin America. There are 12 genera and 58 species in California (many of them non-native) and 3 genera and 10 species in the area covered by this book.

Eremocarpus setigerus   Native annual
Doveweed, Turkey Mullein   May–Oct

Description: 4–12″ tall. It forms a rosette of prostrate, fuzzy, silvery green thick oval leaves. Inconspicuous whitish to yellowish green mealy-looking flowers are clustered in the center of the rosette.

Habitat: 100–4,200′. Dry open fields, roadsides, especially in disturbed areas. GR, FW, CH, LC.

Comments: The seeds are relished by quail and doves but the foliage may be poisonous to geese if eaten in quantity. Sheep and hogs occasionally feed on it with seemingly ill effects. The leaves have a somewhat lemonlike odor when crushed. They contain a narcotic used by Native Americans to stun fish. Stiff hairs make the stems and leaves rough and unpleasant to touch. Irritation from the hairs causes rashes in some people.

RICHARD HANES

Doveweed

Fabaceae
PEA FAMILY
Chet Blackburn

The familiar pea flower consists of *5 petals arranged in a distinctive pattern. The top petal, called the "banner," is usually largest. Two side petals are known as "wings," and the two bottom petals are joined together, forming a structure called the "keel" because of its resemblance to the keel of a boat.* The leaves are usually alternate and compound. The *fruit is a legume,* with 1 or more seeds enclosed in a chamber that is dehiscent (split) on both sides. Many have nitrogen-fixing bacteria in their roots. It is an important family in food production, timber production, and horticulture. It is the third largest flowering plant family, with more than 650 genera and 18,000 species worldwide. In California, there are 50 genera and 386 species. Our area is represented by 15 genera and 103 species.

Balloon Pod Milkvetch

Astragalus whitneyi Native perennial
Balloon Pod Milkvetch,
Whitney's Locoweed May–Sep

Description: 1–12″ tall with sprawling stems. Foliage hairy, flowers purple with white wings. The seedpods are large and conspicuous, inflated, papery, yellowish to pinkish, and mottled reddish purple.

Habitat: 7,000–12,000′. Widespread above 8,500′. Rocky ridges, summits, often in dry gravelly soil. SA, RO, SP.

Comments: The mature seedpods resemble inflated purple-spotted sausages that rattle when shaken. Highly variable. Toxic to livestock. The genus *Astragalus* is one of the largest in the state, with 144 species and varieties, yet only 10 of them occur within our area, and most of those are either uncommon or found only at high elevations east of the Sierra.

JULIE S. CARVILLE

Hoita macrostachya   Native perennial
Large Leather Root   Jun–Sep

Description: Flowering stem to 6′ tall. Much branched with a hollow base. The three leaflets are narrowly oval and together form a more or less triangular compound leaf that is subtended by a conspicuous bract. The numerous purple flowers are closely spaced together.

Habitat: Below 5,000′. Moist places. Seeps, canals, and along streams. LC, UC, MM, RP.

Comments: Formerly (and still widely) known as *Psoralea macrostachya*. Native Americans utilized fiber from the roots to make rope and extracted a yellow dye from them. It can be distinguished from Round Leaf Leather Root, *Hoita orbicularis*, which also grows in our area, by the shape of the leaves and the fact that *H. orbicularis* tends to have a decumbent or arching habit, while *H. macrostachya* is erect.

Large Leather Root

Lathyrus latifolius   Non-native perennial
Perennial Sweetpea,
Everlasting Pea   May–Sep

Description: Sprawling vine to 8′ with a deep taproot, well-developed tendrils, and flattened stems with a distinctive wing. The flowers are red-purple to pink or white.

Habitat: 100–3,500′. Garden escapee on disturbed sites and the edges of towns. FW, LC.

Comments: A well-known, vigorous, and invasive garden plant that has escaped cultivation and is especially common along roads and around old mining towns. Native to central Europe, it is readily recognized by its winged stems. It starts easily from seed. Anyone driving Highway 49 toward the Yuba River Canyon is well acquainted with this plant.

Perennial Sweetpea

Sierra Nevada Pea

Lathyrus nevadensis   Native perennial
Sierra Nevada Pea   Apr–Jun

Description: A 6–24″ delicate-looking, sprawl-ing vine. There are 4–8 pairs of oval leaflets per leaf, the lower ones opposite, the upper ones alternate. The terminal tendril is slightly curled or reduced to a tail-like appendage.

Habitat: 2,000–5,000′. Common on woodland floors and in openings in dry coniferous forests. LC.

Comments: This denizen of Ponderosa Pine woodlands is usually associated with Sierra Iris and Mountain Misery. It can be seen along the trails at Empire Mine State Park, where it grows along with another native pea, Nevada Pea, *Lathyrus lanzwertii,* which typically has nar-rower, more elongate leaflets and rose to lavender-colored flowers instead of the bluish purple flowers of *L. nevadensis.*

Sulphur Pea

Lathyrus sulphureus   Native perennial
Sulphur Pea   Apr–Jul

Description: Sprawling vines to 10′ (usually less). The tendrils are well developed. The flowers are all on one side of the stalk in tight clusters, and are yellow to orange or brown with purplish lines.

Habitat: 200–5,000′. Common and widespread in shaded to partially shaded dry brushy areas. FW, CH, LC.

Comments: The inflorescence is often com-posed of several colors at the same time. The smaller unopened flowers are creamy to pale yellow, the newly opened flowers yellow to burnt orange, and the older flowers burnt orange to brown. This species is usually found growing on banks in open shade, particularly in canyons. Look for it on the various trails in the American River and Yuba River canyons.

Lotus argophyllus var. *fremontii*
Native perennial
Fremont's Silver Lotus   Apr–Jul

Description: 8–40" wide, forming a prostrate mat that is densely covered with silvery hair and small yellow flowers in umbels of 3 to 8. The flowers are attached directly to the stem in headlike clusters. The banner turns brown or purplish with age. The seedpod is covered with silky hair.

Habitat: 900–4,000'. Dry slopes, granite outcrops, often in river canyons. FW, CH, LC, RO.

Comments: This is a plant of rocky outcrops, in sun or shade. The unopened flower clusters are very pale green, providing a contrast with the silvery foliage. It can be seen at Bridgeport, along the Stevens Trail, and the rocky hillsides along Iowa Hill Road.

Fremont's Silver Lotus

Lotus grandiflorus   Native perennial
Largeflower Lotus   Apr–Jul

Description: 1–2' tall. Decumbent to erect with 7 to 9 oval to egg-shaped somewhat hairy leaflets. The stipules at the base of the leaf are glandular. The inflorescence has 3–9 flowers. The calyx is hairy. The light yellow to greenish white flowers tend to turn reddish with age. The banner petal is much larger than the other petals. The conspicuous purplish-brown seedpods are 1–2" long with a sharp tip.

Habitat: 1,200–3,600'. Open wooded or brushy places. CH, LC.

Comments: Uncommon but can be seen along the trails at Empire Mine State Park. The quite large banner petal is the main identification factor. The genus *Lotus* is a variable one and is widespread in the state. There are 13 species found in our two-county area.

Largeflower Lotus

Hill Lotus

Lotus humistratus   Native annual
Hill Lotus   Mar–Jul

Description: To 1″ tall. Forms prostrate mats 3–14″ wide. There are usually 4 leaflets. Stems are reddish. A single small, sessile, yellow flower rises above the leaves. Flowers age to a reddish tone.

Habitat: 100–3,000′. Common and widespread on dry grassy slopes and openings, especially on banks. FW, CH, LC, RP.

Comments: There are several other similar yellow *Lotus* species in our area, but this is the most common. In our area it would most likely be confused with another small yellow-flowered lotus, Calf Lotus, *Lotus wrangelianus,* but can be distinguished from it by the length of the calyx tips. In *L. wrangelianus* the calyx tips are about as long as the rest of the calyx, whereas in *L. humistratus* the calyx tips are twice as long as the rest of the calyx tube.

Streambank Lotus

Lotus oblongifolius   Native perennial
Streambank Lotus, Torrey's Lotus   May–Sep

Description: 1–1½′ tall. An erect to sprawling or ascending plant with 7–11 linear leaflets (rarely 3). The 2–6 flowers of each inflorescence are in umbels, each flower with a yellow banner and white lower wings adjacent to the keel. There are three leaflike bracts just below the umbels. The seedpod is 1–2″ long.

Habitat: 700–7,500′. Wet places. CH, LC, UC, RP.

Comments: The yellow and white flowers make an attractive combination. It can form dense clumps in the right situation. Ranges throughout much of California, north to Oregon, south to Mexico, and east to Nevada. Although the range is extensive, the populations are scattered.

Lotus purshianus   Native annual
Spanish Lotus   Apr–Oct

Description: 4–16″ tall. A variable, much-branched, ascending to erect plant. The foliage is somewhat silky. The flowers occur singly, are whitish to pinkish, and occur on long stalks.

Habitat: 100–6,600′. Moist to dry places, especially disturbed areas. GR, CH, FW, LC, UC, RP.

Comments: The common name of Spanish Lotus is a misnomer and sometimes leads people to think the plant is not native. Why it is called Spanish Lotus is difficult to understand because it does not come from Spain. Miniature Lotus, *Lotus micranthus,* might be confused with Spanish Lotus but is much smaller and blooms earlier (Mar–Apr). Spanish Lotus is primarily a plant of early to midsummer after the grasses have dried, but it can bloom right up to frost.

JULIE S. CARVILLE

Spanish Lotus

Lotus scoparius   Native perennial/small shrub
Deerweed, California Broom   May–Jun

Description: 3–6′ tall with an equal spread. The greenish stems are clustered, lanky, and branched. It is sometimes summer deciduous. The yellow flowers are tinged with red and occur in the late spring.

Habitat: 1,200–2,000′. Locally common in disturbed locations such as roadsides and mine tailings, especially in chaparral areas. CH, FW, LC.

Comments: Drought tolerant, it is a common constituent of chaparral and a fast-growing fire follower and nitrogen fixer. Deer love the young foliage and like many other members of the genus *Lotus,* it is a host plant for a number of butterfly species, including the Acmon Blue, *Plebejus acmon,* and the Persius Dusky Wing, *Erynnis persius.* Look for it on Foresthill Road near the high Foresthill Bridge.

VIRGINIA MORAN • DON JACOBSON

Deerweed

KAREN CALLAHAN

Pine Lupine

Lupinus albicaulis   Native perennial
Pine Lupine, Sickle Keel Lupine   May–Aug

Description: 1–4′ tall, erect. Numerous leaves consist of 5–9 ascending leaflets, giving the plant a narrow appearance. The white or blue flowers are not in whorls but arranged somewhat haphazardly along the tall stem in bunches of 2–3.

Habitat: 1,200–6,600′. Locally common in open coniferous forests. It occurs in the Sierra Nevada, Klamath Mountains, and north to Washington. CH, LC, UC.

Comments: The flowers in our area are usually white, but they are more often blue over much of its range. Some botanists regard this as a form of *L. andersonii.* The seedpods are often occupied by one or more species of weevil that take a heavy toll on seeds. The plant can be seen at Empire Mine State Park and on Iowa Hill Road.

JULIE S. CARVILLE

Bush Lupine

Lupinus albifrons   Native perennial
Bush Lupine, Silver Lupine   Mar–Jul

Description: To 5′ tall, bushy, variable, and with 7–10 narrow silky leaflets. The foliage is light green to silvery. The flowers are numerous, blue to lavender. The banner usually has a lighter center.

Habitat: 100–2,500′. Open brushy places. GR, FW, LC, CH, RP, RO.

Comments: There are a number of Bush Lupine species around the state; this one is the most abundant in our area and is certainly one of the most attractive. Herbaceous at first, it quickly develops a woody base. At least some forms of the plant give off a grape soda odor on hot days. The flowers were made into head wreaths by Native Americans to celebrate the May strawberry festival. It is found throughout lower elevations in our two counties.

Lupinus benthamii Native annual
Spider Lupine, Bentham's Lupine Mar–May

Description: 1–4′ tall. An erect plant with tall elegant flower spikes containing numerous pale to deep blue flowers with a whitish, yellowish, or rosy center. The leaflets are very narrow, often with a silvery appearance, and are somewhat hairy on the undersides.

Habitat: Below 3,000′. Roadsides, openings, and especially dry sunny slopes. GR, CH, FW, LC.

Comments: One of the earliest lupines to bloom and one of the most attractive. Seedlings are brownish and difficult to spot. The 2 cotyledons are somewhat corrugated and reddish brown, blending well with soil. The compound leaf is almost round like a wagon wheel, with the leaflets resembling spokes. It is abundant at lower elevations. It is the tallest annual lupine in our area, although some of the perennials are taller.

JULIE S. CARVILLE

Spider Lupine

Lupinus bicolor Native annual
Miniature Lupine Mar–Jun

Description: 4–16″ tall, erect, with 3–7 narrow leaflets covered with soft hairs. The small blue and white flowers are mostly under ¼″ and appear in small clusters. The pedicels are shorter than the flowers.

Habitat: Below 3,000′. Open grassy places. GR, CH, FW, LC, RP.

Comments: Larger specimens can be confused with Sky Lupine, *Lupinus nanus,* but Miniature Lupine has fewer flowers. With Sky Lupine, the banner (top petal) is as wide as or wider than it is long, whereas in Miniature Lupine the banner is longer than wide. This is one of our most common lupines but because it has fewer flowers and the plant is small, it does not create the conspicuous mass displays so typical of many other lupines.

KAREN CALLAHAN

Miniature Lupine

Brewer's Lupine

JULIE S. CARVILLE

Lupinus breweri　　　Native perennial
Brewer's Lupine　　　Jun–Aug

Description: A 2–12″ high (usually smaller) plant that forms prostrate mats. The leaves are silvery gray, flowers blue with a white or yellow center, and there are hairs on top of the keel.

Habitat: 4,000–12,000′. Dry stony slopes and coarse sandy areas in forest openings. LC, UC, SA, RO.

Comments: Highly variable with a number of forms. One of our most common high-elevation lupines, it typically forms low mats, especially on granitic soils. You won't find it at lower elevations. To quote Burt Wilson of Las Pilitas Native Plant Nursery, "The plant gets its name in honor of William Brewer, a member of a State Geological Survey party in the 1860s, so don't try to make beer out of it."

Broadleaf Lupine

KAREN CALLAHAN

Lupinus latifolius　　　Native perennial
Broadleaf Lupine　　　Apr–Jul

Description: To 5′ tall. There are from 7 to 9 broad rounded leaflets on long pedicels. It has a tall, somewhat open flower spike with a spiraling appearance. The flower colors range from almost white to dark blue (or occasionally pink).

Habitat: Below 7,000′. Brushy places to moist open woodlands, edges of meadows. CH, FW, LC, UC, MM.

Comments: There are 13 recognized botanical varieties in the state but only the varieties *columbianus, confertus,* and *sellulus* occur in our area. Toxic to (but not often eaten by) livestock. Some tribes considered it poisonous, while others, such as the Miwok, boiled leaves before eating them or making them into a relish for manzanita cider. They also lined their leaching baskets with them to hold acorn meal.

Lupinus microcarpus var. *densiflorus*
Native annual
Gully Lupine, Chick Lupine   Mar–Jun

Description: An 8–16″ erect plant with thick, often hollow stems. The 5 to 9 broad spatula-shaped leaflets are hairless above and curl inward. White or yellow flowers (in our area) are in widely spaced whorls around the stems, giving it a pagoda-like appearance.

Habitat: 100–2,000′. Locally abundant along roads, grassy places, brushy slopes, and flood plains. GR, CH, FW, LC, RP.

Comments: A component of many wildflower mixes, they are often hydroseeded along high-ways. This is the most variable lupine in terms of flower color. In our area the predominant colors are white or yellow, but in other parts of the state blue-, purple-, and rose-colored (var. *microcarpus*) forms exist as well.

Gully Lupine

Lupinus nanus   Native annual
Douglas' Lupine, Sky Lupine   Mar–Jun

Description: 8–24″ high with 5–7 linear to spoon-shaped leaflets. The flowers are conspicu-ous, rich blue, with a large white spot and often dark flecks at the petal base.

Habitat: 100–3,600′. Grassy places from the Valley floor into the mountains. GR, CH, FW, LC.

Comments: When you come across a mass display of lupines, it most likely consists of this species. With the exception of the California Poppy (with which it is often pictured), it is probably our most photographed plant. It is sometimes confused with Miniature Lupine, *Lupinus bicolor,* which frequently grows along with it, but *L. nanus* has a larger flower spike and more flowers. The banner is as wide as or wider than it is long, whereas in Miniature Lupine, the banner is longer than wide.

Douglas' Lupine

Meadow Lupine

Lupinus polyphyllus   Native perennial
Meadow Lupine   May–Aug

Description: 2–5′ tall. A robust plant with 5–17 broad leaflets per leaf, and numerous large dark green leaves that are hairless above and have pointed tips. The blue to purplish flowers are about ½″ long. The keel petals are strongly curved with a narrow tip. The seedpod is hairy.

Habitat: 1,500–5,800′. Locally common along streams, on seeps, wet meadows, and other moist places. LC, UC, MM, RP.

Comments: The species names *polyphyllus* means "many leafed" and refers to the lush foliage. It is leafier than most lupines. Always found in wet places, the plant is quick to wilt if moisture is insufficient. This species is one of the parents of the well-known 'Russell hybrid' lupines of horticulture. One place to see them is along the Sierra Discovery Trail in Bear Valley.

Harlequin Lupine

Lupinus stiversii   Native annual
Harlequin Lupine   Apr–Jul

Description: 4–16″ high. There are 6–9 leaflets per leaf. The flowers are multicolored with a yellow banner, rose-pink wings, and a white keel.

Habitat: 800–4,200′. Openings in chaparral and coniferous forests, especially sandy places. CH, FW, LC.

Comments: As a group, lupines are readily recognized, but distinguishing individual species from each other can be difficult. That is not the case with this one, however. Due to the color combination of the flowers, it is not likely to be confused with any other species. It usually occurs as a few plants scattered about in coarse or gravelly soils. When it grows at lower elevations it tends to have a loose, leggy look, while at higher elevations it is dwarfed and compact.

Lupinus succulentus   Native annual
Arroyo Lupine, Succulent Lupine   Mar–Jun

Description: 8–24″ tall. The leaves are on long petioles with 7–9 large oval leaflets per leaf. The flowers are about ½″ long, and purple-blue (occasionally white). The central portion of the banner is rosy red. The stems are succulent (often hollow) and branched.

Habitat: Below 2,000′. Along highways, grasslands, ravines. GR, CH, FW, LC.

Comments: Although the plant is native to California, it is not native to Placer and Nevada Counties, but has been widely planted along highways and other places that have been hydroseeded with native plants and persists for a few years after planting. The inflorescence is more open and has a less tidy appearance than most lupines. Look for a blue lupine with branching succulent stems to identify this species.

Arroyo Lupine

Melilotus alba   Non-native annual/biennial
White Sweetclover   May–Sep

Description: 2–6′ tall, stout, much branched with numerous small white flowers (rarely yellow) in groups along the stem. Leaves are trifoliate, with the leaflets finely toothed and rounded at the top. The fruit is an oval pod.

Habitat: 100–3,000′. Common along streams, roadsides, ditches, and other moist places. GR, FW, LC, MM, RP.

Comments: An important honey plant, bee-keepers (along with the cattle industry) planted it in quantity in the nineteenth century. The results as a forage plant were mixed, however. The nutrient value is high, but as the plant matures a bitterness develops due to a substance known as coumarin, and livestock then avoid it. The name "Sweetclover" is derived from the fragrance that the flowers and foliage emit on warm days.

White Sweetclover

Yellow Sweetclover

Melilotus officinalis   Non-native biennial
Yellow Sweetclover   May–Aug

Description: 2–6′ plant with trifoliate leaves. The flowers are small and yellow, fading to cream, and are arranged into many-flowered terminal and axillary racemes.

Habitat: 200–3,600′. An uncommon volunteer along streams. GR, FW, LC, RP.

Comments: The leaves resemble alfalfa except that the margins are serrate halfway back from the tip. Sometimes it ends up in hay. The foliage is high in coumarin, which causes anticoagulation of blood, resulting in a condition known as "bloat" in cattle. A smaller relative, *Melilotus indica,* is more common and is known as Sourclover. The flowers of *M. indica* are only 0.08–0.12″ long, however, while the flowers of *M. officinalis* are 0.2–0.3″ long.

Cowbag Clover

Trifolium depauperatum   Native annual
Cowbag Clover, Balloon Clover   Mar–May

Description: 4–10″ high. Variable in size and foliage. The flower head is composed of tiny inflated white-tipped flowers that range from bright to dull reddish purple, but sometimes (rarely) with only white flowers.

Habitat: 400–2,000′. Common and widespread around vernal pools and on grassy flats and slopes that are wet in the spring. VP, GR, FW, RP.

Comments: There are four botanical varieties of this species. The plant receives its common name because of the inflated flowers that narrow into tiny nipplelike projections. When held upside down it bears a resemblance to a cow's mammary glands. Viewing one for the first time usually leaves field trip participants in udder amazement.

Trifolium dubium   Non-native annual
Little Hop Clover,
Shamrock Clover   Mar–Jul

Little Hop Clover

Description: 4–20″ high, prostrate to almost erect. Tough wiry stems. The yellow heads are less than ⅓″ thick with fewer than 30 tiny flowers. The heads are on short stalks.

Habitat: 100–6,200′. Common and widespread in grassy places from the Valley floor to upper conifer woodlands. GR, CH, FW, LC, UC, RP, SG.

Comments: Sometimes confused with the Yellow Bur Clover, *Medicago* sp., but they have wedge-shaped leaves and single to few flowers rather than a head of flowers. It can more easily be confused with another introduced but less common species, Hop Clover, *Trifolium campestre*, that also has yellow flowers. However, the flower head in *T. campestre* is larger and the banners on the individual flowers are veined.

Trifolium hirtum   Non-native annual
Rose Clover   Mar–Sep

Rose Clover

Description: 4–16″ high and quickly forming carpets. The leaflets are about ½″ long, round, and often with a lighter band across the middle. The flower heads are round hairy, and filled with pinkish to rose flowers.

Habitat: 100–2,000′. Common weed of roadsides, pastures, and disturbed places. GR, CH, FW, LC.

Comments: Native to southern Europe, its adaptability to a wide range of soils and climates and the fact that it is palatable even after it is dry causes it to be frequently seeded as a range clover and on burn sites. It is becoming increasingly common. However, it not only replaces native clovers but other wildflowers as well. It is frequently misidentified as Red Clover, another species.

PRENTISS FERGUSON

Crimson Clover

Trifolium incarnatum   Non-native annual
Crimson Clover, Indian Clover   May–Aug

Description: 6–24″ plants with broad, dark green leaflets with depressed central veins. The elongated cylinder-like flower head of brilliant red flowers is very showy.

Habitat: 100–2,000′. Roadsides, pastures, and fields from the Valley into the foothills. GR, CH, FW.

Comments: Another non-native clover introduced as a forage plant and, because of its ornamental nature, also included in some "wildflower" mixes. These mixes sometimes contain other non-native plants such as Cornflower and Gaillarida. Too many times a "wildflower mix" is little more than a place to put leftover seeds from the previous year that didn't sell. It does require perfect drainage and is less competitive than some non-natives, so often disappears in a few years.

RICHARD HANES

Lemmon's Clover

Trifolium lemmonii   Native perennial
Lemmon's Clover   Jun–Jul

Description: A 6–8″ plant from a long taproot. The leaves consist of 3 to 7 coarsely toothed leaflets. The flower heads are on long stalks, and are whitish pink.

Habitat: 5,000–7,000′. It is an uncommon plant of open pine forests and sagebrush flats at moderate to high altitudes. SP, probably UC, SA as well.

Comments: This plant was first found to occur in Nevada County by Gordon H. True on April 27, 1972. It is uncommon and endangered. It occurs in Oregon and Nevada but is not common in those states either. This and many Sierra wildflowers are named in honor of John G. Lemmon (1832–1908). Lemmon and his wife, Sara Plummer, were early California botanists who lived in Sierra County. It is listed in some references as *T. gymnocarpon* var. *lemmonii.*

Trifolium longipes   Native perennial
Long-stalked Clover   Apr–Jul

Description: 2–16″ tall. The stems are decumbent or erect, sometimes forming rhizomes. The 3 narrow leaflets are smooth above, slightly hairy below. The midvein is prominent and keeled. The flowers are in an erect head, whitish or tinged with purple.

Habitat: 4,600–6,500′. Common along streams and moist meadows, forest openings. LC, UC, MM, RP.

Comments: There are 4 botanical varieties but only one of them, *T. longipes* var. *nevadense,* occurs in our area. It becomes a very small plant at high elevations. Native Americans steeped the dried flower heads for a few minutes to make a tea and used the seed as an ingredient in bread. It can be seen at Sagehen Creek, Alpine Meadows, and around Squaw Valley.

KAREN CALLAHAN

Long-stalked Clover

Trifolium pratense   Non-native perennial
Red Clover   Apr–Oct

Description: 4–24″ high. The leaves have conspicuous stipules. Each oblong leaflet has a central white chevron. The inflorescence is a large 1″ round head of bright red flowers without an involucre.

Habitat: 200–4,300′. Moist places, mostly in mountain pastures and disturbed places. LC, MM.

Comments: Planted in pastures for animal food, it does best in cooler climates and is not happy in our hot foothills. The plant that is sometimes called "Red Clover" in the foothills is another species, *T. hirtum.* Herbalists are finding increasing uses for it, but the potential side effects are yet to be evaluated. It is abundant in the eastern United States, where it is frequently planted along highways and median strips.

JULIE S. CARVILLE

Red Clover

Whitetip Clover

CHET BLACKBURN

Trifolium variegatum

Native annual/short-lived perennial
Whitetip Clover, Variegated Clover   Apr–Jul

Description: 6–16″ plant. The leaflets are narrowly oblong, the margins coarsely toothed, and the leaf stipules have ragged edges. Each red-purple flower is tipped white or pink.

Habitat: 100–6,100′. Common and widespread in wet places such as seeps, springs, streams, and edges of vernal pools. VP, GR, FW, LC, UC, MM, RP.

Comments: A very diverse and highly variable species with many forms. It is a short-lived perennial that dies back to the root system during the summer and remains dormant until the fall rains. California is blessed with 21 native and 15 non-native species. Of those, at least 30 of them can be found in Nevada and Placer Counties. This is one of the more attractive ones.

Tomcat Clover

JULIE S. CARVILLE

Trifolium wildenovii   Native annual
Tomcat Clover   Mar–Jun

Description: Low herb, 4–16″ high, with minutely toothed narrow leaflets ½–1½″ long. The stipules at the base of the leaf are bristle-tipped. Flowers are in a 1″ wide head, each flower ranging from lavender to pink-purple to dark purple with a darker center. The petals often have white tips.

Habitat: Below 5,000′. Common and wide-spread on upland grassy slopes and flats, dry gravel bars, openings. GR, FW, CH, LC, RP, SG.

Comments: Listed in older references as *Trifolium tridentatum.* This is another variable species found in many forms in many plant communities. The darker colored individuals might be confused with Variegated Clover, *T. variegatum,* but that species always grows in wetter places and the flower heads are more dense.

Trifolium wormskioldii   Native perennial
Springbank Clover, Cow's Clover   May–Oct

Description: 4–12″ high from creeping
rhizomes. Curving, hairless, leafy stems bearing
blunt-tipped leaflets also bear pale purple to
white, two-tone flowers. The flower heads are
about 1″ across. The banners are white, the keel
and wings reddish, and the calyx lobes needlelike.

Habitat: 1,500–6,500′. Wet places such as
meadows and stream banks. CH, FW, FW, LC, UC,
RP, MM.

Comments: Along the coast it grows on seeping
cliffs at almost sea level, but in our area it
prefers wet mountain meadows and stream banks
above 1,500′. The rhizomes were sometimes
cooked along with camas bulbs, other times with
fermented salmon eggs, or eaten raw by Native
Americans.

CHET BLACKBURN

Springbank Clover

Vicia sativa   Non-native annual
Common Vetch, Spring Vetch   Feb–Jun

Description: 1–3′ tall. A variable sprawling/
climbing plant. The 4–8 pairs of leaflets are
blunt-tipped and bear tiny bristles. The 1″ reddish
purple flowers occur singly or in twos in the leaf
axils. The hairy pods are from 1½–3″ long.
Some forms have flowers of a solid color; others
are two-tone with the wings a darker color than
the banner.

Habitat: 100–3,600′. Grassy and open places
from the Valley to the foothills. GR, CH, FW, LC.

Comments: It was originally introduced from
Europe as livestock forage. Like all vetches, this
species has round stems and round styles with
the style "beard" in a tuft or ring at the top of the
style instead of down one side of the style. This
trait distinguishes this genus from the similar
genus, *Lathyrus*.

JULIE S. CARVILLE

Common Vetch

Hairy Vetch

JULIE S. CARVILLE

Vicia villosa   Non-native annual
Hairy Vetch, Winter Vetch   Mar–Jul

Description: Vines to 2–5′ with 8 to 12 pairs of linear to narrow leaflets to 1″ long. Well-developed tendrils. The stems are slightly hairy. There are 20–60 flowers per cluster, usually all on one side of the stalk. Two-tone purplish red flowers (sometimes light blue or white).

Habitat: 100–3,900′. A common weed of roadsides and distured places. GR, RP, CH, FW, LC.

Comments: Variable. Brought from Europe to be used as a rotation crop, but it has escaped and become rampant. The name "Winter Vetch" seems odd, as it blooms well after Spring Vetch and in fact is an early summer bloomer. However, it received the name "Winter Vetch" not because of its blooming season but because in colder parts of the world it is more winter hardy than most vetches.

KAREN CALLAHAN

The blue Spider Lupine contrasts with the white petals of Evening Snow glowing in the late afternoon light along the trail to Codfish Falls, near the American River.

Gentianaceae
GENTIAN FAMILY
Shawna Martinez

Most members of the Gentian family are herbs. The leaves are generally opposite or whorled, simple, and with smooth margins. The flowers are typically bisexual, regular, 4–5 petaled with scalelike appendages inside the flower tube. *The 4–5 petals are united and form a bell-shaped or funnel-shaped tube (a salverform tube in a few). The number of stamens matches the number of petals, and stamens alternate with the petal lobes.* The fruit is generally a capsule. Gentians contain the phytochemicals seco-iridoids and xanthones. The seco-iridoids are bitter, and a gentian is the source of the most bitter compound known. However, none of the gentians are very poisonous, but due to their bitterness they are seldom eaten by animals. There are 70 genera worldwide and about 1,100 species. There are 7 genera in California; 6 of them and 8 species are found in our area.

Centaurium muehlenbergii

June Centaury

Native annual/biennial
May–Aug

Description: 4–12″ high with paired elliptical leaves that are widely spaced along the stem. Bright rose to pink flowers *without* pedicels. The center of the flower is white, the stamens yellow-orange.

Habitat: 100–3,000′. Moist open places and along streams. GR, CH, FW, LC, RP.

Comments: A slender, delicate-looking annual that seems to appear from nowhere on the remaining patches of green during the waning days of spring. It can be distinguished from its close relative *C. venustum* by the flowers not having pedicels, the petal lobes being smaller (0.12–0.2″ long as opposed to 0.2–0.28″ long in *C. venustum*), and its tendency to grow in more moist situations.

JULIE S. CARVILLE

June Centaury

Canchalagua

Centaurium venustum   Native annual
Canchalagua   May–Aug

Description: 6–24″ high. An erect, threadlike, delicate-looking herb. The stems are mainly unbranched. The leaves are opposite, simple, elongate, and pale green. Small rose-colored flowers with red spots on the white throat are clustered at the top.

Habitat: Below 9,000′. Dry habitats in scrub, grassland, forest. GR, CH, FW, LC, UC.

Comments: *Venustum* means "charming," a term that certainly applies to this little plant. One of the earliest printed tracts extolling the virtues of settling in California was *Sketches of California,* published in 1848. Author Frederick Gay provided a variety of reasons for moving to California but also extolled the virtues of a patent medicine he was promoting that was developed from Canchalagua.

Explorer's Gentian

Gentiana calycosa   Native perennial
Explorer's Gentian   Jul–Sep

Description: 6–24″ high. Several erect stems bearing paired egg-shaped leaves and with each stem supporting a single (rarely 2) deep blue flower. The flowers are erect. Between each petal lobe is a blue, broadly forked filament.

Habitat: 4,000–12,000′. Wet mountain meadows, seeps. UC, SA, MM, RP.

Comments: The structure of the flower is unusual. In between each of the 5 petals is a blue, feathery forked appendage known as a filament. The flower opens only on bright days, closing at night and in inclement weather. An attractive plant, it is in cultivation, although its preference for high elevations and cool damp soils would not make it a great choice for many California gardeners.

Gentiana newberryi   Native perennial
Alpine Gentian   Jul–Sep

Description: 2–4″ high. The large white or pale blue to purple solitary flowers are extremely conspicuous and showy. Inside each flower are ragged-looking appendages between each petal. The short, spreading stem harbors spoon-shaped basal leaves with a few linear leaves scattered along the flower stalk.

Habitat: 5,500–12,000′. Moist meadows and banks in the high Sierra. SA, MM.

Comments: The size of plant is somewhat correlated with altitude and moisture. It is more common in the higher parts of the southern Sierra than in our area. It is one of the few host plants for the Sierra Sulphur butterfly, *Colias behrii.*

Alpine Gentian

Gentianopsis simplex   Native annual
Hiker's Fringed Gentian   Jul–Sep

Description: Stems erect, up to 8″. The spoon-shaped lower leaves wither early. The upper linear leaves are paired along the stem. Conspicuous, showy flowers arise singly on each stalk. Petals 4, large, up to 1½″, blue.

Habitat: 4,000–9,500′. Wet meadows and seeps at mostly mid elevations. UC, SA, MM, RP.

Comments: You can usually expect to get mud on your knees while photographing this little gem. It is a plant of soggy places and consequently fragile environments. Elegant in its simplicity, this little annual can be distinguished by its having 4 petals, the edges of which have the appearance of being frayed, especially toward the tips.

Hiker's Fringed Gentian

Whitestem Swertia

KAREN CALLAHAN

Swertia albicaulis   Native perennial
Whitestem Swertia,
Whitestem Elkweed   May–Jul

Description: 4–26″ tall. Stems one to few, surrounded at the base by whorls of white-edged, narrow, swordlike leaves. The upper leaves are opposite. The stem culminates with many small whorls of delicate greenish white to pale blue flowers on long threadlike stems.

Habitat: 1,000–6,000′. Dry, open places. CH, LC, UC, SP.

Comments: There are nine species of *Swertia* in California but this is the only species found in our area. Native Americans ate the taproot raw, roasted, or boiled. They sometimes placed it in soups. The plant is also still widely known by a former name, Whitestem Frasera, *Frasera albicaulis*. It can be seen along the trails at Empire Mine State Park.

KAREN CALLAHAN • KAREN CALLAHAN

All species of milkweeds are host plants for the caterpillars of the Monarch Butterfly (inset). On the right, a Monarch visits Showy Milkweed flowers.

Geraniaceae
GERANIUM FAMILY
Chet Blackburn

Although the family contains herbs and shrubs, ours are all annual herbs or very short-lived perennials. The leaves can be either alternate or opposite, simple to compound, and frequently hairy. ***There are 5 persistent sepals, and 5 deciduous petals with nectar glands at their bases,*** stamens 5 or 10 (rarely 15). The ovary is superior. ***Styles elongated, forming a beaklike style column.*** Worldwide 14 genera and about 750 species exist. There are 3 genera and 30 species in California, of which 2 genera and 10 species are known in Nevada and Placer Counties, though others are likely to appear in the future.

Erodium botrys Non-native annual
Broadleaf Filaree,
Long-beaked Storksbill Mar–Jun

Description: 6–24″ with leafy stems branching from the base. Leaves simple (deeply lobed but not divided) and hairy. Petals are lavender-pink to purple, often with wine-colored veins. The sepals are often red-tipped. Seed beak to 4″.

Habitat: Below 1,300′. Common in grassy disturbed places from the Valley to foothills. GR, CH, FW, SG.

Comments: "Storksbill" and "beak" both refer to the style that remains attached to each seed. *E. botrys* has the longest "beak" of all our "storksbills." The other storksbill that also has undivided leaves, the Short-fruited Storksbill, *Erodium brachycarpum,* is often confused with this one, but it has a shorter storksbill (to 3″) and green-tipped sepals.

JULIE S. CARVILLE

Broadleaf Filaree

RICHARD HANES

Redstem Filaree

Erodium cicutarium   Non-native annual
Redstem Filaree, Cutleaf Storksbill   Dec–Jul

Description: Leafy stems 3–10″ long, mostly prostrate. Leaves twice pinnate, fernlike in appearance, with sharp-pointed lobes. The stems are red (except when in moist shady places). The tips of the sepals have bristles. Small, delicate rose-colored petals with 1 to 9 flowers in a terminal cluster. The storksbill (seedpod) is 1–2″.

Habitat: Valley floor to 4,200′. GR, CH, FW, LC, SG, MM.

Comments: This is the most common and widespread of our storksbills. It is common worldwide and highly regarded as forage. It can be found on six continents. It was a very early introduction into California. John C. Fremont commented on its abundance. *Erodium* comes from a Greek word meaning "Heron's beak."

JULIE S. CARVILLE

Whitestem Filaree

Erodium moschatum   Non-native annual
Whitestem Filaree   Feb–May

Description: 6–18″ high. The leaves form a ground-hugging rosette at first, then later extend upward. The leaves are divided, the leaflets oval-shaped, toothed but not lobed, forming slightly unequal pairs and are coarsely hairy. The sepal tips lack bristles. The petals are rose-purple and clustered into a flower head at the top of the stems. The storksbill is ½–1½″.

Habitat: Below 4,500′. Locally abundant in disturbed places. GR, CH, FW, LC, SG.

Comments: The name *moschatum* means "musklike" and refers to the slightly musky odor given off when the leaves are crushed. This has one of the shortest beaks of the storksbills. It can be differentiated from the Redstem Filaree, which also has a compound leaf, by the shape of its leaflets and the lack of a bristle on the sepals.

Geranium dissectum   Non-native annual
Cutleaf Geranium   Mar–Jun

Description: 1–2′ tall. Stem hairy, weak, and slender. The leaves are deeply lobed almost to the base and sharp pointed. There are 5 pale pink to whitish flower petals that are the same length as the sepals. The petals are notched, the style tip purple.

Habitat: Below 3,500′. Common in moist grassy places in spring. GR, CH, FW.

Comments: A rather gangly, sprawling plant, usually found as a few scattered individuals almost obscured by other plants in disturbed areas. The petals are fragile and shed easily when handled. The lobing on the petals is such that the individual petals almost look heart-shaped. Introduced from Europe.

GORDON J. HARRINGTON

Cutleaf Geranium

Geranium molle   Non-native annual
Dove's Foot Geranium   Mar–Sep

Description: 4–16″ high but seems smaller because of its decumbent habit. The leaves are pubescent, lobed, and roundish in shape. The small but conspicuous rose-pink to red-purple flowers are notched at the tip.

Habitat: Below 3,000′. Open to shaded, usually disturbed areas. GR, CH, FW, LC, SG.

Comments: Often forms attractive carpets in the shade. It is a European native that is now common in the United States from coast to coast. It has leaves as soft as velvet. Another geranium is occasionally found in our area, especially in places with some summer water. That one is called Herb Robert, *Geranium robertianum,* with reddish-tinged foliage and stems, and a very pungent smell when crushed. It has conspicuous rose-purple flowers and a ridiculously small root system.

JULIE S. CARVILLE

Dove's Foot Geranium

Hydrophyllaceae
WATERLEAF FAMILY
Richard Hanes

Usually herbs, rarely shrubs, often bristly or glandular, with flowers arranged often along one side of branches, or at the tip of the stem in coils like fiddlenecks. The leaves can be alternate or opposite, often with basal rosettes, and either entire or pinnately lobed. *The flowers consist of 5 united sepals and 5 united petals,* varying from nearly flat to bell- or funnel-shaped. *Stamens 5 and arise from the base of the corolla. The ovary is superior.* Of 20 genera and 300 species worldwide, 7 genera and 34 species are found in Nevada and Placer Counties. The western United States is the main center of diversity.

Draperia

Draperia systyla   Native perennial
Draperia   May–Aug

Description: 4–16″ high. Stems decumbent to erect. The leaves are simple, opposite, cauline, ovate, and entire. The lower leaves are petioled, the upper leaves sessile. The calyx is linear and very hairy. The corolla is funnel-shaped, white to pink or lavender or pale violet, and hairy outside. The outsides of the petals are also hairy.

Habitat: 2,400–8,000′. Dry slopes in woods. LC, UC.

Comments: An unobtrusive little plant that is often bypassed in the dry shady woods in which it is found. The white globular anthers deep inside the flower tube look like a nest of eggs when looking into the tube. The decumbent stems sometimes root where they touch the ground. Golden-mantled Ground Squirrels love to eat the flowers.

JULIE S. CARVILLE

Eriodictyon californicum

Native perennial to subshrub

Yerba Santa   May–Jul

Description: An evergreen shrub 3–10′ tall
with sticky stems and branches. The leaves are
lance-shaped to oblong, entire to toothed, sticky
or not, with the margin rolled under. The corolla
is white to purple, and tubular.

Habitat: Below 5,500′. Dry rocky slopes and
ridges, roadsides. GR, CH, FW, LC, SG.

Comments: Although a shrub, this plant looks
herbaceous enough that we are treating it in this
wildflower edition. It has long been an important
plant to the Native Americans, who used it as a
remedy for sore throat. Yerba Santa means "Holy
Herb," a name given to it by the Spanish mis-
sionaries after being introduced to its herbal
benefits. *Eriodictyon* flowers are especially
attractive to bees and butterflies.

KAREN CALLAHAN

Yerba Santa

Hesperochiron californicus   Native perennial

Western Centaur   May–Jul

Description: Stems up to 4″ tall arise from the
ground and a low basal rosette of flat, spoon-
shaped leaves from which comparatively large
white flowers emerge. Leaves are entire, petioled,
and hairy. The flowers are solitary, bell- or
funnel-shaped, and white to bluish in color.

Habitat: 3,000–9,000′. Moist places, meadows,
flats, valleys. LC, UC, MM, RP.

Comments: An odd little genus, there are only
2 species of *Hesperochiron* and both are found
in our area. This is the more common one. The
corolla is shaped like an upside-down bell. The
Dwarf Hesperochiron, *Hesperochiron pumilus,*
is less common and can be seen at Soda Springs,
Alpine Meadows, and Sagehen Creek. In *H.
pumilus,* the flower is flattened and the flower
throat is yellow.

JULIE S. CARVILLE

Western Centaur

Woolen-breeches

JULIE S. CARVILLE

Hydrophyllum capitatum var. *alpinum*
Native perennial
**Woolen-breeches,
Ballhead Waterleaf**   May–Jun

Description: 4–16″ tall. Stems very short,
spreading, hairy. Leaves erect, 2–5″ long, ovate
to oblong, deeply lobed. The inflorescence, a
spherical cyme, is near the ground and beneath
the leaves. The petals are white-purple or white
with lavender marks and five projecting anthers.

Habitat: 3,000–8,000′. Moist slopes, meadows,
flats. LC, UC, MM, SP.

Comments: The young shoots and leaves may
be eaten raw or these and the roots may be
cooked. Grazed by deer and livestock in the
early spring. They are often found on slopes still
wet from melting snow. Though relatively large,
the flower heads are partially hidden under the
plant's overhanging foliage.

Western Waterleaf

JULIE S. CARVILLE

Hydrophyllum occidentale   Native perennial
Western Waterleaf   May–Jul

Description: Stems 2–24″ tall, erect and hairy.
Alternate leaves 2–16″, basal, oblong, lobed;
each lobe with a few sharp teeth along its lower
edges. The inflorescence is well above the ground,
branched, and headlike. The petals are violet to
white, with the petal tips slightly bilobed. The
exserted stamens are distinctive.

Habitat: 2,000–9,000′. Dryish or moist shaded
slopes. CH, FW, LC, UC, MM, RP.

Comments: Unlike the previous species, the
head of flowers rises above the foliage. Another
common name for the plant is Wild Heliotrope,
but that name is also applied to at least three other
California natives (*Heliotropum curassivicum,
Phacelia distans, P. tanacetifolia*) as well as
several plants that are not found in California.

Nama lobbii   Native perennial
Lobb's Nama   Jun–Aug

Description: Forms low mats up to 3′ wide.
The stems are prostrate to ascending, 6–20″
high, and freely branched. The sticky stem leaves
are up to 2″, oblanceolate to obovate and white
felt-hairy. The purple to pink flowers are in
clusters, not coiled, and are widely funnel-
shaped to narrowly bell-shaped. Styles 2.

Habitat: 4,300–7,300′. Dry open places. LC, UC.

Comments: Members of the genus *Nama* tend
to appear in great numbers in the year immediately following a fire, then diminish in numbers
over the next few years as other plants take over
the burn site. Their seeds lie dormant until the
next fire removes the vegetative cover. This one
is a perennial but most *Nama* species, including
the other two in our area (*N. californicum* and
N. densum), are annuals.

KAREN CALLAHAN

Lobb's Nama

Nemophila heterophylla   Native annual
Small White Nemophila,
Variable Leaf Nemophila   Apr–Jul

Description: 4–12″ high. Stems bristly-hairy.
The lower stem leaves are opposite, petioled,
and 5–7-lobed. The upper leaves are alternate,
nearly sessile, and 3–5-lobed. The flowers are
solitary in the axils or opposite the leaves, bowl-
shaped, white to bluish, to ½″ wide. Style 1.

Habitat: 100–5,600′. Forests, chaparral, stream
banks. CH, FW, LC, RP.

Comments: Common in moist, rocky, shrubby
places, especially roadcuts, in wooded areas.
The trailing stems are weak and break easily.
Two other small *Nemophila* species occur in our
area. The flowers of *N. pedunculata* are white
or blue but the petals are adorned with small
dark spots or lines. The leaves of *N. spatulata*
are not as deeply lobed as the other two species.

KAREN CALLAHAN

Small White Nemophila

Fivespot

Nemophila maculata Native annual
Fivespot Apr–Jul

Description: 4–12″ high. The stems are bristly-hairy. The cauline leaves are opposite, 5–9-lobed, the upper leaves sessile. The flowers are solitary in the axils or opposite the leaves. At least 1″ wide, bowl-shaped, white with dark veins and spots, petal tips purple-spotted. Style 1.

Habitat: 200–10,000′. Meadows and woodlands. FW, LC, UC, MM, RP.

Comments: A very attractive species. The tip of each of the 5 petals has a conspicuous triangular, almost iridescent purple spot, hence the common name. It is a colorful, long-blooming, and reliable annual that reseeds readily, so it is no surprise that it has become a popular garden plant. Its seeds are readily available at most nurseries.

Baby Blue-eyes

Nemophila menziesii Native annual
Baby Blue-eyes Mar–May

Description: 4–12″ high. Stems bristly-hairy. Cauline leaves opposite, 5–13-lobed. The flowers are solitary in the axils or opposite the leaves, at least 1″ wide, bowl-shaped, bright blue with a white center, and generally blue-veined and black-dotted. Style 1.

Habitat: 50–6,300′. Moist areas. FW, LC, UC, MM, RP.

Comments: Coming across an open field with mass displays of these baby blue–colored flowers is one of the joys of being a Californian. The mass displays may remain strictly Californian, but the plant itself is now available and popular just about everywhere. Seed packets are available at most nurseries. It prefers a location with more moisture than does Fivespot. Easily grown from seed but does not reseed itself reliably.

Phacelia cicutaria   Native annual
Caterpillar Phacelia   Mar–May

Description: Stems 7–23″ tall, ascending to erect, simple to branched, stiff-hairy, glandular. Leaves deeply lobed to compound. Inflorescence a coiled cyme. Calyx long-hairy, glandular. Corolla bell-shaped, yellowish.

Habitat: Below 4,600′. Rocky slopes. GR, CH, FW, LC, RO.

Comments: A favorite with participants on wildflower walks. It is not the dirty white flowers that draw their attention but they are always amused when the resemblance of the coiled flower head to a caterpillar is pointed out. It is a plant of rocky places. It can be confused with Vari-leaved Phacelia, but the foliage is different and this species is an annual, while the Vari-leaved Phacelia is a biennial to short-lived perennial. Both are common at Bridgeport.

KAREN CALLAHAN * KAREN CALLAHAN

Caterpillar Phacelia

Phacelia heterophylla ssp. *virgata*
    Native perennial
Vari-leaved Phacelia   May–Jul

Description: Stems 8–48″ tall. The central stem is erect, the lateral stems ascending. The leaves are mostly basal, and lance-shaped to ovate. The basal leaves are dissected, the upper ones simple to dissected. The inflorescence is a coiled cyme. The corolla is bell-shaped, and white to lavender.

Habitat: Below 9,500′. Slopes, flats, roadsides. FW, LC, UC, SA.

Comments: The plant's hairs on the foliage and stems can be irritating to the skin. The foliage is deeply veined and hairy and is quite variable in shape. The flowers are usually white, but can be purplish to blue as well. It can be seen on the Buttermilk Bend Trail at Bridgeport.

KAREN CALLAHAN

Vari-leafed Phacelia

Ballhead Phacelia

JULIE S. CARVILLE

Phacelia hydrophylloides   Native perennial
Ballhead Phacelia   Jun–Aug

Description: Stems 4–12″, decumbent to ascending, hairy. Leaves oblong to ovate, coarsely toothed to lobed, and velvety soft. The flower head is dense and headlike, with a fuzzy appearance in a tight coil. Corolla bell-shaped, white to purplish blue. Stamens exserted.

Habitat: 5,000–10,000′. From moist to dry places, both in the open and in shade. LC, UC, SA.

Comments: Usually found in conifer forests in bright shade. Young tender shoots are edible. Gathered before flowering, they provide excellent greens. The genus *Phacelia* is well represented in California. Of the approximately 175 species worldwide, more than half of them (94 species) occur in California, and at least 17 of them in Placer and Nevada Counties.

Quick's Phacelia

KAREN CALLAHAN

Phacelia quickii   Native annual
Quick's Phacelia,
Quick's Scorpionweed   May–Jun

Description: Stems 2–7″, decumbent to erect, simple or branched. The hairy leaves are linear to oblanceolate, and entire. The inflorescence is a coiled cyme. The flowers are widely bell-shaped, blue to lavender, drying whitish. The stamens are exserted and the pollen is yellow.

Habitat: 3,000–8,000′. Open granitic areas. LC, UC.

Comments: The genus name *Phacelia* comes from the Greek word *phakelos* meaning "bundle." It refers to the compact, coiled flower heads of members of this genus. The common name Scorpionweed refers to the way the inflorescence coil curls over the top of the plant, reminding some people of the way a scorpion carries its tail curved over its back.

Phacelia stebbinsii   Native annual
Stebbins' Phacelia   May–Jun

Description: Stems 4–16″ high, simple or branching, hairy and glandular. The stem leaves are lance-shaped with entire or lobed margins. The inflorescence is a coiled cyme. The corolla is spreading, bell-shaped, pale blue to white, and sparsely hairy inside. The flower clusters become erect in fruit. The pollen is white. There is one seed per capsule.

Habitat: 3,000–5,000′. Gravelly metamorphic soils. LC, UC.

Comments: This is a rare species that is so far known only from El Dorado, Placer, and Nevada Counties. It has been found on only 11 sites to date. It can be distinguished from similar species by its white instead of yellow pollen and the single seed, whereas similar Phacelias contain 2–10 seeds per capsule.

RICHARD HANES

Stebbins' Phacelia

JULIE S. CARVILLE

A dry meadow at Tahoe blooms with Sulfur Buckwheat, Mountain Pennyroyal, Applegate's Paintbrush, and Scarlet Gilia.

Hypericaceae
ST. JOHN'S WORT FAMILY
Richard Hanes

Cauline leaves entire, without stipules, glandular, in opposite pairs to top of stem. Oil glands present. The flowers are in terminal cymes, regular, and of a yellow-orange color. *Sepals 5 (rarely 4), not joined, petals 5 (rarely 4), and not joined together. The stamens are exserted and numerous, united at the base in 3–5 clusters. The ovary is superior, with 3 styles.* Hypericaceae is the family name used in the *Jepson Manual,* but it is not universally accepted by all botanists, so some references use either Guttiferae or Clusiaceae for the family name. There are 10 genera and 400 species worldwide. There is 1 genus and 4 species in Nevada and Placer Counties.

Tinker's Penny

RICHARD HANES

Hypericum anagalloides

Native annual/perennial

Tinker's Penny   Jun–Aug

Description: Stems 1–10″, prostrate to ascending, forming dense mats from the creeping and rooting stolons. The small, paired leaves are elliptical to round. The flowers are golden yellow, yellow-orange, or salmon colored.

Habitat: 300–9,000′. Wet places, margins of streams, ponds, bogs, and moist meadows. MM, RP.

Comments: Highly variable. The plant roots easily at each node of its prostrate stolons, and thus is capable of forming dense mats, scrambling over the moist ground and even up onto damp streamside rocks and fallen logs adjacent to ponds and bogs. It is also semi-aquatic, able to withstand long periods of submersion, entering shallow waters with its wandering stolons.

Hypericum concinnum   Native perennial
Gold Wire   Jun–Jul

Description: 6–12″ high with numerous wiry stems from a woody crown, forming a bushy plant. The leaves are linear to lance-shaped and usually folded upward, more or less gray-green. The sepals are oval with a pointed tip. The petal margins are black-dotted.

Habitat: 300–4,000′. Dry shrubby slopes. CH, FW, LC, SG.

Comments: An unobtrusive plant that is locally common on roadcuts, along the dry edges of washes, and on sunny to brushy slopes. It looks like a bonsai version of the well-known Klamath Weed. Though overlooked by most field guides, it was not overlooked by the Miwok, who used it as a wash for running sores. Empire Mine State Park is one of many places you can find it.

Gold Wire

Hypericum formosum var. *scouleri*
                                        Native perennial
Scouler's St. John's Wort   Jun–Aug

Description: Stems erect, 8–20″ tall from a running rootstock, sending up a few stems from the base and often branched above. The leaves are ovate to oblong, mostly flat, and the margins black-dotted. The sepals are without a pointed tip. The sepals and petals are also black-dotted.

Habitat: 300–7,500′. Springs, meadows, moist places, usually in partial shade. MM, RP.

Comments: *Hypericum* is derived from two Greek words, *hyper* (above) and *eikon* (picture) and refers to the ancient custom of placing flowers of *H. perforatum* above an image at a midsummer festival to ward off evil spirits at the feast of St. John. Hence also the common name, St. John's Wort (*wort* means "herbaceous plant").

Scouler's St. John's Wort

Klamath Weed

JULIE S. CARVILLE

Hypericum perforatum   Non-native perennial
Klamath Weed, St. John's Wort   Jun–Sep

Description: Tall wiry stems 1–3′ tall. The leaves are linear, sepals linear to lancelike. Leaves, sepals, and petals are all black-gland-dotted.

Habitat: Below 5,000′. Pastures, abandoned fields, disturbed areas. GR, CH, FW, LC.

Comments: The original California infestation occurred near the Klamath River, hence the name Klamath Weed. It has long been a subject of medicinal and herbal research. A derivative from the plant, hyperican, inhibits the human immunodeficiency virus, but the quantity required makes its use impractical. It is taken internally as an antidepressant and externally as a liniment to reduce inflammation. It is poisonous to livestock. Though not usually fatal, it can cause temporary blindness in horses, skin irritations in sheep, and weight loss in cattle.

KAREN CALLAHAN

Hansen's Larkspur and Ramm's Madia flower among spring grasses and Blue Oaks.

Iridaceae
IRIS FAMILY
Kathy Van Zuuk

Plants develop from a rhizome or corm. The parallel-veined leaves are alternate, simple, basal, *long, and flat, and they overlap each other at the base of the stem. The sepals and petals have the same color and size, which gives the appearance of having 6 petals and no sepals. The Iris family differs from the Lily family in having 3 versus 6 stamens, and an inferior versus superior ovary.* The majority of species in this family are found in South Africa and tropical America. There are 80 genera and 1,500 species worldwide, and 11 genera and 31 species in California, although 9 of the genera are introduced, having escaped from cultivation. There are 2 genera and 9 species found in Nevada and Placer Counties. *Iris* is the Greek word for rainbow. Native irises in general are deer resistant.

Iris hartwegii Native perennial
Sierra Iris Mar–Jul

Description: The stem is 1–2′ tall, the rhizome ½″ thick. The flowers are usually pale yellow to cream, but can also be pale lavender, purple, or bluish violet. The corolla tube is above the ovary and is stout. The pedicel below the ovary is very long.

Habitat: 2,000–7,600′. Open to partly shaded slopes. FW, LC, UC.

Comments: This bright little plant is the most common *Iris* in our area, forming colonies in lower conifer forests. Two subspecies occur in our area. Hybrids are common. The only other *Iris* in our area with which it might be confused is *I. macrosiphon,* but *I. hartwegii* has its stout ovary just under the flower at the top of the flower stalk. *I. macrosiphon*'s ovary is located at the bottom of the flower stalk.

JULIE S. CARVILLE
Sierra Iris

Ground Iris

Iris macrosiphon   Native perennial
Ground Iris   Apr–Jun

Description: The stem is less than 10″ tall. The rhizome averages ³/₁₀″ thick. Flowers are yellow to cream or pale lavender to deep purple, with veins that are generally darker. The corolla tube above the ovary is very long. The pedicel below the ovary is very short.

Habitat: Below 3,000′. Open to partly shaded slopes. CH, GR, FW, LC.

Comments: This Iris typically grows at lower elevations than the Sierra Iris and is more typical of foothill woodlands. It is less common than it once was because its preferred habitat of rolling hills of oak woodlands and grasslands is favored by developers. *Iris* is the Greek goddess of the rainbow.

Western Blue Flag

Iris missouriensis   Native perennial
Western Blue Flag   May–Jul

Description: Rhizomes are 0.8–1.2″ thick. The stem is 8–36″ tall. The flowers are dark blue or sometimes paler. The petals have a central dark yellow-orange stripe and dark blue lines on a white background. The corolla tube is above the ovary, and has a very short bowl-like enlargement. The pedicel below the ovary is very long (up to 8″).

Habitat: 3,000–11,000′. Moist places. GR, LC, UC, MM, RP.

Comments: The plant looks very much like the familiar garden iris. It is more typical of higher elevations and is always found where there is abundant moisture, at least up until flowering time. It can be a noxious weed in pastures. Because the leaves have a bitter taste they are not relished by either livestock or deer.

Iris pseudocaris   Non-native perennial
Yellow Water Iris   Apr–Jul

Description: The stem is 3–5′ tall. It has broad, stiff, straplike leaves and bright yellow flowers on a tall stalk. The flowers have black, brown, or dark purple stripes at the base of the petals.

Habitat: Usually below 1,000′. Wet places such as the edges of ponds, and streams. VG, FW, RP.

Comments: A non-native from Europe, the flower of this iris is the origin of the fleur-de-lis. It is also one of the sources of orris root, a compound used as a fixative in making perfumes, soaps, sachets, and other products. In fact, the phrase "orris root" is thought to be a corruption of "iris root." It is widely marketed as a water-garden plant, but has escaped cultivation and is occasionally found along foothill streams, usually below 1,000′. However, there is no reason why it cannot grow at higher elevations.

CHET BLACKBURN

Yellow Water Iris

Sisyrinchium bellum   Native perennial
Blue-eyed Grass   Feb–Jul

Description: The stem is 4–25″ tall, typically with 2 or more branches and flattened, narrow, and mostly basal leaves. The few stem leaves are much shorter. The flowers are bluish to dark purple with 3 petals and 3 sepals, appearing to be 6 star-shaped petals. The flowers occur at the top of flattish stems and have a bright yellow throat.

Habitat: Below 7,900′. Open, generally moist places. GR, FW, LC, UC, SA, MM, RP.

Comments: The only species it could be confused with is Idaho Blue-eyed Grass, which normally grows at higher elevations. The petals of *S. bellum* look wider and are wedge-shaped at the tip with a short spine. *S. idahoense* has narrower petals that look longer; the tip is more tapered and the spine more prominent. *S. idahoense* also has unbranched flower stems.

PRENTISS FERGUSON

Blue-eyed Grass

JULIE S. CARVILLE

Yellow-eyed Grass

Sisyrinchium elmeri   Native perennial
Yellow-eyed Grass   Jul–Aug

Description: The stem is 6–8″ tall. Flowers are deep yellow to yellow-orange with dark brown veins. There are 6 star-shaped "petals" (3 petals plus 3 sepals that look like petals).

Habitat: 4,000–8,500′. Wet meadows. LC, UC, SA, MM, RP.

Comments: A close relative, also called Yellow-eyed Grass, *Sisyrinchium californicum,* is a coastal species that is widely sold at native plant sales and is a prolific seeder, so it might be introduced in wet situations here at lower elevations. Though uncommon, the odds are that if you see a Yellow-eyed Grass in our area that is not in cultivation, it is probably our species. *S. elmeri* has smaller flowers (0.3–0.4″ compared to 0.4–0.7″) and narrower stems (less than 0.08″ compared to more than 0.08″).

RICHARD HANES

Idaho Blue-eyed Grass

Sisyrinchium idahoense   Native perennial
Idaho Blue-eyed Grass   Jul–Aug

Description: The stem is 6–18″ tall and leafless. Leaves are narrow and grasslike. Flowers are located at the top of the erect to ascending stem in a single terminal cluster of blue, ½″ flowers.

Habitat: 2,700–10,000′. Open, moist, grassy places such as mountain meadows and grassy stream banks. LC, UC, SA, RP, MM.

Comments: Fairly common in the Tahoe area. Highly variable. It can be distinguished from *S. bellum* by elevation and by its unbranched flower stems. The herbage and roots of all our local *Sisyrinchium* species probably contain toxic alkaloids. There are about 70 species of *Sisyrinchium,* all found in the Western Hemisphere, and many of them are in cultivation, including our 3 species.

Lamiaceae
MINT FAMILY
Chet Blackburn

Stems square, leaves opposite or whorled, often hairy, and simple. *Most members of family have fragrant to pungent oils in the leaves;* therefore plants in this family are widely used as herbs and for flavoring. There are *5 petals but they are all fused into a single two-lipped corolla.* Stamens 4 or 2. Style 1 with an unequally bilobed tip. The ovary consists of 4 nutlets. Worldwide there are 180 genera and approximately 3,500 species. There are 26 genera and 121 species in California; 17 genera and 39 species occur in Nevada and Placer Counties.

Agastache urticifolia
Nettleleaf Horsemint,
Giant Hyssop

Native perennial

Jun–Sep

Description: Erect plant 3–5' tall with coarsely toothed, triangular, aromatic leaves. The flowers are terminal on the stem in dense, elongated, thimble-shaped clusters lasting only a few days. The color is whitish rose to light purple.

Habitat: 150–10,000'. Dry wooded slopes to open moist meadows, usually in scattered stands. Often associated with conifers or aspen. GR, CH, FW, LC, UC, SA, MM, RP.

Comments: Some people regard the foliage aroma as pleasing, others as unpleasant. It is grazed eagerly by sheep, moderately by cattle, and lightly by horses. Native Americans chewed the leaves for indigestion and stomach pain. It can be seen at the edge of the meadow by the parking lot for the Sierra Discovery Trail.

Nettleleaf Horsemint

KAREN CALLAHAN

Giraffe Head

RICHARD HANES

Lamium amplexicaule   Non-native annual
Giraffe Head, Hen's Bit   Mar–May

Description: Stem 4–16″ long, but it appears shorter because of the decumbent nature of the plant. The lower leaves are on stalks; the upper leaves clasp the stem. The leaves are rounded and pointed, scalloped, or lobed. The lower leaves are somewhat heart-shaped, the upper ones more triangular. Pale pink to purplish flowers.

Habitat: Below 3,000′. Disturbed areas, especially ranchlands and around home sites. GR, CH, FW.

Comments: The individual bright red-purple flowers suggest the profile of a giraffe head with a long neck and big ears. Native to Eurasia but found over most of California at low elevations. Removing the long flowers and blowing through them from the base produces a whistling sound.

Purple Deadnettle

CINDY RUBIN

Lamium purpureum   Non-native annual
Purple Deadnettle   Apr–Sep

Description: 2–12″ tall. The usually purplish stem is decumbent to erect (the local ones are usually erect) from fibrous roots. The opposite wrinkly, hairy leaves take on a purplish color as they near the top of the stem. The flowers are purplish to rose-purple.

Habitat: Less than 3,000′. Disturbed sites, especially roadsides, railroad beds, meadows, and irrigated fields. GR, FW, RP.

Comments: An uncommon introduced plant. The pinkish purple flowers are attached directly to the stem (no petioles) and peer out from between the purplish leaves at the top of the stem. It is a prolific seeder and a pest in parts of the country, but the potential for it becoming a nuisance here is slight because of its need for summer water.

Lepechinia calycina   Native shrubby perennial
Pitcher Sage   Apr–Jun

Description: 1–5′ tall. A small, bushy, aromatic subshrub with large hairy leaves that are shallowly lobed. The lower lip on the large flower is much larger than the upper lip. Petals white, tinged with lavender, about 1″ long.

Habitat: 500–3,000′. Openings and edges of chaparral, brushy or rocky slopes, less common in woodlands. CH, FW.

Comments: Regenerates by seedlings after fire until crowded out by more aggressive shrubs. The leaves have a strong and distinctive sagelike odor. Some regard the aroma as pleasing, others as unpleasant. The common name Pitcher Sage is derived from the resemblance of the flowers to the porcelain pitchers that were often found in nineteenth-century hotel rooms.

KAREN CALLAHAN

Pitcher Sage

Marrubium vulgare   Non-native perennial
Horehound   May–Sep

Description: Plants 1–3′ tall. Flowers appear in circles around the white woolly stem. The gray oval leaves have a crinkled surface and undulating margins.

Habitat: Up to 2,000′. Disturbed sites, especially overgrazed pastures. Sun or shade. GR, CH, FW.

Comments: Formerly grown commercially as a medicinal herb, mostly for respiratory ailments. It has had a variety of medicinal uses from at least as far back as Roman times. It has escaped cultivation and spread widely around the world. The sap is bitter, but was used when sweetened to make horehound candy lozenges. It is reportedly a good bee plant. The seed-bearing fruit is familiar to anyone who has spent much time outdoors in disturbed areas, as it clings tightly to clothing.

CINDY RUBIN

Horehound

Lemon Balm

Melissa officinalis   Non-native perennial
Lemon Balm, Bee Balm   Jun–Sep

Description: Branching 1–3′ tall. The foliage is egg-shaped with scalloped margins, has a somewhat sticky feeling to touch, and has a lemony scent when crushed. The small whitish flowers are in axillary clusters.

Habitat: Below 2,500′. Moist locations, usually along streams and ditches from the Valley floor to lower conifer woodlands. GR, FW, LC, RP.

Comments: A garden escapee from Europe, where it is sometimes used as a culinary potherb and for flavoring foods. The leaves have a lemony taste when fresh, but it dissipates fast, which is probably why most recipes calling for it also call for lemon juice. It has a long history of ethnobotanical uses in cosmetics, perfume, sedatives, sclerosis, and relief from headaches and cramps. "Balm" means to soothe or calm.

VIRGINIA MORAN • CHET BLACKBURN

Field Mint

Mentha arvensis   Native/non-native perennial
Field Mint   Jul–Sep

Description: 1–4′ tall. A highly variable plant, especially in the amount of hairiness. The stems are simple to branching. Dense whorls of flowers occur up and down the stem, but they are often nearly hidden by the long, bright green, sawtooth-margined leaves. Stoloniferous.

Habitat: Below 8,000′. Moist places, wet meadows, stream banks. GR, FW, LC, UC, MM, RP.

Comments: Some races are thought to be native, but others have been introduced from Europe. The genus *Mentha* occurs widely in the Northern Hemisphere but this is the only species that is native to North America. Native Americans made a tea from the leaves, not only for flavor but also as a medicine for colds, fevers, pains, swellings, and colic in children. Some tribes used the leaves as flavoring when cooking meat.

MICHAEL GRAF

Mentha spicata   Non-native perennial
Spearmint   Jun–Sep

Description: 1–4' tall. A pleasantly fragrant plant with whorls of pale lavender flowers in terminal clusters that rise well above the leaves. The plant is nearly hairless, though some are slightly hairy at the stem nodes.

Habitat: Below 5,000', but mostly lower elevations. GR, FW, LC, UC, MM, RP.

Comments: Escaped from cultivation. It is the source of oil of spearmint, used chiefly for flavoring spearmint gum, but also used to make mint jelly, garnish, mint tea, and mint juleps. Heavily grazed where deer are plentiful and rarely able to flower and set seed because a colony is kept closely cropped, but it spreads by stolons as well. In general, deer dislike the taste of plants in the Mint family because of the oils present, but this is a notable exception.

KAREN CALLAHAN

Spearmint

Monardella lanceolata   Native annual
Mustang Mint   Apr–Aug

Description: 6–24" tall. An erect plant that is usually branching but is sometimes simple. The narrow opposite aromatic leaves taper at both ends. The flowers appear in terminal heads.

Habitat: Foothills to 8,000'. Open rocky areas, often on disturbed sites. CH, FW, LC, UC.

Comments: The species name *lanceolata* refers to lance-shaped leaves. The plant has a pungent fragrance. It can be distinguished from our other species by the fact that there is no woody base from last year's growth because this one is an annual. Butterflies are attracted to it. Not especially common in our area, but it has been observed at Hell's Half Acre.

CHET BLACKBURN

Mustang Mint

Mountain Pennyroyal

JULIE S. CARVILLE

Monardella odoratissima   Native perennial
Mountain Pennyroyal,
Western Pennyroyal   Jun–Sep

Description: About 1′ tall, branched plants, often with a woody base forming a mat with age. The leaves are variable in size, texture, and the amount of surface hair, but all are smooth-edged and the same color above as below. The flower color is variable but usually pale purple, white, or lavender. The flowers are crowded into flat heads with colorful bracts beneath.

Habitat: 1,800–10,000′. Sandy or gravelly soils in coniferous forest openings or growing around boulders. CH, FW, LC, UC, SA, SG.

Comments: Hikers sometimes chew leaves of the plant while walking. Native Americans made tea from the flower heads as a treatment for colds, fever, and indigestion. Attractive to bumblebees and butterflies.

Coyote Mint

KAREN CALLAHAN

Monardella villosa   Native perennial
Coyote Mint   Jun–Sep

Description: 9–18″. Many-stemmed, evergreen plants. At least some leaves have uneven (toothed) margins and are usually paler below. It has densely packed heads of purple, pink, or white flowers. The plant has a slightly woody base and eventually forms mats. A variable species.

Habitat: Below 4,000′. Oak woodlands, chaparral, montane forests, often in dry rocky or gravelly places and roadcuts. CH, FW, LC.

Comments: Cultivated in rock gardens and as slope covers. It is a good bumblebee and butterfly plant. Shelton's Coyote Mint, *Monardella sheltonii,* is uncommon but very similar, differing only by a lack of villous pubescence (hairs). The species name *villosa* refers to the short, soft hairs of foliage.

Pogogyne zizyphoroides   Native annual
Sacramento Beardstyle   Mar–Jun

Description: Under 3″ in height. An ascending
to erect branching little plant with small, dense,
terminal, headlike clusters and/or solitary
flowers in the upper leaf axils. The tiny lavender
to purplish flowers are less than ⅕″.

Habitat: Under 3,500′. Vernal pools and wet
grassy places. VP, GR.

Comments: These little plants are more often
detected by smell than sight when being crushed
by someone walking across the bottom of a
drying vernal pool. The seeds sprout in mud
after the water evaporates, and are generally
blooming in late spring. An even smaller species
in our area, *P. serpylloides,* differs by its prostrate to decumbent habit.

CAROL WITHAM

Sacramento Beardstyle

Prunella vulgaris   Non-native perennial
Self Heal, Heal All   Jun–Sep

Description: Stem 4–10″ tall. Low herb spreading rapidly by stolons and seeds. It produces a
thick spike of violet flowers (white and pink
forms also occur).

Habitat: Many habitats below 7,500′. Dry to
moist sites (more often moist) in sun or shade.
GR, CH, FW, LC, UC, MM, RP.

Comments: The native form grows mostly on
ocean bluffs, but the non-native form is more
abundant and widespread, and is the one found
here. The common names come from the fact
that it has long been used in folk medicine,
especially as a remedy for sore throat. A mintlike
drink can be made by steeping fresh leaves in
cold water, but the plant does not have a strong
odor like most plants in this family.

RICHARD HANES

Self Heal

Creeping Sage

Salvia sonomensis   Native perennial
Creeping Sage, Sonoma Sage   Jun–Sep

Description: To 16″ high. A prostrate, mat-forming plant with heavy, semi-evergreen, grayish green lancelike leaves that have a strong odor when crushed. The flowers range from light purple to creamy white.

Habitat: Below 6,500′. Dry slopes, often in full shade and in lean soil. Low trailing stems sometimes drape down and festoon steep banks. Also commonly found under chaparral shrubs such as manzanitas. CH, FW, LC, SG.

Comments: It is in cultivation and is used effectively as a fast-growing ground cover, but it needs porous soil and infrequent watering. The creeping stems will form a mat in time. Highly attractive to bees, especially bumblebees. The flower color in our area is mostly creamy white. It is common at Hell's Half Acre.

California Skullcap

Scutellaria californica   Native perennial
California Skullcap   Jun–Jul

Description: Less than 1′ tall, this is a sprawling plant with creeping rootstocks. The leaves are linear-oblong to oblong-ovate, slightly crenate at the margin to entire. The white snapdragon-like flowers emerge from the leaf axils.

Habitat: 900–6,500′. Under shrubs and on lightly shaded banks and roadcuts. CH, FW, LC.

Comments: Not aromatic like most mints. The name "Skullcap" is derived from the fact that at a certain stage, the unopened sepals look like the old-fashioned skullcaps that people once wore to bed. Some regard it as looking more like a Quaker bonnet. Common along Clark Tunnel Road near Penryn, among other places.

Scutellaria tuberosa   Native perennial
Blue Skullcap, Danny's Skullcap   Apr–Jul

Description: 1–8″ in height. A low erect herb with weak stems emerging from small white tubers. Broadly oval toothed leaves. Fuzzy light to dark blue to purple flowers, the lower lip of which has a central notch.

Habitat: 600–3,300′. Moist soils or dry sites in brushy situations. CH, FW, LC.

Comments: Especially common after fires. Most often found in chaparral, it sprouts from tubers with the winter rains and by July the top growth has disappeared and only the underground tuber remains through the hot dry summer. It can be found on steep hillsides along Yankee Jim's Road leading down into the American River Canyon and at Bridgeport.

PRENTISS FERGUSON

Blue Skullcap

Stachys ajugoides var. *rigida*   Native perennial
Rigid Hedge Nettle   May–Sep

Description: 1–2′ tall. An erect to slightly decumbent stem, usually with cobwebby woolly hairs covering the stems and leaves. The flowers are rose-purple or purple-veined. The upper lip is shorter than the lower lip, which makes it look like a tongue hanging out of the flower's throat. Variable in size, texture, and the amount of surface hair, and also how quilted the leaf surfaces appear.

Habitat: 1,000–8,000′. Locally common in moist meadows, on seeps, and along rocky streams, but also found on drier, rocky slopes. CH, FW, LC, UC.

Comments: It is called hedge nettle because the foliage resembles the nettle plant, but it does not have stinging hairs. Different populations can be very different in appearance.

KAREN CALLAHAN

Rigid Hedge Nettle

JULIE S. CARVILLE

Vinegar Weed

Trichostema lanceolatum   Native annual
Vinegar Weed   Jul–Oct

Description: 4–24″ tall. Branched near the base. Sharp-pointed, glandular, hairy leaves. The blue flowers are most commonly in clusters on one side of the stem, the stamens much exserted.

Habitat: Below 3,000′. Dry, open, generally disturbed habitats. GR, CH, FW, LC.

Comments: The plant has a strong pungent smell that is offensive to some. Cowboys used to crush the leaves in bedrolls to discourage fleas. It is prized by beekeepers because it blooms late and produces copious amounts of nectar, which makes a high-quality honey. Native Americans made it into a tea or rolled the ground-up foliage on the face and chest as a cold remedy.

CHET BLACKBURN

Mountain Blue Curls

Trichostema oblongum   Native annual
Mountain Blue Curls   Jun–Sep

Description: 4–20″ in height (but usually smaller). The plant has softly hairy leaves and small blue and white flowers that are all on one side of the stem.

Habitat: 300–9,000′. Dry margins of meadows and streams. CH, FW, LC, UC, RP.

Comments: The flowers are inconsequential to the naked eye, but the whole plant is highly attractive when viewed through a hand lens. The small-flowered species like this one produce little or no nectar and attract relatively few insects. Instead, the anthers are adjacent to the stigma and self-pollination results from the stigma brushing the anthers as they split apart at maturity. The third species of *Trichostema* found in our area is *T. simulatum,* which can be distinguished from this one by the flowers having petioles.

Lemnaceae
DUCKWEED FAMILY
Chet Blackburn

Diminutive floating leafless aquatics. The roots are threadlike or lacking entirely. The *plant body consists of a leaflike stem or "frond" that is densely green, disk-shaped, and elongated.* The flowers are unisexual and lack both sepals and petals. Both the pistillate (female) and staminate (male) flowers are enclosed in a membranous spathe (something like a Calla Lily) and are minute. The family is not important economically but is prolific and is a major source of food for fish and waterfowl. There are 4 genera and 34 species worldwide. All 4 genera and 16 species occur in California; 2 genera and 8 species are found in our area.

Lemna minor Native perennial
Duckweed spring/summer

Description: A tiny floating aquatic consisting of an oblong green leafless stem called a "frond" to 0.16″ long and bearing a single dangling root. The flowers are diminutive and seldom seen.

Habitat: Below 2,000′. Abundant on the surface of pools, quiet streams, and ditches, often covering the entire surface. AQ.

Comments: Floats on the surface of quiet waters and propagates rapidly by division. Eaten by waterfowl and fish such as carp. The reproductive capability of duckweed is amazing. A few plants carried in on the feet or feathers of a waterfowl or wading bird can end up covering a pond within a month if there is nothing in the pond to feed on it. There are at least four other species in our area (*L. gibba, L. minuscula, L. trisulca,* and *L. turionifera*).

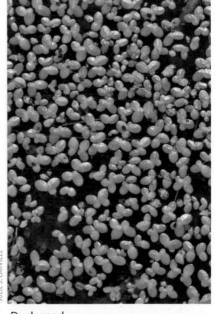

JULIE S. CARVILLE

Duckweed

Lentibulariaceae
BLADDERWORT FAMILY
Chet Blackburn

Carnivorous herbs found in moist or aquatic environments. The leaves range from none to alternate to being arranged in a basal rosette. In aquatic species, the leaves below the surface and above the surface are usually different. There are *2–5 united sepals and 5 united petals. Corolla 2-lipped, with lower lip larger, 3-lobed and spurred at base. Stamens 2.* There are 4 genera and 200 species worldwide of which 2 genera and 5 species are found in California. We have 1 genus and 4 species in our area.

Common Bladderwort

Utricularia vulgaris Native perennial
Common Bladderwort Jun–Sep

Description: A shallowly floating plant with threadlike leaves bearing tiny bladders that capture minute animal life. The flowers are yellow with a pointed spur.

Habitat: Below 5,800′. Aquatic plant of dredge ponds, ditches, sloughs, and streamside pools from the Valley floor to adjacent foothills. AQ, RP.

Comments: Bladderworts possess a unique trap that uses suction to sweep tiny prey into the bladders once a hairlike trigger is touched. All four bladderworts found in the state are found in our area, including two native species, the Flat-leafed Bladderwort, *U. intermedia,* and the Lesser Bladderwort, *U. minor,* both from higher elevation pools, and the non-native Humped Bladderwort, *U. gibba,* which is the most common.

Liliaceae
LILY FAMILY
Chet Blackburn

Perennials with stems originating from bulbs, corms, or scaly rhizomes underground. Leaves with linear veins. *Sepals and petals in 3s and often similar in appearance and color, making the plants appear to have 6 petals and no sepals. Stamens 6 or 3.* Superior ovary. Most take a number of years to flower from seed. It is a large and complex family that, perhaps more than any other, offers job security for plant taxonomists who can make a career of realigning the species into various families. At one time or another, the various members of this family have been placed in more than 80 separate families, and the family is currently undergoing yet another major revision. There are more than 300 genera and 4,600 species worldwide. Of those, 39 genera and 234 species occur in California, with 23 genera and 78 of those species occurring in Nevada and Placer Counties.

Allium amplectens Native perennial
Paper Onion, Narrow-leaf Onion Mar–Jun

Description: Plant 6–24″ tall. The leaves are narrow, linear, and shorter than the flower stalk. They are generally withered and dry by flowering time. Numerous white to pink papery flowers form a ball at the top of a leafless stalk.

Habitat: Below 6,000′. Open or lightly wooded places and rock outcroppings, often on clay and serpentine soils. CH, FW, LC, RO, SG.

Comments: Like all alliums, the plant has a distinctive onion odor when its leaves are crushed. Also called Slim Leaf Onion and Clasping Onion. Locally common in the foothills surrounding the Sacramento Valley. In areas where this and Sanborn's Onion grow together, such as Hell's Half Acre, this species is first to bloom and is fading by the time Sanborn's Onion blooms.

KAREN CALLAHAN

Paper Onion

Sierra Onion

KAREN CALLAHAN • JULIE S. CARVILLE

Allium campanulatum   Native perennial
Sierra Onion   May–Jul

Description: 4–12″ tall. In the spring 2–3 linear leaves emerge that are the same size or slightly shorter than the flower stem. They are slightly concave-convex. The leaves dry by flowering time. The inflorescence is a cluster of 15–40 flat, rose-purple bells to star-shaped flowers forming a loose head subtended by two oval bracts.

Habitat: 2,000–8,500′. Dry gravelly slopes and banks, especially around outcrops in woods. LC, UC, SA, RO, SG.

Comments: Widespread in the Sierra. It prefers dry loose soils at medium to high elevations but is also found on wetter sites. It resembles another *Allium* found within the two counties, *Allium bisceptrum*, but *A. bisceptrum* only occurs in our counties on the eastern side of the Sierra, usually in groves of aspen.

Lemmon's Onion

RICHARD HANES

Allium lemmonii   Native perennial
Lemmon's Onion   May–Jul

Description: 4–8″ flower scape. The 2 sickle-shaped leaves are about the same length as the strongly flattened and winged scape. Flowers are white to pale pink with a greenish or pinkish midvein. The stamens are equal to or slightly longer than the petals.

Habitat: 3,800–6,200′. Drying clay soils. LC, UC, SP.

Comments: Although attractive as individuals, their small flowers don't necessarily stand out among more colorful groups of flowers. The Native Americans used wild onions in much the same way as we use domesticated ones. This species can be seen north of Truckee, south of Hobart Mills, and at places along Prosser Creek.

Allium obtusum   Native perennial
Red Sierra Onion   May–Jul

Description: Scape 4″ or less. One of the leaves is much longer than the scape. The clustered flowers are whitish to greenish with a purplish midrib in the petals.

Habitat: 3,300–11,000′. Sandy granitic or gravelly subalpine and alpine slopes. UC, SA, RO.

Comments: A ground-hugging species that is found only in the Sierra Nevada and the southern Cascades. It is one that is easily overlooked because of its size and less than flamboyant color. There are two varieties; the more common variety *obtusum* is usually white but sometimes pinkish and the less common pinkish purple variety *conspicuum* also has flowers in larger umbels and has an outer bulb coat that is reticulated.

RICHARD HANES

Red Sierra Onion

Allium peninsulare   Native perennial
Peninsular Onion   Mar–Jun

Description: 9–18″ tall with 2–4 leaves almost as long as the scape. The scape is smooth and leafless, terminating in 6 to 25 deep rose-purple, papery flowers. Each petal is about ½″ long.

Habitat: 900–3,500′. Locally common on dry rocky, brush-covered slopes in grasslands and open oak woodlands. Also found on serpentine. GR, CH, FW, SG.

Comments: The name "Peninsular Onion" for this pretty little inland species seems odd until you learn that the plant was first described from a specimen collected on the Baja California Peninsula. The leaves and flower heads were used for food by native people. Until recently, it was especially common on Clark Tunnel Road near Penryn. Clark Tunnel Road is now undergoing massive development.

KAREN CALLAHAN

Peninsular Onion

Pinkstar Onion

Allium platycaule   Native perennial
Pinkstar Onion, Flatstem Onion   May–Aug

Description: 1–6″ tall. Semi-prostrate growth. Flat, sickle-shaped, somewhat waxy leaves. Bright rose flowers form a dense rounded head on a stout, conspicuously flattened stem, rising only a few inches from the ground. The petals are narrow, sharp pointed, and deep rose.

Habitat: 4,200–7,000′. Common on rocky or sandy slopes, the edges of snowmelt, and open mountain slopes. LC, UC, SP.

Comments: Superficially similar to the Sierra Onion but the sickle-shaped leaves and flat stem readily identify it. The Northern Paiute placed the seed heads in hot ashes for a few minutes and then extracted the seeds for food. The leaves were also eaten as a sort of relish. Common at Castle Pass.

Sanborn's Onion

Allium sanbornii   Native perennial
Sanborn's Onion   Jun–Aug

Description: 9–20″ tall. There is one cylindrical leaf about as long as the flower scape. The flowers are many, ranging from white to pink.

Habitat: 1,000–4,400′. Serpentine or shallow volcanic soils. CH, LC, SG.

Comments: There are two varieties; both occur in our area. The variety *sanbornii* has smaller petals (0.2–0.4″), the outer margins of which are irregular to jagged, and the stamens are exserted (rise above the petals). Variety *congdonii* has larger petals (0.3–0.8″) with smooth edges, and the stamens do not rise above the petals. The largest local population of this rare and colorful native onion grows at Hell's Half Acre near Grass Valley.

Allium validum   Native perennial
Swamp Onion, Pacific Onion   Jul–Sep

Description: 1–3′ tall. It forms large clumps. Numerous long, strap-shaped leaves to 3′. Rose to pink-purple flowers occur in flat, upright clusters. The stamens are exserted.

Habitat: 3,400–11,000′. Common on wet meadows and on stream banks. UC, MM, RP.

Comments: This is the largest native onion in our area. The plant has a very strong onion odor. Although Native Americans and early settlers ate the bulbs raw or used it as soup flavoring, it has been implicated in hemolytic anemia in sheep fed foliage from the plant. It can be found on the Sierra Discovery Trail and in the meadows at Sagehen Creek, usually in rather mucky places.

KAREN CALLAHAN

Swamp Onion

Brodiaea californica   Native perennial
California Brodiaea   Late May–Jul, peak Jun

Description: 8–29″ tall. An erect inflorescence bearing open umbels of lilac flowers (rarely white or pink). The midveins of the petals are darker. The petal margins are rolled slightly inward. There are sometimes multiple flower stalks from a single bulb.

Habitat: 200–3,000′. Grassy openings and near streams, mostly in the foothills. Frequently on serpentine soil. Usually on gravelly or clay soils. GR, CH, FW, LC, SG.

Comments: The largest and one of the latest blooming of the brodiaeas. A staminode is a sterile stamen, and is often inconspicuous, but in this species the 3 staminodes are waxy white, almost petal-like, and prominent. Some botanists consider those on serpentine in the northern Sierra foothills as a separate species, *B. sierrae*.

RICHARD HANES

California Brodiaea

Harvest Brodiaea

Brodiaea elegans   Native perennial
Harvest Brodiaea   Jun–Jul

Description: 6–18″ tall. Vivid blue-purple individual flowers form a loose group in open umbels on tall stalks. The 3 white staminodes do not adhere to the stamens but instead are closer to the petals.

Habitat: To 6,000′ but mostly below 2,800′. Abundant in grasslands, meadows, and open woodlands. GR, CH, FW, LC.

Comments: It is called Harvest Brodiaea because it begins blooming at the time of hay harvest. The bright purple flowers stand out against the golden-brown grasses. It is one of the last brodiaeas to bloom, and where it occurs it is usually abundant. Another Harvest Brodiaea, *Brodiaea coronaria,* can be distinguished from this one by the staminodes being purple at the base and adjacent to the fertile stamens but flaring out at the top.

Purdy's Brodiaea

Brodiaea purdyi   Native perennial
Purdy's Brodiaea   Apr–Jun

Description: 3–12″ tall, producing a short scape with blue-violet flowers, usually with a broad purple central stripe on the petals. The conspicuous white staminodes rise from the center of the flower well above the petals. The petals are widely spreading, forming an almost flat cup.

Habitat: 300–1,800′. Open woodlands in heavy soils, frequently on serpentine. GR, CH, FW, LC, SG.

Comments: Almost indistinguishable from the Dwarf Brodiaea, *Brodiaea minor,* which is very similar and more common on grasslands at lower elevations. It differs in the size of the scape, and floral parts, hence it is usually regarded as a separate species. *B. purdyi* is more common in our area, especially above 1,000′. Purdy's Brodiaea also blooms later than Dwarf Brodiaea.

Calochortus albus   Native perennial
Fairy Lanterns, White Globe Lily   Apr–Jun

Description: 15–30″ tall. It forms a pendant, branched, leafy stem bearing globe-shaped, satiny white flowers. The white sepals are about half as long as the white petals. The petals are sometimes tinged pink. The bulb is deep rooted. The seedpods are papery at maturity and contain seed that is also papery.

Habitat: 200–5,000′. Most common in lower foothills. Shaded hillsides, roadcuts, canyon sides, and shrubby banks to open woods. CH, FW, LC.

Comments: One of the area's most common and beloved wildflowers. It loves to grow among rocks where the bulb is often tightly wedged. It can be seen along Independence Trail, the American River Canyon, and almost any other shaded slope in our area.

Fairy Lanterns

Calochortus coeruleus   Native perennial
Beavertail Grass   Late May–Jul

Description: 1–7″ tall. Basal leaves are approximately 6″ long. The flower stalk bears 1–8 white to pale blue flowers. Petal margins are fringed, ranging from smooth to very hairy, often with dark blue and pink markings on the inner petals. Sepals are shorter than the petals and not hairy.

Habitat: 2,000–7,500′. Gravelly openings in woodlands, open brushy flats, and woodland margins. LC, UC.

Comments: Some botanists regard it as a synonym for *C. tolmiei,* a species from the Coast Range. *C. coeruleus* is small but one of our prettiest cat's ears. Not as common in our area as it is farther south. The name *coeruleus* can be misleading, as the flowers are not blue, but white with a subtle bluish tint to them. They are usually found in dry coniferous woodlands in loamy or clay soil.

Beavertail Grass

Leichtlin's Mariposa Lily

JULIE S. CARVILLE

Calochortus leichtlinii   Native perennial
Leichtlin's Mariposa Lily   Jun–Aug

Description: Variable plant 2–24″ tall. The erect stem bears large white flowers, sometimes with a bluish tint. The petals have a large yellow basal spot with a dark purplish red blotch above it. The petals are widely spaced, the anthers arrow-shaped, distinguishing them from other *Calochortus* species.

Habitat: 4,000–11,000′. Meadow edges, rocky ridges, open woodland. LC, UC, SA, MM, RO, SP.

Comments: It resembles the Superb Mariposa Lily, *Calochortus superbus,* that occurs at a lower elevation. The color pattern is different at the petal base, and the petals of this species are widest at the middle, while in *C. superbus* the petals are widest on top. The petals reminded early Spanish settlers of butterflies, hence the Spanish name Mariposa (butterfly) Lily.

Yellow Mariposa Lily

KAREN CALLAHAN

Calochortus luteus   Native perennial
Yellow Mariposa Lily, Gold Nuggets Apr–Jun

Description: Stalk 8–19″ bearing yellow, bowl-shaped flowers. The inside gland markings are variable—from none at all to large crescent-shaped glands. Sepals are greenish yellow, narrower, and do not resemble petals.

Habitat: Below 2,000′, mostly 100–1,200′. Grassy flats and slopes on heavy soils. GR, FW, LC.

Comments: Often found in clay soil that is as hard as cement during the summer, it can be confused with the yellow form of *Calochortus superbus,* but differs in flower size and markings inside the petals. These two species hybridize readily, creating a range of color variations. Some of the best sites where they were once found in large numbers, such as Industrial Boulevard near Lincoln and Clark Tunnel Road near Penryn, are being ravaged by development.

Calochortus monophyllus   Native perennial
Yellow Cat's Ear   Apr–May

Description: Low (4–8″) plant with deep yellow flowers sporting fuzzy petals. Sometimes there is a reddish to rust-colored basal spot on the petals. The sepals are almost as long as the petals but are narrower, yellow inside and green-yellow outside, and not fuzzy.

Habitat: 1,200–4,000′. Brushy flats and open to shady woodlands. CH, FW, LC.

Comments: One of our most common bulbs in lower conifer woodlands and manzanita chaparral. The name "Cat's Ear" is derived from the fuzzy texture of the inside petals. Insects moving across the petals to get to the nectar glands at their base must feel like they are walking on plush carpeting. *Calochortus* means beautiful grass. It can be seen at Hell's Half Acre.

RICHARD HANES

Yellow Cat's Ear

Calochortus nudus   Native perennial
Naked Star Tulip   Jun–Jul

Description: 4–12″ tall. White to pale lavender flowers. The petal tips are usually rounded (but may be flat) with very few hairs above the gland.

Habitat: 4,000–8,000′. Meadow edges and low open woodlands. LC, UC, SG, MM, RP.

Comments: Most *Calochortus* species have numerous hairs around the glands at the base of their petals, and some have very hairy petals as well. This one has just a few hairs around the glands and the petals are relatively unadorned, hence the name "Naked Star Tulip." *C. nudus* and *C. minimus* hybridize readily, forming fertile hybrids. They are most often found on wet meadows, such as the small colony in Bear Valley off Highway 20 and Onion Valley in Placer County.

JULIE S. CARVILLE

Naked Star Tulip

Superb Mariposa Lily

Calochortus superbus Native perennial
Superb Mariposa Lily Late May–Jul

Description: 18–24″ tall. Large, usually white (may be yellow, lavender, or purplish) petals with a reddish haired inverted V-shaped gland near the petal base. The brownish purple gland is bordered by a bright yellow band. There are often numerous red pencil-like markings at the base in the center of the floral cup.

Habitat: Below 5,000′, mostly 600–3,300′. Open grasslands, brush-covered slopes, and occasionally lower conifer forests. GR, CH, FW, LC.

Comments: This is the largest and most conspicuous Mariposa Lily in our area. Yellow individuals of this species might be confused with the Yellow Mariposa Lily, *Calochortus luteus,* but the Superb Mariposa is larger and has the inverted V-shaped gland. The flowers are short-lived. Hybridizes freely with *C. luteus.*

KAREN CALLAHAN · CINDY RUBIN

Common Camas Lily

Camassia quamash Native perennial
Common Camas Lily May–Jul

Description: 1–3′ tall with a leafless stem. The deep blue (rarely white) flowers are about 1″ across.

Habitat: 2,000–8,000′. Wet meadows in full sun. LC, UC, MM.

Comments: This was probably the most important bulb utilized by Native Americans. It was used as a trading item between tribes, and areas where these bulbs were abundant were sometimes fought over. Camas in the Nez Perce language means "sweet." The bulbs often grow in association with the highly poisonous Death Camas, *Zigadenus venenosus.* The two plants don't look much alike in flower, but great care had to be taken when digging out the dormant bulbs. The meadows at Sagehen Creek are well known for their early June displays of this species.

JULIE S. CARVILLE

Chlorogalum pomeridianum Native perennial
Soap Plant   May–Aug

Description: 1–7′ tall from a large underground bulb to 4″ long and 2″ wide that is covered by a dense coat of brown fibers. Many wavy-margined 2–3′ leaves. The tall, almost leafless flowering stem bears many white flowers, often with green-ridged midveins. The petals curve downward.

Habitat: Below 5,000′. Dry, open low hills and plains. GR, CH, FW, LC, UC.

Comments: This plant was a veritable super-market for Native Americans. The crushed bulbs were used as soap and shampoo, and were also used to stupefy fish. Roasting destroys the toxins, rendering the bulbs edible. The fibrous bulb coat was used for making brushes and for holding acorn meal during the leaching process. Thick juices from the bulb were used as glue. The flowers open in the evenings and close by midday. Fertilized by moths.

KAREN CALLAHAN

Soap Plant

Dichelostemma capitatum Native perennial
Blue Dicks   Late Feb–May

Description: 12–24″ tall. Variable with small bluish to purple (rarely white) flowers in upright rounded heads. There are violet to purple bracts with translucent edges below the flower heads. The 6 fertile stamens are enclosed in a tightly packed structure in the center of the flower.

Habitat: Valley floor to 7,000′. Common and widespread in grassy spots from the Central Valley up into conifer woodlands. GR, CH, FW, LC, UC, SG.

Comments: One of the first wildflowers to bloom in the spring. It increases rapidly from both seeds and offsets. Different races flower at different times. It can be confused with Forktooth Ookow, *Dichelostemma congestum,* but it blooms earlier and the flowers are usually withered and setting seed by the time Ookow begins to bloom. The purplish bract is distinctive to this species.

JULIE S. CARVILLE

Blue Dicks

Forktooth Ookow

KAREN CALLAHAN

Dichelostemma congestum   Native perennial
Forktooth Ookow   Apr–Jun

Description: 1–3′ scape bearing a head of blue-purple flowers. The floral tube is only slightly constricted at the top and 3 toothlike projections (staminodes) rise above it. The staminodes are deeply cleft (tips strongly forked). There are 3 fertile stamens.

Habitat: Below 6,000′. Open grasslands, foothill canyons, and mountain slopes. Often volcanic and serpentine soils. GR, CH, FW, LC, SG.

Comments: Localized populations occur in our area. It can be distinguished from Roundtooth Ookow, *Dichelostemma multiflorum,* by forked (not rounded) staminoidea and its usually larger size and darker color. It resembles Blue Dicks but lacks the purple bract below the flower head and usually blooms later.

Wild Hyacinth

JULIE S. CARVILLE

Dichelostemma multiflorum   Native perennial
Wild Hyacinth, Roundtooth Ookow Apr–Jun

Description: From 1–3′ tall, but usually 1′. The rose-purple flowers are in a head but the head is not as tight as Blue Dicks. The staminoidea are rounded (not forked) and petals often have a dark band extending down the center.

Habitat: 100–6,000′. Grasslands, pastures, open woodlands, and open shrubby areas in foothills and mountains. GR, FW, CH, LC.

Comments: It can be recognized by having more open flowers with a wider space between the petals and an obvious constriction between the large ovary and the rest of the floral tube. Most in our area are rose-purple (compared with the blue-purple of Blue Dicks and Forktooth Ookow). It blooms later than Blue Dicks. All of the dichelostemmas used to be included in the genus *Brodiaea.*

Dichelostemma volubile   Native perennial
Snake Lily, Twining Brodiaea   Apr–Jun

Description: Stems 5–6′. Several long leaves lie close to the ground. The pink to reddish stem twists and winds through nearby vegetation, placing the blooms some distance away from the bulb but making them more accessible to pollinators. The pink to rose urn-shaped flowers are clustered in a loose head to 6″ across.

Habitat: 500–5,000′, but mostly below 2,000′. In thickets and open woodlands in the lower foothills, most often in canyons. CH, FW, LC.

Comments: It is not easily confused with any other bulb in our area. The stems are brittle and often break off from the bulb with the slightest touch, but that does not deter the flowering. It will sometimes be found disconnected from the stem, hanging loosely in shrubbery with the plant in full bloom, then continuing on to set seed.

JULIE S. CARVILLE

Snake Lily

Disporum hookeri   Native perennial
Hooker's Fairybell   Mar–May

Description: Plant 1–2½′ tall from a slender horizontal rootstock. The alternate sessile leaves are on branching stems bearing pairs of drooping greenish white flowers followed by scarlet berries.

Habitat: 1,600–5,000′. Shady forest slopes and low conifer woodlands. LC, UC.

Comments: The flowers often go unnoticed because they are almost hidden by the glossy-veined leaves. The berries, at first yellow, then turning to orange-red, are more noticeable than the greenish white flowers but are still mostly hidden by the leaves. The berries look edible, but then, so does broccoli. It can be seen growing along the Rock Creek Nature Trail.

JULIE S. CARVILLE

Hooker's Fairybell

KAREN CALLAHAN

Sierra Fawn Lily

Erythronium multiscapoideum

Native perennial

Sierra Fawn Lily, Adder's Tongue   Mar–May

Description: Up to 15″ tall. From the juncture of the 2 mottled leaves, a stem rises from ground level bearing ½–1″ whitish flowers with an egg yolk yellow base.

Habitat: 1,200–3,400′. On brushy hillsides or slopes in open woodlands. CH, FW, LC, SG.

Comments: The name *multiscapoideum* implies multiple scapes and indeed the plant does look like it has multiple flowering stems. But a closer examination reveals that it is only a single stem branching at ground level. The name Fawn Lily is in reference to the spotting on some species resembling the spotted pattern on fawns. It differs from *E. purpurascens* by its mottled leaves and by being found at lower elevations. Our only Fawn Lily that produces bulblets.

JULIE S. CARVILLE

Plainleaf Fawn Lily

Erythronium purpurascens   Native perennial

Plainleaf Fawn Lily   May–Aug

Description: 3–8″ tall. Two plain (not mottled) tonguelike basal leaves. The leaf edges are turned up and have wavy margins. The stem bears 1–8 white flowers with a yellow base that may become tinged with purple with age.

Habitat: 4,000–8,000′. Along streams, meadows, margins of drying snow fields. LC, UC, MM, RP.

Comments: Grows at a higher elevation than *E. multiscapoideum,* and it does not have mottled leaves. It flowers as soon as the snow melts, but the blooming season is short. There are 13 species of Fawn Lily in California but only 2 of them are found in our area. In California, it ranges from Shasta County south to Tuolumne County. The species from Tulare County is *E. pusaterii.*

Fritillaria agrestis   Native perennial
Stinkbells   Mar–Apr

Description: Up to 24″ from a bulb. Leaves alternate, crowded on the lower part of the stem. Greenish white to brownish purple nodding, bell-shaped flowers.

Habitat: Below 1,500′. Clay soils. GR, FW.

Comments: Uncommon and threatened. Its preferred habitat in our area consists of the lowland clay soils in Western Placer County, where rapid and rampant development is taking place. The common name refers to the strong unpleasant odor the plant gives off, probably to attract certain kinds of insects for pollination.

Stinkbells

Fritillaria atropurpurea   Native perennial
Spotted Mountain Bells   May–Jul

Description: 4–24″ slender stem rising from an underground bulb. The linear leaves are 1–5″ long and arranged as whorls of 2–3 on the middle part of the stem and become alternate as they ascend. The nodding, purplish brown flowers have a wide-open shape. Petals are ½–1″ long and not recurved.

Habitat: 4,000–10,000′. Grows in leaf mold under trees and shrubs. UC, SA, SP.

Comments: This species has the widest geographic distribution of its genus; with the exception of Washington, it occurs in all the states west of the Rocky Mountains and is also found east of the Rockies in North Dakota and Nebraska. Found along the trail at Sagehen Creek and many other trails in the Sierra.

Spotted Mountain Bells

Brown Bells

Fritillaria micrantha   Native perennial
Brown Bells   Mar–Jul

Description: 18–36″ tall. Light green linear leaves in whorls of 3 to 5 along the stem. From 3 to 20 small bell-like flowers along the stem are highly variable in color and range from greenish white to reddish to brown.

Habitat: 1,000–6,000′. Dry benches, slopes, roadside banks, and ravines in shaded forests. FW, LC, UC.

Comments: Fritillaries do not necessarily bloom every year. In the years that they don't bloom they send up one or more succulent leaves but not a flowering stalk. Deer love to nip off ripening seedpods of all fritillaries. Brown Bells is a common resident of wooded slopes at lower elevations. Look for it in the American River Canyon in Placer County and the Yuba River Canyon in Nevada County.

Yellow Bells

Fritillaria pudica   Native perennial
Yellow Bells   Apr–Jun

Description: 3–6″ tall. The bulb consists of 2–4 scales and many "rice grain" bulblets at the base. It has from 2 to 7 alternate, linear to lance-shaped, succulent grooved leaves. There is usually 1 (to several) strongly nodding yellow bell-shaped flowers. The flowers fade to orange or reddish with age.

Habitat: Below 7,500′. Grassy and brushy wooded slopes. LC, UC, SP.

Comments: A tiny plant native over much of the West from British Columbia east to Wyoming and south to New Mexico and central California. The flowers are about the size of a dime. The bulbs were either eaten whole or in a soup by Native Americans. The plant is in cultivation but is a difficult plant to grow and not readily available. A summer dormancy period is essential.

Fritillaria recurva   Native perennial
Scarlet Fritillary   Mar–Jul

Description: 1–3′ stem rising from an underground bulb. The leaves are 2–3″ long and scattered in whorls around the middle. Widely separated nodding flowers are orange-red in color with yellow spotting inside. They are more than 1″ long. The petal and sepal tips are curved back sharply at the tip (recurved).

Habitat: 700–6,000′. Dry hillsides in shrublands or open woodlands, usually in light shade. CH, SG, FW, LC, UC.

Comments: A striking plant, it is the most conspicuous of our native fritillaries. Often seen emerging from the tangled branches of shrubby plants such as ceanothus and manzanita, perhaps because only those protected in that fashion are safe from deer, which love the flowers. A good hummingbird plant.

JULIE S. CARVILLE

Scarlet Fritillary

Hastingsia alba   Native perennial
Bog Hastingsia,
Reed Lily, Rush Lily   Jun–Jul

Description: 1–5′ tall plant with linear elongated leaves to 10″ long and ½″ wide. The tall, erect stem bears many small, densely packed flowers that are white and tinted green or pink. The perianth (petals and sepals) turns papery with age. The style is very short.

Habitat: 1,500–7,500′. Wet meadows, bogs, swampy places, and rocky seeps. AQ, LC, UC, SG, MM.

Comments: The undulating leaves are reminiscent of soap plant. Listed as *Schoenolerion alba* in many books. There are 4 species of *Hastingsia,* all confined to California and Oregon. Two species occur in California, but this is the only one in our area and it is always found in soggy places.

RICHARD HANES

Bog Hastingsia

Humboldt Lily

RICHARD HANES

Lilium humboldtii ssp. *humboldtii*

Native perennial

Humboldt Lily   Jun–Jul

Description: 3–10′ tall with a single, tall, very stout stem bearing whorls of slightly undulating leaves. The flowers are large (to 4″), with pure orange recurved petals and spotted with small purple spots without margins.

Habitat: 300–4,500′. Dry open woods, usually in heavy soil. CH, FW, LC, UC.

Comments: Uncommon and rapidly declining, as the habitat in which it grows is becoming heavily encroached. It also suffers from illegal horticultural collection and has almost disappeared from foothill roadsides. Seed may take up to 10 years to reach flowering size. A favorite deer plant, Humboldt Lily grows in drier places than the Leopard Lily, with which it is often confused.

Leopard Lily

KAREN CALLAHAN

Lilium pardalinum   Native perennial

Leopard Lily   May–Jul

Description: 2–7′ tall, bearing narrow leaves in whorls along the stem. The one to many nodding two-tone orange and reddish flowers are marked with purple spots. Each petal is recurved from the middle upward.

Habitat: 600–6,500′. Moist places, stream banks, damp meadows. LC, UC, MM, RP.

Comments: It is the most widespread of our wet-growing lilies. It sometimes forms large colonies. Sierra Discovery Trail in Bear Valley is a good place to see them in quantity. It is in cultivation and is usually available at native plant sales. It blooms readily and adapts easily to garden conditions, provided that it receives summer water. There are 5 subspecies, 3 of which are rare.

Lilium parvum   Native perennial
Alpine Lily   Jul–Sep

Description: 1–6' tall bearing as many as 25 orange flowers with throats flecked with maroon. The plant has 2–4" light green leaves in whorls scattered along the stem. The bell-shaped flowers are turned upward and outward and are about 1½–2" long.

Habitat: 4,000–9,000'. Wet meadows, willow thickets, stream banks in semi-shaded, coniferous forests. LC, UC, MM, RP.

Comments: Also called Small Tiger Lily, it differs from our other lilies by having smaller flowers, and by the fact that the flowers face upward rather than nodding. It is in cultivation and in spite of the fact that it is from higher elevations, adapts reasonably well to garden conditions and blooms readily, providing that it has lots of moisture.

JULIE S. CARVILLE

Alpine Lily

Lilium washingtonianum   Native perennial
Washington Lily   Jul–Aug

Description: 4–6'. Stem with leaves in whorls around it. There are 2–20 white trumpet-shaped, 3–5" flowers that may become pinkish with age. Inner petals often have violet spots. Fragrant.

Habitat: 3,500–7,500'. Coniferous forests, often in thickets as well as in forest openings. CH, LC, UC, SG.

Comments: This fragrant lily is the largest flowered of our native lilies. It resembles an Easter Lily. Deer love them and often nip them off before blooming, which probably explains why they are most often found in the middle of thickets where deer have difficulty reaching them. There are two subspecies, but only one of them, ssp. *washingtonianum,* grows in our area. The other, ssp. *purpurascens,* is a rare plant in Del Norte, Humboldt, Siskiyou, and Trinity Counties.

JULIE S. CARVILLE

Washington Lily

Hartweg's Doll Lily

Odontostomum hartwegii   Native perennial
Hartweg's Doll Lily,
Odontostomum   Apr–May

Description: 6–18″ tall. Forms a simple or branching stem from a deep corm. The mostly basal linear leaves are up to 12″ in length. The small, oddly shaped whitish to creamy white flowers have petals that sweep strongly backward.

Habitat: 400–2,000′. Dry hard soils in grasslands and open woodlands. Also on serpentine. GR, CH, FW, SG.

Comments: Also called Inside Out Lily. The only species in the genus and found only in California. It is an odd-looking plant, with its reflexed petals making the plant look like a fritillary turned inside out. It is usually found in Blue Oak woodlands and foothill grasslands, both of which are being converted to housing subdivisions at an alarming rate.

Western False Solomon's Seal

Smilacina racemosa   Native perennial
Western False Solomon's Seal   Mar–May

Description: Erect 1–3′ stem from thick, short, whitish, branching rhizomes. The leaves are broad and mostly clasping the arching stem. The flowering stem has numerous white flowers in branched racemes followed by spotted berries that eventually turn red.

Habitat: 1,800–7,100′. Moist woodlands, stream banks, slopes in shaded woods. LC, UC.

Comments: Native Americans cooked the rhizomes after first soaking them for a time to get rid of a disagreeable taste. The cooked rhizomes were also used as a poultice. The berries were eaten raw. This plant differs from *S. stellata* by having a branched inflorescence consisting of many flowers.

Smilacina stellata   Native perennial
Star-flowered False Solomon's Seal,
Slim Solomon's Seal   Apr–Jun

Description: 1–2′ tall from a stout rootstock
supporting a leafy stem. The stem is stout,
smooth, and zigzags slightly. The leaves are sessile
and clasping, folded at the midrib. It produces
3–15 flowers on an unbranched inflorescence,
and spherical red-purple berries in the fall.

Habitat: 3,100–8,000′. Damp woodlands,
stream banks in shady places. CH, FW, LC, UC,
MM, RP.

Comments: Fewer flowers and an unbranched
inflorescence separate this from *S. racemosa*. It
also usually grows in wetter places. It spreads by
rhizomes. The pollinators are primarily metallic
bees, flower flies, and tachinid flies. The berries
provide food for birds and rodents and the
foliage is readily eaten by deer.

Star-flowered False Solomon's Seal

Tofieldia occidentalis   Native perennial
Western Tofieldia, False Asphodel   Jul–Aug

Description: 1–3′ tall. A solitary stem emerges
from a slender rootstock. The linear, sedgelike
leaves are mostly basal and 2–8″ long. The small
rounded inflorescence on a mostly leafless stem
consists of small whitish to yellowish flowers.

Habitat: Below 10,000′. Wet meadows, bogs,
and swampy places. AQ, LC, UC, MM.

Comments: The plant superficially resembles
Bistort, which grows along with it, but can be
distinguished from it by having 6 distinct free
petals as opposed to Bistort's petals all joined
into a single perianth with 5 deep lobes. Both
plants can be seen in the meadows at
Sagehen Creek.

Western Tofieldia

KAREN CALLAHAN

Sweet Trillium

Trillium albidum   Native perennial
Sweet Trillium   Mar–Jun

Description: 8–26″ tall. The 3 leaves are egg-shaped and sometimes subtly brown-spotted. The petals are 1½–4″, white to pinkish, sometimes purplish near the base, are widest at the middle, and usually erect or slightly spreading.

Habitat: 1,600–6,000′. Moist shaded bottomlands and canyon slopes, forest floors, and chaparral. CH, LC, UC.

Comments: Both our trilliums are very slow growing and never abundant. They should not be disturbed. It is popularly believed that picking a trillium stalk even once kills it. Though that is generally not true, removing the flower stalk and its attached foliage will set the plant back and it will probably not bloom the following year.

JULIE S. CARVILLE

Purple Trillium

Trillium angustipetalum   Native perennial
Purple Trillium   Mar–Apr

Description: 8–26″ tall. The rounded leaflets are sometimes spotted darker green or brown. Petals 2–4″, dark red-purple and glossy (sometimes pale yellow). The fruit is hexagonal, almost winged, and dark purple.

Habitat: 300–6,500′. Shaded, vernally damp places. CH, FW, LC, UC.

Comments: The petals are narrower and held more erect than they are in *T. albidum.* Trilliums depend on ants for the dispersal of their seeds. The seed of trilliums have an attachment called an elaisome. The elaisome contains a chemical that is highly attractive to some species of native ants that carry the ripe seed off to their burrows. They then eat the elaisome and discard the rest of the seed in their tunnels, thereby planting them.

Triteleia bridgesii   Native perennial
Bridge's Brodiaea   Apr–Jun

Description: 12–24″ stalk bearing an open umbel of lilac to blue flowers. There is a white zone at the base of the petals and another, much smaller one (sometimes missing) at the tip of the petals. The throat of the floral tube is translucent and shiny. The anthers are noticeably blue, and contrast with the petals.

Habitat: 200–2,000′. Dry bluffs and open woodlands, often in rocky areas and serpentine soils. GR, CH, FW, LC, SG.

Comments: Often confused with Wally Basket, *T. laxa,* but can be distinguished from it by the darker blue anthers and the whitish coloration of the petal bases and tips. Bridge's Brodiaea also tends to bloom later than Wally Basket.

KAREN CALLAHAN

Bridge's Brodiaea

Triteleia hyacinthina   Native perennial
White Brodiaea,
White Wild Hyacinth   Apr–Jul

Description: 15–36″ tall. A variable plant with a close umbel of white to pale blue flowers. The floral cluster may be tight with many flowers or loose with just a few.

Habitat: Valley to 6,000′. Common, especially in areas that are wet in the spring such as meadows, drainage areas, and edges of vernal pools. VP, GR, FW, LC, UC, MM.

Comments: Could be confused with Glassy Brodiaea and Glassy Onion but can be distinguished from them by the lack of the glassy glint at the base of the petals. White Brodiaea has yellow anthers, Glassy Brodiaea has purple. All the *Triteleias* used to be included in the genus *Brodiaea,* but though the botanical name has changed, some of the common names have not.

KAREN CALLAHAN

White Brodiaea

Prettyface

Triteleia ixioides   Native perennial
Prettyface, Golden Brodiaea   Jun–Sep

Description: 6–18″ tall. A flat, ground-hugging cluster of leaves with a scape bearing golden yellow flowers. The flowers are open and flat with broad petal segments. The plant is variable with several botanical varieties, some having dark midveins. The one in our area is var. *scabra,* which is usually solid yellow with no dark midveins, although individuals with dark veins also occur here.

Habitat: Valley floor to 9,000′. Open woodlands in grassy places and on lightly shaded slopes. GR, CH, FW, LC, UC, RP, SG.

Comments: It would not be confused with any other plant in our area, but can be confused with the genus *Bloomeria* that grows farther south.

Wally Basket

Triteleia laxa   Native perennial
Wally Basket,
Ithuriel's Spear, Grass Nut   Apr–Jun

Description: 8–16″ stalk bearing an umbel of blue to purplish (rarely white) flowers.

Habitat: Valley to 5,000′. Grassy places, open woodlands, and chaparral. GR, CH, FW, LC, UC, RP.

Comments: One of the most common and best-known wildflowers. It can be confused with Bridge's Brodiaea but does not have whitish petal bases and whitish petal tips. The defining difference between them is that 3 of Wally Basket's stamens are attached at a lower level than the other 3, whereas in Bridge's Brodiaea all 6 are attached at same level. Wally Basket was formerly known as *Brodiaea laxa.* The plant is in cultivation and a cultivar, *T. laxa* 'Queen Fabiola', has been developed and is readily available from bulb specialists.

Triteleia lilacina   Native perennial
Glassy Hyacinth, Glassy Brodiaea Mar–April

Description: 4–16″ stalks. Open umbels of a
few white flowers. The base of the petals has a
glassy shine because of tiny glasslike beads
found there. The petal tips appear pointed
because of the enfolded edges.

Habitat: 200–1,000′. Prefers shallow volcanic
soils. GR, CH, FW.

Comments: Nearly extirpated in our area
because the tabletop habitats where it prefers to
grow are often developed as view home sites.
Easily mistaken for White Brodiaea, but distinguished by the glassy glint in sunlight and the
petal edges rolled inward. Glassy Brodiaea has
purple anthers, White Brodiaea has yellow
anthers. It might also be confused with the
Glassy Onion, though the latter is not known
north of El Dorado County.

JULIE S. CARVILLE

Glassy Hyacinth

Veratrum californicum   Native perennial
Corn Lily, False Hellebore   Jul–Aug

Description: To 7′ tall. A stout, coarse plant
from a short thick rhizome. The stem is leafy, the
leaves 6–12″, about half as broad, and heavily
veined. Greenish to cream-colored flowers
occur in a tall, terminal-branched cluster.

Habitat: 3,600–11,000′. Stream banks, moist
meadows, forest edges. AQ, LC, UC, MM, RP.

Comments: The herbage and root contain toxic
alkaloids that cause a congenital deformity known
as "Monkey Face" in lambs and abortions in
ewes. Whereas the plants may be toxic to mammals, by midsummer the foliage has often been
left in tatters by chewing insects. The plant has
"monogrammed" petals: There is a V-shaped
spot at the base of each petal. The whole plant
turns yellow in the fall. It may need a mycorrhiza
associated with conifers in the damp soil to survive.

JULIE S. CARVILLE

Corn Lily

KAREN CALLAHAN

Bear Grass

Xerophyllum tenax　　Native perennial
Bear Grass　　May–Aug

Description: 5–6' tall in flower. A short, thick, deeply penetrating woody rhizome bears a stout leafy stem with many tough, rigid grasslike leaves with rough margins. The flowering stalk rises about 1' above the clump of foliage and bears a dense bloom of tiny cream-colored flowers.

Habitat: 4,000–7,000'. Open areas in mixed-conifer forest. UC.

Comments: The flowers have an unpleasant fragrance. They have no nectar, and though they are visited by pollen-eating flies and no doubt some pollination occurs in the process, the majority of the pollination is self-pollination as pollen sheds onto the stigma when the flowers open. Fibers split from the leaves were bleached and used in the finest basketwork by Native Americans. Look for it in the Graniteville area.

KAREN CALLAHAN

Death Camas

Zigadenus venenosus　　Native perennial
Death Camas　　May–Jul

Description: Plant to 2' tall with slender, linear, channeled leaves. Numerous flowers are produced on a thick spike. The stamens are longer than the petals. The petal tips are rounded. The bulbs are onionlike but lack the onion odor. The bulb coat is almost black.

Habitat: 600–7,500'. Wet to moist areas, brush-covered slopes, damp rocky outcrops. GR, CH, FW, LC, UC.

Comments: All parts of the plant are poisonous, but particularly the bulbs, which can be easily confused with the edible Camas Lily when harvested after the top growth has disappeared. An alkaloid, zygadenine, is the toxic agent. Members of the Lewis and Clark expedition suffered serious illness when Death Camas bulbs were made into flour.

Limnanthaceae
MEADOW FOAM FAMILY
Chet Blackburn

Low annual herbs of open moist places. The leaves are alternately arranged and pinnately divided. The *flowers are in parts of 3 (genus Floerkea) or 5 (Limnanthes)*. The ovary is superior. *Fruit usually 5 large nutlike seeds per flower.* It is not a commercially important family at the moment but much research is being done on the oils extracted from the seeds of members of this family that could prove to have economic benefits. This is a strictly North American family consisting of only 2 genera and 10 species, of which both genera and 9 of the species occur in California. Both of the genera and 3 species occur in our area.

Limnanthes alba	Native annual
White Meadow Foam	Apr–Jun

Description: 4–12″ high. The linear leaves are divided once or twice into linear leaflets. The flowers are bowl-shaped and consist of 5 white petals that age slightly pink. Some populations are hairy inside the sepals, others are not. Each flower can produce up to 5 seeds, but the norm is usually 2 to 3.

Habitat: Below 4,000′. Low moist places, including edges of vernal pools. VP, GR, FW, LC, RP.

Comments: A showy plant that is abundant and conspicuous at Hell's Half Acre near Grass Valley. It carpets that site in white at the peak of its bloom. Seeds of this plant contain a high-quality oil that is comparable to that produced by sperm whales. The uses are similar to those of Jojoba. Some experimentation in growing it as a commercial crop has been attempted.

KAREN CALLAHAN

White Meadow Foam

Douglas' Meadow Foam

Limnanthes douglasii   Native annual
Douglas' Meadow Foam   Mar–May

Description: 4–15″ tall. Long-stalked dissected leaves with 5–13 segments that are variously cleft. The flowers are bowl-shaped. The vein on the inner portion of the petals of var. *douglasii* is yellow while in var. *rosea* it is rosy pink, but the petals are occasionally all white in both varieties.

Habitat: Below 3,000′. Wet grassy areas, especially vernal pools. VP, GR, FW, RP.

Comments: A highly variable species with 4 recognized botanical varieties statewide, including 2 in our area. They tend to form rings of color around drying vernal pools. They were once abundant in the vernal pools in the Roseville-Rocklin-Lincoln area.

Douglas' Meadow Foam grows at the edges of drying vernal pools but is also found in creekside habitats, as shown here blooming alongside Seepspring Monkeyflowers.

Linaceae
FLAX PLANT FAMILY
Chet Blackburn

Ours are **slender-stemmed** plants with **short, alternate, threadlike linear** leaves. The leaves are simple and entire. The flower parts are in 5s, and the stamens alternate with the petals. **Petals are rolled in bud and quickly deciduous.** The flowers are bisexual (both stamens and style on the same flower), and both the sepals and petals are free (not joined together). Linen and linseed oil are products derived from a European species, but not ours. There are 13 genera and 300 species worldwide. In California there are 3 genera and 19 species, of which 2 genera and 4 species occur in our area.

Linum bienne   Non-native annual/perennial
Narrowleaf Flax   Mar–Jun

Description: To 2′ tall with linear to lance-shaped leaves with only 1 prominent vein. The 5 petals are small, sky blue, distinctly veined, and 2–3 times larger than the egg-shaped sepals. The seeds are black and very shiny.

Habitat: 900–2,400′. Grassy places in full sun. GR, CH, FW, SG.

Comments: A close relative, *L. usitatissimum,* is the leading source of linen and linseed oil today, and although not grown for these purposes today, this species is genetically similar to it and has had a history of cultivation to produce linen as far back as 9,000 years ago. It is one of the most common wildflowers in the eastern Mediterranean region. It can be seen in abundance in May along the nature trail at the Placer Nature Center.

KAREN CALLAHAN

Narrowleaf Flax

Western Blue Flax

RICHARD HANES

Linum lewisii   Native perennial
Western Blue Flax   May–Jul

Description: 1–3′ tall. Leafy stems of narrow, linear leaves about 1″ long. Delicate sky blue flowers bloom over a long period. The 5 petals are about 1″ long and fragile. They fall off shortly after blooming.

Habitat: 1,000–12,000′. Meadows, coniferous woodlands, exposed ridge tops, coarse ground above timberline. LC, UC, SA, MM, RO, SP.

Comments: This is one of many plants named after Meriwether Lewis. It is native to a large area of the western states, ranging from Alaska to Texas and Mexico. It is often found in harsh environments, which belies its delicate appearance. The Native Americans used the fibers for strings, baskets, fish nets, and similar items. It is in cultivation and is nearly always available at the various native plant sales around the state.

C.S. CARVILLE

Emerald Bay on the west shore of Lake Tahoe. Here the Rubicon Trail follows the shoreline above the lake offering lovely water views and woodland wildflowers.

Loasaceae
LOASA FAMILY
Chet Blackburn

Leaves alternate (in California), pinnately lobed, and often *covered with short barbed or stinging hairs.* There are 5 sepals and either 5 or 10 petals. *The stamens are numerous.* The flower parts are *attached on top of a long inferior ovary.* The fruit is a capsule. There are 15 genera and 200 species worldwide, mostly in the American tropics. There are 3 genera and 33 species found in California, and 1 genus and 6 species in our area.

Mentzelia laevicaulis
Giant Blazing Star

Native biennial
Jun–Oct

Description: 1–5′ tall, stout, branching plant with white stems and long, narrow, deeply cleft leaves. The 2–3″ light yellow petals are lance-shaped.

Habitat: 100–9,000′. Hot, dry, rocky or gravelly places, especially disturbed places. CH, FW, LC, UC, RO, RP.

Comments: Flourishes in summer heat in largely inhospitable places. Blooming begins after most wildflowers have faded and given way to the summer heat. A coarse plant with pretty flowers but is unpleasant to touch because of barbed hairs on the foliage. Other species occur in the eastern edge of our two counties, east of the Sierra. Another Blazing Star, *M. lindleyi,* is a component of wildflower mixes and might appear temporarily.

RICHARD HANES

Giant Blazing Star

Lythraceae
LOOSESTRIFE FAMILY
Chet Blackburn

Ours are hairless herbs with entire simple leaves that are either opposite or whorled. The bisexual flowers are in axils or whorls. There are 4–6 (rarely 8) sepals with an equal number of petals. *There are twice as many stamens as petals arranged in 2 series of different lengths. The ovary is within a 6-ribbed cylinder-like calyx.* Style 1, stigma 2-lobed. The fruit is a capsule. The flower parts are so variable in number that this is one of the hardest families to characterize. Our species have 4–6 petals at the end of a tube that surrounds the ovary but does not adhere to it. Of the 25 genera and 450 species found worldwide, 3 genera and 9 species occur in California, and 1 genus and 3 species are found in our area.

Hyssop Loosestrife

CHET BLACKBURN

Lythrum hyssopifolium

Non-native annual/biennial
Hyssop Loosestrife, Grass Poly   Apr–Oct

Description: 4–20″ tall. Many stems often arise from the base. Stems may be erect, ascending, or prostrate. The small flowers appear in the axils with no (or on very short) petioles. There are 5–6 small petals that are whitish or pale pink to lavender, and shorter than the sepals. Stamens 4, opposite the sepals.

Habitat: Below 5,000′. Common but inconspicuous resident of ditches, gravel bars, and other moist places. VP, GR, FW, LC.

Comments: Distributed worldwide, often a weed in irrigated fields and one of the few non-natives that have invaded vernal pools. In fact, that is where it is most often seen, a small succulent-looking plant with pinkish lavender flowers blooming among the cracks of drying mud.

Lythrum salicaria   Non-native perennial
Purple Loosestrife   Jul–Sep

Description: 1–6′ tall rhizomatous plant with erect stems and simple entire leaves that are opposite or whorled. The steeplelike racemes of crimson to rose-purplish flowers are borne in leafy axils with no pedicels. There are 5–7 petals.

Habitat: Below 3,000′. Wet meadows, shallow water of ponds, marshes, ditches, and lake shores. AQ, RP.

Comments: Considered a noxious weed. It disrupts wetland ecosystems by displacing native plants, which then impacts waterfowl and other birds by reducing the amount of food available to them. Long used as an ornamental plant, some states now ban its sale. The plants demonstrate an interesting phenomenon known as "trimorphy" wherein tops of the stamens are at 2 levels while the stigma is at a third.

FRENTISS FERGUSON

Purple Loosestrife

KAREN CALLAHAN

Pink clarkias and yellow madias flower among the small branches of Pratten's Buckwheat at Hell's Half Acre near Grass Valley.

Malvaceae
MALLOW FAMILY
Richard Hanes

Herbs, shrubs, and small trees, usually covered with starlike hairs. The sap is sticky or mucilaginous. The leaves are alternate, simple, and petioled. The blades are generally palmately veined or lobed. Stipules are present. The inflorescence is often leafy. The flower is radial. *Calyx lobes 5. Petals 5, free. Stamens many, the filaments fused into a tube surrounding the style, and the tube fused in turn to the petal bases.* Pistil 1, ovary superior, style branched. The fruit is composed of 5 to many disk- or wedge-shaped segments, a loculicidal capsule, or a berry. Mature fruit is important for identification. The family includes Hibiscus, Hollyhocks, Cotton, and Okra. There are 100 genera and more than 1,500 species worldwide, 16 genera in California, and 5 genera and 13 species in Nevada and Placer Counties.

Common Mallow

JULIE S. CARVILLE

Malva neglecta   Non-native annual/biennial
Common Mallow, Cheeseweed   May–Oct

Description: 6–24″ tall. Taprooted. Stems decumbent to ascending, 8–24″ long, densely hairy with starlike hairs. Leaves 1–3″ wide, alternate, scalloped. The inflorescence is of 3–6 flowers per axil. Both the calyx and the bractlets just below it are hairy. The flowers are pale lilac or white, with a hairy stalklike base. The stamen tubes are also hairy.

Habitat: Below 9,000′. Disturbed places, gardens. GR, CH, FW, LC, UC.

Comments: Native of Eurasia and North Africa. Euell Gibbons, the famous wild food author, stated that seeds of this plant were the first wild food he had ever eaten. The mucilaginous quality of these seeds is responsible for the name "Cheeseweed." Some species of *Malva* may concentrate selenium and become toxic to livestock.

Modiola caroliniana   Non-native perennial
Carolina Bristlemallow,
Wheel Mallow   Apr–Sep

Description: Under 3″, rooting at the base of its prostrate hairy stems. Small, maplelike leaves. The solitary orange-salmon flower with a yellow center rises from the axils. Flowers are often reddish at the base.

Habitat: Under 1,200′. Disturbed places, such as stream corriders after winter floods. GR, FW, RP.

Comments: Ours all seem to be small, insignificant-looking plants, but there are forms up to 2′ in other parts of the country. Native to tropical Latin America. The seed resembles a wheel hub and is almost as attractive as the flower. The shape of the leaves changes drastically as the season progresses. They are deeply divided in the spring but by fall are almost round but with small scalloped edges.

CHET BLACKBURN

Carolina Bristlemallow

Sidalcea glaucescens   Native perennial
Waxy Checkerbloom   May–Sep

Description: 1–3′ tall. Relatively slender sprawling stems from a thick taproot. Leaves variable and deeply lobed. Saucer-shaped, 1″ flowers with 5 lavender petals containing white lines. The flowers generally occur on only one side of the stalk and at the top.

Habitat: 2,800–9,000′. Dry slopes and open woods. LC, UC, SA.

Comments: Members of the genus *Sidalcea* are sometimes confused with some of the *Clarkia* species, which they superficially resemble, but the two can instantly be distinguished by looking at the center of the flower. In *Sidalcea* and other members of the Mallow family, the pistils and stamens are not separated but are fused into a single column like those in a Hibiscus (which is also in the Mallow family).

JULIE S. CARVILLE

Waxy Checkerbloom

Hartweg's Sidalcea

Sidalcea hartwegii　　　　Native annual
Hartweg's Sidalcea,
Valley Sidalcea　　　　Mar–Jun

Description: Stems 6–12″ erect, slender. Leaf blade with 5–7 linear segments. The inflorescence is panicle-like with 4–6 flowers overlapping. The calyx is densely hairy with star-shaped hairs. The flowers are rose-purple. The fruit is net veined, pitted, and glabrous.

Habitat: Below 3,500′. Grasslands and dry hillsides. GR, CH, FW, SG.

Comments: Many butterflies use plants of the Mallow family as hosts. Those that may occur in our area are: Gray Hairstreak, Painted Lady, West Coast Lady, Common Checkered Skipper, and Large White Skipper. Look for it in mid-May at Hell's Half Acre.

Checkerbloom

Sidalcea malvaeflora ssp. *asprella*
　　　　　　　　　　Native perennial
Checkerbloom　　　　May–Jul

Description: Stems to 24″ long, decumbent. Plant gray-glaucous and hairy with star-shaped and bristly hairs. The leaves are lobed, the lobe tips toothed or entire. The inflorescence is dense to open. The calyx is also densely covered with star-shaped hairs. The petals are bright to deep pink with white veins. The fruit segments are coarsely pitted and net veined.

Habitat: Below 7,500′. Open dry places in forests or scrub. CH, FW, LC, UC.

Comments: As with many members of this genus, the rounded lower leaves with shallow lobes are very different from the deeply divided leaves on the flowering stem. Highly attractive to insects, this plant has a wide variety of pollinators.

Sidalcea oregana Native perennial
Oregon Sidalcea,
Mountain Hollyhock Jun–Aug

Description: Stems erect to 12–32″, and
bristly. The leaves are scalloped to deeply lobed.
The inflorescence is spikelike, dense, and often
branched. The calyx is densely bristly covered
with star-shaped hairs. The petals are rose-pink,
and notched at the apex. The fruit is smooth to
lightly net veined and glandular-hairy.

Habitat: 3,300–9,000′. Meadows, streamsides,
lake shores, and seeps. RP, MM, RP.

Comments: There are 5 subspecies of this
variable plant in California and others in Oregon
and Washington. In California, 3 of the 5 are
listed in the rare plant inventory. The subspecies
that occurs in our area is ssp. *spicata.* It was
collected by W. L. Jepson in Bear Valley and Dog
Valley, Nevada County, during the early 1900s.

Oregon Sidalcea

Sidalcea stipularis Native perennial
Scadden Flat Checkerbloom May–Jul

Description: Stems 12–26″, bristly hairy, erect
to ascending. The leaves cauline (on the stem),
ovate, and scalloped. The stipules are oval or
heart-shaped. The inflorescence is headlike with
rows of bracts with 3 bractlets. The calyx is
bristly. Fruit glabrous, smooth, and beakless.

Habitat: 2,400′. Boggy areas, marsh. AQ.

Comments: A rare species found only in Nevada
County. Only one confirmed population remains,
with a second population located on private
property. The species name is in reference to the
prominent stipules. Discovered by Gordon H.
True on July 10, 1973. Scadden Flat Checkerbloom grows in a perennial freshwater marsh
with sedges and rushes near Grass Valley.

Scadden Flat Checkerbloom

Menyanthaceae
BUCKBEAN FAMILY
Chet Blackburn

Aquatic perennials with horizontal rhizomes, hairless foliage, alternate leaves, *trifoliate blades, and flowers with 5 petals, margins of which are rolled inward.* Stamens 5. The family is sometimes included in the Gentian family. There are 5 genera and up to 40 species worldwide, but only one species in California and it occurs in our area.

Bogbean

Menyanthes trifoliata   Native perennial
Bogbean, Buckbean   Mar–Nov

Description: 4–15″ plant from an underwater creeping rootstock. Leaves all basal, long petioled, and with 3 leaflets. Leaflets oval, 1–3″ long. The attractive flowers are in a raceme, the corolla white, with starlike petals, the inner petals of which are covered with conspicuous hairs.

Habitat: 3,000–9,500′. Aquatic plant of bogs, shallow ponds, and lake shores. AQ.

Comments: The root is edible if boiled in water that is changed several times. Another member of this family is an introduced species that is often used in water gardens and has escaped cultivation. Water Fringe, *Nymphoides peltata*, has fuzzy yellow petals and Water Lily–like leaves (only smaller) and is a very prolific plant in shallow bodies of water. Pretty, but invasive.

JULIE S. CARVILLE

Nymphaeaceae
WATER LILY FAMILY
Chet Blackburn

Aquatic perennial herbs with horizontal rhizomes (sometimes tubers). The leaves are simple, *long-stalked leaves and flowers that reach up to the surface and either float on the surface or project slightly above it. All flower parts numerous.* There are 6 genera and 60 species worldwide. There is 1 native species and 2 introduced species in California. The 1 native species and 1 of the introduced species may be found in our area.

Nuphar luteum ssp. *polysepalum*

Native perennial

Yellow Pond Lily,
Spatterdock, Cow Lily   Apr–Sep

Description: Large, floating, fleshy, leathery, oval-shaped leaves that are deeply cleft at the base. The fleshy globular inflorescence has 8–12 yellow petal-like sepals. Petals 12–18, yellow, about equaling the stamens, which are numerous.

Habitat: 5,000–7,500'. Shallow ponds, margins of lakes, and slow-moving streams. AQ.

Comments: Native Americans boiled or roasted rootstock for stew or ground them into flour. They also roasted the seeds as food. The plant is an important food source for aquatic birds and mammals. An introduced White Water Lily, *Nymphaea odorata,* occurs in Lake Tahoe and other waterways and is the only other member of this family in our area.

JULIE S. CARVILLE

Yellow Pond Lily

Onagraceae
EVENING PRIMROSE FAMILY
Chet Blackburn

Mostly herbs. Leaves either alternate or opposite, and simple. The bisexual *flower parts are in 4s, free.* The petals are often clawed (meaning that the petal near the base becomes very slim and stalklike). There is a *long, slender inferior ovary* with 1 style and a stigma that is either 4-branched or bulblike. The *pollen is enmeshed in cobweblike threads.* Some botanists divide this family into 3 separate families, with Oenotheraceae and Epilobiaceae being the other two. There are 15 genera and 650 species worldwide. California is well represented with 8 genera and 146 species, of which 7 genera and 46 species occur in the area covered by this book.

Enchanter's Nightshade

JULIE S. CARVILLE

Circaea alpina ssp. *pacifica*   Native perennial
Enchanter's Nightshade   May–Sep

Description: 8–20″ slender, fragile-looking plant with paired rounded leaves on thin stalks. The stem is erect, glandular, and bearing tiny unusual flowers with 2 petals, 2 sepals, 2 stamens, and a 2-lobed stigma.

Habitat: 2,400–6,000′. Damp shaded places such as stream edges, alder groves, and willow thickets. LC, UC, RP.

Comments: Occasional, but locally common under moisture-loving trees and shrubs. The two petals are lobed so deeply it could lead to miscounting them as 4 petals. An odd little plant with an odd name. Circe was a Greek goddess thought to be a sorceress or enchantress, who had the ability to turn men into pigs. Some women are said to wonder when she plans on turning them back.

Clarkia biloba   Native annual
Bilobed Clarkia   May–Jun

Description: 1–3′ tall with a simple stem and
linear leaves. There are many flowers on a long
stalk with the buds nodding before bloom, but
then turning to face upward or at a right angle to
the stalk once in flower. The petals are widest at
the tip, are pink to rose, lobed in the middle and
narrowing toward the base.

Habitat: 500–3,500′. Common in openings on
brushy slopes. CH, FW, LC, SG.

Comments: Like most *Clarkias,* where it is
found it tends to be abundant and showy. Iowa
Hill Road, Yankee Jim's Road, and the Yuba
River Canyon are good places to see it. Look for
the nodding buds, and the upward-facing flowers
with widely spaced petals bearing notches at
their tips. The subspecies *brandegeae* is a rare
form found in our area (as shown).

RICHARD HANES

Bilobed Clarkia

Clarkia gracilis   Native annual
Summer's Darling,
Graceful Clarkia   Apr–Jul

Description: 1–3′ plant with linear leaves
scattered along the flowering stem. The flowers
are in the leaf axils but look terminal because the
top of the stem and the rest of the flower buds are
nodding before opening. Flowers form a pink to
rose upright cup with the petals becoming white
toward the base, but sometimes turning bright
red at the base, giving the appearance of a red
eye staring from the center of the flower.

Habitat: 500–1,800′. Occasional to locally
common on gravelly or serpentine soils in open
sunny locations. GR, CH, FW, SG.

Comments: The *Clarkias* without clawed petals
(this is one of them) used to be separated into a
separate genus known as *Godetia* and that name
persists in some references.

CHET BLACKBURN

Summer's Darling

Winecup Clarkia

JULIE S. CARVILLE

Clarkia purpurea   Native annual
Winecup Clarkia   Apr–Jul

Description: 4–24″ variable plant with three distinct subspecies. The flowers are in the leaf axils; the petals are cuplike or fan-shaped. They share the characteristic of a conspicuously ribbed ovary.

Habitat: 100–4,200′. Widespread on grassy or gravelly slopes and flats. Also found on serpentine. GR, CH, FW, SG.

Comments: The ssp. *purpurea* has its lavender to purple flowers in dense heads; the petals usually have a dark spot and are lighter below, and have widely lancelike to ovate leaves. The ssp. *quadrivulnera* has smaller, dark wine red petals, often without a spot, and linear to lancelike foliage. The ssp. *viminea* has larger lavender to purple petals, usually with a big spot at the tips, and linear to narrow lancelike leaves.

Tongue Clarkia

KAREN CALLAHAN

Clarkia rhomboidea   Native annual
Tongue Clarkia   May–Jul

Description: 4–24″ erect plant with opposite elliptical leaves. Pink to deep rose petals that are spatula- to diamond-shaped and spaced widely apart. The petals are narrow toward the base except for two rounded projections near the base. The stamens are conspicuously exserted. The buds are nodding before flowering.

Habitat: 300–5,500′. Brushy or rocky places, open forests in dry conditions. FW, CH, LC, UC.

Comments: The species name *rhomboidea* ("diamond-shaped") refers to the more or less diamond shape of the upper part of the petals. Another California *Clarkia* that is not native to this area, but still often encountered along roadsides because it is always in wildflower seed packets, is *Clarkia amoena.* It has been bred to produce a variety of colors as well as double-flowered forms.

Clarkia unguiculata Native annual
Elegant Clarkia May–Jul

Description: 1–3′ tall, straggly-looking with grayish green leaves rolled inward. The purplish sepals open to form a cuplike structure from which long clawed flowers emerge. The petals are spaced widely apart, and are spidery in appearance, the upper parts rectangular to round, the lower part narrowed into a claw that is often of a different color. The anthers are conspicuous, and sometimes scarlet in color.

Habitat: 100–1,200′. Brushy or rocky slopes or dry open areas in lower foothills. GR, CH, FW.

Comments: When they flower, spring is truly fading into summer. Native Americans used the seeds to make pinole, a meal made from small seeds of many native plants, especially Chia, Red Maids, and grass seed. After grinding and sifting, it was eaten with the fingers.

Elegant Clarkia

Clarkia williamsonii Native annual
Williamson's Clarkia May–Jun

Description: To 3′ tall. Narrow 2″ long leaves. Flower buds erect, and open flowers are bowl-shaped. Each lavender-pink, 1″ long, fan-shaped petal has a white center and dark spot on the outer edge. The fuzzy, 4-lobed red stigma rises above the 8 white anthers in the flower center.

Habitat: Below 6,000′. Open fields, dry places. GR, FW, LC.

Comments: Found only in California in the Sierra Nevada foothills from Fresno north to Nevada County. Some populations in the Yosemite area have wine red flowers. Williamson's Clarkia is uncommon in our area, though a large population is found at Hell's Half Acre. Clarkias are sometimes called Fairy Fans. Over 40 species and subspecies of Clarkia grow in California, many of them rare.

Williamson's Clarkia

JULIE S. CARVILLE

Fireweed

Epilobium angustifolium ssp. *circumvagum*
Native perennial
Fireweed   Jul–Sep

Description: 1–6′ plant with oval, opposite leaves. The long inflorescence is heavily festooned with showy rose to lilac-purple flowers. The white stamens contrast with the rose-colored petals. Fruit 2–3″, splits at maturity, releasing airborne seeds like thistledown.

Habitat: 3,500–7,000′. Stream edges, wet shaded outcroppings, and moist places in mountains. UC, MM, RP, RO.

Comments: Called Fireweed because of its tendency to come back rapidly in abundance on newly burned areas. The plant is more common to the north. It is a plant of the high mountains here. The young stems are edible raw or cooked. Attractive to bees, it has a reputation for making excellent honey.

CAROL WITHAM

Panicled Willowherb

Epilobium brachycarpum   Native annual
Panicled Willowherb   Jun–Oct

Description: 1–3′ tall with stout branching stems bearing linear alternate leaves. The stems have a unique peeling surface. Pale pink to rose petals to ½″.

Habitat: 100–6,500′. Widespread in wet or dry situations, sun or shade, along roadsides, gravel beds, and grassy flats and other disturbed places. GR, CH, FW, LC, UC, RP.

Comments: A tough, prolific, and adaptable plant. Sooner or later, anyone growing plants in containers will have this one show up. It is so common in disturbed areas that most people tend to think it is an introduced weed, not realizing that it is a California native. The flowers are on tall wandlike stems and occur from midsummer until cold weather sets in.

Epilobium canum   Native perennial
California Fuchsia   Jun–Oct

Description: 1–3′ semi-woody perennial spreading by runners. Linear to ovate leaves are green to grayish and alternate on the stem. The red flowers are in a funnel-like tube with the petals cleft toward the tip. The stamens are conspicuously exserted.

Habitat: Below 9,000′. Occasional on rocky outcrops, sandy or gravelly ridges, and dry brushy places in canyons and on mountain slopes. CH, FW, LC, UC, RO.

Comments: This plant remains more widely known by its former name, *Zauschneria californica.* It is a favorite of hummingbirds and gardeners. Many forms are in cultivation, differing in size, leaf color, and flower color. In the Sierra Nevada, plants are usually glandular with lanceolate to ovate green leaves. This is one of the last wildflowers in our area to bloom in the autumn.

KAREN CALLAHAN

California Fuchsia

Epilobium densiflorum   Native annual
Denseflower Willowherb   May–Aug

Description: To 5′ tall. A softly hairy, erect plant with many leaves crowded on the stem. The small pink (sometimes white) flowers bearing darker veins emerge from the axils of the upper leaves. The petals are mostly 2-lobed and sometimes hidden by the foliage.

Habitat: 100–5,800′. Common around vernal pools, seeps, streams, and ditches. VP, GR, FW, LC, UC, RP.

Comments: It arrives on the scene of newly constructed ponds and ditches early on, but is later outcompeted by other plants. It is also frequently found in drying creek beds and washes. It was formerly known as *Boisduvalia densiflora.* There are 14 species of *Epilobium* in our area but they are often overlooked because of their weedy appearance.

CINDY RUBIN

Denseflower Willowherb

Glaucous Willowherb

Epilobium glaberrimum   Native perennial
Glaucous Willowherb   Jul–Aug

Description: 1–2′ tall with multiple ascending stems and clasping, lance-shaped to oval opposite leaves. The foliage is covered with a whitish blue waxy coating. The pink to rose-purple flowers are deeply notched.

Habitat: 2,700–6,300′. Occasional on seeps, along streams, and in meadows of coniferous forests in moist but well-drained situations. LC, UC, MM, RP.

Comments: *Epilobium* is a combination of two Greek words, *epi* (upon) and *lobos* (pod). The name refers to the fact that the flowers are borne at the end of a long ovary. Look for the waxy blue leaves and pink flowers with notched petals. Few wet places above 3,000′ are without this plant.

Water Primrose

Ludwigia peploides   Native perennial
Water Primrose,
Yellow Waterweed   May–Oct

Description: Either floating or growing prostrate with many glossy green, lance-shaped leaves. It can grow to many feet across the surface of the water with its branching stems. The large bright yellow flowers with 5 oval petals are about 1″ across and show some venation.

Habitat: 100–2,000′. Surfaces of permanent ponds and slow-moving streams and ditches or growing prostrate on adjacent mud flats. AQ, RP.

Comments: A beautiful but rampant plant that can quickly cover the surface of a small pond. Ponds in which the surface is mostly covered by *Ludwigia* or other floating plants are not favored by waterfowl, but the seeds and foliage do provide food for waterfowl and muskrats and shelter for fish fry and aquatic insects.

Oenothera elata   Native biennial
Evening Primrose   Jun–Sep

Description: 1–4′ tall. A fast-growing plant with a stout stem covered with short hairs. Large, lance-shaped leaves. The showy clear lemon yellow flowers are up to 3″ across (petals 1–1½″) and fade to an orange-red shade.

Habitat: Below 6,000′. Moist open places. FW, LC, UC, MM.

Comments: All evening primroses open with a sudden quick motion that some claim can not only be seen but can also be heard. They open at night or late evening and close by midday. The flowers have a perfume that attracts moths. It blooms throughout the summer. It reseeds prolifically. There are two subspecies; the one in our area is ssp. *hirsutissima.* The other one, ssp. *hookeri,* is found in the Coast Ranges from central California south.

KAREN CALLAHAN

Evening Primrose

JULIE S. CARVILLE

Rockfringe, *Epilobium obcordatum,* of the Evening Primrose family, creeps over the rocks in vibrant pink at Grouse Ridge.

Orchidaceae
ORCHID FAMILY
Karen Callahan

California orchids are terrestrial perennials with unbranched stems and parallel-veined leaves. They have bilaterally symmetrical flowers of 3 sepals and 3 petals in various arrangements. The flower twists, rotating as it develops. *The stamens and pistil are fused into a column above the ovary and opposite to the lower lip.* The fruit is a capsule and seeds are dustlike. Most orchids have evolved a floral design and scent attractive to specific insect pollinators. With some 30,000 species, the Orchid family is the second largest family of plants. Only the Asteraceae (Sunflower family) has more species. The family worldwide has 800 genera; 11 are found in California, and 9 genera and 18 species in Nevada and Placer Counties.

Phantom Orchid

JULIE S. CARVILLE

Cephalanthera austiniae Native perennial
Phantom Orchid May–Aug

Description: 1–2′ tall. Roots thickened and fibrous. Up to 20 small, waxy white flowers occur along a single white, erect, leafless stalk. The lower lip of the flower has a sticky yellow area. The curved upper petals form a "hood." The flowers are very faintly scented.

Habitat: 900–6,600′. Forest litter, often near small streams, open shade. LC, UC, RP.

Comments: Our only white orchid with no green leaves. Uncommon and seldom seen, at first glance the Phantom Orchid might be taken for a fungus, at least until closer examination reveals the white flowers. The entire plant looks and feels waxy. It is usually found growing in layers of forest duff. The Rock Creek Nature Trail has been a consistently good place to see Phantom Orchids.

Corallorhiza maculata   Native perennial
Spotted Coralroot Orchid   May–Sep

Description: 1–2′ tall. Plant lacks green leaves and can be in shades of red, brown, yellow, or purple. The single erect stalk bears many (8–40) small flowers, each with distinctive spots on the white lower 3-lobed petal.

Habitat: Below 9,000′. Humus of shaded conifer forests, dry or moist. LC, UC.

Comments: Coralroots depend on mycorrhizal soil fungi for nutrients and are apparently restricted to dry acidic soils covered by decomposing litter. Coralroot superficially resembles Pinedrops, *Pterospora andromedea,* in the Heath family. Pinedrops is larger and has sticky, urn-shaped flowers characteristic of the Heath family.

Spotted Coralroot Orchid

Corallorhiza striata   Native perennial
Striped Coralroot Orchid   May–Aug

Description: 1–2′ tall. Plant lacks green leaves. Colors variable: brown, tan, red, or purple. A single erect stalk bears many small striped flowers, each with a darker lower petal curved forward. The flower column is yellow and over the lower lip.

Habitat: 300–6,600′. Humus of shaded or open mixed conifer forests. LC, UC.

Comments: Coralroots do not manufacture their own food as most plants do but instead depend on soil fungi for their nutrients. Coralroot rhizomes may produce several flowering stalks. The Striped Coralroot Orchid often grows along with the Spotted Coralroot Orchid but tends to bloom a few days ahead of it. It is generally less common. The structure of the lower petal serves as a landing pad for pollinators.

Striped Coralroot Orchid

Clustered Ladyslipper Orchid

JULIE S. CARVILLE

Cypripedium fasciculatum   Native perennial
Clustered Ladyslipper Orchid   Apr–Jul

Description: 2–12″ tall. The plant has 2 broad opposite green leaves 2–6″ long. The flower stalks arise from the base of the leaves and bear clusters of 2–4 drooping green and red-brown flowers 1½″ wide. Upper flower petals are pointed, but the lower petals have fused to form the distinctive "lady's slipper."

Habitat: 500–6,000′. Partial shade, moist slopes. LC, UC.

Comments: The pouch's function is to temporarily entrap tiny native wasps and transfer pollen to their bodies. The wasps can only escape by crawling through a narrow passageway that puts them in contact with the anthers and stigma. Nevada County is the southernmost range of this rare orchid. Populations in California are small and reproduce very slowly.

Stream Orchid

KAREN CALLAHAN

Epipactis gigantea   Native perennial
Stream Orchid, Chatterbox   Mar–Oct

Description: Stem to 3′ with 10 or more green leaves. Twelve or more flowers occur along the stem, usually all facing the same direction. The flower color varies from red to brown, green, or white. The petals and sepals are marked with a darker vein pattern.

Habitat: Below 7,800′. Streams, seeps. MM, RP.

Comments: Stream Orchids form colonies both by spreading rhizomes and seeds. They prefer a constant source of water at their roots and are always found in wet places. The species grows throughout California but is not common in our two counties. The plant is pollinated by Syrphid Flies attracted to the honeydew scent of the flowers. It is in cultivation and is not hard to grow, provided its moisture requirements are met.

Epipactis helleborine   Non-native perennial
Broad-leaf Helleborine   May–Sep

Description: Stem 1–3′ tall. Leaves 3 to 30, alternate, plicate. It bears from 15 to 30 pinkish and green flowers that are somewhat star-shaped. The petals are about the same size as the sepals.

Habitat: Below 3,600′. Semi-shady places. FW, LC.

Comments: A European orchid that has been naturalized in parts of California. It is adapted to many habitats and seeds readily. It has attractive flowers and foliage, and is long blooming. It makes either a good garden plant for shaded gardens or a persistent weed in them, depending upon your perspective. There is a large form (to 3′) and a smaller form (under 1′) that seem to retain their size differences even if grown side by side under similar conditions. The flowers are pollinated by wasps.

Broad-leaf Helleborine

Goodyera oblongifolia   Native perennial
Rattlesnake Plantain   Jul–Aug

Description: 8–30″ tall. A basal rosette of as many as 6–8 dark green leaves, with a central greenish white stripe along the midvein, often with other greenish white reticulation across the blade. The erect flowering stem rises above the leaves and bears many small, greenish white, softly hairy flowers.

Habitat: 1,500–6,600′. Dry shaded forest floor. LC, UC.

Comments: Rattlesnake Plantain spreads by rhizomes and forms colonies in undisturbed habitats. The white veins on the dark green leaves make this an easy plant to notice and identify. It is our only native orchid in which the leaves last longer than one season. It is pollinated by bumblebees. It is one of several species of native orchids along the Rock Creek Nature Trail.

Rattlesnake Plantain

Broad-leaf Twayblade

JULIE S. CARVILLE

Listera convallarioides   Native perennial
Broad-leaf Twayblade   May–Aug

Description: 4–8″ high with 2 opposite leaves located near the middle of the stem. The plant is hairless below the flower stem. It produces 7–20 (rarely more) green flowers with a notched translucent lower lip that is larger than the other petals or sepals.

Habitat: 3,000–8,700′. Wet, shady places. MM, RP.

Comments: Twayblades are often found among ferns and mosses growing in light to deep shade and usually under shrubs. It is easy to walk by this little orchid without being aware of its existence. The flower has a trigger that fires pollen on visiting insects. Other species of *Listera* are pollinated by fungus gnats, which are the likely pollinators of this species. There are two other species of twayblade in California, both rare and neither found in our area.

Flat-spurred Piperia

KAREN CALLAHAN

Piperia transversa   Native perennial
Flat-spurred Piperia,
Royal Rein Orchid   May–Aug

Description: To 15″ tall. Plant with 2 to 5 basal leaves about 7″ long that wither before flowering. Many delicate white flowers on a 6–15″ stem. The nectar spurs are about ¼″, are perpendicular to the flower axis, and form a "criss-cross" pattern.

Habitat: Below 7,800′. Mixed oak and conifers, summer dry. LC, UC.

Comments: A similar species, *Piperia elongata*, often grows in the same forested habitat with *Piperia transversa* but is a slightly larger plant with distinctive green flowers. Look for these *Piperia* at Empire Mine State Historic Park near Grass Valley. Pollinated by Geometrid Moths.

Piperia unalascensis   Native perennial
Alaska Rein Orchid   Jun–Aug

Description: Plant 8–10" tall with 2 to 4 slender leaves to 10", the bases of which wrap around the stem. Many tiny, fragrant, pale green flowers, each flower with a slight twist, forming a loose spiral up the slender leafless stem. The flower spur is less than ¼" long.

Habitat: Below 9,000'. Among shrubs in dry forests. LC, UC.

Comments: Alaska Rein Orchid is native from Alaska to Quebec, through the midwestern United States, and throughout most of mountainous California. It can be differentiated from *Piperia transversa* by having spurs about the same length as the lip (not twice as long) and by its loosely flowered inflorescence. The plant used to be known as *Habenaria unalascensis,* a name that is still occasionally used.

JULIE S. CARVILLE • KAREN CALLAHAN

Alaska Rein Orchid

Platanthera leucostachys   Native perennial
White Bog Orchid,
Sierra Rein Orchid   Jun–Sep

Description: 6–36" tall. Green cauline leaves along the stalk. The pure white flowers have a long forward-curving nectar spur below the column and lip. The spur is longer than the lip.

Habitat: Below 10,000'. Wet meadows, seeps. AQ, MM, RP.

Comments: Look for White Bog Orchid in Sierra meadows among Alpine Lily, Corn Lily, and Swamp Onion. Formerly known as *Habenaria dilatata.* All members of the genus *Platanthera* and some members of the genus *Piperia* were included in the genus *Habenaria* until recently. Pollinated by moths with a proboscis long enough to reach into the nectar spur. The flowers on this species are white, whereas the flowers on *P. sparsiflora* are greenish.

RICHARD HANES

White Bog Orchid

Sparsely Flowered Bog Orchid

Platanthera sparsiflora   Native perennial
Sparsely Flowered Bog Orchid   May–Sep

Description: 1½–2′ tall with evenly spaced lance-shaped leaves on a tall stem. It may have more than 100 green to yellowish green flowers. The yellow column occupies most of the interior of the flower. The narrow sepals are reflexed and sometimes twisted, making the flowers look narrow. The nectar spur length is equal to that of the lip.

Habitat: 4,000–10,000′. Along streams, on seeps, and in boggy places. AQ, MM, RP.

Comments: The common name can be misleading because the plant sometimes can bear as many as 120 flowers. Pollinated by moths. This is the most common of the green-flowered bog orchids in California and the only one found in our area.

Western Ladies' Tresses

Spiranthes porrifolia   Native perennial
Western Ladies' Tresses   May–Sep

Description: 6–36″ tall with 3–5 basal leaves. As many as 100 flowers are arranged in a distinctive twisted spiral around the green stem. The flowers are creamy yellowish with recurved lips.

Habitat: Below 7,500′. Wet, meadows. MM, SG, RP.

Comments: Other habitats are rocky wet cliffs and serpentine seeps. The Western Ladies' Tresses can be distinguished from the Hooded Ladies' Tresses by its yellowish-white inflorescence (versus white) and its lance-shaped to egg-shaped lip (versus violin-shaped). The petals and sepals do not unite to form a hood as they do in the Hooded Ladies' Tresses.

Spiranthes romanzoffiana   Native perennial
Hooded Ladies' Tresses   Jul–Oct

Description: 6–18″ tall. The 3–6 basal leaves are 1–5″ long in a grasslike cluster. The stem leaves are few, ½–3″ long. The white flowers are in a twisted spiral around the stem. The sepals and petals are fused to form a tight hood over the downward-curved lip.

Habitat: Below 10,000′. Wet places such as seeps, meadows, shorelines, and temporary streambeds. MM, RP.

Comments: One of the latest blooming orchids in California, the fragrant flowers are pollinated by such native bees as bumblebees, Cuckoo Bees, Leaf-cutting Bees, and Halictid Bees. The flowers are arranged in a tightly wound inflorescence forming a 3-row spiral up the stalk. Both species of *Spiranthes* that occur in California occur in our area.

Hooded Ladies' Tresses

In early spring, yellow-flowered buttercups fill the wet meadow surrounding this Quaking Aspen grove.

Orobanchaceae
BROOM-RAPE FAMILY
Chet Blackburn

Annual or perennial herbaceous root parasites. *Low, fleshy herbs similar to the Snapdragon family but lacking chlorophyll. Parasitic on roots of other plants.* Alternate scales in place of leaves. The bisexual flowers typically have from 2–5 united sepals and 5 united petals. The fruit is a capsule containing many very small seeds. There are 14 genera and 200 species worldwide, and 2 genera with 13 species in California. Both of the California genera and 5 species are in our area.

California Groundcone

Boschniakia strobilacea   Native perennial
California Groundcone   May–Jul

Description: 4–12″ tall. A conelike spike arising from a cormlike basal thickening at the junction of its connection to the host plant. Plant generally reddish brown to dark purple, but can be yellow. The leaves are scalelike. The flowers are 2-lipped, sessile, in a dense spike more or less concealed by bracts.

Habitat: Below 9,500′. Open woods, chaparral, or any place where manzanita would be found. CH, FW, LC, UC, SG.

Comments: Parasitizes roots of manzanitas and Toyon. Seldom seen by the casual observer who normally isn't looking under shrubbery. Easily overlooked because of their resemblance to pine cones. If your eye catches the glimpse of a purplish flower peeking out from what looks like a pine cone, you have found this unusual parasitic plant.

KAREN CALLAHAN

Orobanche fasciculata   Native annual
Clustered Broom-rape   May–Jul

Description: 1–6″ tall. It produces numerous flowers in a cluster of stems. From 5 to 20 slender pale yellow to pale orange or purple flowers are about 1″ long. The calyx lobes are shorter than the tube.

Habitat: Below 10,000′. Brushy to bare places in foothills and coniferous forests. CH, FW, LC, UC, SG, SA, SP.

Comments: Seed germination is apparently triggered by chemicals found on the roots of the host plants, especially on shrubs such as Yerba Santa and Artemisia. The host plant may not be immediately apparent because the roots of the host may extend for some distance. It is usually found in drier places than the Naked Broom-rape.

KAREN CALLAHAN

Clustered Broom-rape

Orobanche uniflora   Native annual
Naked Broom-rape   Mar–Apr

Description: 1–2″ high. A single flower per plant (or rarely 2 or 3) at the tip of a slender scape. The tubular, slightly curved flowers are lavender to pink and may be streaked with yellow, ½–1½″ long. The flowers are 2-lipped, with 2 lobes on top and 3 on the bottom.

Habitat: 200–6,400′. Brushy slopes, rocky outcrops, wet meadows, and generally moist places. GR, CH, FW, LC, UC, SP.

Comments: This leafless plant obtains its nourishment by attaching itself to the roots of other plants such as sedums, saxifrages, and a few members of the Sunflower family. The plants with deep purple flowers have been called var. *purpurea*. Another species, *O. corymbosa,* is found on the eastern edge of our two counties and parasitizes the Sagebrush, *Artemisia tridentata.*

RICHARD HANES

Naked Broom-rape

270

Oxalidaceae
OXALIS FAMILY
Richard Hanes

Mostly perennial herbs, many with fleshy tubers or rhizomes. The leaves are compound and cloverlike, closing and drooping at night. *The flowers are bisexual, with 5 sepals and 5 petals, fused or unfused, with 10 stamens.* The fruit is an explosive capsule. There are 8 genera and about 950 species worldwide, with only 1 genus and 12 species in California. Of those 12 species, 8 are non-natives. There are at least 3 species in Nevada and Placer Counties, all introduced.

Bermuda Buttercup

Oxalis pes-caprae　　　Non-native perennial
Bermuda Buttercup　　　　Nov–Mar

Description: 4–12″ tall. Stems mostly underground, often with bulblets. The leaves are in a loose basal rosette on petioles 4–8″ and are often spotted. The lower surfaces are hairy. Bright lemon yellow flowers in early spring.

Habitat: Below 1,700′. Disturbed areas, grassland. GR, FW.

Comments: Mostly an urban weed. There are at least four species of *Oxalis* in our area, but none of ours is native. The members of the genus *Oxalis* (from the Greek *oxus*, meaning sour) are often called sour clover because of the resemblance of the foliage to clover and the sour taste of the leaves, which contain oxalic acid. This one is from South Africa, and is the largest and most attractive one in our area. There are 3 natives in the state but none east of the Coast Ranges.

Paeoniaceae
PEONY FAMILY
Richard Hanes

Perennial subshrubs, with one to several stems. The leaves are basal and on stems, alternate, and deeply dissected to compounded into 3 parts. The flowers are solitary or few in terminal clusters. There are **5–6 leathery sepals. Petals 5–10. Many stamens. Pistils 2–5, thick walled, surrounded at the base by a lobed nectary disk.** The ovary is superior. The family is included in the Buttercup family, Ranunculaceae, by many botanists. Only 1 genus and 2 species occur in California, and 1 of those species is found in our area.

Paeonia brownii   Native perennial
Western Peony   May–Jun

Description: 6–18″ tall. Low, rounded, and shrublike. There are 5 to 8 leaves per stem, and they are covered with whitish powder. Segment tips are rounded. The flowers are on the re-curved leafy stem. The 5–6 petals are rounded, maroon to bronze in the center, with a margin that is yellowish or greenish.

Habitat: 4,000–6,500′. Open dry pine forest edges and edges of alder thickets, chaparral, and drier parts of meadows. LC, UC, MM, SP.

Comments: There are two species of *Paeonia* in the state but the other, *P. californica,* is confined to Southern California. Native Americans made tea from the roots to treat lung problems. They are bee pollinated. They can be seen at Bear Valley in Nevada County and Sagehen Creek East.

JULIE S. CARVILLE

Western Peony

Papaveraceae
POPPY FAMILY
Vicki Lake

Mostly annual or perennial herbs but includes a few shrubs. The leaves are alternate, without stipules, usually lobed or dissected but sometimes entire. The flowers are regular, bisexual, and the parts free. Showy *petals 4 or 6. Stamens numerous.* Ovary superior. *Sepals 2–3, falling off when a flower opens.* Fruit a capsule. The *sap is often yellowish and milky.* Some botanists put some of the members of this family, such as *Dicentra,* into a separate family, Fumariaceae. There are 40 genera and roughly 400 species worldwide. Represented by 14 genera and 38 species in California; 6 genera and 9 species are known from Nevada and Placer Counties.

Prickly Poppy

Argemone munita Native annual/perennial
Prickly Poppy Mar–Aug

Description: 2–5′ tall. Deeply lobed, silvery leaves. There are numerous yellow spines on the stems and leaves. The large (up to 5″) flowers have 6 petals and a dense yellow center of stamens. The sap is yellow.

Habitat: Below 10,000′. Dry open and disturbed places on the eastern side of the Sierra Nevada. SP.

Comments: A general rule for the protection of our native plants is to "Look but don't touch." This is one plant that enforces that rule. Every part of the aboveground plant except the petals is spiny. Native Americans roasted and mashed the seeds to apply as a salve to burns. Toxic if ingested, especially the seeds. The prickles irritate the skin of some people. Look for it in Ward Canyon near Lake Tahoe.

PRENTISS FERGUSON

Corydalis caseana ssp. *caseana*
Native perennial
Sierra Corydalis, Fitweed   Jun–Aug

Description: Plant 2–3′ high, with waxy blue-green stems and leaves. The inflorescence is narrow and dense, with 50 or more spurred pink to white flowers having purple petal tips. The leaves are bipinnately divided, with numerous short, oval lobes.

Habitat: 4,000–9,000′. Uncommon; shady moist places. UC, MM, RP, SA.

Comments: A denizen of alder thickets and shaded stream banks in coniferous forests, the tops of the plants, stems, leaves, and flowers are toxic, containing isoquinoline alkaloids that may be lethal if eaten in sufficient quantities. Cattle accustomed to the area in which it is found will generally not touch it, but it has caused loss of livestock.

RICHARD HANES

Sierra Corydalis

Dicentra formosa   Native perennial
Wild Bleeding Heart   Mar–Jul

Description: Plant 8–18″ tall, with fernlike foliage that is sometimes whitish blue-green. The flattened heart-shaped flowers occur in nodding clusters above the lacy pinnate leaves. The flowers are mostly rose-pink, although occasionally white ones are found. The outer petals have spreading tips.

Habitat: Below 7,000′. Damp, shaded places. LC, UC, RP.

Comments: A decoction of pounded roots was used medicinally by Native Americans, including as a worm medicine, but it does contain potentially poisonous alkaloids. As with trilliums, the seeds of this plant have oil-bearing appendages that are attractive to ants. Ants disperse the plant by carrying off the seeds, then discarding them after utilizing the oil body attachment.

JULIE S. CARVILLE

Wild Bleeding Heart

Steer's Head

Dicentra uniflora   Native perennial
Steer's Head   May–Jul

Description: Plant 1–3″ tall. The inflorescence
is 1-flowered. The flower is white to pink or
lilac, and nodding. The flattened steer head–like
petals and 2 long reflexed sepals give the flower
a Texas Longhorn appearance. Typically it has a
single pinnately divided leaf, usually whitish blue
on the underside, with 1–3 sections divided into
broad lobes.

Habitat: 5,300–9,500′. Well-drained gravelly
and rocky places. LC, UC, RO.

Comments: Tends to bloom shortly after the
snow melt, hence is not often seen because it is
too early in the season for many hikers to encounter. Be careful…when first exposed to this plant,
it causes a person's face to break out…with a
smile when told the common name. Few common
names seem more appropriate than this one.

Tufted Poppy

Eschscholzia caespitosa   Native annual
Tufted Poppy   Mar–Jun

Description: Plant 2–12″ high, the herbage
sometimes whitish blue. Several stems arise
from a tuft of basal leaves. The leaves are dissected into many narrow divisions. The flowers
are yellow to orange, and the petal bases sometimes orange spotted. The petals are less than 1″
long. The ovary is not subtended by a spreading
outer rim.

Habitat: Below 5,000′. Dry flats and open
chaparral. CH, GR, FW.

Comments: The larger, orange form of this
plant is common in our area and is usually
mistaken for the California Poppy, but lacks the
platformlike rim at the base of the flower that is
conspicuous on the California Poppy. The
masses of "California Poppies" at Bridgeport in
the spring are this species.

Eschscholzia californica
Native annual/perennial
California Poppy   Apr–Sep

Description: 6–24″ tall. Flowers large and bowl-shaped, orange to yellow. (White cultivars have been developed horticulturally.) Petals 1–2½″ long. A double-rimmed round flangelike structure is found below the ovary. Lacy, finely dissected bluish leaves.

Habitat: Below 6,500′. Grassy and open places. CH, GR, FW, LC, UC.

Comments: The California state flower. Native Americans used juice from the root as a wash for headaches and took it as an emetic for stomachaches. A decoction of the flowers was rubbed into hair to kill lice. Flowers underneath a bed were believed to put a child to sleep. Today the plant is used widely as an ornamental in gardens and is common in wildflower mixes.

California Poppy

Eschscholzia lobbii   Native annual
Frying Pans   Mar–May

Description: Plant 4–12″ high. The inflorescence is 1-flowered. Flowers ¾″, pale orange to yellow, the petals less than ½″ long with a single rim below the ovary. The dissected linear leaves occur at the plant base.

Habitat: Below 2,000′. Open grassy places. GR, CH, FW.

Comments: The species description was authored by Edward Lee Greene (1843–1915), a California professor of botany and strong believer of priority in nomenclature. At first glance it looks like a stunted version of the California Poppy, but it can easily be distinguished by the more finely dissected leaves and especially by the fact that the petal tips are triangular rather than rounded. This gives the 4-petaled flower a somewhat square appearance as well.

Frying Pans

Cream Cups

Platystemon californicus   Native annual
Cream Cups   Mar–Jul

Description: Plant 4–12″ high, shaggy and hairy. Single flowers occur on elongated flower stems, each flower with 6 creamy petals that have a bright yellow basal spot, but flower color can range from all yellow, to yellow and cream colored, to almost all white. The unopened buds are nodding. The linear, opposite leaves occur in a cluster at or near the plant base.

Habitat: Below 3,300′. Open fields, sandy soils, and burn sites, including those on serpentine. GR, CH, FW, LC, SG.

Comments: A highly variable plant in appearance, flower color, and size, but only 1 species of *Platystemon* occurs in California. Native Americans ate the leaves as greens. The sap is colorless.

Poppies, lupines, and gilias carpet a hillside of Blue Oaks at the Spenceville Wildlife Area in April.

Phytolaccaceae
POKEWEED FAMILY
Chet Blackburn

Primarily a tropical family with simple, alternate, entire leaves. The flowers are bisexual (rarely unisexual). There are 4–5 persistent sepals, no petals, and 3–10 stamens arranged in 1 or 2 series. The *ovary is several celled within locules.* There are 17 genera and 125 species, almost entirely confined to the American tropics. There are 3 genera of only 3 species in the United States, with 2 of them being confined to Florida. There is 1 introduced species (from the eastern United States) in California, and that species occurs in our area.

Phytolacca americana   Non-native perennial
Pokeweed   Jun–Oct

Description: 1–8′ with succulent hollow stems that turn red as the year progresses. Large, oval-shaped, thin, foul-smelling leaves. The white flowers are on short pedicels in a terminal raceme. Later the ovary changes to a purplish black attractive fruit.

Habitat: 100–3,000′. Occasional to locally common in somewhat moist disturbed areas. FW, LC, RP.

Comments: Native to the eastern United States. All parts of the plant are toxic. The seeds are toxic but the berry flesh is only mildly so. However, young shoots have been eaten widely by many people as "Pokeweed" after boiling twice and discarding the water. Berries have also been made into pies. The cooking breaks down the poison. Juice from the berries was widely used as a dye.

KAREN CALLAHAN

Pokeweed

Plantaginaceae
PLANTAIN FAMILY
Chet Blackburn

Annual or perennial herbs. The *leaves are in a basal rosette, with parallel veining.* The flowers bisexual (rarely unisexual). The inflorescence consists of a leafless stalk bearing a *spike of numerous brownish flowers with 4 sepals, 4 small brown petals (corolla transparent, dry, and papery),* and usually 2 stamens. The fruit is often a capsule and the seeds are often mucilaginous. Of little economic importance except for some negative impact from weedy species. However, 1 species, *Plantago psyllium,* is in cultivation (not in California) and the seeds are used to make a laxative. There are 3 genera and about 270 species worldwide, with 1 genus and 15 species in California, and 4 species in our area.

California Plantain

Plantago erecta
California Plantain

Native annual
Feb–Jun

Description: 2–6″ tall. A small, drab plant with narrow, fuzzy, grasslike leaves. One to many flowering stalks bearing a short, crowded terminal spike of whitish green flowers to silvery white papery flowers, each with 4 slightly curled-back petals and dark stamens.

Habitat: Below 2,200′. Grasslands and open woodlands, including sandy, clay, or serpentine soils. GR, CH, FW, SP, SG.

Comments: Abundant but inconspicuous. Plantain flowers are not normally considered attractive. This one is, but it takes a hand lens to see the beauty. The reflexed, concave translucent petals surround the pistil and stamens as if it were a flimsy negligee trying to seduce its pollinators. Unlike most plantains, this one appears to be insect pollinated, not wind pollinated.

KAREN CALLAHAN

Plantago lanceolata   Non-native perennial
English Plantain, Buckhorn   Apr–Sep

Description: To 18″ tall. The leaves are all clustered at the base and conspicuously ribbed, 4–12″ long, usually less than 1½″ wide, dark green, somewhat hairy, and tapering to a point. One to several flower stalks rise above and are longer than the leaves. Each stalk terminates in a dense flower spike. Rings of small white flowers with exserted stamens work their way up to the top as the season progresses.

Habitat: Below 6,500′. A common weed of lawns, roadsides, pastures, and other disturbed sites. GR, CH, FW, LC, UC.

Comments: Native to Eurasia. A tough plant capable of withstanding much trampling. It can be seen growing even in parking lots and driveways.

CINDY RUBIN

English Plantain

Plantago major   Non-native perennial
Common Plantain   Apr–Sep

Description: 5–15″ tall. A flat rosette of stalked, ribbed, smooth, glossy, 3–7″ egg-shaped leaves from a deep taproot. A leafless erect flower stalk containing tiny greenish white flowers soon replaced by brown seed. A variable plant in size and form.

Habitat: Below 7,000′. Disturbed sites and cultivated fields, usually damp places. GR, CH, FW, LC, UC, RP, MM.

Comments: There are 15 species of plantains in California, and more than half (8) of them are introduced. Both the native and introduced species are important host plants for various species of the Checkerspot butterfly. According to Willis Linn Jepson, Native Americans called it "The White Man's Foot" because of its inevitable appearance in new settlements.

JULIE S. CARVILLE

Common Plantain

Polemoniaceae
PHLOX FAMILY
Richard Hanes

Annual or perennial, herbs, shrubs, or vines. The leaves are simple or compound, cauline (or most in a basal rosette), alternate or opposite. The inflorescence consists of cymes, heads, or solitary flowers or flowers in spiny-bracted heads. *The flower parts in 5s.* The petals are united at the base to form a *slender tube with abruptly spreading petal lobes. The ovary is superior. The stamens alternate with the corolla lobes and the filaments are fused to the corolla tube or throat. Pistil 1 per flower. Style 3-cleft.* There are 19 genera, with 320 species worldwide. Of those, 11 genera and 48 species occur in Nevada and Placer Counties.

KAREN CALLAHAN

Largeflower Collomia

Collomia grandiflora   Native annual
Largeflower Collomia   May–Jul

Description: 4–40″ tall. Stem erect, sometimes branched, hairy, and glandular. The leaves are alternate and sessile. The basal leaves are lance-shaped and toothed. The cauline leaves are lance-shaped to linear, and entire. The calyx is densely glandular-hairy. The funnel-shaped flowers are sessile. The corolla color is yellow-salmon to whitish. The pollen is blue.

Habitat: 2,000–8,200′. Dry, open and wooded slopes. CH, FW, LC, UC.

Comments: Cultivated as an ornamental, it blooms over a long period of time. The flower color is difficult to describe, with terms such as "salmon colored," "light orange," and "peach colored" sometimes used, but none of them providing a completely adequate description of its beautiful coloration.

Collomia heterophylla   Native annual
Vari-leaf Collomia   Apr–Aug

Description: 2–8″ high. Stems erect, branched diffusely, hairy, and glandular. The sessile leaves are alternate, 1–2 pinnately lobed, and hairy. The inflorescence consists of both terminal and axillary clusters. The flower is sessile and funnel-shaped. The corolla is usually pink but white forms also exist.

Habitat: Below 4,000′. Sandy to gravelly open shady areas. CH, FW, LC.

Comments: As both the common name and botanical name suggest, the lacy foliage is variable in shape, with the depth and width of the lobing and the number of lobes all differing from plant to plant and even on the same plant. It is a prolific seed producer and a rapid colonizer in disturbed areas within its range.

RICHARD HANES

Vari-leaf Collomia

Gilia capitata   Native annual
Globe Gilia   Apr–Jul

Description: Stems 6–12″ tall, glandular or with white hairs. The leaves are alternate, the lower ones 1–2 pinnately lobed and the midribs with white hairs. The upper cauline leaves are much reduced. The inflorescence is a spherical terminal head about 1″ in diameter with 5–100 flowers. The calyx is lightly to densely white-woolly, its lobes acute to acuminate. The corolla color is pale to light blue-violet. Both stamens and style are exserted.

Habitat: Below 7,000′. Dry, open, sandy to rocky areas and roadcuts in both sun and shade. CH, FW, LC.

Comments: The rocky hillside of the American River Canyon on Highway 49 just outside of Auburn is one of many places where this plant is commonly found.

KAREN CALLAHAN

Globe Gilia

Bridge's Gilia

Gilia leptalea   Native annual
Bridge's Gilia   Jun–Sep

Description: 1–14″ tall. The plant is glabrous or slightly glandular-hairy. The stems are erect, with spreading branches. The cauline leaves are linear, entire, and alternate along the stem. The lower leaves are rarely pinnately lobed. The inflorescence is loose and spreading, with the flowers mostly in pairs on pedicels. The corolla is funnel-shaped. The throat can be white, yellow, pink, or violet. The petal lobes are ovate-acute, pink or violet. The style and stamens are well exserted.

Habitat: 4,500–9,700′. Open woods. LC, UC.

Comments: Common at the right elevations in our area. There are a few rocky openings along Bowman Lake Road off Highway 20 that are carpeted in pink during late summer from the masses of this little beauty growing there.

RICHARD HANES

Birds-eye Gilia

Gilia tricolor   Native annual
Birds-eye Gilia   Mar–Apr

Description: 4–15″. Many branched stems arise from the base that are long, leafy, and glabrous or white-hairy below. The inflorescence is solitary or in 2–5 flower clusters and glandular. The corolla is short, broad, and bowl-like. The flowers are tricolored, with the lobes dark blue-violet shading to white, the tube yellow to orange, and the top of the throat spotted with dark violet. Stamens and styles are slightly exserted. Pollen is bright blue.

Habitat: Less than 3,600′. Common in open grasslands, open hillsides, and roadsides. GR, CH, FW, LC, SP.

Comments: A small flower, it is attractive both in masses and individually when viewed with a hand lens, except that when staring at it you sometimes get the feeling that it is staring back.

JULIE S. CARVILLE

Ipomopsis aggregata   Native biennial
Scarlet Gilia, Skyrocket   Jun–Sep

Description: Stems erect, 12–32" tall, slightly hairy, simple or branched. The basal leaves are pinnately 9–11-lobed. The cauline leaves 5–7-lobed, alternate. The inflorescence is a one-sided lateral cluster of 1–7 short-pedicelled flowers. The corolla is trumpet-shaped and bright red with yellow mottling. The stamens and style are exserted.

Habitat: 3,300–9,900'. Openings in shrublands and woodlands. CH, LC, UC, SA.

Comments: Pollinated by hummingbirds that are drawn to the eye-catching scarlet flowers. It was previously in the genus *Gilia.* The tips of the tubular flowers flare out to become star-shaped. It favors dry open areas with coarse or sandy soil. One location where it can be found is near Perazzo Creek north of Truckee at 7,200'.

JULIE S. CARVILLE

Scarlet Gilia

Ipomopsis tenuituba   Native perennial
Slender-tubed Skyrocket   Jun–Aug

Description: 10–24" tall. Both basal and stem leaves somewhat hairy, but the basal leaves have usually withered by the time of flowering. The long flowers are tubular, 1–2" long, white to pink, and have long, narrow, slightly recurving petals. Style is included in or just slightly exserted from the flower tube.

Habitat: Above 7,500'. Gravelly to rocky slopes. MM, SA, RO, SP.

Comments: Although it is a perennial, the plant dies after it flowers. The foliage has a somewhat skunklike odor. The Latin name *tenuituba* means "slender trumpet," referring to the flowers. Pollinators for the plant include hummingbirds, Hawk Moths, and Sphinx Moths. It hybridizes readily with Scarlet Gilia, *Ipomopsis aggregata.* Also called Lavender Gilia.

KAREN CALLAHAN

Slender-tubed Skyrocket

Prickly Phlox

Leptodactylon pungens   Native perennial
Prickly Phlox, Granite Gilia   May–Aug

Description: Stems 4–12″ tall. Plant low branching, hairy, and glandular. The leaves are alternate, and 3–7 palmately lobed. The inflorescence is terminal, the flowers sessile and opening in the evening. The flowers are funnel-shaped, with the corolla white or pink with purplish shading. The style is included.

Habitat: 5,000–12,000′. Open rocky or sandy areas. LC, UC, RO, SA.

Comments: The blooms open at night and are pollinated by nocturnal moths. Diurnally the corolla remains closed even during dull weather. The specific name *pungens* can have two meanings when applied to plants: one being prickly or sharp pointed, the other, having a distinctive aroma. This plant has both characteristics.

Bicolored Linanthus

Linanthus bicolor   Native annual
Bicolored Linanthus   Mar–Jun

Description: 2–6″. Plant hairy. Stems erect, the leaves cauline and opposite and palmately lobed, looking like they are in "whorls" around the stem. The inflorescence is a leafy-bracteate head. The flowers are sessile, with usually only 1 flower open at a time. The corolla is trumpet-like, the tube reddish, the throat yellow, and the lobes pink or white. Stamens are exserted.

Habitat: Less than 5,000′. Open grassy areas, chaparral, woodlands. GR, CH, FW.

Comments: Common and widespread in the state. The starlike flowers are at the end of an unusually long floral tube. There are 35 species of *Linanthus* in the state and at least 5 of them are found in our area.

Linanthus ciliatus   Native annual
Whisker Brush   Apr–Jul

Description: To 12″ tall. Plant hairy. Stems
erect, simple, or branched at base. Leaves
cauline, opposite, palmately lobed. Inflorescence
headlike, spherical, flowers sessile. Corolla
trumpetlike, tube white or pink, hairy outside.
Throat yellow, lobes light to deep pink with
darker pink or red spots at base.

Habitat: Below 9,000′. Open or wooded areas.
CH, FW, LC, UC, SA.

Comments: Common. Named for the dense,
whiskery hairs on the leaf lobes. It can be
distinguished from the similar-looking Bicolored
Linanthus, *L. bicolor,* by its having bract margins
that are densely white hairy and the shape of the
flower being more wheel-like than starlike.
Whisker Brush also usually has a darker rose
spot near the base of each petal.

Whisker Brush

Linanthus dichotomus   Native annual
Evening Snow   Mar–May

Description: 2–8″ tall. Relatively large, snowy
white flowers without pedicels. The sepals are
joined together by a translucent membrane for
most of their length but at the top the sepals
separate and flare outward.

Habitat: 400–3,500′. Dry open areas, especially
on serpentine. CH, FW, LC, SG.

Comments: Currently drawing much interest
from researchers. Some botanists separate it into
two subspecies based upon whether flowering is
at night or by day. Most populations are night
bloomers (ssp. *dichotomus*) but some Northern
California populations are day bloomers (ssp.
meridianus). The current *Jepson Manual* does
not recognize the subspecies.

Evening Snow

Needle Navarretia

Navarretia intertexta　　　Native annual
Needle Navarretia　　　May–Jul

Description: To 8″ tall. Stems brown, simple or branched from the base. The leaves are 1–2-pinnate, the axis and lobes needlelike and alternate. The inflorescence is a spiny-bracted head that is hairy below. The bracts and calyx lobes are needlelike. The corolla tube is long, exserted from the calyx, and pale blue to white. Stamens and style are exserted. The stigma is 2-lobed.

Habitat: Below 7,000′. Open, wet areas, meadows, vernal pools. AQ, VP, MM, RP.

Comments: The genus was named for Dr. F. Navarrete, a Spanish physician. This species is common in vernal pools and can be seen in most of the vernal pools in the Roseville-Lincoln area. Most of the other 9 species of *Navarretia* in our area are difficult to identify to the species level.

Downy Navarretia

Navarretia pubescens　　　Native annual
Downy Navarretia　　　Apr–Jun

Description: Stems 2–12″ tall, glandular, brownish red to tan. Upper leaves with white hairs; lower leaves are glabrous. The glandular-hairy inflorescence is clustered in the center of the leaves. Flowers are up to ½″ wide and bloom on solitary stems in shades of deep blue to blue-purple with white in the upper throat. The delicate stamens are attached midway in the throat and rise above the petals. The tiny stigma is 2-lobed.

Habitat: Below 3,500′. In full sun. GR, FW, CH.

Comments: View this little flower through a hand lens to enjoy its surprising beauty. It "hides" among the grasses at the Spenceville Wildlife Area and so is easily overlooked, but once found, it is a delightful discovery.

Phlox diffusa
Spreading Phlox

Native perennial
May–Aug

Description: Stems 1–12″. Woody at the base, with stems prostrate or decumbent and loosely branched. The leaves are arranged in opposite pairs along the stem, are sessile, linear-lanceolate, and entire. The inflorescence is terminal and the flowers solitary. The corolla is trumpetlike, with white, pink, or lavender petal lobes.

Habitat: 3,300–11,000′. Dry, open areas at mid to high elevations. LC, UC, SA.

Comments: The plant forms a ground-hugging mat that is a spectacular sight when in bloom. The numerous flowers grow so closely together that the rest of the plant is barely visible. Pollinated flowers change color from white to pink-purple.

JULIE S. CARVILLE

Spreading Phlox

Phlox gracilis
Slender Phlox

Native annual
May–Aug

Description: 4–8″ tall. Stems erect to decumbent, often branched and glandular-hairy. The leaves are borne on the stem, are opposite below and alternate above, oblanceolate to lanceolate, sessile, and entire. The inflorescence is terminal, with the flowers either solitary or in a cyme. The corolla is trumpetlike, the tube yellowish, and the petal lobes rose to white or violet.

Habitat: 200–6,500′. Dry to moist areas. CH, FW, LC, UC, SA.

Comments: Other phloxes are all perennials with woody bases and bear masses of flowers. This delicate species is common but inconspicuous because of its tendency to occur as scattered plants and because only a few flowers are open at a time. Some botanists place it in a separate genus, *Microsteris*.

JULIE S. CARVILLE

Slender Phlox

Showy Phlox

Phlox speciosa   Native perennial
Showy Phlox   Apr–Jun

Description: To 16″ tall. Stems from a woody base bearing narrow opposite widely spaced leaves up to 3″. The bright pink (rarely lavender or white) flowers are in loose terminal clusters. They can be more than 1″ in diameter and have petals that are notched or more deeply bilobed.

Habitat: 1,000–6,500′. Forest floors, rocky shaded slopes, and roadcuts. FW, LC, UC, SG.

Comments: It often grows in patches of Mountain Misery, *Chamaebatia foliolosa.* The plant tends to be more or less hairy or glandular above. There are 10 species of *Phlox* in the state, and 3 of them occur in our area. There are 2 subspecies of *P. speciosa.* The one that grows in our area is ssp. *occidentalis.* Look for it along the Independence Trail.

Jacob's Ladder

Polemonium californicum   Native perennial
Jacob's Ladder, Low Polemonium Jun–Aug

Description: To 1′ tall. Cespitose. Stems decumbent to erect, less than 12″ long, and glandular-hairy. Ladderlike pinnate leaves with 11–25 hairless leaflets that are lance-shaped to ovate. The inflorescence is open to headlike. The corolla is bell-shaped, the tube white, the throat blue or yellow, and the lobes blue to blue-violet. Stamens and style are exserted.

Habitat: 6,000–10,000′. Open to shaded areas in woodlands. UC, SA.

Comments: The common name refers to the ladderlike arrangement of the leaflets. In the Bible, Jacob wished for a ladder to ascend from earth to heaven. (Heaven was obviously a little closer then than it is now.) This common name is also applied to a number of other species.

Polemonium occidentale   Native perennial
Western Polemonium,
Great Polemonium   Jul–Aug

Description: 6–36″. A single erect stem arises from a short rhizome. Leaves are pinnate with a bare section of the leaf free of any leaflets toward the base. Flowers are blue or pale purple with the throat white or lightly colored. Conspicuous yellow stamens. The blue or purple style is exserted and extends beyond the stamens.

Habitat: 3,000–11,000′. Marshy places, brushy stream margins, seeps, and meadows. LC, UC, SA, MM, RP.

Comments: Formerly known as *P. caeruleum* var. *amygdalinum*. The only other two *Polemonium* species in our area, *P. californicum* and *P. pulcherrimum* var. *pulcherrimum,* prefer drier situations. Our variety is *P. occidentale* var. *occidentale.*

Western Polemonium

Polemonium pulcherrimum
    var. *pulcherrimum*   Native perennial
Showy Polemonium   Jun–Aug

Description: 12″ long suberect stems, glabrous or minutely glandular-hairy. Cespitose. Leaves are mostly basal, pinnate, ovate to round, and glandular; hairs are small. The inflorescence is crowded or headlike. The corolla is wheel-shaped to bell-shaped, the tube is white with a yellow throat, and the lobes are blue to white. The stamens and style are included in the corolla tube.

Habitat: 8,000–11,000′. Dry, rocky slopes. SA, RO.

Comments: Leaflets overlap one another in a fernlike fashion. A specimen (No. 14,997) was collected by W. L. Jepson at Summit Station in Nevada County. It was first described in 1830 by Sir William Jackson Hooker. He was Director of Kew, 1841–1865, and founder and editor of the *Journal of Botany.*

Showy Polemonium

Polygalaceae
MILKWORT FAMILY
Richard Hanes

Leaves simple, alternate, without stipules. The inflorescence is a raceme. *The flower is bilateral, resembling flowers in the Pea family.* Sepals 5, the lateral pair larger and petal-like (winged). *Petals 3 or 5, separate* with 1 lower keel petal, 2 straplike upper petals, and 0 or 2 small lateral petals. *The ovary is superior; pistil and style 1.* The sap is not milky. There are 18 genera and 800 species worldwide. Of those, 1 genus and 6 species are in California, with 1 species in Nevada and Placer Counties.

Milkwort

Polygala cornuta Native perennial
Milkwort Jun–Aug

Description: 4–40″ tall from rhizomes with many slender stems. A subshrub, erect to prostrate and woody below. The leaves are alternate, linear to ovate, to 2½″ long. The flowers are clustered at the end of the stem. Flowers ½″ or less, the upper sepal acute, the outer sepals and wings cream, greenish, or pink in bud, the keel petal dull rose to green after the pollen is shed.

Habitat: 1,000–6,300′. Rocky or gravelly slopes, common forest plant. CH, FW, LC, UC.

Comments: Herbage may be toxic. The genus name *Polygala* literally means "much milk." Some European species were once thought to increase milk flow in cows, hence the common name. The flowers of this family superficially resemble flowers of the Pea family and the plant is often mistaken for a member of that family.

Polygonaceae
BUCKWHEAT FAMILY
Vicki Lake

Annuals to trees, but mostly herbs. Stem nodes are often swollen. The leaves are simple, generally entire, mostly alternate, with or without an *expanded sheathlike base.* The inflorescence is clustered. Flowers generally bisexual, small, radial, and *without petals.* Sepals generally 5 or 6, free or united, sometimes petal-like. Stamens 3–9, free. *Ovary solitary.* Family is well represented in California with 21 genera and over 200 species. Wild buckwheats (*Eriogonum* sp.) comprise one of largest genera in the California flora and are especially attractive to butterflies. In Nevada and Placer Counties, the family is represented by 6 genera and 53 species.

Eriogonum lobbii var. *lobbii*   Native perennial
Lobb's Buckwheat   Jun–Aug

Description: Less than 6" high. Plant prostrate. The base is stout, woody, and few-branched, forming a central rosette of large, gray, densely hairy oval leaves. The inflorescence is umbel-like, the stalks often prostrate. The calyx is white to rose and dark striped. The flowers are creamy white to yellow, turning reddish orange with age.

Habitat: 4,500–11,000'. Open, gravelly, and rocky slopes and ridges. UC, SA, RO, SP, SG.

Comments: Buckwheats are an important component of California's environment and our own local environment. The seeds can be ground and used as flour. Various small mammals and birds eat flowers, foliage, and seeds, and buckwheats are hosts for several butterflies as well as important nectar sources for many insects.

JULES. CARVILLE

Lobb's Buckwheat

Naked-stem Buckwheat

JULIE S. CARVILLE

Eriogonum nudum var. *nudum*
Native perennial
Naked-stem Buckwheat   May–Nov

Description: 6–36″ tall, with long naked stems emerging from a flat basal cluster of dark green, long-petioled oval leaves. The dull green foliage is often wrinkled above and densely hairy on the undersides, giving the undersides a whitish appearance. The inflorescence is a cyme to headlike; the flower cluster bracts are oblong.

Habitat: Below 8,000′. Dry open places, especially with sand or gravel. GR, CH, FW, LC, UC, RO, SG.

Comments: Highly variable, it intergrades with all other varieties of *Eriogonum nudum*. Native Americans used the hollow stems as drinking tubes and pipes for smoking. Although sour tasting, the young stems were eaten as greens.

Pratten's Buckwheat

KAREN CALLAHAN

Eriogonum prattenianum
var. *prattenianum*   Native subshrub
Pratten's Buckwheat   May–Jul

Description: 4–20″ tall, spreading. The leaves are clustered on lower stems, the blades less than 1″ long, elliptic, densely woolly hairy. The inflorescence is headlike and slender, with leaflike bracts whorled near the middle of the flowering stem.

Habitat: 2,500–8,500′. Volcanic substrates on dry, rocky ridges and outcrops. LC, UC, RO.

Comments: An attractive subshrub first collected by Henry Pratten in Nevada City in 1851. It is abundant at Hell's Half Acre but uncommon elsewhere. Pratten spent 2 years in California as part of a geological survey. He collected 200 species of plants, 40 of which were regarded as new species at the time. Of these, 3 were named after him, but only this one retains that honor.

Eriogonum umbellatum   Native subshrub
Sulfur Buckwheat   Jun–Aug

Description: 4–20″ tall. Erect subshrub to spreading mat. Leaves variable by variety, from elliptic to round to spatula-shaped. Long petioles emerge from a basal rosette and as whorls at each branching point. The flowers are yellow, in compound umbels with a whorl of linear leaves below the primary umbel only.

Habitat: 700–10,500′. Common in open forests, chaparral, rock outcrops, and sage shrublands. CH, LC, UC, RO, SP, SA, SG.

Comments: A highly variable species with 17 recognized botanical varieties, 5 of which occur in Nevada and Placer Counties. The Native Americans used the plant medicinally for stomachaches, colds, gonorrhea, and rheumatism. They also ground the seeds into flour. Attractive and almost always available at native plant sales.

JULIE S. CARVILLE

Sulfur Buckwheat

Eriogonum wrightii   Native subshrub
Wright's Buckwheat   Aug–Oct

Description: Ranges from 3–36″ in height, depending on the variety. The plant is densely short hairy. The leaves are linear to widely elliptic and less than 1″ long. The inflorescence is dense above with several long lower branches. Flower bracts are scalelike. The calyx is whitish or pink to rose.

Habitat: 150–10,000′. Dry gravelly or rocky areas. CH, FW, LC, UC, SA, RO.

Comments: Native Americans pounded the seeds into a meal and ate it dry or mixed with water as a beverage. This is another variable species. There are 6 recognized botanical varieties, of which 2 are found in our area. *E. wrightii* ssp. *trachygonum* is common below 2,500′, while ssp. *subscaposum* is usually found at higher elevations.

KAREN CALLAHAN

Wright's Buckwheat

Mountain Sorrel

PRENTISS FERGUSON

Oxyria digyna   Native perennial
Mountain Sorrel   Jul–Sep

Description: 2–20″ high. The bright green kidney-shaped leaves with long stalks are mostly basal. The inflorescence is compact, oblong in outline, and is comprised of many small red to yellow-green flowers in a spike.

Habitat: 7,000–13,000′. Common in alpine rock crevices, on rocky slopes, and talus substrates. RO, SA.

Comments: The leaves and stems have a sour acid taste but are high in vitamin C and can be eaten raw or cooked. If eaten in excess by livestock, the calcium oxalate, the cause of the sour taste, can interfere with calcium absorption. Look for this plant as you hike through rocky areas around 8,000′ in the Lake Tahoe area. It is a true subalpine plant, able to thrive in a very short growing season.

Water Smartweed

MICHAEL GRAF

Polygonum amphibium   Native perennial
Water Smartweed   Jul–Sep

Description: Stems elongate, leafy, unbranched, and rooting at the nodes. The leaves are elongate with margins converging toward the tip. The leaves are broader in their floating form. The inflorescence is less than 6″ long, in terminal spikes or panicles. The flowers are small, rose colored, and attractive.

Habitat: Below 10,000′. Terrestrial, emergent, or floating along shallow lakes, streams, and shores. AQ, MM, RP.

Comments: A fast-growing aquatic plant, either above the surface of shallow waters or with leaves floating in deeper ones. In *Polygonum amphibium* var. *emersum* the stems are terrestrial or emergent in flower, and it is considered a noxious weed. *Polygonum amphibium* var. *stipulaceum* has stems that are floating in flower.

Polygonum bistortoides   Native perennial
Western Bistort   Jun–Aug

Description: 8–28″ tall. Stems several, erect, and slender. The leaves are mainly near the plant base and have long petioles. They are 6–16″ long, reduced upward, oblong or strap-shaped, leathery and whitish underneath. The few leaves on the stem are smaller and lack petioles. The inflorescence spikes are terminal, dense, thick-cylindrical, and less than 2½″ long. The calyx is pink or white. The stamens are exserted.

Habitat: 5,000–10,000′. Wet meadows and along streams. MM, RP.

Comments: The edible parts include the seeds when ground as flour, herbage raw or cooked, and roots raw, boiled, or roasted. The smell of the flowers has been described as that of dirty socks. It can be found in the meadows between Sagehen Creek and Stampede Reservoir.

RICHARD HANES

Western Bistort

Polygonum davisiae   Native perennial
Davis' Knotweed   Jun–Sep

Description: Plant less than 2′ high with several sprawling stems growing from a woody taproot. Light green elliptic leaves are less than 2″ long and decrease in size up the stem. The inconspicuous ¼″ flowers are pale yellow-green to purplish and are found in clusters in the leaf axils.

Habitat: Above 4,500′, especially on dry, rocky ridges and slopes. UC, SA, RO.

Comments: Davis' Knotweed is locally abundant in places of heavy winter snowfall such as Grouse Ridge, Castle Peak, and along the Pacific Crest Trail in Placer County. It typically grows with Mountain Pennyroyal and Sulfur Buckwheat. Its leaves turn bright pink and red as autumn arrives in the high country. The seeds and soft-textured leaves of this knotweed are a favorite food of Blue Grouse.

KAREN CALLAHAN

Davis' Knotweed

Willow Weed

Polygonum lapathifolium   Native annual
Willow Weed,
Smartweed, Knotweed   Jun–Oct

Description: Stem less than 5′ tall, ascending to erect, and swollen at the nodes. The leaves are less than 8″ long and petioled. The stipule below the leaf is veiny and clear brown, the blade lance-shaped and often hairy on the underside. Inflorescence branches are spikelike and nodding, 1–3″ long, drooping, and dense.

Habitat: Below 5,000′. Common in moist places. AQ, RP, MM.

Comments: The common name refers to the fact that the leaves resemble willow leaves. The nodding inflorescence helps separate it from most other knotweeds. It is widespread across North America and Europe. Native Americans used an infusion from the plant as a purgative for fever and stomach trouble.

Lady's Thumb

Polygonum persicaria   Non-native annual
Lady's Thumb   Jun–Nov

Description: Stems erect or spreading, 1–3′ long. Leaves narrow, less than 8″ long, lance-shaped, and generally with a dark purplish spot near the middle. The leaf nodes are sheathed, the stipules tipped with short bristles. Flowers are small, pink or rose colored.

Habitat: Below 5,000′. Common in moist, disturbed places. GR, FW, MM, RP.

Comments: Native to Europe. It is similar in appearance to the Willow Weed, *P. lapathifolium,* but *P. persicaria* has a shorter and more deeply colored flower spike. The leaves of this species have a darkened area near the center of the leaves (the "thumb"), whereas Willow Weed leaves are consistently green. The sheaths at the base of the leaf on this species are tipped with short bristles, which Willow Weed lacks.

Polygonum phytolaccifolium   Native perennial
Alpine Knotweed   Jun–Sep

Description: 3–8' tall with an erect, stout stem emanating from a large, fleshy caudex. The large-petioled leaves, 4–9" long, are lance-shaped to ovate with a rounded base, possess a conspicuous midrib, and taper to a sharp point at the tip. Many small whitish flowers are on an erect to hanging panicle that comes out of the leaf axils, or are terminal or are at the end of the stem.

Habitat: 5,000–9,300'. Meadows, along streams, and moist rocky places in forests. UC, MM.

Comments: The sheer size of the plant, as well as the high elevation at which is grows, should prevent confusion with any of the other knotweeds in our area. Edible parts include seeds (ground as flour) and herbage (raw). It is common at the edge of the parking lot for the Sierra Discovery Trail.

Alpine Knotweed

Rumex acetosella   Non-native perennial
Sheep Sorrel   Apr–Oct

Description: Less than 18" tall with a slender, erect stem. The fleshy leaves are in a basal rosette during the early stages of growth, then alternating along the stem later. The leaves are 1–4" long with the arrow-shaped blades having 2 basal lobes. The very small flowers are nodding, yellow becoming reddish as they age, and borne in clusters at the ends of the stems. Male and female flowers are on separate plants.

Habitat: Below 7,000'. Common in moist, often disturbed, open places. GR, FW, LC, UC, MM, RP.

Comments: Native Americans used a poultice of leaves and blossoms to help heal sores, and chewed fresh leaves as a stomach aid. The leaves were eaten by children for their tangy, sour taste. This non-native plant creeps using an extensive, shallow system of roots and rhizomes.

Sheep Sorrel

Curly Dock

KAREN CALLAHAN

Rumex crispus   Non-native perennial
Curly Dock   Most of year

Description: A robust plant, 2–5′ high. Stems erect, often reddish and slightly ridged. The leaves are mostly basal, 4–12″ long, lancelike, with curly or wavy margins. The flowers are small, numerous, reddish, and crowded on a large spikelike terminal and axillary clusters. The tiny red-brown seeds are heart-shaped and enclosed in papery winged structures.

Habitat: Below 8,500′. Abundant in moist disturbed areas. GR, CH, FW, MM, RP.

Comments: Native to Eurasia. The herbage can be eaten after removing the tart acids. Boiling in a series of water baths removes the bitter taste of oxalic acid. Native Americans used mashed root pulp for swellings and sores. Green Dock, *Rumex conglomeratus,* resembles Curly Dock but has a less dense, often interrupted, flower spike.

JULIE S. CARVILLE

Bright yellow Sulfur Buckwheat and deep red Applegate's Paintbrush bring vibrant color to a talus slope at Tahoe.

Portulacaceae
PURSLANE FAMILY
Karen Callahan

A family of annual or perennial herbs with a few succulent subshrubs. The leaves are fleshy or succulent, simple, alternate or opposite. The *symmetrical, bisexual flowers have 3–18 petals, usually 2 sepals, one to many stamens, and a superior ovary.* The seed capsule opens from the top, releasing shiny black or brown seeds. The family includes many edible and horticultural species. There are 20 genera and 400 species worldwide, 6 genera and 51 species in California. Of those, 6 genera and 21 species are found in our area.

Calandrinia ciliata   Native annual
Red Maids   Mar–May

Description: A low plant 2–15″ high, with narrow fleshy 1–3″ leaves on spreading stems. The flowers are ½″ in size; the 5 petals are a bright magenta with white-streaked centers.

Habitat: Below 6,000′. Open, grassy. GR, FW, LC.

Comments: The flower opens fully in the midday sun, closes each evening, and remains closed on cloudy days. Some references regard Red Maids as an introduced species. The black seeds, which have a high oil content, are a valuable food for mammals and birds. They were collected and included in pinole, a gruel prepared by the Native Americans, and the foliage was eaten as greens. It is an early colonizer on disturbed weedy areas and immediately following a fire.

JULIE S. CARVILLE

Red Maids

Pussypaws

Calyptridium umbellatum   Native perennial
Pussypaws   May–Aug

Description: The plant has a 2–10″ basal rosette of spreading stems bearing fleshy leaves and pink, yellow, or white terminal flower clusters. There are 2 large papery sepals, and 4 petals that wither quickly.

Habitat: 4,500–12,900′. Sandy, rocky forest openings. LC, UC, SA, RO.

Comments: A widespread and variable species on both the east and west sides of the Sierra. The flower clusters resemble fuzzy kitten paws. In response to temperature, the stems elevate during the midday heat. A related, taller, more brightly colored species, *C. monospermum,* grows on rocky cliffs along Bowman Lake Road. It differs from *C. umbellatum* by having axillary, rather than terminal, scapes and by the bracts under the inflorescence being ovate.

Western Spring Beauty

Claytonia lanceolata   Native perennial
Western Spring Beauty   Apr–Jul

Description: Plant less than 10″ tall and growing from a deep corm. 1–2 narrow basal leaves, often withering before the flowers appear, and a pair of succulent lance-shaped leaves on the flower stem. The inflorescence is a raceme of white to pink flowers; 2 sepals, 5 petals, often with darker pink stripes and yellow at the base.

Habitat: 5,000–8,000′. Woodlands, meadows. UC, MM.

Comments: Typically grows near melting snowbanks. A widespread and variable species. As the flowers began to fade, entire families of Native Americans often camped for days in the meadows where the Western Spring Beauty was common. They dug the corms with digging sticks made from deer antlers or a hard wood. The corms can be up to the size of a walnut.

Claytonia perfoliata Native annual
Miner's Lettuce Mar–Jul

Description: A succulent plant from 1–14" tall. The basal leaves are wider than long and ovate to deltate in shape. The flower stems have a circular leaf below the raceme of white to pink flowers.

Habitat: Below 6,500'. Vernally moist, shaded. GR, CH, FW, LC, UC.

Comments: What appears to be an upper circular leaf under the flowers is actually a pair of fused leaves. Another species, *Claytonia parviflora*, closely resembles *C. perfoliata* and is also called Miner's Lettuce. The basal leaves of *C. parviflora* are long and linear and differentiate the two species. Both species are abundant in our area and highly variable. Native Americans and settlers used Miner's Lettuce as food, but people should avoid eating the leaves after the flowers form, as this reportedly can cause an upset stomach.

JULIE S. CARVILLE

Miner's Lettuce

Lewisia cantelovii Native perennial
**Cantelow's Lewisia,
Wet Cliff Lewisia** May–Jun

Description: 6" or taller and forming a spreading basal rosette of many succulent, spoon-shaped, toothed leaves. Flowering stems bear 6–12 leaves and 1 to many dime-sized flowers. The flowers are pale pink with darker pink lines.

Habitat: 1,500–3,000'. Wet cliffs. LC, RO.

Comments: Wet Cliff Lewisia grows on nearly vertical moss-covered cliffs. This is a rare species endemic to the northern Sierra. A closely related form, *Lewisia serrata*, has a smaller inflorescence and distinct leaf serration. *L. serrata* is not recognized as a separate species in the *Jepson Manual* and is found only in the American River watershed. Many of the rare and slow-growing *Lewisias* are threatened by horticultural collecting.

RICHARD HANES

Cantelow's Lewisia

Kellogg's Lewisia

Lewisia kelloggii   Native perennial
Kellogg's Lewisia   Jun–Jul

Description: Plant to 4″ tall. Many spoon-shaped 1½–3½″ succulent leaves form a dense rosette. The flowers consist of 5–9 pink or white petals about 1″ across, 2 gland-toothed sepals, and 2 sepal-like bracts.

Habitat: 5,700–8,700′. Decomposed granite, volcanic gravel. UC, RO.

Comments: The plant has a very short blooming period, sometimes just a matter of days, before drying out and disappearing before the arrival of the summer heat. It has a thick, partially under-ground stem at the base of the leaves called a caudex. Though its range extends from Plumas County south to Mariposa County, it is a rare plant throughout its range. The plant resembles Bitterroot, *Lewisia rediviva*, which has not yet been found in our two counties.

Sierra Lewisia

Lewisia nevadensis   Native perennial
Sierra Lewisia   May–Jul

Description: Plant 4″ tall. The several to many basal linear leaves are 1–5″ long. The flowering stems do not rise above the leaves. There is 1 terminal flower per stem. The flowers are distinctly oval, white to pinkish, with 5–10 petals and 2 green sepals.

Habitat: 4,500–12,000′. Wet banks and meadows. UC, MM.

Comments: The plant is common in grassy fields and wet meadows on both the eastern and western sides of the Sierra Nevada. There are 16 *Lewisia* species in California. The large roots of most of them were used as a food source by Native Americans who removed the outer part of the root and then boiled it to remove most of the bitterness. Look for this plant at Loney Meadow and Bear Valley.

Lewisia pygmaea   Native perennial
Alpine Lewisia, Dwarf Lewisia   May–Aug

Description: Plant less than 4″ high. A tuft of fat linear basal leaves grows from the caudex. The leaves are longer than the flower stems. The flower stems are less than 3″ and bear 1–7 flowers per stem that are nestled among the leaves. The flowers are white, pink, or magenta, have 5–9 petals, and 2 toothed sepals.

Habitat: 5,100–13,500′. Dry or moist. UC, SA.

Comments: Alpine Lewisia lives in the harshest environments, yet has the widest range of any *Lewisia* species. It is variable in size, flower color, and shape. The flowers last about 1 month. Often found in bare, gravelly soil. *L. longipetala* is a rare species resembling this one but has only 1–2 flowers per stem, as opposed to 1–7 flowers, and the 2 sepals are less than one-third the size of the corolla compared to half the size.

Alpine Lewisia

Lewisia triphylla   Native perennial
Three-leaf Lewisia   May–Aug

Description: Plant 1–6″ tall. The basal leaves are typically lost by the time of flowering but the 3 (from 2–5) linear, succulent, opposite leaves remain on the flowering stem. The succulent stem terminates with from 1–10 small (½″) white to pinkish flowers. Each flower has from 5–9 petals and 2 green sepals.

Habitat: 4,000–10,000′. Wet. UC, SA, MM.

Comments: The plant grows in wet sand, gravel, and in alpine meadows. The name could be misleading, as it sometimes has either more or fewer than 3 stem leaves. The arrangement of the leaves on the stem often resembles a trident. The center of the flower cup is yellow; the petals often have pink central stripes.

Three-leaf Lewisia

Common Purslane

CINDY RUBIN

Portulaca oleracea   Non-native annual
Common Purslane   Jun–Sep

Description: Plant to 6″ high. The sprawling fleshy stems radiate out from the roots to distances of up to 12″. The succulent leaves are smooth and wedge-shaped, about ¼″ in size. The small 5-petaled yellow flowers are borne in the leaf axils and open only in sunshine.

Habitat: Below 4,200′. Disturbed areas. GR, FW, LC.

Comments: Considered a weed, Purslane has been cultivated for food and medicine for centuries. It is certainly known by anyone who gardens. It seeds prolifically and the seeds can remain dormant for years. The vitamin-rich plant is called "*pourpier*" by the French and "*verdolaga*" by Mexicans and other Latin Americans. In Bolivia it is combined with cheese and made into a salad called "*k'allu*" but is only eaten during its tender stage.

KAREN CALLAHAN • KAREN CALLAHAN

Checkerspot caterpillars feed on plants of the Figwort family, but the adult butterflies use nectar from flowers of several plant families.

Potamogetonaceae
PONDWEED FAMILY
Chet Blackburn

Perennial aquatic herbs from rhizomes or detached winter buds submersed in quiet fresh or brackish water. There are *two kinds of leaves, submersed and floating. The submersed leaves are narrow to linear. The floating leaves are broad, lying flat on the water surface. The flowers are in spikes on an axillary peduncle. Stamens 4, pistils 4. They may or may not have petals or sepals.* The stems are jointed and numerous. Worldwide, 3 genera and about 95 species exist. There are 2 genera and 20 species in California, of which 1 genus and 11 species occur in our area.

Potamogeton natans Native perennial
Broad-leaf Pondweed Jun–Aug

Description: An aquatic plant consisting of both floating and submerged leaves. The stems branch from a horizontal rhizome. Submersed leaves are linear, leathery, and without blades. The more conspicuous floating leaves are broadly elliptic to rounded with a more or less heart-shaped base. The tiny flowers are on clublike spikes that emerge out of the water. The emerging stalk is about 5″ long, while the clublike portion is about 2″ long.

Habitat: 4,000–8,000′. Marshy ponds and lakes. AQ.

Comments: It is an important food source for waterfowl. It can occur in depths up to 10′. Easily recognized by the leaf blades floating at an odd angle from the leaf petioles rather than straight out from them.

Broad-leaf Pondweed

Primulaceae
PRIMROSE FAMILY
Karen Callahan

Perennials or annuals. The leaves are generally opposite, usually simple, whorled or basal, and frequently dotted with glands. The flowers are *symmetrical, usually 4–5 petals, sepals, and stamens, usually attached at the base of the ovary. Calyx deeply lobed.* Fruit, a 1-chambered capsule. The family includes many ornamentals (e.g., Cyclamens, Primroses). Most are from the Northern Hemisphere. Of 25 genera and 600 species worldwide, 9 genera occur in California and 6 in Nevada and Placer Counties.

Scarlet Pimpernel

Anagallis arvensis　　　Non-native annual
Scarlet Pimpernel　　　Mar–Jul

Description: Plant 1–6″ tall and 4–12″ across. Creeping 4-sided stems bearing shiny, smooth-edged leaves to ¾″. The flowers are ¼″, with 5 salmon-colored to reddish orange petals. The petals are red to purplish at their bases.

Habitat: Below 3,000′. Disturbed. GR, CH, FW, LC.

Comments: The flowers close on cloudy or rainy days, hence the other common name, "Poor Man's Weatherglass." Because cloudiness precedes rainfall, they close as stormy weather approaches. The plant contains saponins and glycoside that can be toxic to livestock and humans. When eaten by humans it causes an intense headache and nausea for 24 hours. It has caused the loss of livestock (including horses) when eaten in quantity.

PRENTISS FERGUSON

Dodecatheon alpinum   Native perennial
Alpine Shooting Star   Jul–Aug

Description: Plant to 12″ high. The linear to oblanceolate leaves are 1–5″ long and gradually narrow at the base. The flower usually consists of 4 reflexed petals that are magenta to lavender and yellow at the base. The anthers are dark and exserted.

Habitat: 6,400–12,000′. Wet places. MM, RP.

Comments: This species can be distinguished from a similar Sierran species, Jeffrey's Shooting Star, by its lack of glandular hairs on the stems (*D. jeffreyi* has them) and the generally narrow leaves. The flowers are pollinated by bees, but not in the traditional way. As the bees gather pollen, they grab the petals and vibrate the flowers with the buzzing of their wings. Other "buzz pollinated" plants occur in the Nightshade family, *Solanaceae*.

Alpine Shooting Star

Dodecatheon hendersonii   Native perennial
Henderson's Shooting Star   Mar–May

Description: Plant 5–16″. Several flower stalks emerge from a cluster of rounded basal leaves. The inflorescence is an umbel. The flowers consist of 4–5 reflexed petals that are magenta, lavender, or white and with yellow and white marks at the petal base.

Habitat: Below 6,000′. Shade to semi-shade. CH, FW, LC, SG.

Comments: An early bloomer and common in vernally moist places, this foothill plant usually goes dormant by early summer. The flowers are nodding before pollination. The developing seed capsules point upward after pollination. This is true of all the Shooting Stars. Shooting Stars are sometimes called "Mosquito Bills" because of the resemblence of the exserted stamens to the needlelike proboscis of a mosquito.

Henderson's Shooting Star

Sierra Primrose

JULIE S. CARVILLE

Primula suffrutescens   Native perennial
Sierra Primrose   Jul–Sep

Description: Plant 6–12″ tall. Creeping stems from a woody base form a low mat. The spoon-shaped leaves are less than 2″ long and toothed on the margins. The flowers are less than 1″ in diameter, with 5 magenta petals and a yellow center.

Habitat: 8,000–13,500′. Rocky places. UC, SA, RO.

Comments: Only hikers to the high country will have the opportunity to see California's only native *Primula*. Uncommon, it grows in isolated colonies near melting snowbanks in rock crevices. The colonies, however, may be large and, in good years, spectacular. Their growing season is short, so the plant must rush to manufacture the food it needs, flower, and set seed. The Sierra Primrose does not adapt to lower elevation gardens. Look for it in rocky slopes near Sagehen Creek, Castle Peak, and Grouse Ridge.

Starflower

KAREN CALLAHAN

Trientalis latifolia   Native perennial
Starflower   Apr–Jun

Description: Plant 4–10″ tall. It has a single stem with a whorl of 3–8 ovate leaves from a deep-seated tuber. Rising above the whorl are 1 or more threadlike flower stems, each with a ½″ star-shaped flower. The flower has 5–8 pale pink to white petals and pointed green sepals.

Habitat: Below 4,500′. Semi-shaded forest. LC.

Comments: This is a maverick in the Primrose family. Instead of sticking to the usual 4 or 5 petals that are characteristic of the rest of the family, this one may have as many as 8. The number varies from plant to plant. It is a lover of shaded, summer-dry, coniferous forests where years of accumulated leaf litter hides the bare soil. One of the many places it can be seen is along the Rock Creek Nature Trail.

Ranunculaceae
BUTTERCUP FAMILY
Julie Carville

Perennial/annual herbs/vines. *Usually numerous pistils and stamens. Petals either 0/5 or more, unfused, often with petal-like sepals.* The petals/sepals are either simple, uniform, and glossy or the petals/sepals are nonuniform, nonglossy, and often spurred as in columbines and delphiniums. The ovary is superior. The leaves are generally alternate, simple or palmately compound, basal, and on stem with a sheathing base. *The fruit is often a follicle/achene cluster. The plant parts and seeds are toxic unless processed.* There are 60 genera and approximately 1,700 species worldwide. Of those, 12 genera and 43 species are known to occur in our area.

Aconitum columbianum   Native perennial
Monkshood   Jun–Aug

Description: 2–5′ tall. The showy flowers are in a raceme, dark or light bluish purple, or occasionally white. The upper sepal forms a petal-like hood resembling a monk's cowl. The leaves are palmately 3–7-lobed and wedge-shaped. The fruit is a follicle.

Habitat: 900–9,600′. Moist, semi-shaded woodlands, wet meadows, and streamsides. MM, RP.

Comments: This is a plant that likes its own kind. Single specimens standing alone are seldom seen, but instead are inevitably found in groups. Look for the tiny balls (bulblets) at the base of the leaf stems. These fall to root and form a new clonal plant. All parts of the plant are very toxic. The plant juice was used by Native Americans to poison arrowheads. Bumblebees are the main pollinators.

RICHARD HANES

Monkshood

Red Baneberry

RICHARD HANES

Actaea rubra   Native perennial
Red Baneberry   May–Jul

Description: 1–3′ tall. Dainty flowers, with tiny threadlike petals, sepals, and stamens clustered in a raceme at the top of the stems. The crinkly leaves are up to 2′ long, composed of 2–3 sharp-tipped leaflets. The balls of fuzzy-looking white flowers are followed by shiny red (rarely white) poisonous berries.

Habitat: Below 10,000′. Moist, semi-shaded forests, streamsides, seeps. LC, UC, RP.

Comments: Not common. They are usually found along seeps and in wet woodlands. Native Americans boiled the roots and applied them to sores. They also drank a decoction of roots to increase milk flow in women after childbirth. The berries are poisonous, though apparently rarely fatal. However, as few as 6 berries can cause severe discomfort.

Western Pasque Flower

JULIE S. CARVILLE

Anemone occidentalis   Native perennial
Western Pasque Flower   Jul–Aug

Description: 6–24″ tall, it has a densely hairy stem initially, but later is often without hairs. The bowl-shaped flower is up to 2″ wide with 5 or more petal-like sepals. The undersides are tinged purple. There is a single flower per stem. The leaves are finely divided into narrow, lacy segments.

Habitat: 5,500–10,000′. Sunny slopes, often near melting snowbanks. UC, SA, MM.

Comments: The fruiting styles elongate to form a woolly 1½″ long structure, resembling a Sesame Street Muppet. Anemones have no petals, but the sepals are petal-like. Compare it with Drummond's Anemone, with its shorter 4–12″ stems, its sepals with blue undersides, and its styles of tiny woolly nubbins.

Aquilegia formosa   Native perennial
Crimson Columbine   May–Aug

Description: 1–3′ tall. The upper leaves are linear, the lower leaves larger and divided. The flowers consist of flaring sepals and tubular petals, with nectar in the swollen petal tip. The fruit is an erect follicle.

Habitat: To 10,000′. Meadows, streamsides, woods. FW, LC, UC, SA, MM, RP, RO, SP.

Comments: Honeybees chew tiny holes at the top of the flower tubes, stealing the nectar without pollinating the flower. Bumblebees unfurl their "tongues" up the tube for nectar and in doing so pollinate it. Native Americans chewed the seeds, then rubbed them on their bodies and clothing as a kind of perfume. They also ate the seeds to relieve stomachaches. The leaves were chewed for sore throats and coughs or brewed into a tea for colds.

Crimson Columbine

Caltha leptosepala var. *biflora*
                                   Native perennial
Marsh Marigold   May–Jul

Description: 6–12″ tall. The shiny 3½″ wide leaves grow from the base of the plant and are rounded. The flower is up to 1¼″ wide, with 5 or more petal-like sepals and numerous yellow pistils and stamens. The fruit is an achene up to 1″ long and forms dense clusters.

Habitat: 4,500–10,000′. Stream banks, marshy areas, full sun. MM, RP.

Comments: The leaves are toxic unless cooked. Native Americans chewed the plant to make a poultice and applied it to inflamed wounds. There are good displays at Sagehen Creek West, 7.5 miles north of Truckee, and at Winnemucca Lake near Carson Pass.

Marsh Marigold

Chaparral Clematis

JULIE S. CARVILLE

Clematis lasiantha   Native perennial
Chaparral Clematis, Pipestem   Apr–Jun

Description: A deciduous vine to 15' or more. Flowers are usually solitary, up to ¾" wide, with white to creamy petal-like sepals but no petals. Leaves are divided into 3–5 leaflets with lobed edges. The style in fruit is 1½" long and feathery.

Habitat: Below 6,000'. Chaparral, open woodlands, hillsides. CH, FW, LC.

Comments: It is very noticeable in fruit due to its prominent feathery styles. It is often found climbing oaks. Native Americans pulverized the burned plant remains to apply to burns and sores. The stems and bark were also pounded, boiled, and used in a steam bath for colds, and the roots were burned and inhaled or chewed for colds. A related species, Virgin's Bower, *Clematis ligusticifolia,* is more common in wetter places such as the American River Canyon near Auburn.

Mountain Larkspur

JULIE S. CARVILLE

Delphinium glaucum   Native perennial
Mountain Larkspur,
Tower Larkspur   Jul–Sep

Description: 3–8' tall. This is the tallest of our larkspurs. The stems are hollow and covered with a powdery material. The leaves are large, 3-lobed, palmate, and hairy below. The leaflets are sharply lobed. The flowers are bluish to blue-purple.

Habitat: 5,000–10,000'. Stream banks, wet meadows, full sun. LC, UC, MM, RP.

Comments: Delphinium is derived from the Latin for "dolphin." The flower bud looks like a tiny dolphin atop a slender stem. The petal-like sepals of delphiniums, which surround the petals, are larger and more conspicuous than the tiny petals. Prized as a garden plant in Europe, distribution of plants and seeds is banned in Canada, because this species is the number-one cause of cattle poisoning in western Canada.

Delphinium gracilentum   Native perennial
Slender Larkspur,
Pine Forest Larkspur   May–Jul

Description: Stems often horizontal 6–24″ long
and unbranched. The leaves are mainly on the
lower third of the stem, usually 5-lobed, generally
rounded. The 1″ flowers are blue, white, or pink.

Habitat: 500–8,000′. Shady, damp forests.
LC, UC.

Comments: The genus *Delphinium* is easy to
recognize, but identification of the individual
species is very difficult. The differences between
them are subtle and they hybridize readily,
making the task of keying them frustrating. Of
the 28 California species, 9 grow in our area.
The roots of this species are tuberlike and the
stem breaks away easily from the tuber, a trait
shared only by *D. nuttallianum, D. patens,* and
D. depauperatum in our area.

KAREN CALLAHAN

Slender Larkspur

Delphinium hansenii   Native perennial
Hansen's Larkspur   Apr–Jul

Description: 18–36″ tall, hairy at the base,
with the hairs curving backward. The leaves and
leaf stems are hairy and usually wither by flowering time. The flower sepals are blue-violet, blue-
pink, or white, and are curved. The upper petals
are white with violet edges. The flowers are
hairy. The fruit is a hairy, erect follicle.

Habitat: Below 4,000′. Oak woodlands, open
grassy areas, chaparral, rocky slopes. CH, FW, RO.

Comments: This species has a woody root,
which is not easily detached from the stem, a
trait it shares with only *D. variegatum* ssp.
variegatum in our area. Hansen's Larkspur is
found mostly in foothill woodlands and chaparral.

KAREN CALLAHAN

Hansen's Larkspur

Nuttall's Larkspur

KAREN CALLAHAN

Delphinium nuttallianum   Native perennial
Nuttall's Larkspur   May–Jul

Description: 6–18″ tall. Stems slightly hairy near the base, hairy to glandular-hairy above. The leaves are divided into 3–5 lobes. The flowers are blue to pale purple. The 5 sepals are of roughly equal length and hairy. The upper petals are whitish, the lower petals translucent. The seeds have an inflated, collarlike structure near the largest end.

Habitat: 5,000–10,000′. Open woods, sagebrush, damp to dry grassy areas, streamsides. GR, CH, LC, UC, SA, RP, SP, SG.

Comments: Named for Thomas Nuttall, an eastern botanist who came west in 1834, and was one of the earliest botanists to study the western states' plants. Native Americans used the flowers to make a blue dye for coloring arrows and other things, and also used them in special ceremonies.

Spreading Larkspur

KAREN CALLAHAN

Delphinium patens   Native perennial
Spreading Larkspur,
Zigzag Larkspur   Mar–Jun

Description: 4–20″ tall. Stem is usually without hairs, and it usually has a definite zigzag. Stem is easily detached from the tuberous root. The leaves are usually without hairs and are 3–5-lobed. The upper petals are white with blue lines. The 5 sepals are dark blue, large, and look like petals. The spur points upward.

Habitat: Below 3,500′. Grasslands, woodlands, forests. GR, FW, LC.

Comments: Called Zigzag Larkspur because of the bends in the flower stems, but that is not a reliable trait for identification. It is most often found on slopes in oak-studded canyons. It begins blooming earlier than the other larkspurs in our area.

Delphinium variegatum   Native perennial
Royal Larkspur   Mar–May

Description: 6–36″ tall. The leaves and stems are very hairy, the leaves divided and forked. The flowers are showy, deep royal blue to deep blue-purple, with the sepals being the most intense color. The upper petals are narrow and whitish, the lower two are blue-purple with white hairs. Summer and winter dormant, it develops rapidly in the spring.

Habitat: Below 3,000′. Open woodlands, grasslands. GR, CH, FW.

Comments: One of the showiest and largest flowers of our native delphiniums. It is primarily a grasslands species but is occasional in chaparral and woodlands in the low foothills. It is common in the grasslands on the western end of the two counties, especially in the Roseville-Lincoln area.

Royal Larkspur

Isopyrum occidentale   Native perennial
Western Rue Anemone   Feb–Apr

Description: 3–10″ tall, stems slender and grayish black. The leaves are light green, similar to Meadow Rue and Columbine leaves, but more delicate. The flowers consist of 4–6 petal-like sepals that are white to pink to pinkish purple. The fruit is an achene.

Habitat: Below 5,600′. Shady, wooded slopes. RP, FW, LC.

Comments: A lovely and delicate-looking member of the Buttercup family. It flowers early in the spring, and the flowering is of such short duration that many hikers miss it. It prefers growing at the base of mossy rocks in oak woodlands. This charming, early spring bloomer is a heart thriller, as it sweetly announces spring's arrival along streams and in damp woodland habitats.

Western Rue Anemone

Waterfall Buttercup

Kumlienia hystricula   Native perennial
Waterfall Buttercup   Feb–Apr

Description: 3–10″ tall. The leaves are rounded, shallowly lobed, and alternate. The 1–3 flowers cluster at the top of the stem and consist of 5–12 tiny yellow to greenish thread-like petals, and 5 or more white, petal-like sepals. The fruit is an achene.

Habitat: Below 6,000′. Streamsides, in streams, wet places among rocks. AQ, RP.

Comments: How can a delicate-looking plant like this exist in the environment it has selected? It grows around vernal waterfalls that can be raging torrents in the winter fully capable of moving boulders, so how do the delicate plants and seeds keep from being washed away? It is a single-species genus. It can be found at a trailside waterfall along Stevens Trail near Colfax.

Plantain Buttercup

Ranunculus alismifolius var. *alismifolius*
                              Native perennial
Plantain Buttercup   May–Jul

Description: Stems 6–20″ long. It grows erect or lies on the ground. The leaves are 2–5″ long, narrow and undivided. The flowers have 5 or more shiny yellow petals, ½–1″ wide, with yellowish green reflexed sepals. The fruit is an achene.

Habitat: 4,300–7,600′. Wet meadows, stream banks. MM, RP, SP.

Comments: Native Americans cooked buttercup seeds by shaking them with hot rocks in flat, wide baskets to break down toxins. The roasted seeds taste like popcorn. Named by Pliny, a Roman naturalist who lived 2,000 years ago, *Ranunculus* comes from the Latin for "little frog." *Ranunculus* refers to the wet environment these early spring bloomers share with little froggies.

Ranunculus aquatilis   Native perennial
Water Buttercup   May–Aug

Description: Both submerged and floating
stems. It has two types of leaves. The underwater
leaves are greenish brown in threadlike filaments.
The emergent leaves are palmately 3-lobed. The
flowers are white with a yellow center, are
floating or submerged, and have 4–12 petals.
The fruit is an achene.

Habitat: Below 9,600′. Ponds, slow-moving
streams, marshes, at virtually every elevation. AQ.

Comments: Some flowers bloom underwater but
most float on the surface where they are pollinated by flying insects. Waterfowl love this plant.
Many aquatic plants have filament-like leaves that
provide more leaf exposure for gathering light in
a light-deficient environment, yet do not shade the
foliage below them. Native Americans boiled and
ate the entire plant. Can be seen at Sagehen Creek.

JULIE S. CARVILLE

Water Buttercup

Ranunculus muricatus
                    Non-native annual/biennial
Prickleseed Buttercup   May–Jun

Description: 3–20″ tall, erect or horizontal.
The flower is small with yellow petals. The fruit
is a flat, oval achene with a curved hook at the
tip, and on the side of each achene are tiny
curved prickles. Achenes are in a cluster.

Habitat: Below 2,300′. Streamsides, wet fields
and lawns, vernal pools. VP, GR, FW, RP.

Comments: Using a hand lens will make the
achene prickles easier to see. It grows at the
Spenceville Wildlife Area near streams and
seeps. Native to Europe. Of the 15 buttercup
species likely to be found in our area, only 5 are
non-native. The other 4 are *R. acris, R. arvensis,
R. repens,* and *R. testiculatus.*

KAREN CALLAHAN

Prickleseed Buttercup

Western Buttercup

Ranunculus occidentalis   Native perennial
Western Buttercup   Apr–Jun

Description: 4–24″ tall on thin, usually hairy, stems. The leaves are 3-parted and deeply lobed with toothed edges. The flower has 5 or 6 shiny petals, and tiny green, reflexed sepals that fall off during flowering. The fruit is a flat, oval achene with a strongly curved tip.

Habitat: 300–7,500′. Wet meadows, streamsides. CH, FW, LC, UC, MM, RP, SP.

Comments: Common, an early bloomer that announces spring's arrival. It has a delicate appearance. Native Americans roasted the seeds and added them to pinole. It is difficult to distinguish from another common species, *R. canus* (you have to measure the fruit), but *R. canus* generally (but not always) has more than 5 petals and larger flowers.

Fendler's Meadow Rue

Thalictrum fendleri   Native perennial
Fendler's Meadow Rue   May–Aug

Description: 2–6′ tall. The fernlike leaves are mostly 3-lobed into rounded segments that are thin and delicate, like columbine leaves. The male and female flowers are on separate plants. The plant has no petals, only green sepals.

Habitat: 4,000–10,000′. Woodland, damp meadows. FW, LC, UC, SA, MM, RP.

Comments: Also called "Earring Plant" for its pinkish to greenish yellow filaments with their dangling, pink anthers. As a wind-pollinated plant it lacks petals. Compare the male plant with the swollen achenes of female plants. Native Americans made an infusion from this plant for colds and gonorrhea. They are obviously sociable plants, as they are often found growing close together for good communication, which leads to romance!

Rosaceae
ROSE FAMILY
Julie Carville

Trees, shrubs, and perennial/annual herbs. The flowers *usually have 5 separate, uniform petals and sepals,* often with a tiny bract between each sepal, *five to numerous stamens and one to usually numerous pistils. Often with a hypanthium,* a cup or tubelike structure made up of fused lower parts of sepals, petals, and stamens. The leaves are usually alternate, *with stipules,* simple, palmately or pinnately compound. The fruits come in many forms, from achene or follicle to swollen rose hip or strawberry with seeds attached to the outside. Many commercial fruits are in this family, including apples, peaches, plums, raspberries, cherries, and almonds. It is a large and important family with about 110 genera and 3,000 species worldwide. In our area, there are 25 genera and 63 species.

Chamaebatia foliolosa   Native subshrub
Mountain Misery, Kit-kit-dizzy   May–Jul

Description: 8–24″ tall. A ground-carpeting, evergreen subshrub. The leaves are pinnately compound, glandular, fragrant, and very finely divided. The flowers are approximately 1″ wide, with white petals and numerous yellow stamens.

Habitat: Above 2,000′. Mixed conifer forests. LC.

Comments: Known by anyone who has spent any time in our pine forests. Mountain Misery forms dense carpets in the dappled shade under many of our coniferous trees. There are different stories as to how this plant came by its common name. The most prevalent one suggests that the wiry stems wrapped around and grabbed the axles of the pioneers' wagon wheels, causing frustrating delays. Its resinous leaves are flammable and on warm days they emit an artichoke-like fragrance.

KAREN CALLAHAN

Mountain Misery

Mock Strawberry

Duchesnea indica   Non-native perennial
Mock Strawberry   May–Aug

Description: Less than 6″ high. Trailing stems form leafy runners that root at the nodes. The leaves are 3-palmate, dark green above and hairy beneath. The solitary flowers are in the leaf axils. There are toothed bractlets between the sepals. The hypanthium is cup-shaped and contains numerous pistils and stamens.

Habitat: Below 1,600′. Disturbed places. FW, RP.

Comments: Strongly resembles a small strawberry, but the flowers are yellow instead of white. The "strawberry" is edible but rather tasteless. The name honors French botanist A. N. Duchesne, who died in the early 1800s. The plant is native to Southeast Asia and has become naturalized from gardens.

Mountain Strawberry

Fragaria virginiana   Native perennial
Mountain Strawberry   May–Jul

Description: Under 6″ in height. Forms a ground cover with red runners that root at the swellings (nodes) along the stems to form new plants. The leaves are serrated, hairy, and palmately 3-lobed. The flowers are white to pinkish and about 1″ wide.

Habitat: 4,000–10,000′. Damp woods. LC, UC, SA, RP.

Comments: *Fragaria* is Latin for "fragrant." Wild strawberries have an intense flavor. The leaves can be brewed into tea as a soothing drink or a gargle for a sore throat. The fruits are high in vitamin C. Native Americans ate the boiled roots and drank the fluid as tea to treat diarrhea, as well as to treat kidney and bladder problems. The tea was also brewed and drunk for jaundice and scurvy, and to calm nerves.

Geum triflorum   Native perennial
Prairie Smoke   Apr–Aug

Description: 6–20″ tall. The basal leaves form a tuft and are odd-pinnately lobed. The leaflets are wedge-shaped and usually 2–3-lobed. Before flowering the stem bears 1–3 nodding buds of reddish pink sepals and bractlets. The creamy, pink-tinged flowers become erect and visible when in bloom. It grows in patches.

Habitat: 3,900–9,600′. Dry places. LC, UC, MM, SP.

Comments: Petals and sepals drop off after fertilization to show off the vertical fuzzy styles, giving this plant its other name, "Old Man's Whiskers." A similar species, Bigleaf Avens, *Geum macrophyllum,* grows in wet meadows from 3,500–10,000′. It has yellow flowers and a large terminal leaflet. Both species resemble potentillas but the seeds differ.

RICHARD HANES

Prairie Smoke

Horkelia fusca   Native perennial
Dusky Horkelia   May–Aug

Description: 4–24″ in height. A grayish green plant with reddish hairy stems. The leaves are up to 6″ long and divided into 5 to 10 pairs of leaflets on the lower leaves. The upper leaves are made up of fewer leaflets. The flowers are in tight clusters at the end of the stems. The flowers are ½″ wide, white to pinkish, with wedge-shaped lobed petals and reddish sepals and bractlets.

Habitat: Below 10,000′. Woods, sunny openings, dry to moist habitats. CH, LC, UC, SA, SP.

Comments: An inconspicuous flower, but it has lovely detail through a hand lens, with its red nectar guides to draw pollinators to the center of the flower for pollination. It grows in Shirley Canyon at North Tahoe.

JULIE S. CARVILLE

Dusky Horkelia

Plumas Ivesia

Ivesia sericoleuca　　　　Native perennial
Plumas Ivesia　　　　Jun–Aug

Description: 6–20″ tall. An herbaceous plant with hairy, decumbent to ascending stems. The leaves are densely pinnate with 2–35 leaflets per side. The flowers are white, up to ½″ wide, with petals extending well beyond the sepals. The flowers grow in open clusters.

Habitat: 4,900–7,200′. Drying open meadows, volcanic soils. MM, SP.

Comments: Plumas Ivesia is found in the Truckee River drainage area near Sagehen Creek. It is endemic to California and is listed as rare and endangered by the California Native Plant Society. Looking for its unusual, densely compacted, pinnate leaves is a good way to initially spot it, then the flowers will confirm the species.

Shrubby Cinquefoil

Potentilla fruticosa　　　　Native subshrub
Shrubby Cinquefoil　　　　Jun–Aug

Description: Shrubby, 1–3′ tall. Many branched. The small leaves are deeply lobed with 2–3 narrow leaflets per side. The bright yellow flowers are 1″ wide, and often appear to almost cover the plant.

Habitat: 6,500–11,800′. Sunny, moist, rocky hillsides and meadows, often in volcanic soils. SA, MM, RO.

Comments: This showy little shrub has a silky texture and is commonly sold in nurseries. *Potentilla* is derived from the Latin for "little powerful one," which well describes this medicinally useful genus. The whole plant is used as a gentle astringent, internally or externally. A tea produced from it allegedly reduces fevers and diarrhea and is applied externally to heal sunburn and poison oak rashes, and so would be useful for backpackers.

Potentilla glandulosa　　　Native perennial
Sticky Cinquefoil　　　　　Apr–Sep

Description: 2–36″ tall on stems with spreading hairs. The leaves are pinnate, glandular-hairy, and bearing 4 to 9 leaflets. The flowers are pale yellow to whitish, approximately ½″ wide.

Habitat: Up to 12,500′. Dry to moist meadows, open forest. GR, CH, FW, LC, UC, SA, MM, SP.

Comments: Cinquefoils are often confused with buttercups because of their yellow, similar-looking petals. Cinquefoils have green sepals with tiny green bracts between each sepal, whereas buttercups don't have these tiny bracts between the sepals. Native Americans used the plant as a poultice for swellings and prepared a tea from the whole plant that was drunk as a tonic. A variable species with 4 subspecies in our area.

KAREN CALLAHAN

Sticky Cinquefoil

Sanguisorba minor　　　Non-native perennial
Garden Burnet, Small Burnet　　　May–Jul

Description: 12–30″ tall. Stem erect. Long compound leaves bearing 6 to 10 pairs of leaflets. The inflorescence is composed of 5–30 flowers. Tiny greenish flowers with purple-tinged styles appear in clublike, rounded heads on an erect stalk that extends well above the foliage.

Habitat: 100–3,000′. Open grassy and/or disturbed places. GR, CH, FW, LC.

Comments: Used in salads. Native to the Mediterranean region. Western Burnet, *Sanguisorba occidentalis,* a native species, also occurs in our area. Its leaflets are deeply pinnately cut, as opposed to being merely toothed; it is an annual (sometimes biennial) as opposed to perennial. *Sanguisorba* means "blood absorbing" and refers to folk usage of the foliage in making decoctions to arrest hemorrhage.

CHET BLACKBURN

Garden Burnet

Sibbaldia

Sibbaldia procumbens   Native perennial
Sibbaldia   Jun–Aug

Description: 1–4″ high with long, mat-forming stems. The leaves are 3-lobed, wedge-shaped, and terminal. Each 3-branched leaflet has 3 teeth at its tip. The 5-petalled, pale yellow flowers are small, with petals tapering to a pointed tip. The 5 green sepals also have pointed tips and are longer than the petals.

Habitat: 6,000–12,000′. Rocky, moist areas, mostly at high elevations. SA, MM, RO.

Comments: These small, ground-hugging plants with pretty leaves and nonshowy flowers are easily overlooked. Sibbaldia's hairy leaves retain heat and protect it from intense sunlight, and its mat-forming growth protects it from strong winds in its high-elevation habitat. It resembles a cinquefoil, but cinquefoils have numerous stamens and Sibbaldia has only 5 to 10.

MICHAEL GRAF

JULIE S. CARVILLE

Cold nights bring fall color to a mountain lake at Grouse Ridge before snow blankets the mountains in white.

Rubiaceae
MADDER FAMILY
Chet Blackburn

Herbs, shrubs, and trees. Stems square and roughly prickled. Leaves in whorls or pairs. The flowers are bisexual with *mainly 4 minute sepals, and 4 petals* (sometimes 5 in *Kelloggia*) *in a shape resembling a tiny cross. Stamens 4 and alternate from the petals.* The inferior ovary turns into twin rounded seeds. Mostly tropical in distribution. It is an important family, providing such products as coffee, quinine, and many ornamental plants. There are 50 genera and 6,000 species worldwide, 6 genera and 52 species in California, and 5 genera and 20 species in the area covered by this book.

Galium aparine	Non-native annual
Goose-grass, Common Bedstraw	Mar–Jul

Description: A sprawling plant to 3′. Rambling, weakly 4-angled hairy stems with leaves in whorls, 6–8 leaves per whorl. The flowers are small, greenish white, appear in the nodes, and usually produce 2 rounded spiny seeds per flower.

Habitat: 100–5,000′. Common and widespread in shaded woods and rocky places. CH, FW, LC, RP.

Comments: The plant climbs on other plants for support. The leaves and stems have an abundance of small hairs with little hooks at their tips. Placing a strand on clothing produces an instant but nondescript corsage. It used to be fed to penned geese in Europe, where it probably originated. A distant relative of the Coffee plant, the spiny bean-shaped seeds of *Galium* can be made into a coffee substitute, which lacks caffeine but is said to have a pleasing taste.

RICHARD HANES

Goose-grass

KAREN CALLAHAN

Climbing Bedstraw

Galium porrigens var. *tenue*   Native perennial
Climbing Bedstraw,
Narrowleaf Bedstraw   Jan–Jul

Description: Climbing to 5′. Stems woody at the base. Stems and leaves bear downward-pointing hairs that feel rough to the touch. The delicate, dark green leaves are small (0.08–0.25″). The flowers are yellowish green and inconspicuous.

Habitat: 100–2,000′. Brushy shady places. CH, FW, LC, RP.

Comments: Usually seen climbing up a shrub or scrambling over a rock, this is a miniature version of Common Bedstraw. *Galium* is a large genus in California, with 46 species, and at least 12 of them occur in Nevada and Placer Counties. Only 3 in our area have a woody base, including this one, but this is the only one with a woody base that is found below 2,400′.

JULIE S. CARVILLE

Kelloggia

Kelloggia galioides   Native perennial
Kelloggia   May–Aug

Description: 6–24″ tall from spreading rhizomes. Opposite, narrow, lance-shaped leaves are widely spaced along the stem, with smaller leaves emerging from their leaf bases. Small white to pink funnel-shaped flowers occur on long stalks.

Habitat: 3,000–9,000′. Dry open areas in coniferous forests. LC, UC, SA.

Comments: Common but often overlooked because of its small size. Nevertheless it should not be confused with any other plant. The 4 distinctive pinkish white petals emerge from a fuzzy bulging calyx that as a unit resembles a small Pussy Willow.

Sherardia arvensis   Non-native annual
Common Field Madder   Feb–Jul

Description: Under 6″. Multiple sprawling 4-angled stems from the base bear whorls of small leaves in whorls of 6. The pink-purple to lavender or lilac flowers are in small groups with leaflike bracts surrounding them. They appear at the ends of the flowering stems. What looks like 4 petals are actually 4 deeply cut lobes on a united floral tube.

Habitat: 100–4,000′. Disturbed open places such as lawns and fields. GR, CH, FW, LC.

Comments: This is a tiny flower often found in lawns because it is too short to fall victim to the lawn mower. Native to the Mediterranean region. Its early blooming habit and heavy crop of seeds allow it to thrive in places dominated by much taller herbaceous vegetation later in the season.

JULIE S. CARVILLE

Common Field Madder

KAREN CALLAHAN • JULIE S. CARVILLE

California Pitcher Plant blooms in July (inset of flower) along with Bog Hastingsia, Seepspring Monkeyflower, Western Tofieldia, and Bog Orchid in a Nevada County fen.

Sarraceniaceae
PITCHER PLANT FAMILY
Chet Blackburn

Insectivorous perennial herbs. Leaves are **modified into hollow tubular structures adapted to trapping insects.** The flowers are nodding on a leafless stalk. Sepals and petals 5 (in ours) and free. There are many stamens. There are 3 genera and 15 species worldwide, and 1 native genus and 1 native species in California. Another species, Purple Pitcher Plant, *Sarracenia purpurea,* has been introduced in a few other parts of California but not, as yet, here. *Darlingtonia californica* ranges from Northern California to Southern Oregon. Nevada County has the southernmost populations of *Darlingtonia.* Plants are attractive to collectors, but rarely survive transplantation from their natural habitat.

Cobra Lily

Darlingtonia californica   Native perennial
Cobra Lily, California Pitcher Plant   Apr–Jul

Description: To 2′ tall. The leaves are modified to catch insects. The conspicuous veined leaf forms a funnel with a hood. The top of the hood is bent over to form an opening between two fishtail-like appendages. Large single nodding flowers rise above the hoods on a durable stalk with yellow sepals and red petals.

Habitat: 5,000–7,000′ in our area, lower in the northern coastal area. Marshy and boggy places standing in shallow, cold water. AQ, MM, RP.

Comments: A carnivorous plant. The leaf looks like a cobra with a walrus moustache. The moustachelike appendages and the inside of the hood secrete nectar to attract insects, then trap them inside. This is a sensitive species threatened by horticultural collecting and timber harvesting. (Flower shown on previous page.)

Saxifragaceae
SAXIFRAGE FAMILY
Julie Carville

Perennial herbs. The leaves are *usually simple, alternate or basal, and palmately veined.* The flowers are usually small, *on upright leafless stems. The petals are usually white or pink, with 5 separate petals, 5 or 10 stamens, often with red anthers, 2 pistils. The fruit has 2 follicles, which as they mature become fleshy and reddish and separate at the pointed tips, looking like a tiny "bird's beak,"* a helpful clue to identifying members of this family. Saxifrage is Latin for "rock breaker," a reference to the strong roots of some species that work their way into cracks in rock cliffs and ledges. There are 40 genera and about 600 species worldwide, with 16 genera and 64 species found in California and 8 genera and 24 species in our area.

Boykinia major   Native perennial
Mountain Brookfoam   Jun–Sep

Description: 1–3' tall, with unbranched stems bearing brown glandular hairs. The maplelike leaves are rounded, approximately 7" wide, alternate and basal on 4–8" long glandular-hairy petioles with leaflike stipules that are approximately ³⁄₈" long. Its lobed leaves are serrated with gland-tipped teeth and are without hairs except for beneath the veins. The small flowers, about ¼–½" wide, are in dense clusters. There are 5 white roundish to elliptical petals and 5 tiny sepals.

Habitat: Below 7,500'. Moist, shady, wet meadows, streams, and damp woods. MM, RP.

Comments: Compare the large stipules of this one with our other Brookfoam with its bristled, brownish stipules, looser flower clusters, and more shallowly lobed leaves.

RICHARD HANES

Mountain Brookfoam

Brookfoam

Boykinia occidentalis   Native perennial
Brookfoam   Jun–Jul

Description: 8–12″ tall. The leaves are rounded, approximately 5″ wide, lobed, with tiny brownish and bristled stipules. Small flowers, about ¼″ wide in loose clusters, rise up on fragile-looking branched stalks above the foliage. The flowers have 5 white triangular petals.

Habitat: Below 5,000′. Moist shaded banks. RP.

Comments: The roots are often embedded in mossy rock crevices on the banks of permanent streams, where they receive constant moisture. Native Americans ate the raw leaves as a remedy for tuberculosis. The dried leaves were sometimes placed inside basket caps for fragrance. It can be seen growing in the rocks along and in Rock Creek at the Rock Creek Nature Trail.

Indian Rhubarb

Darmera peltata   Native perennial
Indian Rhubarb, Umbrella Plant   Apr–Jun

Description: 1–3′ tall from a thick rhizome. The leaves are up to 2′ wide. The white or pink flowers are at the top of a leafless stalk in a rounded cluster at the top of the stem. The plant blooms before the leaves are full size, and often before the leaves even appear.

Habitat: Below 6,600′. Stream banks. RP.

Comments: The very showy, large leaves and flower clusters stand out among the rocks in streams and at stream edges. The leaves turn red to yellow in the fall. Native Americans ate the young shoots raw. The fleshy leaf stalks were also peeled and eaten raw, the flavor being similar to celery. Pulverized roots were mixed with acorn meal to whiten the meal. It occurs in almost every permanent rocky stream draining the western side of the Sierra.

Heuchera micrantha   Native perennial
Crevice Heuchera, Alumroot   May–Jul

Description: Grows 12–40″ tall. The maplelike leaves are roundish, lobed, and mainly basal but on long petioles. The leaf stems are adorned with long hairs. Stipules at the base of the leaf stem are 2-lobed and hairy edged. Sprays of flowering stalks bear clusters of tiny white flowers.

Habitat: Below 7,000′. Moist rocky habitats, especially on cliffs. RO.

Comments: The name Alumroot comes from the astringent nature of *Heuchera* roots. Native Americans ate steamed leaves in the spring, and made an infusion of roots for liver problems and sore throats. A poultice of mashed roots and Douglas-fir pitch was applied to wounds. The leaves and roots were chewed and applied to sores or wounds.

KAREN CALLAHAN

Crevice Heuchera

Heuchera rubescens   Native perennial
Pink Alumroot   May–Aug

Description: Grows 4–12″ tall. The leaves are roundish, lobed, and mainly basal. The leaf stems are glandular-hairy. Clusters of tiny, pale pink to white flowers with pinkish red sepals appear on multiple stalks.

Habitat: 3,500–12,000′. Dry, rocky habitats on ledges, often right out of crevices. LC, UC, SA, RO.

Comments: A beautiful plant in the late-afternoon light. Native Americans dried and ground the astringent roots and applied them to open wounds to stop bleeding. Chopped roots were also boiled and the liquid drunk as a tonic to relieve colic in babies or to relieve high fevers. It was also drunk for venereal diseases, liver troubles, diarrhea, and vomiting from stomach flu, or used as a gargle for sore throat. An infusion of the root was used as an eyewash.

JULIE S. CARVILLE

Pink Alumroot

Prairie Star

Lithophragma parviflorum var. *trifoliatum*
Native perennial
Prairie Star   Apr–Jun

Description: 6–14″ tall. The leaves are rounded and deeply lobed, each lobe sharply toothed. The flowers are pink (sometimes white) on a leafless stem, the petals usually deeply lobed.

Habitat: Below 2,000′. Open grassy areas and open woodlands. GR, CH, FW.

Comments: A variable species. The white-flowered form is sometimes called Woodland Star and mistaken for *L. heterophylla,* a species that is more likely to be found in the Coast Ranges. Several other *Lithophragmas* occur in our area and are sometimes called Woodland Star as well. They include *L. bolanderi, L. glabrum,* and *L. tenellum.* The flowers are slightly fragrant.

KAREN CALLAHAN

Brewer's Bishop's Cap

Mitella breweri   Native perennial
Brewer's Bishop's Cap   Apr–Aug

Description: 4–12″ tall. The leaves are basal, rounded, shallowly lobed, and up to 3″ across. The unusual flowers are tiny and yellowish green. The petals are linear and fringed. The sepals are fused to form a saucer shape. Yellowish anthers nestle in the sepal "saucer."

Habitat: 500–11,500′. Semi-shady, moist areas, often near streams or seeps. FW, LC, UC, SA, MM, RP.

Comments: Named after William Brewer, the botanist hired by the governor to survey California's flora and fauna from 1860 to 1864. His account of the trip in his book, *Up and Down California,* is wonderful. The common name Bishop's Cap refers to the resemblance of the fruit capsule to the cap worn by Catholic bishops.

JULIE S. CARVILLE

Parnassia californica   Native perennial
California Grass of Parnassus   Jul–Oct

Description: Grows 6–20″ tall. The leaves are basal and oval to lance-ovate with a tapering base. There is a single flowering stalk. The flowers are creamy white with greenish veins, ½–1″ wide. Fringed staminodes occur at the base of the petals.

Habitat: Below 12,000′. Wet meadows, seeps, streamsides. MM, RP.

Comments: Grass of Parnassus is unusual for a member of the Saxifrage family because instead of the usual cluster of tiny flowers atop each stem, there is only one large flower per stem. This flower has 5 stamens and 5 staminodes, which are infertile stamens (without anthers) that are covered with tiny fringes.

California Grass of Parnassus

Saxifraga californica   Native perennial
California Saxifrage   Feb–Jun

Description: Grows 4–12″ tall. The leaves are oblong and basal and, unlike most members of the Saxifrage family, they are unlobed. The white flowers bloom atop leafless, reddish, glandular-hairy stems. The sepals are reddish, as are the stamens. The fruit is 2-beaked.

Habitat: Up to 4,000′. Damp to drying slopes, ledges, and grassy places. GR, CH, FW, RP.

Comments: They commonly grow around mossy rocks and grassy hillsides in the spring, but are summer dormant and disappear at the onset of summer heat. It blooms in March at the Spenceville Wildlife Area west of Grass Valley and along the rocky river canyons.

California Saxifrage

Hooker's Saxifrage

CHET BLACKBURN

Saxifraga integrifolia   Native perennial
Hooker's Saxifrage,
Whole-leaf Saxifrage   Feb–Apr

Description: 6–12″ tall. The leaf blades are egg-shaped to spoon-shaped, and succulent. The edges are smooth or nearly so. A single erect reddish flower stem arises from the basal leaf cluster. The flowers are in dense headlike clusters; the petals are white and egg-shaped.

Habitat: 100–2,000′. Vernally moist valley grasslands, chaparral openings, and open Blue Oak woodlands. GR, CH, FW.

Comments: The plant can be distinguished from the California Saxifrage by its having entire (meaning not serrated) leaves, a denser inflorescence, and the lack of red stamens. It also is generally found at lower elevations than the California Saxifrage. Locally common, especially in the Auburn area.

Brook Saxifrage

RICHARD HANES • JULIE S. CARVILLE

Saxifraga odontoloma   Native perennial
Brook Saxifrage,
Streambank Saxifrage   Jun–Aug

Description: Grows 8–20″ tall. The leaves are simple, rounded, lobed, and adorned with sharp teeth. Tiny, delicate flowers (¼″ wide) bloom in a loose cluster on leafless stems. Each white petal has a pair of yellow dots. The anthers are bright red.

Habitat: Above 5,000′. Streamsides. MM, RP.

Comments: This one can by separated from the other saxifrages in our area by looking at the leaves. The leaf blade is roundish, often with a heart-shaped base, and is as broad as it is long. All our other saxifrages have leaves that are noticeably longer than wide. The yellow dots on the flowers are also unique. Use a hand lens to appreciate the delicate beauty of this flower.

Saxifraga oregana   Native perennial
Bog Saxifrage   May–Aug

Description: 1–3′ tall with glandular-hairy, thick stems and a rosette of hairy, succulent foliage. The leaves are oval in a basal cluster. The white to greenish white flowers are ¼″ wide with red-orange anthers. The flowers form a tight, elongated cluster at the end of fleshy stems. The petals may be of different sizes. The ovary ripens into a red, fleshy, 2-beaked structure so characteristic of the Saxifrage family.

Habitat: 3,500–11,000′. Streamsides and wet meadows. AQ, UC, MM, RP, SA.

Comments: Use a hand lens to view the glandular-hairy stems. The flowers form buds nestled in a basal leaf rosette, then the stem elongates and later the flowers bloom on the tall stalk. Abundant in boggy areas at Sagehen Creek, north of Truckee.

JULIE S. CARVILLE

Bog Saxifrage

Tellima grandiflora   Native perennial
Fringe Cups   Apr–Jul

Description: 1–3′ tall. The heart-shaped leaves are basal, shallowly lobed, and coarsely toothed. The inflorescences are on hairy stems rising from a rhizome. The flowers are white or greenish white with fringed petals, aging to reddish brown.

Habitat: Below 5,000′. Stream banks, moist wooded or rocky areas. FW, LC, RP, RO.

Comments: Out of bloom, Fringe Cups might be mistaken for an Alumroot, since the foliage is very similar. But there is no doubt which plant it is once the flower stalk emerges. Native Americans cooked and ate the whole plant to restore a lagging appetite. The plant is in cultivation and makes a great addition to a shade garden. It can be seen in its native habitat at the Rock Creek Nature Trail.

DON JACOBSON • CINDY RUBIN

Fringe Cups

Scrophulariaceae
FIGWORT FAMILY
Julie Carville

Annuals, perennials, and shrubs. The leaves are usually alternate, unlobed, and simple, and usually lack stipules. *The flowers are generally showy and are tubular, bilateral, and two-lipped, with the upper lip usually 2-lobed (but sometimes fused) and the lower lip 3-lobed. A single pistil and usually 4 stamens, with the fifth stamen as an infertile staminoid,* which is a filament with no anther. The family name is derived from a species in this family used to cure scrofula, a disease of the lymph glands. There are 200 genera and 3,000 species worldwide. It is well represented in California with 32 genera, and in our area with 23 genera and 106 species.

Brewer's Snapdragon

Antirrhinum vexillo-calyculatum
ssp. *breweri*　　　　　Native annual
Brewer's Snapdragon　　　　Jun–Aug

Description: 4–24″ plant with well-branched, glandular-hairy stems. The flowers are in the axils of the linear leaves. The flowers are up to ½″ long and lavender-violet, with a rounded basal pouch. The upper lip is erect. The flower tube and upper lip have violet lines. There are hairs on the larger lower lip above the lobes. The anthers are yellow.

Habitat: Below 6,600′. Open, rocky areas, often on serpentine. FW, LC, UC, RO, SG.

Comments: The stems are sometimes weak and clinging to other plants. The garden snapdragon also belongs to the genus *Antirrhinum*; checking out these smaller flowers with a hand lens will reveal the similarities. The other *Antirrhinum* in our area, *A. cornutum,* has small white flowers.

CHET BLACKBURN

Castilleja applegatei   Native perennial
Applegate's Paintbrush   Apr–Aug

Description: 4–24″ tall. The leaves are wavy edged with lobes or are linear. They are glandular-hairy (sticky). The flower bracts range from green and red to entirely red to orangish to pinkish with red or yellowish tips. The upper petals are yellowish green with reddish edges.

Habitat: 900–12,000′. Dry meadows, open woods, and sagebrush. CH, FW, LC, UC, SA.

Comments: A common, variable species, it is also called the Wavy-leafed Indian Paintbrush. Named for Elmer Applegate (1867–1949), who studied Oregon's wildflowers. Paintbrush flowers are tubular and sit inside brightly colored bracts. Each flower is composed of 2 upper petals fused into 1 petal, with 3 rudimentary "lower petals" (3 tiny nubbins).

JULIE S. CARVILLE

Applegate's Paintbrush

Castilleja attenuata   Native annual
Valley Tassels   Mar–Jun

Description: Grows 4–12″ tall with hairy stems. The leaves are linear and lobed. The flower bract tips are yellowish to white. The lower flower lip forms a white pouch that is purple dotted, and resembles a little face.

Habitat: Below 4,000′. Grassy places. GR, FW, LC, SG.

Comments: The genus *Castilleja* is named after Domingo Castillejo, a Spanish botanist. Valley Tassels was formerly named *Orthocarpus attenuatus,* before the *Jepson Manual* regrouped many species of *Orthocarpus* into the *Castilleja* genus. All of the *Castillejas* are semi-parasitic. They derive a portion of their nutrients from other plants, but also manufacture their own food.

CAROL WITHAM

Valley Tassels

Purple Owl's Clover

RICHARD HANES

Castilleja exserta   Native annual
Purple Owl's Clover   Mar–May

Description: 4–16″ tall. An erect to sprawling plant with glandular-hairy stems and narrow lobed leaves. The flower bracts and flowers are deep pinkish purple, appearing on dense spikes. The upper flower tip forms a hooked beak with a little rounded, velvety cap. The lower petals are inflated and white tipped.

Habitat: Below 5,200′. Sunny, grasslands. GR.

Comments: Purple Owl's Clover often covers grassy hillsides with glorious color—a truly lovely sight to behold! Apparently someone in the past with an overly vivid imagination thought that the flowers peeking out from between the bracts resembled owls because of the two eyelike dark spots on the flowers' inflated lower lips, and pointed earlike upper lips, hence the common name.

Giant Red Paintbrush

JULIE S. CARVILLE

Castilleja miniata   Native perennial
Giant Red Paintbrush,
Scarlet Paintbrush   May–Sep

Description: 1–3′ tall (sometimes taller). The alternate leaves are lance-shaped, not lobed, with 3 prominent veins. The flower bracts are variable in color from bright red to reddish purple to pale red to orange.

Habitat: Up to 11,500′. Streamsides and wet meadows. GR, UC, SA, MM, RP.

Comments: Common. The name *miniata* means "cinnabar red," cinnabar being a bright red pigment. This is one of our tallest and most brightly colored paintbrushes. Not all of the red parts of the plants are really flowers. Some are modified leaflike structures called floral bracts that surround the flowers. Paintbrushes photosynthesize in their green leaves, but also parasitize neighboring shrubs.

Castilleja nana   Native perennial
Alpine Paintbrush   Jun–Sep

Description: 1–6″ tall. The stem leaves are
5–7-lobed. The flower bracts are yellow-green
or purplish; the flowers are pale yellow blotched
with purple and sporting tiny black "eyes" at
their tips.

Habitat: 6,400–12,000′. Dry alpine meadows,
sandy slopes, rocky places, and summits. SA,
MM, RO, SP.

Comments: Alpine Paintbrush is unlike any
other paintbrush, with its varying and odd mix of
yellowish whitish purplish color combinations
that blend in with its harsh environment. It is
parasitic on sagebrush (*Artemisia*) roots and
also photosynthesizes in its green leaves. It is
beautiful through a hand lens. The species name
nana means "dwarf." It can be found at Donner
Summit, Castle Peak, Mount Lola, and Ward Peak.

KAREN CALLAHAN

Alpine Paintbrush

Castilleja pilosa   Native perennial
Hairy Paintbrush,
Parrothead Paintbrush   Jun–Aug

Description: Grows 1–12″ tall, forms mats. The
whole plant is very soft hairy and nonglandular.
The leaves are linear-lanceolate and lobed to
entire. The lower bracts are pink to purplish
(sometimes greenish) with white edges, and the
tips of the bracts are rounded. Flowers are pale
yellow-green.

Habitat: 3,900–11,200′. Dry sagebrush flats to
mountain summits. UC, SA, MM, SP.

Comments: There are 36 species of *Castilleja*
in California, and almost half of them are found
in our area. Other common species in our area
include Pale Owl's Clover, *C. lineariloba*, Woolly
Indian Paintbrush, *C. foliolosa*, Lemmon's
Paintbrush, *C. lemmonii,* and Cream Sacs,
C. rubicundula.

JULIE S. CARVILLE

Hairy Paintbrush

Frosty Paintbrush

KAREN CALLAHAN

Castilleja pruinosa   Native perennial
Frosty Paintbrush   May–Aug

Description: 12–28″ tall on often branching stems that have tiny branched hairs on them. The leaves are narrowly lancelike, the upper leaves with 0–3 lobes and of a dark grayish color. The flower bracts are bright red to orange-red.

Habitat: 1,600–7,000′. Dry, open serpentine and gabbro soils, rocky habitats, or forest edges. FW, LC, RO, SG.

Comments: This paintbrush has adapted to growing on serpentine and gabbro soils that are toxic to many plants. This is one of more than 200 species of California plants that are restricted wholly or in large part to serpentine soils where competition for survival is less intense for those that are able to adapt to soils high in magnesium, chromium, nickel, and other toxic metals.

Chinese Houses

RICHARD HANES

Collinsia heterophylla   Native annual
Chinese Houses   Mar–Jul

Description: 6–20″ tall. Leaves opposite, narrowly triangular, and toothed, up to 3″ long. Gorgeous ¾–1″ flowers in a series of dense whorls around the stem. The upper 2 petals are white (or lavender to rose-purple to reddish magenta) with purple lines and spots, and are a dark rose-purple at the upper edge. The lower 2 petals are solid purple or of the same color as the upper ones. There is a third lower petal, the central one, but it is folded and hidden behind the other 2 lower petals.

Habitat: Below 3,300′. Shady, grassy places. GR, CH, FW.

Comments: The whorled arrangement of the flowers is suggestive of a Chinese pagoda, hence the common name. Variable, it hybridizes with other *Collinsias*.

Collinsia parviflora
Blue-eyed Mary

Native annual
Mar–Jul

Description: 1″ to (rarely) 16″ tall, erect to branching, few to no glandular hairs on stem. Leaves opposite, linear to lance-shaped, and smooth edged. Flowers tiny (¼″), upper lobes white with bluish tips, lower lobes bluish.

Habitat: 2,600–11,500′. Moist, shady places. GR, FW, LC, UC, SA, MM.

Comments: Check out this tiny flower with a hand lens. It's one of nature's little miracles! Although normally blue, as the name suggests, magenta flowers and white flowers are also known. There is variation in flower size in different populations of this plant. The larger flowered plants are mostly pollinated by insects, whereas populations of the smaller flowered plants are less visited by insects and mostly self-pollinated.

JULIE S. CARVILLE

Blue-eyed Mary

Collinsia sparsiflora
Few-flowered Blue-eyed Mary

Native annual
Apr–Jun

Description: 2–10″ tall, with finely hairy to nonhairy and nonglandular stems. The leaves are linear, oblong, and smooth edged. The ½″ flower is purple, but with the upper petals white at the base. The flowers are in opposite pairs.

Habitat: Below 4,000′. Grassy areas, chaparral, and open woods. GR, CH, FW, LC.

Comments: This species can be distinguished from *C. parviflora* by its long pedicels, giving it a less compact appearance. It can additionally be distinguished by the fact that in *C. parviflora* the upper filaments and the middle corolla lobe (hidden by the other two bottom "petals") are not hairy, whereas in this species they are hairy. *C. parviflora* also tends to have a "bluer" shade of blue.

KAREN CALLAHAN

Few-flowered Blue-eyed Ma

Sticky Chinese Houses

Collinsia tinctoria   Native annual
Sticky Chinese Houses,
Tincture Plant   May–Aug

Description: 8–24″ tall with hairy stems. The leaves are opposite, clasping the stem, and are glandular-pubescent. The flowers are in a series of whorls around the stem. The flower is greenish white, or pale lavender-white to yellowish with purple dots or lines.

Habitat: 1,900–8,200′. Dry to moist, open habitats, forests, and rocky areas. CH, FW, LC, UC, RO.

Comments: Hybridizes with *Collinsia heterophylla,* making identification sometimes difficult. The species name *tinctoria* means staining, and refers to the fact that breaking or squeezing the stem or foliage leaves a reddish stain on the hands. The stain does not show up immediately, but appears after a few minutes.

KAREN CALLAHAN

Torrey's Blue-eyed Mary

Collinsia torreyi   Native annual
Torrey's Blue-eyed Mary   May–Aug

Description: 2–10″ tall on leafy, glandular-hairy stems. The flowers are ½″, densely glandular, and arranged in open whorls. The upper petals are pale lavender or whitish with a yellow base and purple dots. The lower petals are deep blue to blue-lavender.

Habitat: 3,000–10,000′. Damp or drying open sandy soils, forest openings. CH, LC, UC, SA.

Comments: Torrey's Blue-eyed Mary blooms along the trail to Paige Meadows at the North Shore of Lake Tahoe and in some years blooms in profusion in the dryish, open meadows at Sagehen Creek, north of Truckee. It can be distinguished from the other two "Blue-eyed Mary" species by its hairy glandular inflorescence, and this one grows at a much higher elevation than the other two species.

RICHARD HANES

Digitalis purpurea
Foxglove

Non-native biennial/perennial
May–Sep

Description: 1–6' tall. The leaves are hairy and large, up to 12" long. They form a rosette at the base of the plant as well as growing in an alternate arrangement along the flowering stem. The conspicuously large and colorful flowers cascade down the erect stalk. The flowers can be pink, purple, or white, and are tubular and 2-lipped with spots inside the tube.

Habitat: Below 3,300'. Woodlands. GR, FW, LC.

Comments: It is well known as the original source of digitalis, a drug that strengthens the contraction of the heart muscle, slows the heart rate, and helps eliminate fluid from body tissues. All parts of the plant are toxic and could be fatal if ingested.

RICHARD HANES

Foxglove

Kickxia elatine
Sharp-pointed Kickxia, Fluellen

Non-native annual
Jun–Sep

Description: A tiny, sticky, soft-hairy little plant that grows trailing on the ground with branching stems. The central stem is erect; the numerous lateral stems are ascending to prostrate. The leaves are widely arrowhead-shaped, and the hairy flowers are borne singly in the leaf axils and are yellowish to bluish with a violet upper lip.

Habitat: Below 3,300'. Disturbed places in the sun such as gravel bars, highway medians and shoulders, railroad rights-of-way, and parking lots. GR, CH, FW, RP.

Comments: Native to the Mediterranean region, it is more common than is generally realized but is inconspicuous enough to be easily overlooked. The flowers are small but fascinating when viewed with a hand lens, with their long spurs and two-toned pair of lobes.

CINDY RUBIN

Sharp-pointed Kickxia

JULIE S. CARVILLE

Pansy Monkeyflower

Mimulus angustatus　　　　Native annual
Pansy Monkeyflower　　　　Apr–Jun

Description: Grows on ¼″ stems from a tight cluster of basal, hairy leaves. The flower is magenta-purple with a purple spot on each petal. The flower tube is an outlandish 1–2″ long, extending well beyond the tiny calyx.

Habitat: 800–4,000′. Wet depressions in spring. VP, CH, FW, LC.

Comments: A gorgeous little flower that blooms in profusion at Hell's Half Acre near Grass Valley. It is the most common of the 3 small monkeyflowers found at that site. Although small, the flower is nonetheless large in relation to the foliage. It occurs there mostly in low, vernally wet depressions in disturbed (bare) soil and on gopher mounds. *Mimulus* is the diminutive of the Latin *mimus* for "little actor" or "mime," referring to its little flower face.

CHET BLACKBURN

Sticky Bush Monkeyflower

Mimulus aurantiacus "aurantiacus"
　　　　　　　　　　Native subshrub
Sticky Bush Monkeyflower　　　　May–Jul

Description: 2–4′ tall with woody stems that are glandular-hairy above. The leaves are narrow and sticky, paler beneath, and with hairs topped with tiny "hair stars." The flowers are showy, ½–1″ long, the petals shallowly notched one-quarter of their length at the tips and orangish yellow to salmon colored.

Habitat: Below 5,200′. Dry slopes. CH, FW, LC, RO.

Comments: Look for leaf "hair stars" with a hand lens. This form is the more common one at lower elevations. It was known as *Diplaucus aurantiacus* before the release of the current *Jepson Manual* in 1993. It is also in cultivation. All the bush monkeyflowers are good hummingbird plants.

Mimulus aurantiacus "bifidus"

Native subshrub

Bush Monkeyflower   May–Jul

Description: 2–4′ tall, woody stems, hairy above. The leaves are narrow and paler on the undersides. The flowers are showy and 2–3″ long, pale cream to salmon colored, with petals deeply notched one-quarter to one-half their length.

Habitat: Below 5,200′. Dry slopes. CH, FW, LC, UC, RO.

Comments: The flowers look like lovely little azaleas. This plant blooms abundantly along Highway 49, especially on the hillsides near the bridge over the South Yuba River. It was formerly known as *Diplaucus bifidus*. Bush monkeyflowers have now been lumped together as a single species even though they are very different from each other in appearance.

Bush Monkeyflower

Mimulus bicolor   Native annual

Yellow and White Monkeyflower   Apr–Jun

Description: Grows 4–12″ tall. The upper 2 petals of the flower are white (rarely lavender to purple), while the lower 3 petals are yellow with red spots.

Habitat: 1,000–4,000′. Moist places, grassy areas. GR, CH, FW, LC.

Comments: A striking little flower often hidden among grasses. At least 24 of the 65 species of *Mimulus* found in the state occur in Placer and Nevada Counties. Anyone interested in our wildflowers soon comes across this genus and can't help but be charmed by its members. From the larger bush monkeyflowers down to the tiny species with flowers that are bigger than the rest of the plant, they are lovely and colorful members of our native flora.

Yellow and White Monkeyflower

Scarlet Monkeyflower

Mimulus cardinalis   Native perennial
Scarlet Monkeyflower   Apr–Oct

Description: 1–3′ tall. The plant has soft, oval, hairy leaves in opposite pairs along the stem, the upper ones clasping the stem. The whole plant is sticky to the touch. The 2″ flowers are bright red, the upper petals erect and the lower petals bent back at the sides. The protruding stamens are topped with anthers that are creamy and toothed.

Habitat: Below 8,000′. Seep areas. FW, LC, MM, RP, SP.

Comments: Native Americans steeped the plant in boiled water to use as a wash for newborns. They also ate the tender stalks raw. It is a striking plant of wet areas. Its red petals make it a favorite of hummingbirds. It is also a food source of Buckeye and Checkerspot butterflies.

KAREN CALLAHAN

Seepspring Monkeyflower

Mimulus guttatus   Native annual/perennial
Seepspring Monkeyflower   Mar–Sep

Description: 2–36″ tall. The stems root at the nodes. The leaves are oval and clasp the upper stems. The flowers are often large and showy, 1″ long, and with or without red, purple, or brown spots on the lower petals. The lower petals are also adorned with yellow hairs.

Habitat: Below 11,000′. Widespread in wet places. VP, GR, FW, LC, UC, SA, MM, RP.

Comments: Common and variable. The annual form grows to about 4″ tall, with several small flowers, red spotted on lower petals. The flowers fall off after fertilization, exposing the pistil. Native Americans ate the leaves raw or cooked. The crushed leaves were applied as a poultice to wounds, and a tea was brewed to ease stomachaches.

JULIE S. CARVILLE

Mimulus kelloggii   Native annual
Kellogg's Monkeyflower   Mar–Jun

Description: 2–12″ in height. The leaves are
oval-shaped, sometimes purplish on the veins and
on the undersides. The flowers are a deep rose-
pink ½–¾″ wide with a long, very slender tube.
The lower petals are shorter than the upper ones
and the flower throat is yellow with red dots.

Habitat: 160–5,200′. Damp to dry open hillsides,
flats, disturbed areas in full sun. GR, CH, FW.

Comments. One of the prettiest of the monkeyflowers. It is especially gorgeous when viewed
through a hand lens. Albert Kellogg was a botanist
and doctor who lived in the 1800s and helped to
establish the California Academy of Sciences in
San Francisco. It can be seen along the Stevens
Trail near Colfax and on the banks along Yankee
Jim's Road.

JULIE S. CARVILLE

Kellogg's Monkeyflower

Mimulus layneae   Native annual
Layne's Monkeyflower   May–Aug

Description: 2–8″ tall with glandular-hairy,
simple or branched stems. The leaves are linear
to oblanceolate and up to 1″ long. The flowers
are up to ¾″ long, magenta to rose with a white
throat and rose spots, and a dark spot in the
crease of the lower petal. The anthers are hairy
and the stigma fringed. The calyx lobes are
unequal and spreading.

Habitat: 600–6,000′. Sandy, gravelly flats and
ridges. CH, SG, LC, UC.

Comments: A strongly scented little plant
colonizing disturbed areas, often found along
roadsides. It more often appears as scattered
individuals rather than in large masses as some
of the other smaller monkeyflowers do. It is one
of three small monkeyflowers found at Hell's
Half Acre, but is the least common of the three.

CINDY RUBIN

Layne's Monkeyflower

Lewis' Monkeyflower

Mimulus lewisii Native perennial
Lewis' Monkeyflower Jun–Sep

Description: 1–3′ tall in clusters, hairy stems with large opposite clasping leaves. The leaves have prominent parallel ribs. The 1–2″ flowers are pink with yellow hairs and ridges down the throat.

Habitat: 4,000–10,000′. Stream banks, seeps. UC, SA, MM, RP.

Comments: Named after Meriwether Lewis (1774–1809) of the Lewis and Clark expedition. Its hinged, disklike stigma rests against the throat of the top 2 petals. Touch the stigma with a blade of grass and it will close. If it has been pollinated, it will stay closed, but if not pollinated, it reopens in a few minutes to await another chance! Look for Sphinx Moths, hovering like tiny hummingbirds, as they pollinate the flowers.

Skunky Monkeyflower

Mimulus mephiticus Native annual
Skunky Monkeyflower Jun–Aug

Description: 1–6″ tall, glandular-hairy with a strong "offensive" odor. The narrow, veined leaves are very sticky haired. The flowers are either pink or yellow, depending upon the particular population, and some populations contain both forms. The flowers are brightly marked with yellow ridges and red spots on the lower petals and have a protruding stigma. The petals are nearly equal and the calyx is sticky haired.

Habitat: 5,000–11,500′. Sandy, gravelly granitic soil. SA, SP.

Comments: Mephitic means "smells offensive." Its protruding stigma (and sometimes anthers) helps to distinguish it from other similar-looking species. Yellow-flowered Skunkys can be distinguished by their flower stems, which are shorter than the flower tube, unlike other yellow species.

Mimulus moschatus   Native perennial
Musk Monkeyflower   May–Aug

Description: 2–12″ in height, often in little clumps. It has weak, drooping stems bearing shallow, toothed, woolly leaves. The flowers are yellow with narrow hairy throats; the floor of the tube throat is deeply grooved.

Habitat: Below 9,500′. Seeps and stream banks, moist to dry areas, shaded/sunny areas among trees. LC, UC, SA, RP.

Comments: Often found in shaded alder groves, it is easy to identify by its equal-sized petals and the slimy, often cold feeling of the leaves. Native Americans boiled young plant leaves for food. The species is in cultivation, but in a touch of irony, is more often found in cultivation in Europe, where it is grown in pots, than in California gardens.

JULIE S. CARVILLE

Musk Monkeyflower

Mimulus primuloides ssp. *primuloides*
                                       Native perennial
Primrose Monkeyflower   Jun–Aug

Description: 3–6″ tall. Spreading by rhizomes. The leaves are in a basal rosette and covered with long scattered hairs. The naked flower stems support a single yellow flower per stem (like a little primrose). The fragile-looking flowering stem is long and slender. The petals are notched and the bottom 3 petals contain maroon to reddish spots of varying size.

Habitat: 2,000–11,000′. Wet meadows, stream banks, and seeps. LC, UC, SA, MM, RP.

Comments: A tiny plant from high elevations that is often hidden among other vegetation. The leaves collect dew at night. In the morning tiny rainbows can be seen if you position yourself at the correct angle to the sun.

JULIE S. CARVILLE

Primrose Monkeyflower

Candelabra Monkeyflower

Mimulus pulsiferae   Native annual
Candelabra Monkeyflower   Jun–Jul

Description: 2–6″ tall with stems spreading or upright. The elliptic stem leaves are up to ³⁄₄″ long and arranged in pairs along the reddish stems. The basal leaves are egg-shaped. The small ¹⁄₄–¹⁄₂″ bright yellow flowers have maroon spots on their lower petals.

Habitat: 1,500–6,000′. Seasonally wet areas. FW, LC, UC, MM, RP.

Comments: This plant can be distinguished from other species by tiny glandular hairs on the flower, which can be seen with a magnifying glass. The flower stems curve out and up from the axils of its leaves like a candelabra. The plant can be seen at Hell's Half Acre in May growing alongside the magenta-purplish and more common species, the Pansy Monkeyflower.

Torrey's Monkeyflower

Mimulus torreyi   Native annual
Torrey's Monkeyflower   Apr–Oct

Description: 2–12″ tall. It has tiny (best seen with a hand lens) hairy leaves that are narrowly elliptic to almost egg-shaped with a deep central vein. The flowers are a light magenta to a reddish purple. The ridges of the throat are yellow and bordered by purple.

Habitat: 1,800–6,800′. Dry openings in coniferous forests. LC, UC.

Comments: Resembles Layne's Monkeyflower, *M. layneae*, but can be separated by the following characteristics: *M. torreyi* has a green calyx that is not conspicuously ribbed, the floral tube is narrower, which gives the flower a more elongated appearance, and the ridges in the throat are yellow with a purple margin. In *M. layneae* the calyx is ribbed and generally purplish, and the throat ridges are whitish with purple spotting.

Mimulus tricolor
Tricolored Monkeyflower

Native annual
Apr–Jun

Description: 1–6″ in height. Leaves oval to lancelike. The flower is pink-purple, has a white throat with yellow staining and dark spots, and a triangular spot on each petal.

Habitat: Below 2,000′. Edges of vernal pools. VP.

Comments: This species is more common in the Sacramento and San Joaquin Valleys and enters our area only on the extreme western edge. It is found in some of the vernal pools in the Roseville-Lincoln area, but the rapid loss of vernal pool habitats to development has made it increasingly difficult to find. The small seed capsules are very hard, remain closed during the hot, dry dormant season, and open to release the seed only after prolonged exposure to water, an adaptation to their vernal pool habitat.

PRENTISS FERGUSON

Tricolored Monkeyflower

Parentucellia viscosa
Yellow Glandweed, Yellow Bartsia

Non-native annual
Apr–Jun

Description: 6–18″ tall. Sticky hairy, un-branched stems. The leaves are lance shaped, toothed, arranged in pairs, and attached directly to the stem. The yellow flowers emerge from leafy bracts on the upper portion of the flowering stem. The 2 petal lobes on the upper lip are joined together, while the lower 3 petal lobes are separate for a third or more of their length.

Habitat: Under 1,000′. Vernally wet places. GR, FW.

Comments: An uncomfortably sticky plant native to the Mediterranean region. It has been established sparingly, especially in the Lincoln area, along roadsides where road runoff increases moisture availability. They are more abundant in wet years. It is semi-parasitic, attaching itself to the roots of nearby plants.

KAREN CALLAHAN

Yellow Glandweed

Little Elephant Head

Pedicularis attolens   Native perennial
Little Elephant Head   Jun–Sep

Description: 6–18″ tall. The leaves are deeply divided and almost fernlike. The ¼–½″ flowers are clustered at the top of the stem in a tight spike. They are pink with upward twisted "trunks" formed by the upper petals.

Habitat: 5,000–12,800′. Wet meadows, streamsides. AQ, SA, MM, RP.

Comments: Little Elephant Head vaguely resembles an elephant's head with a tiny upturned "trunk." It can be distinguished from its larger relative, the Elephant Head, *P. groenlandica,* by having smaller leaves and flowers and its later blooming season. Bees know the difference. The pollen from this smaller species is deposited on the bee's thorax, while the pollen from Elephant Head is deposited on its abdomen.

JULIE S. CARVILLE

Indian Warrior

Pedicularis densiflora   Native perennial
Indian Warrior   Jun–Aug

Description: 6–24″ tall. The dark green fernlike leaves are sometimes tinted red. The stems are purplish with brown hairs. The conspicuous flowers range from red to dark red to purple-red, and occur in dense spikes. The individual flowers are tubular (1¼″ long) with a straight upper beak. The lower lip is composed of 3 lobes.

Habitat: Below 7,000′. Shady, damp to dry wooded areas. CH, FW, LC, SP.

Comments: Indian Warrior is parasitic on the roots of shrubs, mostly on members of the Heath family such as Manzanita and Madrone. This allows it to live in shady environments because it is not solely dependent upon sunlight for photosynthesis to survive. The colonies under a favored host tend to expand over the years.

RICHARD HANES

Pedicularis groenlandica　Native perennial
Elephant Head　Jun–Aug

Description: 1–3′ tall. The fernlike leaves start out reddish before turning green. They are most abundant on the lower part of the stem. The flowers (½–¾″) look like little pink elephant heads. The upper petals create a "trunk," while the lower petals form "floppy elephant ears." The reproductive parts are hidden in the "trunk."

Habitat: 3,300–12,000′. Wet meadows, streamsides. UC, SA, MM, RP.

Comments: The resemblance of the flower to an elephant's head is uncanny and amusing. A herd of them placed along a flowering stem is a sight that makes a safari into their soggy surroundings well worth getting one's shoes wet. Native Americans made an infusion of the powdered leaves and stems to relieve coughs.

JULIE S. CARVILLE

Elephant Head

Pedicularis semibarbata　Native perennial
Dwarf Lousewort　May–Jul

Description: 2–6″ tall. Stems mainly underground. The leaves are in a basal rosette, up to 6″ long, bipinnate and somewhat resembling a fern. The flowers are in whorls around the stem, and are yellowish with purplish tips and a short upper lip. They may be hidden under the green leafy floral bracts.

Habitat: 5,000–11,500′. Forest floor in shade or sun. LC, UC.

Comments: Both its botanical and common names come from an old belief that livestock that ate members of this genus were more prone to lice infestation. "Wort" comes from "wyrt," the Old English name for "herbaceous plant" and "pedicularis" is Latin for "lice." The plant is common in the Lake Tahoe area. It is a preferred host of the Checkerspot butterfly.

RICHARD HANES

Dwarf Lousewort

Azure Penstemon

Penstemon azureus   Native perennial
Azure Penstemon   May–July

Description: 8–27″ tall with a woody base. The opposite, clasping bluish green leaves are widest on the upper part of the stem. They are oval and entire. The flowers are tubular, with flaring petals, 2 upper and 3 lower. The unopened buds are yellow, turning blue as they prepare to open. The staminode (a filament without an anther) is hairless.

Habitat: 1,000–8,000′. Dry, sunny areas, gravelly/sandy soils. UC, SA, RO, SG.

Comments: Penstemons have 4 stamens and 1 staminode and are identified in flower keys (a binary system to deduce names of plants) by whether the staminode is glabrous (without hairs) or hairy. When a staminode is hairy it looks like a little toothbrush.

RICHARD HANES

Hotrock Penstemon

Penstemon deustus   Native perennial
Hotrock Penstemon   May–Aug

Description: 6–24″ tall. The mostly basal leaves are leathery and lancelike with jagged edges. The flowers are in clusters. Individual flowers are ½″ wide, and white to creamy with red to maroon lines on the lower petals. The upper petals appear shriveled. They grow in whorls around the stem and are glandular and aromatic.

Habitat: 2,000–10,000′. Rocky, sandy, dry places. UC, SA, RO.

Comments: This is Lake Tahoe's only white penstemon. Its leathery leaves help reduce evaporation in its dry habitat. Native Americans mashed the raw leaves and used the extracted juice as medicine for venereal disease or as a poultice for mosquito and tick bites and other sores. The roots were dried into a powder and applied to sores.

PRENTISS FERGUSON

Penstemon heterodoxus   Native perennial
Whorled Penstemon   Jul–Sep

Description: 2–8″ tall. The leaves are entire
(not toothed or lobed) and sometimes folded.
The flowers are glandular-hairy, blue-purple,
and appear in whorls around the stem. The
staminode is hairy.

Habitat: 6,000–12,800′. Mountain slopes,
meadows. SA, MM.

Comments: Its glandular-hairy flowers distinguish it from the nonglandular, hairless flowers
of *Penstemon rydbergii;* otherwise they look
almost identical. *P. heterodoxus* also grows at a
higher elevation. There are 53 species of penstemons in California, and at least 9 of them occur
in Nevada and Placer Counties. Many of them
have been introduced into cultivation and/or
used in producing hybrid penstemons.

Whorled Penstemon

Penstemon heterophyllus var. *purdyi*
    Native perennial
Foothill Penstemon   May–Jun

Description: 1–5′ tall. The lower leaves are
narrow, 1–4″ long, and alternate along the stem.
The upper leaves are much shorter and are
opposite on the stem. The very showy flowers
are in clusters of individual flowers about 1¼″
long, with a color range that is hard to describe
but gorgeous. It ranges from blue to violet, with
shades of magenta. The staminode is hairless.

Habitat: Up to 5,200′. Grassy hillsides, forest
openings. CH, FW, LC, RO.

Comments: One of our prettiest penstemons.
The species name *heterophyllus* refers to its
variable leaves. It is common, especially in
exposed rocky canyons. It can be seen along the
Buttermilk Bend Trail at Bridgeport and in the
American River Canyon.

Foothill Penstemon

Gay Penstemon

Penstemon laetus   Native perennial
Gay Penstemon   May–Jul

Description: 6–30″ tall, woody at the base. The leaves are linear to lance-shaped and entire. The flower tube is narrow, blue, and glandular. The staminode is glabrous.

Habitat: 1,300–8,200′. Open scrub or partial shade of forest. LC, UC, SA.

Comments: A delicate-looking penstemon, its tubular flowers are narrower than those of most penstemons. It can be confused with *Penstemon gracilentus,* which grows in the same environment and looks almost identical, but *P. laetus* has a glabrous staminode, while *P. gracilentus* has a hairy staminode. The Native Americans used this plant in steam baths to soothe grief—it is interesting to note that its common name, gay, is the opposite of grief.

KAREN CALLAHAN

Mountain Pride

Penstemon newberryi   Native perennial
Mountain Pride   Jun–Aug

Description: 5–12″ in height, mat forming, and is a subshrub with woody stems and leathery leaves. The flowers are bright rose-pink, glandular, and have white hairs on the lower petal ridges. The staminode is hairy. The anther sacs are white-woolly.

Habitat: 4,200–11,500′. Rock outcrops, talus slopes, sandy, dry soils. LC, UC, SA, RO.

Comments: Forms natural rock gardens and is highly desired for its beauty in homemade rock gardens as well. The flowers are striking against their rocky, sandy habitat. John Newberry was a nineteenth-century botanist and physician. Many doctors in the 1800s were fine botanists because their practice often depended upon knowledge of herbs used as medicines, which often sparked an interest in plants in general.

JULIE S. CARVILLE

Penstemon personatus   Native perennial
Close-throated Beardtongue   Jun

Description: 12–20″ tall, the stems are either short haired or without hairs, but covered with a coating that can be rubbed off. The leaves are largest in the middle of the stem, oval-shaped, and usually smooth edged. The flower is blue-purple, the outside glandular but without hairs, and densely hairy inside. The throat is nearly closed. The staminode is hairy.

Habitat: 5,000–6,000′. Forests. LC, UC.

Comments: Rare. The species name *personatus* means "with a two-lipped mouth." The term personate is often used in botany to describe two-lipped flowers such as the penstemons. This species differs markedly from most penstemons by having a nearly closed throat instead of the normally open one.

KAREN CALLAHAN • KAREN CALLAHAN

Close-throated Beardtongue

Penstemon rydbergii var. *oreocharis*
                            Native perennial
Meadow Penstemon   May–Aug

Description: 8–24″ tall. The leaves are smooth edged and lance-shaped without stem hairs, except for a few on the lower parts of stems. It produces from 1–10 flowering stalks, each with 3 to 4 whorls of flowers. The flowers are purple to bluish purple; white to yellow hairs are on the lower petal into the throat. The staminode is very hairy.

Habitat: 4,000–10,200′. Meadows. MM.

Comments: It is very similar to *P. heterodoxus,* the Whorled Penstemon. See the comments under that species regarding how to separate them. Meadow Penstemon fills the meadows of Paige Meadows at North Tahoe with acres of color in a good year. It is also common in the meadows between Sagehen Creek and Stampede Reservoir.

RICHARD HANES

Meadow Penstemon

Showy Penstemon

Penstemon speciosus   Native perennial
Showy Penstemon   Jun–Aug

Description: 2–24″ tall and shrublike. The blue-green leaves are linear to lance-shaped, and up to 3″ in length. They are leathery, smooth edged, and often folded lengthwise. It produces showy clusters of flowers, each flower up to 1¾″ long, with a white to pinkish throat. The staminode is hairless, except for a few hairs at the tip of the filament.

Habitat: 4,000–10,900′. Rocky slopes, summits. LC, UC, SA, RO, SP.

Comments: Common at Tahoe. It can be found on the trail to Mt. Rose and on Donner Summit. At ridgelines, it grows matted with short stems and dense clusters of flowers. The matting reduces damage from high-elevation winds and keeps the plant close to the ground's warmth.

California Figwort

Scrophularia californica   Native perennial
California Figwort   Jun–Aug

Description: 1½–4′ tall. The leaves are triangular to egg-shaped, up to 7½″ long. The small flower is a ½″ long "face," the upper petals brownish maroon, the lower petals paler to yellowish green. The lower petal is bent backward. The staminoid is club-shaped to round, brownish to maroon.

Habitat: Below 5,000′. Moist to dryish areas, disturbed places. CH, FW, LC.

Comments: Easy to identify because of its unusually colored small flowers, which seem disproportionately small compared with the tall stems and large leaves. Native Americans made a poultice of its leaves or used its plant juice to relieve sore eyes. They boiled the root and drank it to reduce fevers.

Triphysaria eriantha   Native annual
Butter and Eggs, Johnny Tuck   Mar–May

Description: 4–14″ tall. The leaves are deeply
lobed into narrow segments. The long flower
tube is hairy, thin, and white. The 2 upper petals
are purple and form a pointed beak, while the 3
lower petals form inflated sacs that are mostly
yellow but white at the flower's center. The flower
bracts and upper leaves are purple tipped.

Habitat: Below 4,200′. Grassy, open meadows.
GR, CH, FW, MM.

Comments: One of our most common spring
flowers, it often grows as extensive carpets in
sunny meadows. It is listed in older books as
Orthocarpus erianthus. The common name is
odd, as it doesn't really look like either eggs or
butter. *Triphysaria* is Greek for "three bladders"
and refers to its petal sacs; *eriantha* means
"woolly flowered" in reference to its hairiness.

KAREN CALLAHAN

Butter and Eggs

Verbascum blattaria   Non-native biennial
Moth Mullein   May–Oct

Description: 1–4′ tall. The first-year leaves
form a basal rosette with leaves reaching up to
9½″ long. They are crinkly and with little teeth
along the edges. In the second year it sends up a
single leafy flowering stalk bearing toothed
triangular leaves that grow smaller toward the
top. The flowers appear in the top portion of the
stem. They are yellow with orange anthers, but a
white form is also rather common.

Habitat: Below 5,200′. Disturbed places, open
grassy meadows. GR, CH, FW.

Comments: Native to Eurasia. Its leaves and
flowers have been used in fabric dyeing. It was
also thought to be an insect repellant.

RICHARD HANES

Moth Mullein

Woolly Mullein

Verbascum thapsus   Non-native biennial
Woolly Mullein   Jun–Sep

Description: 1–6′ tall and densely hairy with large, dull green, woolly leaves. It forms a dense rosette the first year and in the second year sends up a leafy, winged flower stalk. The small yellow flowers are clustered in long terminal spikes that have a long blooming period.

Habitat: Below 7,300′. Disturbed places. CH, FW, LC, UC, MM, SP.

Comments: Hairs on the plant are stellate (tiny hairs at the tip of the main hair form a tiny star). Although considered attractive, this plant is invasive in disturbed areas. It was introduced by way of Europe, although it is native to Asia. The plant dies after the seeds ripen. Herbalists use flower-steeped oil as a remedy for earaches.

JULIE S. CARVILLE

Persian Speedwell

Veronica persica   Non-native annual
Persian Speedwell   Jan–Aug

Description: About 1″ in height. A prostrate, spreading, weedy plant. The leaves are ovate to rounded, have marginal teeth, and are hairy. The blue flowers are ³⁄₈″ wide with deep blue lines, white centers, and 4 petals.

Habitat: Below 3,300′. Lawns, gardens, disturbed areas. GR, CH, FW, LC.

Comments: Native to Asia Minor, it has become established in most of the United States. It is one of the first plants to flower in spring and is lovely when viewed through a hand lens. A larger native species, American Brooklime, *V. americana,* is often found blooming from May through August at stream edges, lake margins, and in wet meadows. It also has blue to blue-violet 4-petaled flowers with dark lines, but is usually a darker blue.

KAREN CALLAHAN

Solanaceae
NIGHTSHADE FAMILY
Chet Blackburn

Herbs, shrubs, vines, and trees. The leaves are alternate and simple. The flowers are bisexual. The calyx consists of 4–6 (usually 5) persistent sepals, and a ***corolla consisting of 5 united petals. The fruit is a berry or capsule.*** It is an important family commercially, producing such products as tomatoes, potatoes, tobacco, peppers, and numerous drugs. There are 75 genera and about 3,000 species worldwide, especially well represented in the tropics. In California there are 12 genera and 58 species, but more than half of them are introduced non-natives. There are 5 genera and 16 species in Nevada and Placer Counties.

Nicotiana attenuata　　　　Native annual
Coyote Tobacco, Indian Tobacco　　May–Oct

Description: 1–6′ tall with a slender stalk and ovate to lance-shaped sticky (not always) leaves 2–6″ long. The flowers are white, long, and trumpetlike.

Habitat: 600–9,000′. Open, well-drained slopes, washes, and disturbed places, generally on the dry side. CH, FW, LC, UC, MM.

Comments: Particularly common following a fire. It can be confused with Bigelow's Tobacco, but Bigelow's has longer petal segments and the leaves are sessile (attached directly to the stem), whereas Coyote Tobacco has a definite petiole. It tends to appear on disturbed sites in large numbers and then disappear within a relatively short time. Among other uses, Native Americans chewed and smoked it, much as we now do with traditional tobacco.

CHET BLACKBURN

Coyote Tobacco

Black Nightshade

Solanum nigrum Non-native annual
Black Nightshade Mar–Jul

Description: 6–24″ tall. A bushy plant with many branches bearing smooth, elliptic to egg-shaped wavy leaves that taper to a tip. The flowers are starlike, resembling tomato flowers except that they are white to pale blue. They are followed by green berries that later turn into smooth, shiny black berries.

Habitat: Below 1,200′. Prefers rich soils and shady, moist, disturbed areas. GR, FW, RP.

Comments: The plant does not produce nectar but instead is pollinated by the buzzing action of insects shaking the pollen free. Native to Europe. The foliage and green fruit contain toxins, but heat from cooking may destroy the poisonous glycoalkaloids.

CHET BLACKBURN

Purple Nightshade

Solanum xanti Native perennial
Purple Nightshade, Blue Witch Mar–Sep

Description: 1–3′ tall. Herbaceous stems from a woody root. Thin, lance-shaped to egg-shaped leaves to 2″, often lobed at the base. Violet to blue, saucer-shaped flowers hang in terminal clusters and are up to 1″ in size. Each flower has a tight cluster of conspicuous bright yellow anthers. The flowers are followed by smooth, green, poisonous berries.

Habitat: Below 8,000′. Dry slopes, rocky soils, and open woodlands. CH, FW, LC, UC.

Comments: The plant is in cultivation and is on many "deer resistant," "fire resistant," and "drought tolerant" plant lists. There are 20 species of *Solanum* found in California, but more than half of them (13) have been introduced.

KAREN CALLAHAN

Urticaceae
NETTLE FAMILY
Vicki Lake

Annuals to soft-wooded trees, ***sometimes with stinging hairs.*** Flowers typically unisexual, small, and greenish. ***Typically 4 sepals and no petals. 1 style.*** Herbs with watery juice. There are 5 genera and 8 species in California, 50 genera and 700 species worldwide. Of those, there are 2 genera and 3 species in Nevada and Placer Counties.

Urtica dioica ssp. *holosericea*

Native perennial

Hoary Nettle   Jun–Sep

Description: 3–10′ tall, an erect plant with a gray-green stem. The large leaves are opposite, lance- to narrowly ovate-shaped, coarsely serrate, and have many stinging hairs. The stem and lower leaf surfaces have moderate to dense nonstinging hairs. The flowers are small and in separate dense clusters of male and female flowers.

Habitat: Below 10,000′. Stream banks and other moist areas such as margins of deciduous woodlands. FW, MM, RP.

Comments: Wind pollinated. The "sting" is caused by the injection of formic acid. The young stems and leaves are edible after boiling. They are most often found at the edge of woodlands, especially in dappled shade, and along creeks.

GORDON J. HARRINGTON

Hoary Nettle

364

Valerianaceae
VALERIAN FAMILY
Richard Hanes

Perennial or annual herbs, sometimes strongly scented. The basal and cauline leaves are *opposite,* simple, and pinnately lobed. The inflorescence is dense, either in the form of a cyme or headlike. The calyx is fused to the ovary top. *Flowers irregular. Corolla united,* funnel-shaped or 2-lipped, with generally 5 lobes and the base spurred or swollen. *Stamens 1–3, ovary inferior.* There are 17 genera and 300 species worldwide, 5 genera and 10 species in California, and 4 genera and 5 species in Nevada and Placer Counties.

Red Valerian

Centranthus ruber   Non-native perennial
Red Valerian, Jupiter's Beard   Apr–Aug

Description: 12–36″ tall. The stems are decumbent to erect, hollow, simple or branched, and woody at the base. The leaves on the stem are widely oblong to elliptic-lanceolate with entire margins. The inflorescence is terminal and densely clustered with flowers. The corolla is funnel-shaped, a tube less than ³⁄₄″ long, and slender. It is long spurred and purplish red, though sometimes lavender or white. Stamens 1.

Habitat: Below 1,500′. Disturbed urban places, rocky areas, and roadsides. GR, FW, RO.

Comments: *Centranthus* is derived from Greek, meaning "spurred flower." It is grown as an ornamental and touted for attracting butterflies. It has escaped cultivation and is locally common in areas such as the rocky cliffs along Taylor Road by the Newcastle Tunnel.

Plectritis ciliosa   Native annual
Long-tubed Plectritis,
Long-spurred Plectritis   Mar–May

Description: Stems erect, 2–30″ tall. The basal
and cauline leaves are sessile, simple, opposite,
entire, and narrow. The inflorescence is terminal, clustered, and headlike. The corolla is less
than ⅓″, 2-lipped, with the lower lip having 2
red spots. The spur is elongated, slender,
pointed, and extends well beyond the ovary.
Stamens 3.

Habitat: Below 5,000′. Open, partly shaded or
moist areas. GR, CH, FW, LC.

Comments: Look for the two little red dots on
each side of the middle petal lobe as a way to
distinguish it from White Plectritis, *P. macrocera,*
which is the only other *Plectritis* in our area.
Both are common here and occupy similar
habitats.

JULIE S. CARVILLE

Long-tubed Plectritis

Valeriana californica   Native perennial
California Valerian   Jun–Sep

Description: 8–24″ tall. Stems glabrous to
slightly hairy. Basal leaves simple or compound,
deeply 3-lobed, while leaves along the stem are
3–9-lobed. Clusters of small white to pinkish
flowers each with 3 protruding anthers begin as
tiny, pinkish buds.

Habitat: 4,500–10,000′. Moist wooded habitats.
LC, UC, SA, MM.

Comments: It is abundant along the Sagehen
Creek trail to Stampede Reservoir. The original
plant collection was on a ridge south of Donner
Pass at 8,500′ in Nevada County. The European
garden Valerian, *V. officinalis,* is a medicinal
sedative used as a calmative in nervousness and
hysteria (a favorite herb of members of the
Editorial Committee as they approached
publication).

MICHAEL GRAF

California Valerian

366

Verbenaceae
VERVAIN FAMILY
Karen Callahan

Trees, shrubs, and herbs. Opposite or whorled simple leaves. *The stems are often 4-sided. Flowers in spikelike clusters or heads. The corolla consists of 5 petals united to form a slender tube, opening wide at the top, and 4–5-lobed.* The ovary is superior, and there are 4–5 stamens. The fruit is a dry nutlet, capsule, or drupe. The family includes many weedy species but also some important horticultural species (Vervain, *Lantana, Vitex*). The family is also of economic importance because the highly prized teak wood comes from a tree in this family. There are 90 genera worldwide, 5 in California, and 2 genera and 4 species in Nevada and Placer Counties.

Western Verbena

Verbena lasiostachys   Native perennial
Western Verbena   Jun–Sep

Description: Plant 1–3′ tall, decumbent to erect, one to many 4-sided branching stems. The leaves are coarse but softly hairy, 1–4″ long, and toothed. The inflorescence is a spike of blue to purple flowers, with individual flowers less than ½″. The seeds are composed of 4 nutlets.

Habitat: Below 8,200′. Open areas, wet or dry. CH, FW, LC, UC.

Comments: Also called Western Vervain, a common name for many species in the family. Found in almost every county in California, but not common here. The flowers are pretty but very small. They are nonetheless attractive to butterflies. Although native, it has a "weedy" look to it and is often mistaken for a member of the Mint family because it has conspicuously square stems.

Violaceae
VIOLET FAMILY
Julie Carville

Annuals or perennials. Flowers *bilateral with 5 petals: 2 upper petals, 2 dark-veined side petals, and 1 veined lower petal that is spurred or pouched,* holding nectar for pollinators. Leaves alternate or basal. Flowers in most species are of two types: The spring flower has showy petals and seeks pollination; the later season flower is *cleistogamous,* forming a bud that never opens. It self-fertilizes to create a clone of the mother plant. Fruit is a 3-parted *capsule,* which upon opening looks like 3 little canoes with the seeds lined up inside. Violet flowers and leaves are edible as a salad and are high in vitamin C. Native Americans used the leaves like aspirin for relief of headaches and burned the roots as incense. Worldwide there are 15 genera and 600 species, 1 genus in California, and 15 species in our area.

Viola adunca
Western Dog Violet

Native perennial
Mar–Aug

Description: 2–6" tall. The leaves are oval-shaped at the base and are on long stems. The flowers are deep to pale violet with the 2 side petals white and fuzzy at the base; the lower 3 petals form a pouch and are often white at the base with the lower petal long spurred.

Habitat: Up to 11,500'. Stream edges, damp forest edges. FW, LC, UC, SA, MM, RP.

Comments: A lovely little violet resembling the domesticated common violet. It usually has a white throat with purple lines. Both leaves and flowers of violets are edible. Native Americans applied an infusion of the leaves to sore and swollen joints. A poultice of the chewed leaves was applied to sore eyes, and the whole plant was used to dye arrows blue.

KAREN CALLAHAN

Western Dog Violet

Great Basin Violet

JULIE S. CARVILLE

Viola beckwithii   Native perennial
Great Basin Violet,
Beckwith's Violet   Mar–May

Description: 2–9″ tall. The stems are clustered and leafy from a short erect rhizome. The grayish green leaves are divided into oblong to linear, fleshy segments. The lower petals are whitish purple with a yellowish base. The 2 upper petals are reddish purple.

Habitat: 3,000–9,000′. Dry, gravelly places, especially among sagebrush. SP.

Comments: With its pansylike flowers, it is the most multicolored of our violets. It is common on the eastern side of the Sierra. It is a plant of seasonally moist places, especially sagebrush flats and slopes, where it becomes summer dormant. It can be seen at the Martis Lake Wildlife Area in Placer County near North Star Ski Resort.

Douglas' Violet

JULIE S. CARVILLE

Viola douglasii   Native perennial
Douglas' Violet   Mar–May

Description: 2–8″ tall. Foliage clustered and rising from a short rhizome. The leaves are divided into numerous linear lobes. The flowers are large and golden yellow with dark brown veining. The upper petals are dark maroon on the back.

Habitat: Below 2,500′. Grassy areas, moist slopes, especially on thin soils, including serpentine. GR, FW, SG.

Comments: Grows in the western Sierra Nevada foothills but it is becoming scarce in our area as the result of increased development on the sites it favors. It used to be common on the thin soils along the top of the ridge on Indian Hill Road in Auburn, but that population has now been subdivided out of existence.

Viola glabella   Native perennial
Stream Violet   Mar–Aug

Description: 4–12″ tall. The leaves are heart-shaped. The glossy 2 or 3 leaves are toothed and branch out near the top of each stem, leaving the bottom portion of the stem leafless. The flowers are bright yellow on long peduncles (leafless flower stems). The top 2 petals are solid yellow, while the bottom 3 have brownish to purplish linear markings.

Habitat: Up to 8,600′. Stream banks, damp, shady seeps. LC, UC, RP.

Comments: Some of our native violets are summer dormant but this one requires moisture all year. In our area it is often found in alder or willow thickets. It can be identified by the long peduncles that grow to about 3″ in length.

RICHARD HANES

Stream Violet

Viola lobata   Native perennial
Pine Violet   Apr–Jul

Description: 2–18″. The leaves are divided into wide, fingerlike lobes (except for the subspecies *integrifolia*). The yellow flowers grow out of the upper leaf axils on naked stems (peduncles). They may or may not have purple veins.

Habitat: Below 7,600′. Dry, open woods. FW, LC, UC, SG.

Comments: Found most often in open pine woodlands. The common subspecies in our area is *Viola lobata* ssp. *lobata,* which has deeply divided leaves, but there is also an uncommon subspecies in our area, *Viola lobata* ssp. *integrifolia,* which has diamond-shaped to triangular leaves. The subspecies *lobata* can be seen at the Rock Creek Nature Trail along with 3 other species of native violets.

JULIE S. CARVILLE

Pine Violet

Macloskey's Violet

Viola macloskeyi   Native perennial
Macloskey's Violet   May–Aug

Description: 1–6″ tall, mat forming, and spreading by stems that lie on the ground and root at the nodes. The leaves are heart-shaped to rounded. The flowers are white. The upper 2 petals are bent back and often touching at the tips. The lower 3 petals are veined in purple with the 2 side petals often white-fuzzy.

Habitat: 3,300–11,200′. Seeps, stream banks, wet meadows. UC, SA, MM, RP.

Comments: Our only pure white violet and one of our smaller violets. It is a plant of high-elevation wet places. Our area is particularly rich in native violet species. Of the 21 species of native violets found in California, 14 of them occur in Placer and Nevada Counties.

Mountain Violet

Viola purpurea   Native perennial
Mountain Violet, Oak Violet   Apr–Aug

Description: 1–5″ in height. Clumps of grayish green leaves form mats. The leaves are smooth edged to toothed and often purplish underneath, fleshy, and deeply veined. The flowers are yellow, the upper 2 petal backs purple.

Habitat: 1,300–10,200′. Dry, sandy soils, full sun, dry forest. FW, LC, UC, SA, SP, SG.

Comments: Very common. Its long taproot helps it survive in dry, hot soils. Although one of its common names is Oak Violet, it is more likely to be found growing under pines than oaks. But that is only one inconsistency associated with the plant. The other is the species name *purpurea,* which means purple. Why would this violet have that species name when the flowers are clearly yellow? The answer lies both on the undersurface of the leaves and the back of the top two petals.

Viola sheltonii   Native perennial
Shelton's Violet, Fan Violet   Apr–Jul

Description: 2–6″ tall. A small violet with blue-green fan-shaped leaves deeply cleft into 3 lobes, which are themselves further deeply cleft. The leaves are often purplish on the underside. The flowers are dark veined, just slightly so on the upper petals, but more deeply on the lower 3 petals.

Habitat: 2,600–8,200′. Oak woodlands, pine and fir forests, gravel slopes. FW, LC, UC.

Comments: Besides the deeply slashed, decidedly unviolet-like leaves, there is another odd characteristic about this little plant. No two petals are alike. Each differs in either size or shape from the other four. Look for it at the intersection of Highway 20 and Conservation Road, which leads to the Rock Creek Nature Trail.

Shelton's Violet

Viola tomentosa   Native perennial
Woolly Violet   Jun–Aug

Description: Usually 1–6″ high with stems up to 6″ long, lying prostrate in sunny areas but more erect in shaded places. There are densely matted white hairs on the stems and leaves. The felty leaves are long and narrow, not violet-like. The flower is yellow with a tiny spur. The upper pair of petals may have dark lines near the base.

Habitat: 5,000–6,600′. Dry, gravelly areas. LC, UC.

Comments: No other violet in our area has woolly leaves. It's a beautiful little flower and plant. It seems to prefer exposed soils and does not thrive in thick duff. A rare plant here and elsewhere. There are no cleistogamous flowers. As mentioned earlier, most violets have 2 types of flowers, the ones that we notice, and later, budlike flowers that do not open and that self-pollinate.

Woolly Violet

Zygophyllaceae
CALTROP FAMILY
Richard Hanes

Herbs and shrubs, rarely trees. Many members are drought tolerant and alkaline tolerant and often armed with spines. The leaves are usually opposite and pinnately compound, *once divided.* The stems are branched. *The flowers occur as 1–2 in axils, are regular, sepals 5, petals 5, stamens 10, the ovary superior, pistil and style 1.* Fruit a capsule or splitting into 5–10 nutlets. There are 26 genera, 250 species worldwide; 5 genera, 8 species in California; and 1 species in Nevada and Placer Counties.

Puncture Vine

Tribulus terrestris Non-native annual
Puncture Vine, Caltrop Apr–Oct

Description: Stem prostrate, hairy, spreading radially to 3′. The leaves are opposite and pinnate. The flowers are solitary in the leaf axils, are less than ¼″, with yellow petals. The fruit is 5-lobed, splitting into 5 nutlets, each with 2–4 stout spines that are ⅓″ long.

Habitat: Below 3,000′. Dry disturbed areas, roadsides, vacant lots, and railways. GR, CH, FW.

Comments: Toxic to livestock, it is nonetheless used widely by Chinese herbalists in a variety of ways, from use as an aphrodisiac to treating headaches and eye problems to raising testosterone levels. The fruits can puncture thin shoes and bicycle tires. Caltrops were the ancient equivalent of what are called tire spikes today. They were devices made of sharp spikes that were thrown on roads to impede cavalry and foot soldiers.

The South Yuba River begins its life in the high Sierra, where it seeps out of a hillside below Roller Pass. Its newborn waters nourish creekside wildflowers and willows.

*C*hecklist of Plants by Family of Nevada and Placer Counties

Richard Hanes and Chet Blackburn

The following is a checklist of plants presently known to occur within Nevada and Placer Counties, California. The authors were conservative in including names on the checklist and more species undoubtedly occur in Nevada and Placer Counties than those shown. Only those species that are known for certain to occur in the two-county area, either by vouchered specimens or reliable sightings, are included. There are plants that occur in adjacent counties in similar habitat that may also occur here, but have not yet been reported by reliable sources. We have not included plants from the Calflora Web site that were listed as "probably present" or "presence implied by the *Jepson Manual* distribution." It should be noted that any checklist is dynamic by nature as species, particularly non-natives, expand their ranges.

The botanical names conform to the taxonomy used in the *Jepson Manual*. The common names of species shown in bold type are those depicted and described in this book. An asterisk (*) at the end of a common name indicates a non-native species.

Ferns and Fern Allies

Azollaceae – Mosquito Fern Family
Azolla filiculoides .... Water Fern
Azolla mexicana .... Water Fern

Blechnaceae – Deer Fern Family
Woodwardia fimbriata .... Giant Chain Fern

Dennstaedtiaceae – Bracken Family
Pteridium aquilinum var. *pubescens* .... Bracken Fern

Dryopteridaceae – Wood Fern Family
Athyrium alpestre var. *americanum* .... Alpine Lady Fern
Athyrium filix-femina var. *cyclosorum* .... Lady Fern
Cystopteris fragilis .... Fragile Fern
Dryopteris arguta .... California Wood Fern
Polystichum imbricans ssp. *imbricans* .... Imbricate Sword Fern
Polystichum lonchitis .... Northern Hollyfern
Polystichum munitum .... Sword Fern
Polystichum scopulinum .... Mountain Holly Fern

Equisetaceae – Horsetail Family
Equisetum arvense .... Common Horsetail
Equisetum ×ferrissii .... Ferris' Horsetail
Equisetum hyemale ssp. *affine* .... Scouring Rush
Equisetum laevigatum .... Smooth Horsetail
Equisetum telmateia var. *braunii* .... Giant Horsetail

Isotaceae – Quillwort Family
Isoetes bolanderi .... Bolander's Quillwort
Isoetes howellii .... Howell's Quillwort
Isoetes nuttallii .... Nuttall's Quillwort
Isoetes occidentalis .... Western Quillwort
Isoetes orcuttii .... Orcutt's Quillwort

Lycopodiaceae – Club-moss Family
Lycopodiella inundata .... Bog Club-moss

Marsileaceae – Marsilea Family
Marsilea obligospora .... Nelson's Pepperwort
Marsilea vestita .... Water Clover
Pilularia americana .... American Pillwort

Ophioglossaceae – Adders Tongue Family
Botrychium crenulatum .... Scalloped Moonwort
Botrychium lunaria .... Moonwort
Botrychium minganense .... Mingan Moonwort
Botrychium multifidum .... Leather Grapefern

Polypodiaceae – Polypody Family
Polypodium calirhiza .... Nested Polypody

Pteridaceae – Brake Family
Adiantum aleuticum .... Pacific Fivefinger Fern
Adiantum jordanii .... California Maidenhair Fern
Aspidotis californica .... California Lace Fern
Aspidotis densa .... Indian's Dream
Cheilanthes cooperae .... Cooper's Lip Fern
Cheilanthes gracillima .... Lace Fern
Cryptogramma acrostichoides .... Parsley Fern, Rock Brake
Pellaea andromedifolia .... Coffee Fern
Pellaea brachyptera .... Sierra Cliff-brake
Pellaea breweri .... Brewer's Cliff-brake
Pellaea bridgesii .... Bridge's Cliff-brake
Pellaea mucronata var. *californica* .... Bird's Foot Fern
Pellaea mucronata var. *mucronata* .... Bird's Foot Fern
Pentagramma pallida .... Silverback Fern
Pentagramma triangularis .... Goldback Fern

Selaginellaceae – Spike-moss Family
Selaginella hansenii .... Hansen's Selaginella
Selaginella wallacei .... Little Selaginella
Selaginella watsonii .... Watson's Spike-moss

Thelypteridaceae – Thelypteris Family
Thelypteris nevadensis .... Sierra Wood Fern

Flowering Plants

Aceraceae – Maple Family
Acer glabrum var. *diffusum* .... Mountain Maple
Acer glabrum var. *torreyi* .... Mountain Maple
Acer macrophyllum ....Bigleaf Maple
Acer negundo var. *californicum* .... California Box Elder

Alismataceae – Water Plantain Family
Alisma lanceolatum .... Common Water Plantain*
Alisma plantago-aquatica ....**Common Water Plantain**
Damasonium californicum ....**Fringed Water Plantain**
Echinodorus berteroi .... Burhead
Sagittaria cuneata ....Arum-leaf Arrowhead
Sagittaria latifolia ....**Broadleaf Arrowhead**
Sagittaria sanfordii .... Sanford's Arrowhead

Amaranthaceae – Amaranth Family
Amaranthus albus .... Tumbleweed*
Amaranthus blitoides .... Prostrate Pigweed
Amaranthus californicus .... California Amaranth
Amaranthus deflexus .... Low Amaranth*
Amaranthus palmeri ....Palmer's Amaranth
Amaranthus powellii ....Powell's Amaranth
Amaranthus retroflexus .... Rough Pigweed, Redroot Pigweed*

Anacardiaceae – Sumac Family
Rhus trilobata .... Skunkbush
Schinus molle ....Peruvian Pepper Tree*
Toxicodendron diversilobum .... Poison Oak

Apiaceae – Carrot Family
Ammi visnaga .... Bisnaga*
Angelica breweri ....Brewer's Angelica
Anthriscus caucalis ....Bur-chervil*
Apiastrum angustifolium .... Wild Celery
Berula erecta ....Water Parsnip
Cicuta douglasii .... Western Water Hemlock
Cicuta maculata .... Water Hemlock
Conium maculatum ....**Poison Hemlock***
Coriandrum sativum ....Coriander, Cilantro*
Cymopterus terebinthinus .... Cymopterus
Daucus carota ....**Queen Anne's Lace, Wild Carrot***
Daucus pusillus .... Rattlesnake Weed
Eryngium alismaefolium ....Alisma-leaf Coyote Thistle
Eryngium castrense ....**Great Valley Button Celery**
Foeniculum vulgare ....**Fennel***
Heracleum lanatum ....**Cow Parsnip**
Ligusticum grayi ....**Gray's Lovage**
Lomatium californicum ....California Lomatium
Lomatium caruifolium var. *denticulatum* .... Alkali Desert Parsley
Lomatium dasycarpum ssp. *tomentosum* .... Hog Fennel
Lomatium dissectum .... Fernleaf Lomatium

Lomatium dissectum var. *multifidum* .... Fernleaf Lomatium
Lomatium macrocarpum .... Sheep Parsnip
Lomatium marginatum var. *marginatum* .... Butte Desert Parsnip
Lomatium nevadense var. *nevadense* .... Sierra Lomatium
Lomatium torreyi .... Torrey's Lomatium
Lomatium triternatum .... Lewis' Lomatium
Lomatium utriculatum .... **Foothill Lomatium**
Orogenia fusiformis .... Indian Potato
Osmorhiza brachypoda .... California Sweet Cicely
Osmorhiza chilensis .... **Mountain Sweet Cicely**
Osmorhiza occidenalis .... Western Sweet Cicely
Perideridia bacigalupii .... Bacigalupi's Yampah
Perideridia bolanderi ssp. *bolanderi* .... **Bolander's Yampah**
Perideridia bolanderi ssp. *involucrata* .... Yampah
Perideridia gairdneri .... Gairdner's Yampah
Perideridia howellii .... Howell's Yampah
Perideridia kelloggii .... Kellogg's Yampah
Perideridia lemmonii .... Lemmon's Yampah
Perideridia parishii .... Parish's Yampah
Perideridia parishii ssp. *latifolia* .... Parish's Yampah
Podistera nevadensis .... Sierra Podistera
Sanicula bipinnata .... **Poison Sanicle**
Sanicula bipinnatifida .... **Purple Sanicle, Shoe Buttons**
Sanicula crassicaulis .... **Gamble Weed, Pacific Sanicle**
Sanicula graveolens .... Sierra Snakeroot
Sanicula tuberosa .... **Tuberous Sanicle, Turkey Pea**
Scandix pecten-veneris .... Venus Needle*
Sphenosciadium capitellatum .... **Ranger's Buttons, White Heads**
Tauschia hartwegii .... **Hartweg's Tauschia**
Tauschia kelloggii .... Kellogg's Tauschia
Torilis arvensis .... **Hedge Parsley***
Torilis nodosa .... Knotted Hedge Parsley*
Yabea microcarpa .... California Hedge Parsley

Apocynaceae – Dogbane Family
Apocynum androsaemifolium .... **Bitter Dogbane, Spreading Dogbane**
Apocynum cannabinum .... Indian Hemp
Vinca major .... **Periwinkle***

Araliaceae – Ginseng Family
Aralia californica .... **Elk Clover, California Spikenard**
Hedera helix .... English Ivy*

Aristolochiaceae – Pipevine Family
Aristolochia californica .... **Pipevine, Dutchman's Pipe**
Asarum hartwegii .... **Hartweg's Ginger**
Asarum lemmonii .... **Lemmon's Ginger**

Asclepiadaceae – Milkweed Family
Asclepias californica .... California Milkweed
Asclepias cordifolia .... **Purple Milkweed**
Asclepias eriocarpa .... Indian Milkweed, Kotolo
Asclepias fascicularis .... **Narrow-leaf Milkweed**

Asclepias speciosa .... **Showy Milkweed**

Asteraceae – Sunflower Family
Achillea millefolium .... **Yarrow**
Achyrachaena mollis .... Blow Wives
Acroptilon repens .... Russian Knapweed*
Adenocaulon bicolor .... **Pathfinder, Trail Plant**
Ageratina occidentalis .... **Western Eupatorium, Western Snakeroot**
Agoseris aurantiaca .... Orange Agoseris
Agoseris elata .... Tall Agoseris
Agoseris glauca var. *laciniata* .... False Dandelion
Agoseris glauca var. *monticola* .... Mountain Agoseris
Agoseris grandiflora .... **Large-flower Agoseris, California Dandelion**
Agoseris heterophylla .... Annual Agoseris
Agoseris retrorsa .... **Spearleaf Agoseris**
Ambrosia artemisiifolia .... Common Ragweed*
Ambrosia psilostachya .... Western Ragweed
Anaphalis margaritacea .... **Pearly Everlasting**
Antennaria argentea .... Silver Pussytoes
Antennaria corymbosa .... Flat-top Pussytoes
Antennaria dimorpha .... Cushion Pussytoes
Antennaria geyeri .... Geyer's Pussytoes
Antennaria luzuloides .... Silver-brown Pussytoes
Antennaria media .... Alpine Pussytoes
Antennaria pulchella .... Beautiful Pussytoes
Antennaria rosea .... **Rosy Pussytoes**
Antennaria umbrinella .... Brown Pussytoes
Anthemis cotula .... Mayweed*
Anthemis tinctoria .... Golden Marguerite
Arctium minus .... Burdock*
Arnica amplexicaulis .... Streambank Arnica
Arnica chamissonis ssp. *foliosa* .... Meadow Arnica
Arnica cordifolia .... **Heart-leaf Arnica**
Arnica discoidea .... Rayless Arnica
Arnica diversifolia .... Lawless Arnica
Arnica latifolia .... Broadleaf Arnica
Arnica longifolia .... Seep-spring Arnica
Arnica mollis .... **Soft Arnica, Hairy Arnica**
Arnica nevadensis .... Sierra Arnica
Arnica parryi .... Frogflower, Parry's Arnica
Arnica tomentella .... Recondite Arnica
Artemisia arbuscula .... Low Sagebrush
Artemisia arbuscula ssp. *arbuscula* .... Little Sagebrush
Artemisia arbuscula ssp. *thermopola* .... Little Sagebrush
Artemisia cana ssp. *bolanderi* .... Silver Sagebrush
Artemisia douglasiana .... **California Mugwort**
Artemisia dracunculus .... Tarragon
Artemisia ludoviciana ssp. *candicans* .... Silver Wormwood, Tarragon
Artemisia ludoviciana ssp. *incompta* .... Gray Mugwort
Artemisia michauxiana .... Lemon Sagewort
Artemisia norvegica ssp. *saxatilis* .... Mountain Sagewort
Artemisia rothrockii .... Rothrock Sagebrush

Artemisia spiciformis .... Snowfield Sagebrush
Artemisia tridentata ssp. *tridentata* .... Common Sagebrush
Artemisia tridentata ssp. *vaseyana* ....Mountain Sagebrush
Aster alpigenus var. *andersonii* .... **Alpine Aster**
Aster ascendens .... Longleaf Aster
Aster breweri .... Brewer's Aster
Aster chilensis .... **Common Aster**
Aster eatonii .... **Eaton's Aster**
Aster foliaceus .... Leafyhead Aster
Aster integrifolius .... Entire-leafed Aster
Aster occidentalis var. *occidentalis* .... Western Aster
Aster oregonensis ....Oregon White-topped Aster
Aster radulinus .... Broadleaf Aster
Baccharis pilularis ....Coyote Bush
Balsamorhiza deltoidea .... **Deltoid Balsamroot**
Balsamorhiza hookeri var. *lanata* .... Hooker's Balsamroot
Balsamorhiza macrolepis .... Flat Scale Balsamroot
Balsamorhiza macrolepis var. *platylepis* .... Flat Scale Balsamroot
Balsamorhiza sagittata .... Arrow-leaf Balsamroot
Bidens frondosa ....Beggar Ticks, Sticktight
Blennosperma nanum .... **Common Blennosperma, Stickyseed**
Brickellia californica .... California Bricklebush
Brickellia grandiflora .... Golden Sashay
Brickellia greenei ....Greene's Bricklebush
Calycadenia mollis .... Soft Western Rosinweed
Calycadenia multiglandulosa .... Sticky Western Rosinweed
Calycadenia spicata .... **Spiked Rosinweed**
Calycadenia truncata .... Rosinweed
Carduus acanthoides .... Spiney Plumeless Thistle*
Carduus nutans ....Musk Thistle*
Carduus pycnocephalus .... **Italian Thistle***
Carthamus lanatus ....Woolly Distaff Thistle*
Centaurea calcitrapa .... Purple Star Thistle*
Centaurea cyanus .... Bachelor's Button, Cornflower*
Centaurea diffusa ....Diffuse Knapweed*
Centaurea maculosa .... Spotted Knapweed*
Centaurea melitensis .... Tocalote*
Centaurea solstitialis .... **Yellow Star Thistle***
Centaurea sulphurea ....Sicilian Star Thistle*
Chaenactis douglasii .... **Dusty Maidens**
Chaenactis douglasii var. *alpina* .... Alpine Dusty Maidens
Chaenactis douglasii var. *douglasii* .... Douglas' Dusty Maidens
Chaenactis glabriuscula ....Yellow Pincushion
Chaenactis nevadensis .... Sierra Chaenactis
Chamomilla suaveolens ....**Pineapple Weed***
Chondrilla juncea ....**Skeleton Weed***
Chrysothamnus nauseosus ....Common Rabbitbrush
Chrysothamnus nauseosus ssp. *albicaulis* .... Whitestem Rabbitbrush
Chrysothamnus parryi ssp. *nevadensis* .... Nevada Parry's Rabbitbrush
Chrysothamnus viscidiflorus ssp. *viscidiflorus* .... Yellow Rabbitbrush
Cichorium intybus ....**Chicory***
Cirsium andersonii .... **Anderson's Thistle, Rose Thistle**

Cirsium arvense ....Canada Thistle*
Cirsium canovirens .... Gray-green Thistle
Cirsium douglasii var. *breweri* .... Swamp Thistle
Cirsium occidentale var. *californicum* ....**California Thistle**
Cirsium occidentale var. *candidissimum* .... Snowy Thistle
Cirsium occidentale var. *venustum* .... Venus Thistle
Cirsium scariosum .... Elk Thistle
Cirsium vulgare ....**Bull Thistle***
Cnicus benedictus .... Blessed Thistle*
Conyza bonariensis .... Hairy Fleabane*
Conyza canadensis ....**Canadian Horseweed**
Conyza coulteri .... Coulter's Horseweed
Coreopsis stillmanii ....Stillman's Tickseed
Crepis acuminata .... Longleaf Hawksbeard
Crepis bakeri .... Baker's Hawksbeard
Crepis capillaris .... Smooth Hawksbeard*
Crepis intermedia .... Limestone Hawksbeard
Crepis modocensis .... Modoc Hawksbeard
Crepis occidentalis ....Western Hawksbeard
Crepis pleurocarpa ....Naked-stem Hawksbeard
Cynara cardunculus ....Cardoon, Artichoke Thistle*
Dugaldia hoopesii ....Hoope's Sneezeweed
Ericameria arborescens .... Golden Fleece
Ericameria bloomeri ....Bloomer's Goldenbush
Ericameria cuneata var. *cuneata* .... Cliff Goldenbush
Ericameria discoidea ....Whitestem Goldenbush
Ericameria greenei ....Greene's Goldenbush
Ericameria suffruticosa .... Heath Goldenbush
Erigeron annuus ....Easter Daisy Fleabane*
Erigeron barbellulatus .... Shining Daisy
Erigeron bloomeri var. *bloomeri* .... Scabland Fleabane
Erigeron breweri var. *breweri* .... Brewer's Fleabane
Erigeron compositus ....Cutleaf Daisy
Erigeron coulteri ....**Coulter's Daisy**
Erigeron divergens ....Diffuse Daisy
Erigeron eatonii .... Eaton's Fleabane
Erigeron eatonii var. *nevadincola* ....Nevada Daisy
Erigeron eatonii var. *sonnei* .... Sonne's Daisy
Erigeron foliosus .... Daisy Fleabane
Erigeron foliosus var. *hartwegii* ....**Foothill Daisy Fleabane**
Erigeron inornatus var. *inornatus* ....California Rayless Daisy
Erigeron linearis ....Narrow-leaved Fleabane
Erigeron miser ....**Starved Daisy**
Erigeron nevadincola ....Nevada Daisy
Erigeron peregrinus ....Wandering Daisy
Erigeron peregrinus ssp. *callianthemus* ....Wandering Daisy
Erigeron petrophilus var. *sierrensis* .... Northern Sierra Daisy
Erigeron petrophilus var. *viscidulus* .... Klamath Rock Daisy
Erigeron philadelphicus ....Philadelphia Daisy
Erigeron pumilus var. *intermedius* .... Shaggy Fleabane
Erigeron reductus var. *reductus* .... California Rayless Daisy
Erigeron strigosus ....Prairie Fleabane*

Eriophyllum lanatum .... **Woolly Sunflower**
Eriophyllum lanatum var. *achillaeoides* ....Yarrowleaf Woolly Sunflower
Eriophyllum lanatum var. *croceum* .... Sierra Woolly Sunflower
Eriophyllum lanatum var. *grandiflorum* ....Woolly Sunflower
Eriophyllum lanatum var. *integrifolium* .... Oregon Sunshine
Euthamia occidentalis ....Western Goldenrod
Filago gallica ....Fluffweed*
Gaillardia aristata .... Indian Blanket*
Gnaphalium californicum ....California Everlasting
Gnaphalium californicum × *beneolens* .... unknown
Gnaphalium canescens ....Everlasting Cudweed
Gnaphalium canescens ssp. *beneolens* ...... **White Everlasting, Feltleaf Everlasting**
Gnaphalium canescens ssp. *microcephalum* ....White Everlasting
Gnaphalium canescens var. *thermale* .... Smallhead Cudweed
Gnaphalium luteo-album ....Weedy Cudweed*
Gnaphalium palustre ....Marsh Cudweed, Lowland Cudweed
Gnaphalium purpureum .... Purple Cudweed
Gnaphalium stramineum .... Cotton-batting Plant
Grindelia camporum .... Great Valley Gumplant
Grindelia hirsutula var. *davyi* .... **Davy's Gumweed**
Grindelia squarrosa ....Curly Cup Gumweed*
Hazardia whitneyi .... Whitney's Hazardia
Hedypnois cretica .... Crete Weed*
Helenium bigelovii .... **Bigelow's Sneezeweed**
Helenium puberulum .... **Rosilla**
Helianthella californica .... California Helianthella
Helianthella californica var. *nevadensis* ....**California Helianthella**
Helianthus annuus ....Common Sunflower
Helianthus bolanderi .... Bolander's Sunflower
Hemizonia congesta ssp. *luzulifolia* ....White Hayfield Tarweed
Hemizonia fitchii ....**Fitch's Tarweed, Fitch's Spikeweed**
Heterotheca grandiflora .... Telegraph Weed
Heterotheca villosa var. *hispida* .... Hairy Golden Aster
Hieracium albiflorum .... **White Hawkweed**
Hieracium albiflorum × *cynoglossoides* .... unknown
Hieracium argutum .... Southern Hawkweed
Hieracium aurantiacum .... Orange Hawkweed*
Hieracium gracile .... Alpine Hawkweed
Hieracium horridum .... Shaggy Hawkweed
Hieracium scouleri .... Scouler's Hawkweed
Holocarpha virgata ssp. *virgata* ....Virgate Tarweed
Holozonia filipes ....Hareleaf
Hypochaeris glabra .... **Smooth Cat's Ear***
Hypochaeris radicata ....Rough Cat's Ear*
Iva axillaris ssp. *robustior* ....Wormwood
Lactuca biennis ....Tall Blue Lettuce*
Lactuca saligna ....Willow Lettuce*
Lactuca serriola .... **Prickly Lettuce***
Lagophylla glandulosa ....Glandular Hareleaf
Lagophylla ramosissima ....Clustered Hareleaf
Lagophylla ramosissima ssp. *congesta* .... Rabbitfoot
Lagophylla ramosissima ssp. *ramosissima* ....Clustered Hareleaf

Lapasana communis .... Nipplewort*
Lasthenia californica .... **California Goldfields**
Lasthenia fremontii .... Fremont's Goldfields
Layia fremontii .... **Tidy Tips**
Layia glandulosa ....White Layia
Layia pentachaeta ssp. *pentachaeta* .... Sierra Tidy Tips
Leontodon taraxacoides .... Hawkbit*
Leontodon taraxacoides ssp. *longirostris* .... Hawkbit*
Leontodon taraxacoides ssp. *taraxacoides* .... Hawkbit*
Lessingia leptoclada .... Sierra Leptoclada
Lessingia nemaclada .... Slenderstem Lessingia
Lessingia virgata .... Wand Lessingia
Leucanthemum vulgare .... **Ox-eye Daisy***
Machaeranthera canescens var. *canescens* ....**Hoary Aster**
Machaeranthera canescens var. *shastensis* ....Hoary Aster
Madia bolanderi .... Bolander's Tarweed
Madia citriodora .... Lemon-scented Tarweed
Madia elegans ....**Common Madia**
Madia elegans ssp. *densifolia* .... Showy Tarweed
Madia elegans ssp. *elegans* .... Common Tarweed
Madia elegans ssp. *vernalis* .... Spring Madia
Madia elegans ssp. *wheeleri* .... Wheeler's Madia
Madia exigua .... Threadstem Tarweed
Madia glomerata .... Mountain Tarweed
Madia gracilis .... Slender Tarweed
Madia minima .... Dwarf Madia
Madia rammii .... **Ramm's Madia**
Malacothrix floccifera .... **Woolly Malacothrix**
Micropus californicus var. *californicus* .... **Slender Cottonweed, Q-Tips**
Microseris acuminata ....Foothill Microseris
Microseris nutans .... **Nodding Microseris**
Microseris sylvatica ....Sylvan Scorzonella
Monolopia lanceolata .... Common Monolopia
Nothocalais alpestris .... Alpine Dandelion
Onopordum acanthium ssp. *acanthium* ....Scottish Thistle*
Onopordum tauricum .... Taurian Thistle, Scotch Thistle*
Pentachaeta exilis ssp. *exilis* .... Slender Pentachaeta
Phalacroseris bolanderi .... Bolander's Mock Dandelion
Psathyrotes annua .... Annual Psathyrotes
Pseudobahia heermannii .... Heermann's Golden Sunburst
Psilocarphus brevissimus var. *brevissimus* .... **Dwarf Woolly-heads**
Psilocarphus oregonus .... Oregon Woolly-heads
Psilocarphus tenellus var. *tenellus* .... Slender Woolly Marbles
Pyrrocoma apargioides .... Alpine Flames
Pyrrocoma hirta var. *lanulosa* .... Tacky Goldenrod
Pyrrocoma racemosa var. *paniculatus* ....Pyrrocoma
Rafinesquia californica .... California Chicory
Raillardella argentea .... **Silky Raillardella, Silvermat**
Rigiopappus leptocladus ....Rigiopappus
Rudbeckia occidentalis var. *occidentalis* .... **Western Coneflower**
Senecio aronicoides .... California Butterweed
Senecio canus .... Woolly Butterweed

Senecio clarkianus .... Clark's Butterweed
Senecio cymbalarioides .... Rocky Mountain Butterweed
Senecio hydrophiloides .... Sweet Marsh Ragwort
Senecio hydrophilus .... Marsh Ragwort
Senecio integerrimus .... Tower Butterweed
Senecio integerrimus var. *exaltatus* .... Tower Butterweed
Senecio integerrimus var. *major* .... **Single-Stem Butterweed**
Senecio jacobaea .... Tansy Ragwort, Stinking Willie*
Senecio pauciflorus .... Rayless Alpine Ragwort
Senecio pseudaureus var. *pseudaureus* .... Streambank Butterweed
Senecio serra var. *serra* .... Tall Ragwort
Senecio streptanthifolius .... Cleft-leafed Groundsel
Senecio triangularis .... **Arrowhead Butterweed**
Senecio vulgaris .... **Common Groundsel, Old Man of Spring***
Silybum marianum .... **Milk Thistle***
Solidago californica .... California Goldenrod
Solidago canadensis ssp. *elongata* .... **Canada Goldenrod**
Solidago multiradiata .... Northern Goldenrod
Solidago spectabilis .... Showy Goldenrod
Soliva sessilis .... Common Soliva*
Sonchus arvensis .... Perennial Sow Thistle*
Sonchus asper ssp. *asper* .... Prickly Sow Thistle*
Sonchus oleraceus .... **Common Sow Thistle***
Stenotus acaulis .... Stemless Mock Goldenrod
Stephanomeria elata .... Santa Barbara Wirelettuce
Stephanomeria lactucina .... **Largeflower Stephanomeria**
Stephanomeria tenuifolia .... Narrow-leaved Wirelettuce
Stephanomeria virgata .... Tall Stephanomeria
Stephanomeria virgata ssp. *pleurocarpa* .... Tall Stephanomeria
Tanacetum parthenium .... Feverfew*
Tanacetum vulgare .... Tansy*
Taraxacum officinale .... Common Dandelion*
Tragopogon dubius .... Yellow Salsify*
Tragopogon porrifolius .... **Purple Salsify, Oyster Plant***
Tragopogon pratensis .... Meadow Salsify*
Uropappus lindleyi .... Silver Puffs
Whitneya dealbata .... **Whitneya, Mock Leopardbane**
Wyethia angustifolia .... **Narrowleaf Mule Ears, California Compass Plant**
Wyethia bolanderi .... **Bolander's Mule Ears**
Wyethia helenioides .... **White Mule Ears, Silver Mule Ears**
Wyethia mollis .... **Mountain Mule Ears, Woolly Mule Ears**
Xanthium spinosum .... Spiny Cocklebur
Xanthium strumarium .... **Common Cocklebur**

Berberidaceae – Barberry Family
Berberis aquifolium .... Oregon Grape
Berberis aquifolium var. *repens* .... Creeping Barberry

Betulaceae – Birch Family
Alnus incana ssp. *tenuifolia* .... Mountain Alder
Alnus rhombifolia .... White Alder
Corylus cornuta var. *californica* .... California Hazelnut

Boraginaceae – Borage Family

Amsinckia eastwoodiae .... Valley Fiddleneck
Amsinckia lycopsoides .... Bug-gloss Fiddleneck
Amsinckia menziesii var. *intermedia* .... **Common Fiddleneck**
Amsinckia menziesii var. *menziesii* .... Rancher's Fiddleneck
Borago officinalis .... Borage*
Cryptantha affinis .... **Side-grooved Cryptantha**
Cryptantha ambigua .... Wilke's Cryptantha
Cryptantha circumscissa .... Cushion Cryptantha
Cryptantha echinella .... Prickly Cryptantha
Cryptantha flaccida .... Flaccid Cryptantha
Cryptantha glomeriflora .... Truckee Cryptantha
Cryptantha humilis .... Roundspike Cryptantha
Cryptantha muricata .... Prickly Cryptantha
Cryptantha nubigena .... Sierra Cryptantha
Cryptantha pterocarya .... Winged-nut Cryptantha
Cryptantha simulans .... Pine Cryptantha
Cryptantha torreyana .... Torrey's Cryptantha
Cynoglossum grande .... **Grand Hound's Tongue**
Cynoglossum occidentale .... Western Hound's Tongue
Hackelia amethystina .... Amethyst Stickseed
Hackelia californica .... California Stickseed
Hackelia floribunda .... Many-flowered Stickseed
Hackelia micrantha .... Smallflower Stickseed
Hackelia nervosa .... Sierra Stickseed
Hackelia velutina .... **Velvety Stickseed**
Heliotropioum curassavicum .... Heliotrope
Lithospermum californicum .... **California Stoneseed, California Puccoon**
Lithospermum ruderale .... Western Gromwell
Mertensia ciliata .... Tall-fringed Bluebells
Myosotis discolor .... Yellow & Blue Scorpion Grass*
Myosotis scorpioides .... Yelloweye Forget-me-not*
Pectocarya pusilla .... Little Pectocarya
Plagiobothrys bracteatus .... Bracted Popcorn Flower
Plagiobothrys canescens .... Valley Popcorn Flower
Plagiobothrys cognatus .... Cognate Popcorn Flower
Plagiobothrys cusickii .... Cusick's Popcorn Flower
Plagiobothrys fulvus .... Hairy Popcorn Flower
Plagiobothyrs glyptocarpus var. *modestus* .... Cedar Crest Popcorn Flower
Plagiobothrys greenei .... Greene's Popcorn Flower
Plagiobothrys hispidulus .... Harsh Popcorn Flower
Plagiobothrys hispidus .... Cascade Popcorn Flower
Plagiobothrys nothofulvus .... **Popcorn Flower**
Plagiobothrys scriptus .... Scribe Popcorn Flower
Plagiobothrys stipitatus var. *micranthus* .... Stalked Popcorn Flower
Plagiobothrys stipitatus var. *stipitatus* .... Common Vernal Pool Allocarya
Plagiobothrys tenellus .... Delicate Popcorn Flower
Plagiobothrys tener .... Slender Popcorn Flower
Plagiobothrys torreyi .... Torrey's Popcorn Flower
Plagiobothrys torreyi var. *diffusus* .... Torrey's Popcorn Flower

Brassicaceae – Mustard Family

Alyssum alyssoides	Sweet Alyssum*
Arabidopsis thaliana	Mouse-ear Cress*
Arabis breweri	**Brewer's Rock Cress**
Arabis davidsonii	Davidson's Rock Cress
Arabis ×divaricarpa	Hybrid Drummond's Rock Cress
Arabis drummondii	Drummond's Rock Cress
Arabis glabra	Tower Mustard
Arabis hirsuta	Hairy Rock Cress
Arabis holboellii var. *retrofracta*	Holboell's Rock Cress
Arabis holboellii var. *pinetorum*	Pine Rock Cress
Arabis lemmonii var. *depauperata*	Soldier Rock Cress
Arabis lyalli	Lyall's Rock Cress
Arabis perennans	Perennial Rock Cress
Arabis platysperma	Broad-seeded Rock Cress
Arabis platysperma var. *howellii*	Howell's Rock Cress
Arabis puberula	Blue Mountain Rock Cress
Arabis rectissima var. *rectissima*	Bristly-leafed Rock Cress
Arabis repanda	Yosemite Rock Cress
Arabis rigidissima var. *demote*	Carson Range Rock Cress
Arabis sparsiflora	Elegant Rock Cress
Arabis sparsiflora var. *arcuata*	Elegant Rock Cress
Arabis suffrutescens	Woody Rock Cress
Athysanus pusillus	Dwarf Athysanus
Barbarea orthoceras	**American Wintercress, Yellow Rocket**
Barbarea vulgaris	Common Wintercress*
Brassica nigra	**Black Mustard***
Brassica rapa	Field Mustard*
Capsella bursa-pastoris	**Shepherd's Purse***
Cardamine breweri var. *breweri*	Brewer's Bitter-cress
Cardamine californica	**Milk Maids, Toothwort**
Cardamine cordifolia var. *lyallii*	Heartleaf Bitter-cress
Cardamine nuttallii	Nuttall's Bitter-cress
Cardamine oligosperma	Western Bitter-cress
Cardamine pachystigma var. *dissectiflora*	Dissected Leaf Toothwort
Cardamine pachystigma var. *pachystigma*	Serpentine Bitter-cress
Cardamine pennsylvanica	Pennsylvania Bitter-cress
Cardaria chalepensis	Lens-podded Hoary Cress
Cardaria draba	Heart-podded Hoary Cress*
Cardaria pubescens	White Top*
Coronopus didymus	Wart Cress*
Cusickiella douglasii	Alkali Draba, Alkali Cusickiella
Descurainia californica	Sierra Tansy Mustard
Descurainia incana	Soft Mountain Tansy Mustard
Descurainia incisa ssp. *filipes*	Erect-fruited Mountain Tansy Mustard
Descuraina incisa ssp. *incisa*	Mountain Tansy Mustard
Descurainia pinnata var. *halictorum*	Tansy Mustard
Descurainia sophia	Flixweed*
Diplotaxis tenuifolia	Wall Rocket*
Draba albertina	Alberta Whitlow Grass
Draba densifolia	Denseleaf Draba
Draba oligosperma var. *oligosperma*	Few-seeded Draba

Draba paysonii var. *treleasei* .... Trelease's Draba
Draba verna .... **Whitlow Grass**
Erysimum capitatum .... **Western Wallflower**
Erysimum capitatum ssp. *perenne* .... Mountain Wallflower
Erysimum cheiranthoides .... Wormseed Mustard*
Hesperis matronalis .... Dame's Rocket*
Hirschfeldia incana .... **Short-pod Mustard, Summer Mustard***
Idahoa scapigera .... Oldstem Idaho
Isatis tinctoria .... Woad*
Lepidium campestre .... Field Cress*
Lepidium densiflorum .... Miner's Pepper
Lepidium latifolium .... Broad-leafed Pepperweed*
Lepidium nitidum .... Common Peppergrass
Lepidium perfoliatum .... Shield Cress*
Lepidium strictum .... Prostrate Cress
Lepidium virginicum .... Virginia Peppergrass
Lepidium virginicum var. *pubescens* .... Hairy Tongue Cress
Lesquerella occidentalis ssp. *occidentalis* .... Western Bladderpod
Lunaria annua .... Money Plant*
Phoenicaulis cheiranthoides .... **Dagger Pod**
Raphanus raphanistrum .... Jointed Charlock, Yellow Wild Radish*
Raphanus sativus .... **Wild Radish***
Rorippa curvipes .... Bluntleaf Yellow Cress
Rorippa curvisiliqua .... Western Yellow Cress
Rorippa nasturtium-aquaticum .... **Water Cress**
Rorippa palustris .... Bog Yellow Cress
Rorippa palustris var. *occidentalis* .... Western Bog Yellow Cress
Rorippa sinuata .... Spreading Yellow Cress
Rorippa subumbellata .... Tahoe Yellow Cress
Rorippa tenerrima .... Modoc Yellow Cress
Sinapis arvensis .... Charlock, Field Mustard*
Sisymbrium altissimum .... Tumble Mustard*
Sisymbrium officinale .... Hedge Mustard*
Streptanthus cordatus .... Heartleaf Jewelflower
Streptanthus polygaloides .... **Milkwort Jewelflower**
Streptanthus tortuosus ....**Mountain Jewelflower**
Streptanthus tortuosus var. *orbiculatus* .... Mountain Jewelflower
Streptanthus tortuosus var. *suffrutescens* .... Bush Mountain Jewelflower
Subularia aquatica var. *americana* .... Awlwort
Thelypodium crispum .... Wavyleaf Thelypodium
Thlaspi arvense .... Fan Weed, Field Pennycress*
Thysanocarpus curvipes ....**Fringepod, Lacepod**
Thysanocarpus radians .... Ribbed Fringepod
Tropidocarpum gracile .... Lacepod

Cabombaceae – Watershield Family
Brasenia schreberi .... Watershield

Callitrichaceae – Water Starwort Family
Callitriche heterophylla .... Water Starwort
Callitriche verna .... Vernal Water Starwort

Calycanthaceae – Sweetshrub Family
Calycanthus occidentalis .... Western Sweetshrub, Spicebush

Campanulaceae – Bluebell Family
Campanula prenanthoides .... **California Harebell**
Downingia bacigalupii .... Bach's Downingia
Downingia bicornuta .... **Horned Downingia**
Downingia bicornuta var. *picta* .... Horned Downingia
Downingia cuspidata .... Toothed Downingia
Downingia elegans .... Elegant Downingia
Downingia montana .... Sierra Calicoflower
Downingia ornatissima .... Folded Downingia
Downingia pusilla .... Dwarf Downingia
Githopsis specularioides .... **Bluecup**
Heterocodon rariflorum .... Heterocodon
Legenere limosa .... Legenere
Nemacladus capillaris .... Common Nemacladus
Nemacladus interior .... Sierra Nemacladus
Porterella carnosula .... **Porterella**

Caprifoliaceae – Honeysuckle Family
Linnaea borealis ssp. *longiflora* .... **Twinflower**
Lonicera cauriana .... Sweetberry Honeysuckle
Lonicera conjugialis .... Double Honeysuckle
Lonicera hispidula var. *vacillans* .... Hairy Honeysuckle
Lonicera interrupta .... Chaparral Honeysuckle
Lonicera involucrata var. *involucrata* .... Twinberry
Sambucus melanocarpa .... Black Elderberry
Sambucus mexicana .... Blue Elderberry
Sambucus racemosa var. *microbotrys* .... Red Elderberry
Symphoricarpos albus var. *laevigatus* .... Snowberry
Symphoricarpos mollis .... Creeping Snowberry, Trip Vine
Symphoricarpos rotundifolius var. *rotundifolius* .... Roundleaf Snowberry
Viburnum ellipticum .... Oval-leaf Viburnum

Caryophyllaceae – Pink Family
Agrostemma githago .... Corn-cockle*
Arenaria aculeata .... Prickly Sandwort
Arenaria congesta .... **Ballhead Sandwort**
Arenaria congesta var. *subcongesta* .... Ballhead Sandwort
Arenaria congesta var. *suffrutescens* .... Ballhead Sandwort
Arenaria kingii var. *glabrescens* .... **King's Sandwort**
Arenaria serpyllifolia ssp. *serpyllifolia* .... Thymeleaf Sandwort*
Cerastium arvense .... Field Chickweed
Cerastium fontanum ssp. *vulgare* .... Common Chickweed*
Cerastium glomeratum .... **Mouse-ear Chickweed***
Gypsophila paniculata var. *paniculata* .... Baby's Breath*
Herniaria hirsuta ssp. *hirsuta* .... Hairy Rupturewort*
Lychnis coronaria .... Rose Campion*
Minuartia californica .... California Sandwort
Minuartia douglasii .... **Douglas' Sandwort**
Minuartia nuttallii ssp. *gracilis* .... Nuttall's Sandwort
Moehringia macrophylla .... Largeleaf Sandwort

Petrorhagia dubia	**Wild Carnation***
Petrorhagia prolifera	Childing Pink*
Pseudostellaria jamesiana	Sticky Starwort
Pseudostellaria sierrae	Sierra Starwort
Sagina apetala	Dwarf Pearlwort
Sagina decumbens ssp. *occidentalis*	Western Pearlwort
Sagina saginoides	Alpine Pearlwort
Saponaria officinalis	Bouncing Bet, Soapwort*
Scleranthus annuus ssp. *annuus*	Knawel*
Silene bernardina	Palmer's Catchfly
Silene bridgesii	Bridge's Catchfly
Silene californica	**Indian Pink**
Silene dichotoma	Branching Campion*
Silene douglasii	**Douglas' Catchfly**
Silene gallica	**Windmill Pink***
Silene invisa	Short-petaled Campion
Silene lemmonii	**Lemmon's Catchfly**
Silene menziesii	Menzies' Campion
Silene occidentalis	Western Catchfly
Silene sargentii	Sargent's Campion
Spergula arvensis ssp. *arvensis*	Corn Spurry*
Spergularia macrotheca	Largeflower Sand Spurry
Spergularia rubra	**Ruby Sand Spurry***
Stellaria calycantha	Northern Starwort
Stellaria crispa	Ruffled Starwort
Stellaria longipes var. *longipes*	**Long-stalked** Starwort
Stellaria media	**Common Chickweed***
Stellaria nitens	Shining Chickweed
Stellaria obtusa	Obtuse Starwort
Stellaria umbellata	Umbrella Chickweed

Celastraceae – Staff-tree Family

Paxistima myrsinites	Oregon Boxwood

Ceratophyllaceae – Hornwort Family

Ceratophyllum demersum	Hornwort

Chenopodiaceae – Goosefoot Family

Atriplex rosea	Tumbling Oracle*
Atriplex truncata	Wedgescale
Chenopodium album	Lambs Quarters*
Chenopodium ambrosioides	Mexican Tea*
Chenopodium atrovirens	Dark-green Goosefoot
Chenopodium berlandieri	Pitseed Goosefoot
Chenopodium botrys	Jerusalem Oak*
Chenopodium desiccatum	Aridland Goosefoot
Chenopodium incanum var. *occidentale*	Pigweed
Chenopodium incognitum	Masked Goosefoot
Chenopodium pumilio	Small Goosefoot*
Chenopodium strictum var. *glaucophyllum*	White-leafed Goosefoot*
Halogeton glomeratus	Saltlover*
Kochia scoparia	Summer Cypress*
Monolepis nuttalliana	Poverty Weed

Salsola soda .... Tumbleweed*
Salsola tragus .... Russian Thistle*
Sarcobatus vermiculatus .... Black Greasewood

Convolvulaceae – Morning Glory Family
Calystegia malacophylla ssp. *malacophylla*
.... **Woolly Morning Glory, Sierra Morning Glory**
Calystegia occidentalis ssp. *occidentalis* .... **Western Morning Glory**
Calystegia stebbinsii .... **Stebbins' Morning Glory**
Convolvulus arvensis .... **Bindweed***

Cornaceae – Dogwood Family
Cornus glabrata .... Brown Dogwood
Cornus nuttallii .... Mountain Dogwood
Cornus sericea ssp. *occidentalis* .... Western Creek Dogwood
Cornus sericea ssp. *sericea* .... American Dogwood
Cornus sessilis .... Black-fruited Dogwood

Crassulaceae – Stonecrop Family
Crassula aquatica .... Pygmyweed
Crassula connata .... Sand Pygmyweed
Crassula tillaea .... Moss Pygmyweed*
Dudleya cymosa .... **Canyon Dudleya**
Parvisedum congdonii .... Congdon's Stonecrop
Parvisedum pumilum .... **Sierra Stonecrop**
Sedum lanceolatum .... Lanceleaf Sedum
Sedum obtusatum ssp. *obtusatum* .... **Sierra Sedum**
Sedum roseum ssp. *integrifolium* .... **King's Crown, Rose Sedum**
Sedum spathulifolium .... **Pacific Sedum**

Cucurbitaceae – Cucumber Family
Marah fabaceus .... **Common Manroot**
Marah watsonii .... Watson's Manroot

Cupressaceae – Cypress Family
Calocedrus decurrens .... Incense Cedar
Cupressus macnabiana .... McNab Cypress
Juniperus californica .... California Juniper
Juniperus communis .... Common Juniper
Juniperus occidentalis .... Sierra Juniper
Juniperus occidentalis var. *australis* .... Sierra Juniper
Juniperus occidentalis var. *occidentalis* .... Western Juniper

Cuscutaceae – Dodder Family
Cuscuta californica .... **California Dodder**
Cuscuta californica var. *breviflora* .... Shortflower Dodder
Cuscuta howelliana .... Boggs Lake Dodder
Cuscusta subinclusa .... Canyon Dodder

Cyperaceae – Sedge Family
Bulbostylis capillaris .... Threadleaf Beakside
Carex abrupta .... Abrupt-beaked Sedge
Carex amplifolia .... Ample-leaf Sedge
Carex angustata .... Narrow Spike Sedge
Carex aquatilis .... Sitka Sedge

Carex aquatilis var. *dives* .... Sitka Sedge
Carex athrostachya ....Slenderbeak Sedge
Carex aurea .... Goldenfruit Sedge
Carex barbarae .... Santa Barbara Sedge
Carex bolanderi ....Bolander's Sedge
Carex brainerdii .... Brainerd's Sedge
Carex canescens ....Hoary Sedge
Carex capitata .... Capitate Sedge
Carex cusickii .... Cusick's Sedge
Carex davyi .... Davy's Sedge
Carex densa .... Dense Sedge
Carex deweyana ssp. *leptopoda* ....Shortscale Sedge
Carex diandra .... Lesser Panicled Sedge
Carex disperma .... Softleaf Sedge
Carex douglasii .... Douglas' Sedge
Carex echinata ssp. *echinata* .... Stellate Sedge
Carex feta .... Greensheath Sedge
Carex filifolia var. *erostrata* .... Shorthair Sedge
Carex fissuricola .... Cleft Sedge
Carex fracta ....Fragile-sheath Sedge
Carex gracilior .... Slender Sedge
Carex hassei .... Hasse's Sedge
Carex helleri .... Heller's Sedge
Carex heteroneura .... Variable-nerve Sedge
Carex hirtissima .... Fuzzy Sedge
Carex hoodii ....Hood's Sedge
Carex illota .... Smallhead Sedge
Carex integra .... Smoothbeak Sedge
Carex jonesii ....Jones' Sedge
Carex laeviculmis .... Smoothstem Sedge
Carex lanuginosa ....Woolly Sedge
Carex lasiocarpa .... Woolly-fruit Sedge
Carex lemmonii ....Lemmon's Sedge
Carex lenticularis var. *impressa* ....Few-ribbed Sedge
Carex lenticularis var. *lipocarpa* ....Fat-fruited Sedge
Carex leporinella .... Sierra Hare Sedge
Carex limosa .... Shore Sedge
Carex luzulifolia ....Littleleaf Sedge
Carex luzulina var. *ablata* ....Cold-loving Sedge
Carex mariposana .... Mariposa Sedge
Carex microptera ....Smallwing Sedge
Carex multicaulis .... Manystem Sedge
Carex multicostata ....Many Ribbed Sedge
Carex nebrascensis .... Nebraska Sedge
Carex nervina .... Sierra Nerved Sedge
Carex nigricans .... Black Alpine Sedge
Carex nudata .... Naked Sedge
Carex praegracilis .... Field Sedge
Carex preslii .... Presl's Sedge
Carex raynoldsii ....Raynolds' Sedge
Carex rossii .... Ross' Sedge

Carex scopulorum var. *bracteosa* .... Bracted Sedge
Carex senta .... Rough Sedge
Carex serratodens .... Bifid Sedge
Carex sheldonii .... Sheldon's Sedge
Carex simulata .... Shortbeak Sedge
Carex specifica .... Narrow Fruited Sedge
Carex spectabilis .... Showy Sedge
Carex straminiformis .... Straw-like Sedge
Carex subfusca .... Rusty Sedge
Carex subnigricans .... Blackish Sedge
Carex tumulicola .... Foothill Sedge
Carex utriculata .... Beaked Sedge
Carex vernacula .... Native Sedge
Carex vesicaria .... Inflated Sedge
Carex whitneyi .... Whitney's Sedge
Cyperus difformis .... Variable Flatsedge
Cyperus eragrostis .... Tall Sedge*
Cyperus erythrorhizos .... Redroot Cypress
Cyperus esculentus .... Yellow Nutgrass
Cyperus niger .... Brown Umbrella Sedge
Cyperus squarrosus .... Bearded Flatsedge
Cyperus strigosus .... False Nutsedge
Dulichium arundinaceum .... Three Way Sedge
Eleocharis acicularis var. *acicularis* .... Needle Spikerush
Eleocharis acicularis var. *bella* .... Beautiful Spikerush
Eleocharis macrostachya .... Pale Spikerush
Eleocharis montevidensis .... Montevideo Spikerush
Eleocharis obtusa .... Blunt Spikerush
Eleocharis pachycarpa .... Black Sand Spikerush*
Eleocharis pauciflora .... Few-flowered Spikerush
Eleocharis rostellata .... Beaked Spikerush
Eriophorum criniger .... Slender Cotton Grass
Eriophorum gracile .... Cotton Grass
Rhynchospora alba .... White Beakrush
Rhynchospora capitellata .... Brown Beakrush
Scirpus acutus var. *occidentalis* .... Tule
Scirpus americanus .... American Bulrush
Scirpus congdonii .... Congdon's Bulrush
Scirpus diffusus .... Diffuse Rush
Scirpus microcarpus .... Smallfruit Bulrush
Scirpus pungens .... Common Threesquare
Scirpus setaceous .... unknown*
Scirpus subterminalis .... Water Bulrush

Dipsacaceae – Teasel Family
Dipsacus fullonum .... Wild Teasel*

Droseraceae – Sundew Family
Drosera anglica .... Long-leaved Sundew
Drosera rotundifolia .... **Round-leaved Sundew**

Elatinaceae – Waterwort Family
Elatine chilensis .... Waterwort

Ericaceae – Heath Family

Allotropa virgata	**Sugar Stick**
Arbutus menziesii	Pacific Madrone
Arctostaphylos mewukka	Indian Manzanita
Arctostaphylos mewukka ssp. *truei*	True's Manzanita
Arctostaphylos nevadensis	Pinemat Manzanita
Arctostaphylos patula	Greenleaf Manzanita
Arctostaphylos patula × *nevadensis*	unknown
Arctostaphylos viscida ssp. *viscida*	Whiteleaf Manzanita
Cassiope mertensiana	**White Heather**
Chimaphila menziesii	Little Prince's Pine
Chimaphila umbellata	**Prince's Pine, Pipsissiwa**
Gaultheria ovatifolia	Oval-leaf Gaultheria, Oregon Wintergreen
Kalmia polifolia	Bog Laurel
Kalmia polifolia ssp. *microphylla*	Small-leaf Bog Laurel
Ledum glandulosum	Western Labrador Tea
Leucothoe davisiae	Sierra Laurel
Orthilia secunda	**One-sided Wintergreen, Sidebells**
Phyllodoce breweri	**Mountain Heather**
Pleuricospora fimbriolata	**Fringed Pinesap**
Pterospora andromedea	**Pinedrops**
Pyrola asarifolia ssp. *asarifolia*	Bog Wintergreen
Pyrola picta	**White-veined Wintergreen**
Rhododendron occidentale	Western Azalea
Sarcodes sanguinea	**Snow Plant**
Vaccinum caespitosum	Dwarf Bilberry
Vaccinum macrocarpon	Cranberry*
Vaccinum parvifolium	Red Huckleberry
Vaccinum uliginosum ssp. *occidentale*	Western Blueberry

Euphorbiaceae – Spurge Family

Chamaesyce maculata	Spotted Spurge*
Chamaesyce nutans	Eyebane*
Chamaesyce ocellata	Valley Spurge
Chamaesyce serpyllifolia	Thymeleaf Spurge
Eremocarpus setigerus	**Doveweed, Turkey Mullein**
Euphorbia crenulata	Chinese Caps
Euphorbia oblongata	Eggleaf Spurge*
Euphorbia palmeri	Woodland Spurge
Euphorbia peplus	Petty Spurge*
Euphorbia spathulata	Spatula Spurge

Fabaceae – Pea Family

Amorpha californica var. *californica*	California False Indigo
Astragalus austiniae	Austin's Locoweed
Astragalus bolanderi	Bolander's Locoweed
Astragalus canadensis var. *brevidens*	Short-toothed Milkvetch
Astragalus gambelianus	Gambel's Dwarf Milkvetch
Astragalus pauperculus	Depauperate Milkvetch
Astragalus purshii	Pursh's Sheep-pod
Astragalus purshii var. *tinctus*	Woollypod Milkvetch
Astragalus whitneyi	**Balloon Pod Milkvetch, Whitney's Locoweed**
Astragalus whitneyi var. *lenophyllus*	Balloon Pod Milkvetch

Cercis occidentalis .... Western Redbud
Colutea arborescens .... Bladder Senna*
Cytisus scoparius .... Scotch Broom*
Hoita macrostachya .... **Large Leather Root**
Hoita orbicularis .... Round Leaf Leather Root
Lathyrus brownii .... Brown's Brush Pea
Lathyrus hirsutus .... Caley Pea*
Lathyrus jepsonii .... Jepson's Pea
Lathyrus jepsonii var. *californicus* .... Bluff Pea
Lathyrus lanzwertii .... Nevada Pea
Lathyrus lanzwertii var. *aridus* .... Dryland Nevada Pea
Lathyrus latifolius .... **Perennial Sweetpea, Everlasting Pea***
Lathyrus nevadensis var. *nevadensis* .... **Sierra Nevada Pea**
Lathyrus sulphureus .... **Sulphur Pea**
Lathyrus sulphureus var. *argillaceus* .... Dubious Pea
Lotus argophyllus var. *fremontii* .... **Fremont's Silver Lotus**
Lotus corniculatus .... Birdfoot Trefoil*
Lotus crassifolius var. *crassifolius* .... Buck Lotus
Lotus grandiflorus var. *grandiflorus* .... **Largeflower Lotus**
Lotus humistratus .... **Hill Lotus**
Lotus incanus .... Woolly Lotus
Lotus micranthus .... Miniature Lotus
Lotus nevadensis var. *nevadensis* .... Sierra Nevada Lotus
Lotus oblongifolius var. *oblongifolius* .... **Streambank Lotus, Torrey's Lotus**
Lotus pinnatus .... Pinnateleaf Lotus
Lotus purshianus var. *purshianus* .... **Spanish Lotus**
Lotus scoparius .... **Deerweed, California Broom**
Lotus stipularis var. *ottleyi* .... Stipulate Lotus
Lotus uliginosus .... Marsh Lotus*
Lotus wrangelianus .... Calf Lotus
Lupinus adsurgens .... Silky Lupine
Lupinus albicaulis .... **Pine Lupine, Sickle Keel Lupine**
Lupinus albifrons var. *albifrons* .... **Bush Lupine, Silver Lupine**
Lupinus andersonii .... Anderson's Lupine
Lupinus angustiflorus .... Narrowflower Lupine
Lupinus apertus .... Summit Lupine
Lupinus arbustus .... Spur Lupine
Lupinus argenteus .... Silvery Lupine
Lupinus argenteus var. *heteranthus* .... Silvery Lupine
Lupinus argenteus var. *meionanthus* .... Tahoe Lupine
Lupinus benthamii .... **Spider Lupine, Bentham's Lupine**
Lupinus bicolor .... **Miniature Lupine**
Lupinus breweri .... **Brewer's Lupine**
Lupinus grayii .... Sierra Lupine
Lupinus latifolius .... **Broadleaf Lupine**
Lupinus latifolius var. *columbianus* .... Broadleaf Lupine
Lupinus lepidus .... Elegant Lupine
Lupinus lepidus var. *confertus* .... Elegant Lupine
Lupinus lepidus var. *lobbii* .... Lobb's Lupine
Lupinus lepidus var. *sellulus* .... Stool Lupine
Lupinus microcarpus var. *densiflorus* .... **Gully Lupine, Chick Lupine**
Lupinus nanus .... **Douglas' Lupine, Sky Lupine**

Lupinus obtusilobus .... Bluntlobe Lupine
Lupinus pachylobus .... Bigpod Lupine
Lupinus polyphyllus ....Meadow Lupine
Lupinus polyphyllus var. *burkei* .... **Meadow Lupine**
Lupinus rivularis .... Riverbank Lupine
Lupinus stiversii .... **Harlequin Lupine**
Lupinus succulentus .... **Arroyo Lupine, Succulent Lupine**
Medicago arabica .... Spotted Burclover*
Medicago lupulina .... Black Medick*
Medicago polymorpha .... Yellow Burclover*
Medicago sativa .... Common Alfalfa*
Melilotus alba .... **White Sweetclover***
Melilotus indica .... Sourclover*
Melilotus officinalis .... **Yellow Sweetclover***
Pickeringia montana var. *montana* .... Chaparral Pea
Robinia pseudoacacia ....Black Locust*
Sesbania punicea .... Scarlet Wisteria, Rattlebox*
Spartium junceum .... Spanish Broom*
Thermopsis macrophylla .... Golden Pea
Trifolium albopurpureum .... Rancheria Clover
Trifolium albopurpureum var. *olivaceum* ....Olive Clover
Trifolium andersonii .... Fiveleaf Clover
Trifolium barbigerum .... Bearded Clover
Trifolium beckwithii .... Beckwith's Clover
Trifolium bifidum .... Deceiving Clover
Trifolium breweri .... Brewer's Clover
Trifolium campestre .... Hop Clover*
Trifolium ciliolatum .... Tree Clover
Trifolium cyathiferum .... Bowl Clover
Trifolium depauperatum .... **Cowbag Clover, Balloon Clover**
Trifolium dubium ....**Little Hop Clover, Shamrock Clover***
Trifolium glomeratum .... Clustered Clover*
Trifolium gracilentum .... Pinpoint Clover
Trifolium hirtum .... **Rose Clover***
Trifolium hybridum .... Hybrid Clover*
Trifolium incarnatum .... **Crimson Clover, Indian Clover***
Trifolium kingii var. *productum* .... Shasta Clover
Trifolium lemmonii .... **Lemmon's Clover**
Trifolium longipes .... **Long-stalked Clover**
Trifolium macraei .... Chilean Clover
Trifolium microcephalum .... Smallhead Clover
Trifolium microdon .... Valparaiso Clover
Trifolium monanthum var. *monanthum* .... Mountain Carpet Clover
Trifolium obtusiflorum .... Creek Clover
Trifolium oliganthum .... Fewflower Clover
Trifolium pratense .... **Red Clover***
Trifolium repens .... White Clover*
Trifolium subterraneum .... Subterranean Clover*
Trifolium variegatum .... **Whitetip Clover, Variegated Clover**
Trifolium wildenovii .... **Tomcat Clover**
Trifolium wormskioldii .... **SpringbankClover, Cow's Clover**
Ulex europaea .... Gorse*

Vicia americana var. *americana* .... American Vetch
Vicia benghalensis ....Purple Vetch*
Vicia hirsuta .... Tiny Vetch*
Vicia sativa ssp. *nigra* .... Narrowleaf Vetch*
Vicia sativa ssp. *sativa* .... **Common Vetch, Spring Vetch***
Vicia villosa var. *varia* .... Winter Vetch*
Vicia villosa ssp. *villosa* .... **Hairy Vetch, Winter Vetch***

Fagaceae – Oak Family
Chrysolepis sempervirens .... Bush Chinquapin
Lithocarpus densiflorus var. *densiflorus* .... Tanbark Oak
Lithocarpus densiflorus var. *echinoides* .... Tanbark Scrub Oak
Quercus berberidifolia .... Scrub Oak
Quercus chrysolepis .... Canyon Live Oak, Maul Oak
Quercus douglasii .... Blue Oak
Quercus durata .... Leather Oak
Quercus garryana var. *breweri* ....Oregon White Oak
Quercus kelloggii .... California Black Oak
Quercus lobata .... Valley Oak
Quercus vaccinifolia .... Huckleberry Oak
Quercus wislizenii var. *wislizenii* .... Interior Live Oak
Quercus wislizenii var. *frutescens* .... Interior Live Oak

Garryaceae – Silktassel Family
Garrya flavescens .... Ashy Silktassel
Garrya fremontii .... Mountain Silktassel

Gentianaceae – Gentian Family
Centaurium muehlenbergii ....**June Centaury**
Centaurium venustum ....**Canchalagua**
Gentiana calycosa ....**Explorer's Gentian**
Gentiana newberryi var. *newberryi* ....**Alpine Gentian**
Gentiana newberryi var. *tiogana* .... Sierra Alpine Gentian
Gentianella amarella ssp. *acuta* .... Northern Gentian
Gentianopsis simplex .... **Hiker's Fringed Gentian**
Swertia albicaulis .... **Whitestem Swertia, Whitestem Elkweed**
Swertia albicaulis var. *nitida* .... Whitestem Swertia
Swertia radiata .... Monument Plant

Geraniaceae – Geranium Family
Erodium botrys .... **Broadleaf Filaree, Long-beaked Storksbill***
Erodium brachycarpum .... Short-fruited Storksbill*
Erodium cicutarium .... **Redstem Filaree, Cutleaf Storksbill***
Erodium moschatum .... **Whitestem Filaree***
Geranium carolinianum .... Carolina Geranium
Geranium dissectum ....**Cutleaf Geranium***
Geranium molle ....**Dove's Foot Geranium***
Geranium retrorsum .... New Zealand Geranium*
Geranium richardsonii .... Richardson's Geranium
Geranium robertianum .... Herb Robert*

Grossulariaceae – Gooseberry Family
Ribes amarum .... Bitter Gooseberry
Ribes aureum .... Golden Currant

Ribes cereum var. *cereum* .... Wax Currant
Ribes inerme var. *inerme* .... White-stemmed Gooseberry
Ribes lacustre .... Swamp Currant
Ribes lasianthum .... Alpine Gooseberry
Ribes montigenum .... Mountain Gooseberry
Ribes nevadense .... Mountain Pink Currant
Ribes roezlii var. *roezlii* .... Sierra Gooseberry
Ribes velutinum .... Plateau Gooseberry
Ribes viscosissimum .... Sticky Currant

Haloragaceae – Water-milfoil Family
Myriophyllum sibiricum .... Siberian Water-milfoil
Myriophyllum spicatum .... Eurasian Milfoil*
Myriophyllum verticillatum .... Whorl-leaf Water-milfoil

Hippocastanaceae – Buckeye Family
Aesculus californica .... California Buckeye

Hydrocharitaceae – Waterweed Family
Elodea canadensis .... Common Waterweed, Anacharis
Elodea nuttallii .... Nuttall's Waterweed
Najas guadalupensis .... Common Water Nymph

Hydrophyllaceae – Waterleaf Family
Draperia systyla .... **Draperia**
Eriodictyon californicum .... **Yerba Santa**
Hesperochiron californicus .... **Western Centaur**
Hesperochiron pumilus .... Dwarf Hesperochiron
Hydrophyllum capitatum var. *alpinum* ...... **Woolen-breeches, Ballhead Waterleaf**
Hydrophyllum occidentale .... **Western Waterleaf**
Nama californicum .... California Waterleaf
Nama densum .... Purplemat
Nama lobbii .... **Lobb's Nama**
Nemophila heterophylla .... **Small White Nemophila, Variable Leaf Nemophila**
Nemophila maculata .... **Fivespot**
Nemophila menziesii .... **Baby Blue-eyes**
Nemophila parviflora var. *austinae* .... Small-flowered Nemophila
Nemophila pedunculata .... Meadow Nemophila
Nemophila spatulata .... Sierra Nemophila
Phacelia cicutaria var. *cicutaria* .... **Caterpillar Phacelia**
Phacelia curvipes .... Washoe Phacelia
Phacelia egena .... Rock Phacelia
Phacelia hastata .... Silverleaf Phacelia
Phacelia hastata ssp. *compacta* .... Timberline Phacelia
Phacelia heterophylla ssp. *virgata* .... **Vari-leaved Phacelia**
Phacelia humilis .... Low Phacelia
Phacelia hydrophylloides .... **Ballhead Phacelia**
Phacelia imbricata ssp. *imbricata* .... Imbricate Phacelia
Phacelia marcescens .... Persistent-flower Phacelia
Phacelia mustelina .... Death Valley Roundleaf Phacelia
Phacelia mutabilis .... Changeable Phacelia
Phacelia procera .... Tall Phacelia
Phacelia quickii .... **Quick's Phacelia, Quick's Scorpionweed**

Phacelia racemosa .... Racemose Phacelia
Phacelia ramosissima var. *eremophila* .... Branched Phacelia
Phacelia ramosissima var. *subglabra* .... Branching Phacelia
Phacelia stebbinsii .... **Stebbins' Phacelia**
Phacelia vallicola .... Mariposa Phacelia

Hypericaceae – St. John's Wort Family
Hypericum anagalloides .... **Tinker's Penny**
Hypericum concinnum .... **Gold Wire**
Hypericum formosum var. *scouleri* .... **Scouler's St. John's Wort**
Hypericum perforatum .... **Klamath Weed, St. John's Wort***

Iridaceae – Iris Family
Iris hartwegii ssp. *hartwegii* .... **Sierra Iris**
Iris hartwegii ssp. *pinetorum* .... Hartweg's Pine Iris
Iris macrosiphon .... **Ground Iris**
Iris missouriensis .... **Western Blue Flag**
Iris psuedacoris .... **Yellow Water Iris***
Iris tenuissima .... Longtube Iris*
Sisyrinchium bellum .... **Blue-eyed Grass**
Sisyrinchium elmeri .... **Yellow-eyed Grass**
Sisyrinchium halophilum .... Nevada Blue-eyed Grass
Sisyrinchium idahoense var. *occidentale* .... **Idaho Blue-eyed Grass**

Juglandaceae – Walnut Family
Juglans californica var. *hindsii* .... Hind's Walnut, Northern California Black Walnut

Juncaceae – Rush Family
Juncus acuminatus .... Tapertip Rush
Juncus ambiguus .... Saline Toad Rush
Juncus articulatus .... Jointleaf Rush
Juncus balticus .... Baltic Rush
Juncus bryoides .... Moss Rush
Juncus bufonius .... Toad Rush
Juncus bufonius var. *occidentalis* .... Roundfruit Toad Rush
Juncus capitatus .... Leafybract Dwarf Rush
Juncus chlorcephalus .... Greenhead Rush
Juncus confusus .... Colorado Rush
Juncus covillei .... Coville's Rush
Juncus covillei var. *obtusatus* .... Coville's Rush
Juncus drummondii .... Drummond's Rush
Juncus dubius .... Mariposa Rush
Juncus effusus .... Bog Rush
Juncus effusus var. *pacificus* .... Pacific Bog Rush
Juncus ensifolius .... Swordleaf Rush
Juncus hemiendytus var. *abjectus* .... Center Basin Rush
Juncus hemiendytus var. *hemiendytus* .... Vernal Pool Rush
Juncus howellii .... Howell's Rush
Juncus kelloggii .... Kellogg's Rush
Juncus leiospermus var. *ahartii* .... Ahart's Dwarf Rush
Juncus leiospermus var. *leiospermus* .... Red Bluff Dwarf Rush
Juncus longistylis .... Longstyle rush
Juncus macrandrus .... Long-anther Rush

Juncus marginatus var. *marginatus*	Red-anther Rush
Juncus mertensianus	Merten's Rush
Juncus mexicanus	Mexican Rush
Juncus nevadensis	Sierra Rush
Juncus occidentalis	Slender Rush
Juncus orthophyllus	Straightleaf Rush
Juncus oxymeris	Pointed Rush
Juncus parryi	Parry's Rush
Juncus phaeocephalus	Brownhead Rush
Juncus saximontanus	Rocky Mountain Rush
Juncus tenuis	Slender Rush
Juncus tiehmii	Tiehm's Rush
Juncus uncialis	Inch-high Rush
Juncus xiphioides	Iris-leaf Rush
Luzula comosa	Hairy Woodrush
Luzula divaricata	Spreading Woodrush
Luzula parviflora	Small-flowered Woodrush
Luzula subcongesta	Donner Woodrush

Juncaginaceae – Arrow-weed Family

Lilaea scilloides	Flowering Quillwort
Triglochin maritima	Seaside Arrowgrass

Lamiaceae – Mint Family

Agastache urticifolia	**Nettleleaf Horsemint, Giant Hyssop**
Glecoma hederacea	Ground Ivy*
Lamium amplexicaule	**Giraffe Head, Hen's Bit***
Lamium purpureum	**Purple Deadnettle***
Lepechinia calycina	**Pitcher Sage**
Lycopus americanus	Cutleaf Water Horehound
Lycopus uniflorus	Northern Bugleweed
Marrubium vulgare	**Horehound***
Melissa officinalis	**Lemon Balm, Bee Balm***
Mentha arvensis	**Field Mint**
Mentha ×*piperata*	Peppermint*
Mentha pulegium	Pennyroyal*
Mentha spicata var. *spicata*	**Spearmint***
Monardella candicans	Sierra Monardella
Monardella follettii	Follett's Monardella
Monardella glauca	Pale Monardella
Monardella lanceolata	**Mustang Mint**
Monardella odoratissima ssp. *odoratissima*	**Mountain Pennyroyal, Western Pennyroyal**
Monardella odoratissima ssp. *pallida*	Pallid Mountain Monardella
Monardella sheltonii	Shelton's Coyote Mint
Monardella villosa	**Coyote Mint**
Monardella viridis	Green Monardella
Pogogyne douglasii	Douglas' Pogogyne
Pogogyne serpylloides	**Thymeleaf Pogogyne, Vernal Pool Mint**
Pogogyne zizyphoroides	**Sacramento Beardstyle**
Prunella vulgaris var. *lanceolata*	Self Heal
Prunella vulgaris var. *vulgaris*	**Self Heal, Heal All***
Pycnanthemum californicum	Mountain Mint

Salvia sonomensis .... **Creeping Sage, Sonoma Sage**
Salvia virgata .... Meadow Sage
Scutellaria antirrhinoides .... Nose Skullcap
Scutellaria bolanderi ssp. *bolanderi* .... Bolander's Skullcap
Scutellaria californica .... **California Skullcap**
Scutellaria galericulata .... Marsh Skullcap
Scutellaria siphocampyloides .... Grayleaf Skullcap
Scutellaria tuberosa .... **Blue Skullcap, Danny's Skullcap**
Stachys ajugoides .... Hedge Nettle
Stachys ajugoides var. *ajugoides* .... Ajuga Hedge Nettle
Stachys ajugoides var. *rigida* .... **Rigid Hedge Nettle**
Stachys albens .... Whitestem Hedge Nettle
Trichostema lanceolatum .... **Vinegar Weed**
Trichostema oblongum .... **Mountain Blue Curls**
Trichostema simulatum .... Siskiyou Blue Curls

Lauraceae – Laurel Family
Umbellularia californica .... California Bay Tree

Lemnaceae – Duckweed Family
Lemna aequinoctialis .... Lesser Duckweed
Lemna gibba .... Swollen Duckweed
Lemna minor .... **Duckweed**
Lemna minuscula .... Least Duckweed
Lemna trisulca .... Ivy-leaf Duckweed
Lemna turionifera .... Turion Duckweed
Lemna valdiviana .... Valdivia's Duckweed
Wolffia columbiana .... Water Meal

Lentibulariaceae – Bladderwort Family
Utricularia gibba .... Humped Bladderwort*
Utricularia intermedia .... Flat-leafed Bladderwort
Utricularia minor .... Lesser Bladderwort
Utricularia vulgaris .... **Common Bladderwort**

Liliaceae – Lily Family
Allium acuminatum .... Tapertip Onion
Allium amplectens .... **Paper Onion, Narrow-leaf Onion**
Allium anceps .... Twinleaf Onion
Allium bisceptrum var. *bisceptrum* .... Aspen Onion
Allium campanulatum .... **Sierra Onion**
Allium jepsonii .... Jepson's Onion
Allium lemmonii .... **Lemmon's Onion**
Allium membranaceum .... Paper Onion
Allium obtusum .... **Red Sierra Onion**
Allium parvum .... Dwarf Onion
Allium peninsulare var. *peninsulare* .... **Peninsular Onion**
Allium platycaule .... **Pinkstar Onion, Flatstem Onion**
Allium sanbornii var. *congdonii* .... Congdon's Onion
Allium sanbornii var. *sanbornii* .... **Sanborn's Onion**
Allium tribracteatum .... Three-bracted Onion
Allium triquetrum .... Three-cornered Leek*
Allium unifolium .... One-leaf Onion

Allium validum	**Swamp Onion, Pacific Onion**
Allium vineale	Wild Garlic*
Brodiaea appendiculata	Hoover's Brodiaea
Brodiaea californica var. *californica*	**California Brodiaea**
Brodiaea coronaria	Harvest Brodiaea
Brodiaea elegans ssp. *elegans*	**Harvest Brodiaea**
Brodiaea elegans ssp. *hooveri*	Harvest Brodiaea
Brodiaea minor	Dwarf Brodiaea
Brodiaea purdyi	**Purdy's Brodiaea**
Calochortus albus	**Fairy Lanterns, White Globe Lily**
Calochortus coeruleus	**Beavertail Grass**
Calochortus leichtlinii	**Leichtlin's Mariposa Lily**
Calochortus luteus	**Yellow Mariposa Lily, Gold Nuggets**
Calochortus minimus	Sierra Mariposa Lily
Calochortus monophyllus	**Yellow Cat's Ear**
Calochortus nudus	**Naked Star Tulip**
Calochortus superbus	**Superb Mariposa Lily**
Calochortus venustus	Butterfly Mariposa Lily
Calochortus vestae	Coast Range Mariposa Lily
Camassia quamash ssp. *breviflora*	Small-flowered Camas Lily
Camassia quamash ssp. *quamash*	**Common Camas Lily**
Chlorogalum grandiflorum	Red Hills Soaproot
Chlorogalum pomeridianum var. *pomeridianum*	**Soap Plant**
Clintonia uniflora	Bride's Bonnet
Dichelostemma capitatum ssp. *capitatum*	**Blue Dicks**
Dichelostemma congestum	**Forktooth Ookow**
Dichelostemma multiflorum	**Wild Hyacinth, Roundtooth Ookow**
Dichelostemma volubile	**Snake Lily, Twining Brodiaea**
Disporum hookeri	**Hooker's Fairybell**
Erythronium multiscapoideum	**Sierra Fawn Lily, Adder's Tongue**
Erythronium purpurascens	**Plainleaf Fawn Lily**
Fritillaria agrestis	**Stinkbells**
Fritillaria atropurpurea	**Spotted Mountain Bells**
Fritillaria eastwoodiae	Butte County Fritillary
Fritillaria micrantha	**Brown Bells**
Fritillaria pudica	**Yellow Bells**
Fritillaria recurva	**Scarlet Fritillary**
Hastingsia alba	**Bog Hastingsia, Reed Lily, Rush Lily**
Lilium humboldtii ssp. *humboldtii*	**Humboldt Lily**
Lilium kelleyanum	Kelley's Lily
Lilium pardalinum ssp. *pardalinum*	**Leopard Lily**
Lilium pardalinum ssp. *shastense*	Shasta Lily
Lilium parvum	**Alpine Lily**
Lilium washingtonianum ssp. *washingtonianum*	**Washington Lily**
Narthecium californicum	Bog Asphodel
Odontostomum hartwegii	**Hartweg's Doll Lily, Odontostomum**
Smilacina racemosa	**Western False Solomon's Seal**
Smilacina stellata	**Star-flowered False Solomon's Seal, Slim Solomon's Seal**
Smilax californica	Greenbriar
Streptopus amplexifolius var. *americanus*	Twisted Stalk
Tofieldia occidentalis ssp. *occidentalis*	**Western Tofieldia, False Asphodel**
Trillium albidum	**Sweet Trillium**

Trillium angustipetalum .... **Purple Trillium**
Trillium chloropetalum .... Giant Trillium
Triteleia bridgesii .... **Bridge's Brodiaea**
Triteleia hyacinthina .... **White Brodiaea, White Wild Hyacinth**
Triteleia ixioides var. *analina* .... Prettyface
Triteleia ixioides var. *ixioides* .... **Prettyface, Golden Brodiaea**
Triteleia ixioides var. *scabra* .... **Prettyface, Golden Brodiaea**
Triteleia laxa .... **Wally Basket, Ithuriel's Spear, Grass Nut**
Triteleia lilacina .... **Glass Hyacinth, Glassy Brodiaea**
Triteleia montana .... Mountain Brodiaea
Veratrum californicum var. *californicum* .... **Corn Lily, False Hellebore**
Xerophyllum tenax .... **Beargrass**
Zigadenus exaltatus .... Giant Death Camas
Zigadenus paniculatus .... Sand Corn
Zigadenus venenosus var. *venenosus* .... **Death Camas**

Limnanthaceae – Meadow Foam Family
Floerkea proserpinacoides .... False Mermaid
Limnanthes alba ssp. *alba* .... **White Meadow Foam**
Limnanthes alba ssp. *versicolor* .... Shasta Meadow Foam
Limnanthes douglasii .... **Douglas' Meadow Foam**
Limnanthes douglasii var. *rosea* .... Rosy Meadow Foam
Limnanthes striata .... Foothill Meadow Foam

Linaceae – Flax Family
Hesperolinon micranthum .... Smallflowered Dwarf Flax
Linum bienne .... **Narrowleaf Flax***
Linum lewisii .... **Western Blue Flax**
Linum usitatissimum .... Common Flax*

Loasaceae – Loasa Family
Mentzelia albicaulis .... Whitestem Stickleaf
Mentzelia congesta .... Clustered Blazing Star
Mentzelia dispersa .... Nevada Stickleaf
Mentzelia laevicaulis .... **Giant Blazing Star**
Mentzelia montana .... Mountain Blazing Star
Mentzelia veatchiana .... Veatch's Blazing Star

Lythraceae – Loosestrife Family
Lythrum hyssopifolium .... **Hyssop Loosestrife, Grass Poly***
Lythrum portula .... Broadleaf Loosestrife*
Lythrum salicaria .... **Purple Loosestrife***

Malvaceae – Mallow Family
Abutilon theophrasti .... Velvet Leaf*
Malva neglecta .... **Common Mallow, Cheeseweed***
Malva nicaeensis .... Bull Mallow*
Malva parviflora .... Cheeseweed, Little Mallow*
Modiola caroliniana .... **Carolina Bristlemallow, Wheel Mallow***
Sidalcea diploscypha .... Fringed Sidalcea
Sidalcea glaucescens .... **Waxy Checkerbloom, Glaucous Checker-mallow**
Sidalcea hartwegii .... **Hartweg's Sidalcea, Valley Sidalcea**
Sidalcea malvaeflora ssp. *asprella* .... **Checkerbloom**
Sidalcea oregana .... **Oregon Sidalcea, Mountain Hollyhock**

Sidalcea oregana ssp. *oregana* .... Oregon Sidalcea, Mountain Hollyhock
Sidalcea oregana ssp. *spicata* .... Spicate Oregon Sidalcea
Sidalcea pedata .... Birdfoot Checkerbloom
Sidalcea stipularis .... **Scadden Flat Checkerbloom**
Sphaeralcea munroana ....Munroe's Globe Mallow

Martyniaceae – Unicorn Plant Family
Proboscidea louisianica .... Common Unicorn Plant*
Proboscidea lutea .... Unicorn Plant*

Menyanthaceae – Bogbean Family
Menyanthes trifoliata .... **Bogbean, Buckbean**

Molluginaceae – Carpetweed Family
Mollugo verticillata .... Carpetweed*

Moraceae – Fig Family
Ficus carica .... Fig Tree*
Maclura pomifera .... Osage Orange*
Morus alba ....White Mulberry*

Nymphaeaceae – Water Lily Family
Nuphar luteum ssp. *polysepalum* .... **Yellow Pond Lily, Spatterdock, Cow Lily**
Nymphaea odorata .... White Water Lily*

Oleaceae – Olive Family
Fraxinus dipetala .... California Ash
Fraxinus latifolia ...... ,,Oregon Ash
Olea europaea .... ,,,,,,,,,,,. Olive*

Onagraceae – Evening Primrose Family
Camissonia andina .... Sundrops
Camissonia graciliflora ....Hill Suncup
Camissonia subacaulis .... Northern Suncup
Camissonia tanacetifolia .... Tansyleaf Suncup
Circaea alpina ssp. *pacifica* .... **Enchanter's Nightshade**
Clarkia amoena .... Farewell to Spring
Clarkia arcuata .... Kellogg's Clarkia
Clarkia biloba ssp. *biloba* .... **Bilobed Clarkia**
Clarkia biloba ssp. *brandegeae* ....Bilobed Clarkia
Clarkia cylindrica .... Speckled Clarkia
Clarkia dudleyana .... Dudley's Clarkia
Clarkia gracilis ssp. *gracilis* .... **Summer's Darling, Graceful Clarkia**
Clarkia heterandra .... Mountain Clarkia
Clarkia purpurea ssp. *purpurea* ....Purple Clarkia
Clarkia purpurea ssp. *quadrivulnera* .... **Winecup Clarkia**
Clarkia purpurea ssp. *viminea* ....Purple Clarkia
Clarkia rhomboidea .... **Tongue Clarkia**
Clarkia stellata ....Starry Clarkia
Clarkia unguiculata .... **Elegant Clarkia**
Clarkia williamsonii .... **Williamson's Clarkia**
Epilobium anagallidifolium .... Pimpernel Willowherb
Epilobium angustifolium ssp. *circumvagum* .... **Fireweed**
Epilobium brachycarpum .... **Paniceled Willowherb**
Epilobium canum ....**California Fuchsia**

Epilobium canum ssp. *latifolium* .... Broadleaf California Fuchsia
Epilobium ciliatum ssp. *ciliatum* .... Fringed Willowherb
Epilobium ciliatum ssp. *glandulosum* .... Glandular Willowherb
Epilobium densiflorum .... **Denseflower Willowherb**
Epilobium glaberrimum ssp. *fastigiatum* .... Glaucous Willowherb
Epilobium glaberrimum ssp. *glaberrimum* .... **Glaucous Willowherb**
Epilobium halleanum .... Slender Willowherb
Epilobium hornemannii ssp. *hornemanni* .... Hornemann's Willowherb
Epilobium howellii .... Yuba Pass Willowherb
Epilobium lactiflorum .... Milkflower Willowherb
Epilobium minutum .... Minute Willowherb
Epilobium obcordatum .... Rockfringe
Epilobium oreganum .... Oregon Fireweed
Epilobium oregonense .... Oregon Willowherb
Epilobium pygmaeum .... Smooth Willowherb
Epilobium torreyi .... Narrowleaf Willowherb
Gayophytum decipiens .... Deceptive Groundsmoke
Gayophytum diffusum .... Groundsmoke
Gayophytum diffusum ssp. *parviflorum* .... Spreading Groundsmoke
Gayophytum eriospermum .... Woolly-seeded Groundsmoke
Gayophytum heterozygum .... Zigzag Groundsmoke
Gayophytum humile .... Dwarf Groundsmoke
Gayophytum racemosum .... Blackfooted Groundsmoke
Gayophytum ramosissimum .... Pinyon Groundsmoke
Ludwigia palustris .... Marsh Purslane
Ludwigia peploides .... **Water Primrose, Yellow Waterweed**
Ludwigia peploides ssp. *montevidensis* .... Water Primrose*
Oenothera caespitosa ssp. *marginata* .... Fragrant Evening Primrose
Oenothera elata ssp. *hirsutissima* .... **Evening Primrose**
Oenothera elata ssp. *hookeri* .... Hooker's Evening Primrose
Oenothera villosa ssp. *strigosa* .... Hairy Evening Primrose

Orchidaceae – Orchid Family
Cephalanthera austiniae .... **Phantom Orchid**
Corallorhiza maculata .... **Spotted Coralroot Orchid**
Corallorhiza striata .... **Striped Coralroot Orchid**
Cypripedium fasciculatum .... **Clustered Ladyslipper Orchid**
Epipactis gigantea .... **Stream Orchid, Chatterbox**
Epipactis helleborine .... **Broad-leaf Helleborine***
Goodyera oblongifolia .... **Rattlesnake Plantain**
Listera convallarioides .... **Broad-leaf Twayblade**
Piperia colemanii .... Coleman's Rein Orchid
Piperia cooperi .... Cooper's Rein Orchid
Piperia elongata .... Denseflower Rein Orchid
Piperia leptopetala .... Rein Orchid
Piperia transversa .... **Flat-spurred Piperia, Royal Rein Orchid**
Piperia unalascensis .... **Alaska Rein Orchid**
Platanthera leucostachys .... **White Bog Orchid, Sierra Rein Orchid**
Platanthera sparsiflora .... **Sparsely Flowered Bog Orchid**
Spiranthes porrifolia .... **Western Ladies' Tresses**
Spiranthes romanzoffiana .... **Hooded Ladies' Tresses**

Orobanchaceae – Broom-rape Family
Boschniakia strobilacea .... **California Groundcone**
Orobanche californica ssp. *grayana* .... Gray's Broom-rape
Orobanche californica ssp. *jepsonii* .... Jepson's Broom-rape
Orobanche corymbosa .... Flat-top Broom-rape
Orobanche fasciculata ....**Clustered Broom-rape**
Orobanche uniflora .... **Naked Broom-rape**

Oxalidaceae – Oxalis Family
Oxalis corniculata ....Creeping Oxalis*
Oxalis laxa .... Dwarf Woodsorrel*
Oxalis pes-caprae .... **Bermuda Buttercup***

Paeoniaceae – Peony Family
Paeonia brownii .... **Western Peony**

Papaveraceae – Poppy Family
Argemone munita .... **Prickly Poppy**
Corydalis caseana ssp. *caseana* .... **Sierra Corydalis, Fitweed**
Dendromecon rigida .... Bush Poppy
Dicentra formosa .... **Wild Bleeding Heart**
Dicentra uniflora .... **Steer's Head**
Eschscholzia caespitosa .... **Tufted Poppy**
Eschscholzia californica .... **California Poppy**
Eschscholzia lobbii .... **Frying Pans**
Platystemon californicus ....**Cream Cups**

Philadelphaceae – Mock Orange Family
Philadelphus lewisii ....Wild Mock Orange

Phytolaccaceae – Pokeweed Family
Phytolacca americana .... **Pokeweed***

Pinaceae – Pine Family
Abies concolor .... White Fir
Abies magnifica .... Red Fir
Pinus albicaulis .... Whitebark Pine
Pinus attenuata .... Knobcone Pine
Pinus contorta ssp. *murrayana* .... Lodgepole Pine
Pinus jeffreyi ....Jeffrey Pine
Pinus lambertiana .... Sugar Pine
Pinus monticola .... Western White Pine
Pinus ponderosa .... Ponderosa Pine
Pinus sabiniana .... Gray Pine
Pinus washoensis .... Washoe Pine
Pseudotsuga menziesii ....Douglas-fir
Tsuga mertensiana .... Mountain Hemlock

Plantaginaceae – Plantain Family
Plantago coronopus .... Oatleaf Plantain*
Plantago erecta ....**California Plantain**
Plantago lanceolata ....**English Plantain, Buckhorn***
Plantago major ....**Common Plantain***

Poaceae – Grass Family

Achnatherum hymenoides	Indian Ricegrass
Achnatherum lemmonii	Lemmon's Needlegrass
Achnatherum lettermanii	Letterman's Needlegrass
Achnatherum nelsonii ssp. *dorei*	Mountain Needlegrass
Achnatherum nevadensis	Sierra Needlegrass
Achnatherum occidentalis	Western Needlegrass
Achnatherum occidentalis ssp. *californicum*	California Needlegrass
Achnatherum occidentalis ssp. *occidentalis*	Western Needlegrass
Achnatherum occidentalis ssp. *pubescens*	Elmer's Needlegrass
Achnatherum stillmanii	Stillman's Needlegrass
Achnatherum thurberianum	Thurber's Needlegrass
Aegilops triuncialis	Barbed Goatgrass*
Agropyron desertorum	Crested Wheatgrass*
Agrostis capillaris	Colonial Bent*
Agrostis elliottiana	Elliott's Bentgrass
Agrostis exarata	Spiked Bentgrass
Agrostis gigantea	Giant Bentgrass*
Agrostis hendersonii	Henderson's Bentgrass
Agrostis idahoensis	Idaho Bentgrass
Agrostis microphylla	Little-leaf Bentgrass
Agrostis oregonensis	Oregon Bentgrass
Agrostis pallens	Leafy Bentgrass
Agrostis scabra	Tickle Grass, Rough Bentgrass
Agrostis stolonifera	Creeping Bent*
Agrostis thurberiana	Thurber's Bentgrass
Agrostis variabilis	Mountain Bentgrass
Agrostis viridis	Bentgrass*
Aira caryophyllea	Silver European Hairgrass*
Alopecurus aequalis	Short-awn Foxtail
Alopecurus pratensis	Meadow Foxtail*
Alopecurus saccatus	Pacific Foxtail
Andropogon glomeratus var. *scabriglumis*	Bushy Beardgrass
Andropogon virginicus var. *virginicus*	Broomsedge Bluestem*
Anthoxanthum odoratum	Sweet Vernal Grass*
Aristida oligantha	Common Three-Awn
Arrhenatherum elatius	Tuber Oatgrass*
Arundo donax	Giant Reed*
Avena barbata	Slender Wild Oat*
Avena fatua	Wild Oat*
Avena sativa	Cultivated Oat*
Beckmannia syzigachne	Slough Grass
Brachypodium distachyon	Purple Falsebrome*
Briza maxima	Rattlesnake Grass*
Briza minor	Quaking Grass*
Bromus arenarius	Australian Chess*
Bromus carinatus var. *carinatus*	California Brome
Bromus ciliatus	Fringed Brome
Bromus diandrus :	Ripgut Grass*
Bromus hordeaceus	Soft Cheatgrass*
Bromus inermis ssp. *inermis*	Smooth Brome*
Bromus japonicus	Japanese Chess*

Bromus laevipes .... Chinook Brome
Bromus madritensis ssp. *madritensis* .... Spanish Brome*
Bromus madritensis ssp. *rubens* .... Foxtail Grass*
Bromus orcuttianus .... Orcutt Brome
Bromus secalinus .... Cheatgrass*
Bromus sterilis .... Poverty Brome*
Bromus suksdorfii .... Suksdorf's Brome
Bromus tectorum .... Downy Brome, Cheatgrass*
Bromus vulgaris .... Narrowleaf Brome
Calamagrostis breweri .... Shorthair Reedgrass
Calamagrostis canadensis .... Bluejoint
Calamagrostis rubescens .... Pine Grass
Chloris verticillata .... Tumble Finger Grass*
Cinna latifolia .... Drooping Woodreed
Cortaderia selloana .... Uruguayan Pampas Grass*
Crypsis schoenoides .... Swamp Prickle Grass*
Cynodon dactylon .... Bermuda Grass*
Cynosurus echinatus .... Hedgehog Dogtail*
Dactylis glomerata .... Orchard Grass*
Danthonia californica var. *americana* .... California Oatgrass
Danthonia intermedia .... Intermediate Oatgrass
Danthonia unispicata .... One-spike Oatgrass
Deschampsia cespitosa ssp. *cespitosa* .... Tufted Hairgrass
Deschampsia danthonioides .... Annual Hairgrass
Deschampsia elongata .... Slender Hairgrass
Digitaria ischaemum .... Smooth Crabgrass*
Digitaria sanguinalis .... Large Crabgrass*
Distichlis spicata .... Saltgrass
Echinochloa crus-galli .... Barnyard Grass*
Ehrharta calycina .... Veldt Grass*
Elymus elymoides ssp. *californicus* .... Squirreltail
Elymus glaucus ssp. *glaucus* .... Blue Wildrye
Elymus glaucus ssp. *jepsonii* .... Jepson's Blue Wildrye
Elymus lanceolatus ssp. *lanceolatus* .... Northern Wheatgrass
Elymus multisetus .... Big Squirreltail
Elymus sierrae .... Sierra Wildrye
Elymus stebbinsii .... Stebbins' Wheatgrass
Elymus trachycaulus ssp. *subsecundus* .... Bearded Wheatgrass
Elymus trachycaulus ssp. *trachycaulus* .... Slender Wheatgrass
Elytrigia intermedia ssp. *intermedia* .... Intermediate Wheatgrass*
Elytrigia repens .... Quackgrass*
Eragrostis cilianensis .... Stinkgrass*
Eragrostis mexicana ssp. *virescens* .... Non-sticky Lovegrass
Eragrostis pectinacea var. *pectinacea* .... Spreading Lovegrass
Festuca arundinacea .... Tall Fescue*
Festuca elmeri .... Elmer's Fescue
Festuca idahoensis .... Idaho Fescue, Blue Fescue
Festuca kingii .... King's Fescue
Festuca occidentalis .... Western Fescue
Festuca pratensis .... Meadow Fescue*
Festuca rubra .... Red Fescue
Festuca subulata .... Bearded Fescue

Festuca viridula .... Mountain Bunchgrass
Gastridium ventricosum .... Nit Grass*
Glyceria borealis .... Northern Mannagrass
Glyceria elata .... Tall Mannagrass
Glyceria grandis .... American Mannagrass
Glyceria striata .... Fowl Meadowgrass
Hesperostipa comata .... Needle and Thread Grass
Holcus lanatus .... Common Velvet Grass*
Hordeum brachyantherum ssp. *brachyantherum* .... Meadow Barley
Hordeum brachyantherum ssp. *californicum* .... California Meadow Barley
Hordeum jubatum .... Foxtail Barley
Hordeum murinum ssp. *gussoneanum* .... Mediterranean Barley*
Hordeum murinum .... Hare Barley*
Hordeum murinum ssp. *leporinum* .... Hare Barley*
Koeleria macrantha .... Junegrass
Leersia oryzoides .... Rice Cutgrass
Leptochloa fascicularis .... Spangletop
Leymus cinereus .... Gray Wildrye
Leymus triticoides .... Wet Meadow Wildrye
Lolium multiflorum .... Italian Ryegrass*
Lolium perenne .... Perennial Ryegrass*
Lolium temulentum .... Darnel*
Melica aristata .... Awned Melic
Melica bulbosa .... Onion Grass
Melica californica .... California Melic
Melica fugax .... Small Melic
Melica geyeri .... Geyer's Onion Grass
Melica harfordii .... Harford Onion Grass
Melica stricta .... Nodding Melic
Melica subulata .... Alaska Onion Grass
Melica torreyana .... Torrey's Melic
Muhlenbergia andina .... Foxtail Muhly
Muhlenbergia asperifolia .... Scratch Grass
Muhlenbergia filiformis .... Pull-up Muhly
Muhlenbergia jonesii .... Jones' Muhly
Muhlenbergia montana .... Mountain Muhly
Muhlenbergia richardsonis .... Mat Muhly
Muhlenbergia rigens .... Deergrass
Muhlenbergia schreberi .... Nimblewell*
Nassella cernua .... Nodding Needlegrass
Nassella lepida .... Foothill Needlegrass
Nassella pulchra .... Purple Needlegrass
Oryza sativa .... Domestic Rice*
Panicum acuminatum var. *acuminatum* .... Marsh Panicum, Western Panicum
Panicum capillare .... Witchgrass
Panicum dichotomiflorum .... Fall Panicum*
Panicum hillmanii .... Hillman's Panic Grass*
Pascopyrum smithii .... Western Wheatgrass
Paspalum dilatatum .... Dallis Grass*
Paspalum distichum .... Knot Grass
Paspalum urvillei .... Vasey's Grass*
Pennisetum clandestinum .... Kikuyu Grass*

Phalaris aquatica .... Harding Grass*
Phalaris arundinacea .... Reed Canary Grass
Phalaris caroliniana ....Carolina Canary Grass*
Phalaris lemmonii .... Lemmon's Canary Grass
Phalaris minor ....Mediterranean Canary Grass*
Phalaris paradoxa .... Hood Canary Grass*
Phleum alpinum .... Mountain Timothy
Phleum pratense .... Cultivated Timothy*
Poa annua ....Annual Bluegrass*
Poa bolanderi ....Bolander's Bluegrass
Poa bulbosa .... Bulbous Bluegrass*
Poa compressa .... Canadian Bluegrass*
Poa cusickii ssp. *cusickii* .... Cusick's Bluegrass
Poa cusickii ssp. *epilis* .... Skyline Bluegrass
Poa fendleriana ssp. *longiligula* .... Longtongue Muttongrass
Poa glauca ssp. *rupicola* .... Timberline Bluegrass
Poa keckii .... Keck's Bluegrass
Poa leptocoma ssp. *leptocoma* .... Bog Bluegrass
Poa palustris .... Fowl Bluegrass*
Poa pratensis ssp. *pratensis* ....Kentucky Bluegrass*
Poa pringlei ....Pringle's Bluegrass
Poa secunda ssp. *juncifolia* .... Rush Bluegrass
Poa secunda ssp. *secunda* .... One-sided Bluegrass
Poa sierrae .... Sierra Bluegrass
Poa stebbinsii .... Stebbins' Bluegrass
Poa tenerrima .... Delicate Bluegrass
Poa trivialis .... Rough Bluegrass*
Poa wheeleri .... Wheeler's Bluegrass
Polypogon australis .... Chilean Beard Grass*
Polypogon interruptus ....Ditch Beard Grass*
Polypogon maritimus .... Mediterranean Beard Grass*
Polypogon monspeliensis ....Annual Beard Grass*
Puccinellia distans .... European Alkali Grass*
Scribneria bolanderi .... Scribneria
Secale cereale ....Rye*
Setaria faberi .... Japanese Bristlegrass*
Setaria gracilis .... Bristle Foxtail
Setaria pumila .... Bristly Foxtail*
Setaria viridis ....Green Foxtail*
Sorghum bicolor ....Sorghum, Sudan Grass*
Sorghum halepense ....Johnson Grass*
Sporobolus vaginiflorus .... Poverty Grass*
Taeniantherum caput-medusae ....Medusa Head*
Torreyochloa erecta .... Spiked Mannagrass
Torreyochloa pallida var. *pauciflora* .... Pale False Mannagrass
Trisetum canescens .... Nodding Oatgrass, Tall Trisetum
Trisetum spicatum ....Narrow Oatgrass
Trisetum wolfii ....Beardless Oatgrass
Ventenata dubia ....Ventenata Grass*
Vulpia bromoides .... Brome Fescue*
Vulpia microstachys var. *microstachys* .... Small Fescue
Vulpia microstachys var. *confusa* ....Confusing Fescue

Vulpia microstachys var. *pauciflora* .... Few-flowered Fescue
Vulpia myuros var. *hirsuta* .... Foxtail Fescue*
Vulpia myuros var. *myuros* .... Rattail Fescue*

Polemoniaceae – Phlox Family
Allophyllum divaricatum .... Straggling Allophyllum
Allophyllum gilioides ssp. *gilioides* .... Purple Allophyllum
Allophyllum gilioides ssp. *violaceum* .... Violet Allophyllum
Allophyllum integrifolium .... White Allophyllum
Collomia grandiflora .... **Largeflower Collomia**
Collomia heterophylla .... **Vari-leaf Collomia**
Collomia linearis .... Tiny Trumpet
Collomia tinctoria .... Staining Collomia
Eriastrum filifolium .... Lavender Woolly-star
Eriastrum wilcoxii .... Wilcox's Woolly-star
Gilia capillaris .... Miniature Gilia, Smoothleaf Gilia
Gilia capitata ssp. *capitata* .... **Globe Gilia**
Gilia capitata ssp. *mediomontana* .... Foothill Gilia
Gilia capitata ssp. *pedemontana* .... Blue Field Gilia
Gilia capitata ssp. *staminea* .... Globe Gilia
Gilia leptalea ssp. *bicolor* .... Purplethroat Gilia
Gilia leptalea ssp. *leptalea* .... **Bridge's Gilia**
Gilia sinistra .... Clockwise Gilia
Gilia tricolor ssp. *diffusa* .... Birds-eye Gilia
Gilia tricolor ssp. *tricolor* .... **Birds-eye Gilia**
Gymnosteris parvula .... Small-flower Gymnosteris
Ipomopsis aggregata .... **Scarlet Gilia, Skyrocket**
Ipomopsis aggregata ssp. *formosissima* .... Wherrey's Scarlet Gilia
Ipomopsis congesta .... Ballhead Ipomopsis
Ipomopsis tenuituba .... **Slender-tubed Skyrocket**
Leptodactylon pungens .... **Prickly Phlox, Granite Gilia**
Linanthus bicolor .... **Bicolored Linanthus**
Linanthus bolanderi .... Bolander's Linanthus
Linanthus ciliatus .... **Whisker Brush**
Linanthus dichotomus .... **Evening Snow**
Linanthus filipes .... Filiform Linanthus
Linanthus harknessii .... Harkness' Linanthus
Linanthus liniflorus .... Narrowleaf Flaxflower
Linanthus montanus .... Mustang Clover
Linanthus pygmaeus var. *continentalis* .... Pygmy Linanthus
Navarretia breweri .... Brewer's Navarretia
Navarretia divaricata ssp. *divaricata* .... Mountain Navarretia
Navarretia divaricata ssp. *vividior* .... Mountain Navarretia
Navarretia eriocephala .... Hoary Navarretia
Navarretia filicaulis .... Thinstem Navarretia
Navarretia intertexta ssp. *intertexta* .... **Needle Navarretia**
Navarretia intertexta ssp. *propinqua* .... Great Basin Navarretia
Navarretia leucocephala .... White-flowered Navarretia
Navarretia leucocephala ssp. *minima* .... White-flowered Navarretia
Navarretia myersii .... Pincushion Navarretia
Navarretia prolifera .... Burr Navarretia
Navarretia prolifera ssp. *lutea* .... Yellow Burr Navarretia

Navarretia pubescens	**Downy Navarretia**
Navarretia subuligera	Awl-leaf Pincushion
Navarretia tagetina	Marigold Navarretia
Navarretia viscidula	Sticky Navarretia
Phlox austromontana	Mountain Phlox
Phlox diffusa	**Spreading Phlox**
Phlox douglasii ssp. *rigida*	Douglas' Phlox
Phlox gracilis	**Slender Phlox**
Phlox speciosa	**Showy Phlox**
Phlox speciosa ssp. *occidentalis*	Showy Phlox
Polemonium californicum	**Jacob's Ladder, Low Polemonium**
Polemonium occidentale	**Western Polemonium, Great Polemonium**
Polemonium pulcherrimum var. *pulcherrimum*	**Showy Polemonium**

Polygalaceae – Milkwort Family

Polygala cornuta var. *cornuta*	**Milkwort**

Polygonaceae – Buckwheat Family

Chorizanthe membranacea	Pink Spineflower
Chorizanthe polygonoides var. *polygonoides*	Knotweed Spineflower
Eriogonum baileyi var. *baileyi*	Bailey's Buckwheat
Eriogonum baileyi var. *praebens*	Bailey's Buckwheat
Eriogonum cernuum	Nodding Buckwheat
Eriogonum cespitosum	Cushion Buckwheat
Eriogonum collinum	Hill Buckwheat
Eriogonum douglasii var. *douglasii*	Douglas' Buckwheat
Eriogonum elatum	Tall Buckwheat
Eriogonum elatum var. *villosum*	Tall Buckwheat
Eriogonum incanum	Frosty Buckwheat
Eriogonum lobbii var. *lobbii*	**Lobb's Buckwheat**
Eriogonum luteolum var. *luteolum*	Greene's Buckwheat
Eriogonum marifolium	Marumleaf Buckwheat
Eriogonum microthecum var. *ambiguum*	Meadow Buckwheat
Eriogonum nudum var. *deductum*	Naked Buckwheat
Eriogonum nudum var. *nudum*	**Naked-stem Buckwheat**
Eriogonum nudum var. *oblongifolium*	Hairy Buckwheat
Eriogonum nudum var. *pubiflorum*	Hairy-flowered Buckwheat
Eriogonum ochrocephalum	White Woolly Buckwheat
Eriogonum ovalifolium var. *nivale*	Oval-leaf Buckwheat
Eriogonum ovalifolium var. *vineum*	Cushenbury Buckwheat
Eriogonum prattenianum var. *prattenianum*	**Pratten's Buckwheat**
Eriogonum rosense	Mt. Rose Buckwheat
Eriogonum roseum	Rose Buckwheat
Eriogonum spergulinum var. *reddingianum*	Spurry Buckwheat
Eriogonum spergulinum var. *spergulinum*	Spurry Buckwheat
Eriogonum strictum ssp. *proliferum*	Blue Mountain Buckwheat
Eriogonum tripodum	Tripod Buckwheat
Eriogonum umbellatum	**Sulfur Buckwheat**
Eriogonum umbellatum var. *covillei*	Coville's Sulfur Buckwheat
Eriogonum umbellatum var. *furcosum*	Desert Sulfur Buckwheat
Eriogonum umbellatum var. *nevadense*	Nevada Sulfur Buckwheat
Eriogonum umbellatum var. *polyanthum*	Manyflower Sulfur Buckwheat
Eriogonum umbellatum var. *torreyanum*	Donner Pass Buckwheat

Eriogonum ursinum .... Bear Valley Buckwheat
Eriogonum vimineum .... Wicker Buckwheat
Eriogonum wrightii ssp. *subscaposum* .... **Wright's Buckwheat**
Eriogonum wrightii ssp. *trachygonum* .... Bastard Sage
Oxyria digyna .... **Mountain Sorrel**
Polygonum amphibium var. *stipulaceum* .... **Water Smartweed**
Polygonum arenastrum .... Common Knotweed*
Polygonum bistortoides .... **Western Bistort**
Polygonum bolanderi .... Bolander's Knotweed
Polygonum californicum .... California Knotweed
Polygonum cuspidatum .... Japanese Knotweed*
Polygonum davisiae .... **Davis' Knotweed**
Polygonum douglasii ssp. *douglasii* ....Douglas' Knotweed
Polygonum douglasii ssp. *johnstonii* .... Johnston's Knotweed
Polygonum douglasii ssp. *majus* .... Large Douglas' Knotweed
Polygonum douglasii ssp. *spergulariiforme* .... Scatter Knotweed
Polygonum hydropiper .... Marsh Pepper*
Polygonum lapathifolium .... **Willow Weed, Smartweed, Knotweed**
Polygonum minimum .... Leafy Dwarf Knotweed
Polygonum parryi .... Parry's Knotweed
Polygonum pensylvanicum .... Pinkweed*
Polygonum persicaria .... **Lady's Thumb***
Polygonum phytolaccifolium .... **Alpine Knotweed**
Polygonum polygaloides .... Denseflower Knotweed
Polygonum polygaloides ssp. *confertiflorum* .... Denseflower Knotweed
Polygonum polygaloides ssp. *kelloggii* .... Kellogg's Knotweed
Polygonum punctatum .... Water Knotweed
Polygonum sachalinense .... Giant Knotweed*
Polygonum shastense .... Shasta Knotweed
Pterostegia drymarioides .... Pterostegia
Rumex acetosella .... **Sheep Sorrel***
Rumex conglomeratus .... Green Dock*
Rumex crispus .... **Curly Dock***
Rumex obtusifolius .... Bitter Dock
Rumex paucifolius .... Alpine Sheep Sorrel
Rumex pulcher .... Fiddle Dock*
Rumex salicifolius var. *salicifolius* ....Willow-leafed Dock
Rumex salicifolius var. *transitorius* .... Willow Dock
Rumex salicifolius var. *triangulivalvis* .... Triangular-fruited Willow Dock

Pontederiaceae – Pickerweed Family
Eichhornia crassipes .... Water Hyacinth

Portulacaceae – Purslane Family
Calandrinia ciliata .... **Red Maids**
Calyptridium monandrum .... Pussypaws, Sand Cress
Calyptridium monospermum .... One-seeded Pussypaws
Calyptridium umbellatum .... **Pussypaws**
Claytonia exigua ssp. *exigua* .... Common Claytonia
Claytonia lanceolata .... **Western Spring Beauty**
Claytonia megarhiza .... Fell-fields Claytonia
Claytonia parviflora ssp. *grandiflora* .... Miner's Lettuce
Claytonia parviflora ssp. *parviflora* .... Miner's Lettuce

Claytonia perfoliata ssp. *mexicana* .... Miner's Lettuce
Claytonia perfoliata ssp. *perfoliata* .... **Miner's Lettuce**
Claytonia rubra ssp. *depressa* .... Redstem Miner's Lettuce
Claytonia rubra ssp. *rubra* .... Redstem Miner's Lettuce
Lewisia cantelovii .... **Cantelow's Lewisia, Wet Cliff Lewisia**
Lewisia kelloggii .... **Kellogg's Lewisia**
Lewisia longipetala .... Long-petaled Lewisia
Lewisia nevadensis .... **Sierra Lewisia**
Lewisia pygmaea ....**Alpine Lewisia, Dwarf Lewisia**
Lewisia serrata .... Saw-toothed Lewisia
Lewisia triphylla .... **Three-leaf Lewisia**
Montia chamissoi .... Toad Lily
Montia fontana .... Water Montia
Montia linearis .... Linearleaf Montia
Montia parvifolia .... Showy Rock Montia
Portulaca oleracea .... **Common Purslane***

Potamogetonaceae – Pondweed Family
Potamogeton alpinus ssp. *tenuifolius* ....Alpine Pondweed
Potamogeton epihydrus ssp. *nuttallii* .... Nuttall's Pondweed
Potamogeton filiformis .... Slenderleaf Pondweed
Potamogeton foliosus var. *foliosus* .... Leafy Pondweed
Potamogeton gramineus .... Grassleaf Pondweed
Potamogeton illinoensis .... Shining Knotweed
Potamogeton natans .... **Broad-leaf Pondweed**
Potamogeton nodosus .... Longleaf Pondweed
Potamogeton praelongus .... White-stemmed Pondweed
Potamogeton pusillus .... Small Pondweed
Potamogeton robbinsii .... Robbins' Pondweed

Primulaceae – Primrose Family
Anagallis arvensis .... **Scarlet Pimpernel***
Androsace occidentalis var. *simplex* .... Western Androsace
Centunculus minimus .... Chaffweed
Dodecatheon alpinum .... **Alpine Shooting Star**
Dodecatheon hendersonii .... **Henderson's Shooting Star**
Dodecatheon jeffreyi .... Jeffrey's Shooting Star
Primula suffrutescens .... **Sierra Primrose**
Trientalis latifolia .... **Starflower**

Ranunculaceae – Buttercup Family
Aconitum columbianum .... **Monkshood**
Actaea rubra .... **Red Baneberry**
Anemone drummondii .... Drummond's Anemone
Anemone occidentalis .... **Western Pasque Flower**
Aquilegia formosa .... **Crimson Columbine**
Caltha leptosepala var. *biflora* .... **Marsh Marigold**
Clematis lasiantha .... **Chaparral Clematis, Pipestem**
Clematis ligusticifolia .... Virgin's Bower
Delphinium andersonii .... Anderson's Larkspur
Delphinium depauperatum .... Dwarf Larkspur
Delphinium glaucum ....**Mountain Larkspur, Tower Larkspur**
Delphinium gracilentum ....**Slender Larkspur, Pine Forest Larkspur**

Delphinium hansenii ssp. *hansenii* .... **Hansen's Larkspur**
Delphinium hesperium .... Western Larkspur
Delphinium nuttallianum .... **Nuttall's Larkspur**
Delphinium patens .... **Spreading Larkspur, Zigzag Larkspur**
Delphinium polycladon .... High Mountain Larkspur
Delphinium variegatum ssp. *variegatum* .... **Royal Larkspur**
Isopyrum occidentale .... **Western Rue Anemone**
Kumlienia hystricula .... **Waterfall Buttercup**
Myosurus apetalus .... Bristly Mousetail
Myosurus minimus .... Little Mousetail
Ranunculus acris .... Blister Buttercup, Tall Buttercup*
Ranunculus alismifolius var. *alismifolius* .... **Plantain Buttercup**
Ranunculus alismifolius var. *alismellus* .... Small Plantain Buttercup
Ranunculus andersonii .... Anderson's Buttercup
Ranunculus aquatilis .... **Water Buttercup**
Ranunculus aquatilis var. *capillaceus* .... Water Buttercup
Ranunculus aquatilis var. *hispidulus* .... Water Buttercup
Ranunculus arvensis .... Corn Buttercup*
Ranunculus bonariensis var. *trisepalus* .... Vernal Buttercup
Ranunculus californicus .... California Buttercup
Ranunculus canus .... Sacramento Valley Buttercup
Ranunculus cymbalaria var. *saximontanus* .... Rocky Mountain Buttercup
Ranunculus eschscholtzii .... Alpine Buttercup
Ranunculus eschscholtzii var. *oxynotus* .... Alpine Buttercup
Ranunculus flammula .... Crowfoot, Creeping Buttercup
Ranunculus glaberrimus .... Sagebrush Buttercup
Ranunculus glaberrimus var. *ellipticus* .... Sagebrush Buttercup
Ranunculus hebecarpus .... Downy Buttercup
Ranunculus muricatus .... **Prickleseed Buttercup***
Ranunculus occidentalis .... **Western Buttercup**
Ranunculus orthorhyncus var. *orthorhyncus* .... Birdsfoot Buttercup
Ranunculus repens .... Creeping Buttercup*
Ranunculus testiculatus .... Bur Buttercup*
Ranunculus uncinatus .... Woodland Buttercup
Thalictrium fendleri var. *fendleri* .... **Fendler's Meadow Rue**
Thalictrium fendleri var. *polycarpum* .... Fendler's Meadow Rue
Thalictrum sparsiflorum .... Few-flowered Meadow Rue

Rhamnaceae – Buckthorn Family
Ceanothus cordulatus .... Mountain Whitethorn
Ceanothus cuneatus var. *cuneatus* .... Buckbrush
Ceanothus diversifolius .... Pinemat
Ceanothus fresnensis .... Fresno Ceanothus
Ceanothus integerrimus .... Deerbrush
Ceanothus lemmonii .... Lemmon's Ceanothus
Ceanothus prostratus .... Squaw Mat, Mahala Mat
Ceanothus tomentosus .... Woolly-leaf Ceanothus
Ceanothus velutinus .... Tobacco Bush
Rhamnus alnifolia .... Alder Buckthorn
Rhamnus crocea .... Spiney Redberry
Rhamnus ilicifolia .... Hollyleaf Redberry
Rhamnus purshiana .... Cascara

Rhamnus rubra .... Sierra Coffeeberry
Rhamnus tomentella ssp. *tomentella* .... Hoary Coffeeberry

Rosaceae – Rose Family
Adenostoma fasciculatum .... Chamise
Agrimonia gryposepala .... Common Agrimony
Amelanchier alnifolia var. *pumila* .... Pacific Serviceberry
Amelanchier alnifolia var. *semiintegrifolia* .... Pacific Serviceberry
Amelanchier utahensis .... Utah Serviceberry
Aphanes occidentalis .... Western Dewcup
Cercocarpus betuloides var. *betuloides* .... Birch-leaf Mountain-mahogany
Cercocarpus ledifolius var. *ledifolius* .... Curl-leaf Mountain-mahogany
Chamaebatia foliolosa .... **Mountain Misery, Kit-kit-dizzy**
Crataegus monogyna .... Single-seeded Hawthorne*
Duchesnea indica .... **Mock Strawberry***
Fragaria vesca .... Wood Strawberry
Fragaria virginiana .... **Mountain Strawberry**
Geum macrophyllum .... Bigleaf Avens
Geum triflorum .... **Prairie Smoke**
Heteromeles arbutifolia .... Toyon
Holodiscus discolor .... Creambush
Holodiscus microphyllus var. *microphyllus* .... Rock Spiraea
Horkelia fusca ssp. *capitata* .... Bighead Horkelia
Horkelia fusca ssp. *parviflora* .... **Dusky Horkelia**
Horkelia tridentata ssp. *flavescens* .... Threetooth Horkelia
Horkelia tridentata ssp. *tridentata* .... Threetooth Horkelia
Ivesia gordonii .... Alpine Ivesia
Ivesia pygmaea .... Dwarf Ivesia
Ivesia sericoleuca .... **Plumas Ivesia**
Ivesia shockleyi var. *shockleyi* .... Shockley's Ivesia
Ivesia unguiculata .... Yosemite Ivesia
Oemleria cerasiformis .... Oso Berry
Physocarpus capitatus .... Ninebark
Potentilla biennis .... Biennial Cinquefoil
Potentilla drummondii ssp. *breweri* .... Brewer's Cinquefoil
Potentilla drummondii ssp. *bruceae* .... Bruce's Cinquefoil
Potentilla drummondii ssp. *drummondii* .... Drummond's Cinquefoil
Potentilla flabellifolia .... Fan Foil, Fanleaf Cinquefoil
Potentilla fruticosa .... **Shrubby Cinquefoil**
Potentilla glandulosa ssp. *ashlandica* .... Sticky Cinquefoil
Potentilla glandulosa ssp. *glandulosa* .... **Sticky Cinquefoil**
Potentilla glandulosa ssp. *hansenii* .... Hansen's Cinquefoil
Potentilla glandulosa ssp. *nevadensis* .... Nevada Cinquefoil
Potentilla gracilis ssp. *fastigiata* .... Fivefinger Cinquefoil
Potentilla grayi .... Gray's Cinquefoil
Potentilla millefolia .... Cutleaf Cinquefoil
Potentilla palustris .... Marsh Cinquefoil
Potentilla rivalis .... Brook Cinquefoil
Prunus andersonii .... Desert Peach
Prunus cerasifera .... Cherry Plum*
Prunus emarginata .... Bittercherry
Prunus subcordata .... Sierra Plum

Prunus virginiana var. *demissa* .... Western Chokecherry
Purshia tridentata var. *tridentata* .... Antelope Bush
Rosa bridgesii .... Pygmy Rose
Rosa californica .... California Wild Rose
Rosa canina .... Dog Rose*
Rosa eglanteria .... Sweet-brier*
Rosa gymnocarpa .... Wood Rose
Rosa pinetorum .... Pine Rose
Rosa pisocarpa ....Cluster Rose
Rosa woodsii var. *ultramontana* .... Interior Rose
Rubus discolor .... Himalayan Blackberry*
Rubus glaucifolius .... Raspberry
Rubus laciniatus..Cutleaf Blackberry*
Rubus leucodermis .... Blackcap Raspberry
Rubus parviflorus .... Thimbleberry
Rubus ursinus ....California Blackberry
Sanguisorba minor ssp. *muricata* .... **Garden Burnet, Small Burnet***
Sanguisorba occidentalis .... Western Burnet
Sibbaldia procumbens .... **Sibbaldia**
Sorbus californica .... California Mountain Ash
Sorbus scopulina var. *scopulina* .... Green's Mountain Ash
Spiraea densiflora .... Mountain Spiraea
Spiraea douglasii .... Douglas' Spiraea

Rubiaceae – Madder Family
Cephalanthus occidentalis var. *californicus* .... Buttonwillow
Crucianella angustifolia .... Crosswort*
Galium ambiguum var. *ambiguum* ....Yolla Bolly Bedstraw
Galium aparine .... **Goose-grass, Common Bedstraw**
Galium bifolium .... Low Mountain Bedstraw
Galium bolanderi ....Bolander's Bedstraw
Galium divaricatum ....Lamarck's Bedstraw*
Galium grayanum var. *grayanum* .... Gray's Bedstraw
Galium hypotrichium .... Alpine Bedstraw
Galium mexicanum var. *asperulum* .... Rough Bedstraw
Galium mollugo .... Hedge Bedstraw
Galium munzii ....Munz's Bedstraw
Galium nuttallii .... Climbing Bedstraw
Galium parisiense .... Wall Bedstraw*
Galium porrigens .... Climbing Bedstraw
Galium porrigens var. *tenue* .... **Climbing Bedstraw, Narrowleaf Bedstraw**
Galium sparsiflorum ssp. *sparsiflorum* ....Sequoia Bedstraw
Galium tricornutum ....Rough Corn Bedstraw
Galium trifidum var. *pacificum* .... Pacific Bedstraw
Galium trifidum var. *pusillum* ....Small Bedstraw
Galium triflorum .... Sweet-scented Bedstraw
Kelloggia galioides .... **Kelloggia**
Sherardia arvensis ....**Common Field Madder***

Rutaceae – Rue Family
Ptelea crenulata ....Hop Tree

Salicaceae – Willow Family
Populus alba .... White Poplar*
Populus balsamifera ssp. *trichocarpa* .... Black Cottonwood
Populus fremontii ssp. *fremontii* .... Fremont's Cottonwood
Populus tremuloides .... Quaking Aspen
Salix alba .... White Willow*
Salix arctica .... Arctic Willow
Salix babylonica .... Weeping Willow*
Salix eastwoodiae .... Sierra Willow
Salix exigua .... Narrowleaf Willow, Sandbar Willow
Salix geyeriana .... Geyer's Willow
Salix goodingii .... San Joaquin Willow
Salix jepsonii .... Jepson's Willow
Salix laevigata .... Red Willow
Salix lasiolepis .... Arroyo Willow
Salix lemmonii .... Lemmon's Willow
Salix ligulifolia .... Strapleaf Willow
Salix lucida .... Shining Willow
Salix lucida ssp. *lasiandra* .... Shining Willow
Salix lutea .... Yellow Willow
Salix melanopsis .... Dusky Willow
Salix orestera .... Grayleaf Sierra Willow
Salix scouleriana .... Scouler's Willow

Santalaceae – Sandalwood Family
Comandra umbellata ssp. *californica* .... Bastard Toad-flax

Sarraceniaceae – Pitcher Plant Family
Darlingtonia californica .... **Cobra Lily, California Pitcher Plant**

Saxifragaceae – Saxifrage Family
Boykinia major .... **Mountain Brookfoam**
Boykinia occidentalis .... **Brookfoam**
Darmera peltata .... **Indian Rhubarb, Umbrella Plant**
Heuchera micrantha .... **Crevice Heuchera, Alumroot**
Heuchera rubescens .... **Pink Alumroot**
Heuchera rubescens var. *alpicola* .... Pink Alumroot
Heuchera rubescens var. *glandulosa* .... Jack o' the Rocks
Lithophragma bolanderi .... Bolander's Woodland Star
Lithophragma glabrum .... Bulbous Woodland Star
Lithophragma parviflorum var. *parviflorum* .... Prairie Star
Lithophragma parviflorum var. *trifoliatum* .... **Prairie Star**
Lithophragma tenellum .... Slender Woodstar
Mitella breweri .... **Brewer's Bishop's Cap**
Mitella pentandra .... Five-point Bishop's Cap
Parnassia californica .... **California Grass of Parnassus**
Parnassia fimbriata .... Fringed Grass of Parnassus
Saxifraga aprica .... Sierra Saxifrage
Saxifraga bryophora .... Bud Saxifrage
Saxifraga californica .... **California Saxifrage**
Saxifraga ferruginea .... Rusty Hair Saxifrage
Saxifraga integrifolia .... **Hooker's Saxifrage, Whole-leaf Saxifrage**
Saxifraga mertensiana .... Wood Saxifrage

Saxifraga nidifica var. *nidifica* ....Peak Saxifrage
Saxifraga odontoloma ....**Brook Saxifrage, Streambank Saxifrage**
Saxifraga oregana ....**Bog Saxifrage**
Saxifraga tolmiei .... Tolmie's Saxifrage
Tellima grandiflora ....**Fringe Cups**

Scrophulariaceae – Figwort Family
Antirrhinum cornutum ....Spurred Snapdragon
Antirrhinum leptaleum ....Spurred Snapdragon
Antirrhinum vexillo-calyculatum ssp. *breweri* ....**Brewer's Snapdragon**
Antirrhinum vexillo-calyculatum ssp. *intermedium* ....Sail-flower Snapdragon
Bacopa rotundifolia ....Roundleaf Water Hyssop*
Bellardia trixago ....Bellardia*
Castilleja affinis .... Common Paintbrush
Castilleja ambigua ....Johnny Nip
Castilleja applegatei ssp. *disticha* ....Wavy-leaf Paintbrush
Castilleja applegatei ssp. *pallida* .... Brewer's Paintbrush
Castilleja applegatei ssp. *pinetorum* ....**Applegate's Paintbrush**
Castilleja attenuata ....**Valley Tassels**
Castilleja exserta ssp. *exserta* ....**Purple Owl's Clover**
Castilleja foliolosa .... Woolly Indian Paintbrush
Castilleja lacera .... Cutleaf Owl's Clover
Castilleja lemmonii .... Lemmon's Paintbrush
Castilleja lineariloba .... Pale Owl's Clover
Castilleja miniata ssp. *miniata* ....**Giant Red Paintbrush, Scarlet Paintbrush**
Castilleja nana ....**Alpine Paintbrush**
Castilleja parviflora .... Mountain Paintbrush
Castilleja pilosa ....**Hairy Paintbrush, Parrothead Paintbrush**
Castilleja pruinosa ....**Frosty Paintbrush**
Castilleja rubicundula .... Cream Sacs
Castilleja rubicundula ssp. *lithospermoides* .... Cream Sacs
Castilleja subinclusa ssp. *subinclusa* .... Longleaf Paintbrush
Castilleja tenuis .... Hairy Owl's Clover
Collinsia heterophylla ....**Chinese Houses**
Collinsia linearis ....Narrowleaf Blue-eyed Mary
Collinsia parviflora ....**Blue-eyed Mary**
Collinsia sparsiflora var. *collina* ....Spinster's Blue-eyed Mary
Collinsia sparsiflora var. *sparsiflora* ....**Few-flowered Blue-eyed Mary**
Collinsia tinctoria ....**Sticky Chinese Houses, Tincture Plant**
Collinsia torreyi var. *brevicarinata* .... Torrey's Blue-eyed Mary
Collinsia torreyi var. *torreyi* ....**Torrey's Blue-eyed Mary**
Collinsia torreyi var. *wrightii* ....Wright's Collinsia
Cordylanthus mollis ssp. *hispidus* .... Hispid Bird's Beak
Cordylanthus pilosus ssp. *hanseni* .... Hairy Bird's Beak
Cordylanthus pilosus ssp. *trifidus* .... Hairy Bird's Beak
Cordylanthus tenuis ssp. *tenuis* .... Slender Bird's Beak
Digitalis purpurea ....**Foxglove***
Gratiola ebracteata ....Bractless Hedge Hyssop
Gratiola heterosepala ....Bogg's Lake Hedge Hyssop
Gratiola neglecta ....Clammy Hedge Hyssop
Keckiella breviflora var. *breviflora* .... Gaping Penstemon
Keckiella breviflora var. *glabrisepala* .... Gaping Penstemon

Keckiella lemmonii .... Lemmon's Penstemon
Kickxia elatine .... **Sharp-pointed Kickxia, Fluellen***
Kickxia spuria .... Female Kickxia*
Limosella acaulis .... Broad-leaved Mudwort
Limosella aquatica .... Mudwort
Linaria genistifolia ssp. *dalmatica* .... Dalmatian Toadflax*
Lindernia dubia var. *anagallidea* .... False Pimpernel
Lindernia dubia var. *dubia* .... Yellowseed False Pimpernel
Mimulus angustatus .... **Pansy Monkeyflower**
Mimulus aurantiacus "aurantiacus" .... **Sticky Bush Monkeyflower**
Mimulus aurantiacus "bifidus" .... **Bush Monkeyflower**
Mimulus bicolor .... **Yellow and White Monkeyflower**
Mimulus breviflorus .... Shortleaf Monkeyflower
Mimulus breweri .... Brewer's Monkeyflower
Mimulus cardinalis .... **Scarlet Monkeyflower**
Mimulus douglasii .... Mouse-eared Monkeyflower
Mimulus floribundus .... Long-flowering Monkeyflower
Mimulus glaucescens .... Shield-bracted Monkeyflower
Mimulus guttatus .... **Seepspring Monkeyflower**
Mimulus jepsonii .... Common Large Monkeyflower, Jepson's Monkeyflower
Mimulus kelloggii .... **Kellogg's Monkeyflower**
Mimulus layneae .... **Layne's Monkeyflower**
Mimulus leptaleus .... Sierra Monkeyflower
Mimulus lewisii .... **Lewis' Monkeyflower**
Mimulus mephiticus .... **Skunky Monkeyflower**
Mimulus moschatus .... **Musk Monkeyflower**
Mimulus nanus .... Dwarf Monkeyflower
Mimulus pilosus .... Downy Monkeyflower
Mimulus primuloides ssp. *primuloides* .... **Primrose Monkeyflower**
Mimulus pulsiferae .... **Candelabra Monkeyflower**
Mimulus rubellus .... Little Red-stem Monkeyflower
Mimulus suksdorfii .... Suksdorf's Monkeyflower
Mimulus tilingii .... Mountain Monkeyflower
Mimulus torreyi .... **Torrey's Monkeyflower**
Mimulus tricolor .... **Tricolored Monkeyflower**
Orthocarpus cuspidatus ssp. *cryptanthus* .... Shortflower Owl's Clover
Orthocarpus luteus .... Yellow Owl's Clover
Parentucellia viscosa .... **Yellow Glandweed, Yellow Bartsia***
Pedicularis attolens .... **Little Elephant Head**
Pedicularis densiflora .... **Indian Warrior**
Pedicularis groenlandica .... **Elephant Head**
Pedicularis racemosa .... Leafy Lousewort
Pedicularis semibarbata .... **Dwarf Lousewort**
Penstemon azureus ssp. *angustissimus* .... Azure Penstemon
Penstemon azureus ssp. *azureus* .... **Azure Penstemon**
Penstemon deustus .... **Hotrock Penstemon**
Penstemon deustus var. *pedicellatus* .... Hotrock Penstemon
Penstemon gracilentus .... Slender Beardtongue
Penstemon heterodoxus var. *heterodoxus* .... Whorled Penstemon
Penstemon heterophyllus var. *heterophyllus* .... Foothill Penstemon
Penstemon heterophyllus var. *purdyi* .... **Foothill Penstemon**
Penstemon laetus var. *laetus* .... **Gay Penstemon**

Penstemon laetus var. *leptosepalus* .... Gay Penstemon
Penstemon newberryi var. *newberryi* .... **Mountain Pride**
Penstemon personatus .... **Close-throated Beardtongue**
Penstemon roezlii .... Regel's Mountain Penstemon
Penstemon rydbergii .... Meadow Penstemon
Penstemon rydbergii var. *oreocharis* .... **Meadow Penstemon**
Penstemon speciosus .... **Showy Penstemon**
Penstemon sudans .... Susanville Beardtongue
Scrophularia californica var. *heterophyllus* .... California Figwort
Tonella tenella .... Smallflower Tonella
Triphysaria eriantha ssp. *eriantha* .... **Butter and Eggs, Johnny Tuck**
Triphysaria pusilla .... Dwarf Owl's Clover
Verbascum blattaria .... **Moth Mullein***
Verbascum thapsus .... **Woolly Mullein***
Veronica americana .... American Brooklime
Veronica anagallis-aquatica .... Water Speedwell*
Veronica arvensis .... Common Speedwell*
Veronica chamaedrys .... Germander Speedwell*
Veronica cusickii .... Cusick's Speedwell
Veronica hederifolia .... Ivyleaf Speedwell*
Veronica peregrina ssp. *xalapensis* .... Purslane Speedwell
Veronica persica .... **Persian Speedwell***
Veronica serpyllifolia var. *humifusa* .... Sprawling Speedwell
Veronica wormskjoldii .... American Alpine Speedwell

Simarubiaceae – Quassia Family
Ailanthus altissima .... Tree of Heaven*

Solanaceae – Nightshade Family
Chamaesaracha nana .... Dwarf Chamaesaracha
Datura stramonium .... Jimson Weed*
Nicotiana acuminata var. *multiflora* .... Manyflower Tobacco*
Nicotiana attenuata .... **Coyote Tobacco, Indian Tobacco**
Physalis lancifolia .... Ground Cherry*
Physalis philadelphica .... Tomatillo*
Solanum americanum .... Smallflower Nightshade
Solanum carolinense .... Carolina Horsenettle*
Solanum dimidiatum .... Torrey's Nightshade*
Solanum dulcamara .... Bittersweet*
Solanum elaeagnifolium .... White Horse-nettle*
Solanum lanceolatum .... Lanceleaf Nightshade*
Solanum nigrum .... **Black Nightshade***
Solanum parishii .... Parish's Purple Nightshade
Solanum rostratum .... Buffalo Berry*
Solanum triflorum .... Cutleaf Nightshade*
Solanum xanti .... **Purple Nightshade, Blue Witch**

Sterculiaceae – Cacao Family
Fremontodendron californicum ssp. *californicum* .... Flannelbush
Fremontodendron californicum ssp. *decumbens* .... Pine Hill Flannelbush

Styracaceae – Styrax Family
Styrax officinalis var. *redivivus* .... Snowdrop Bush

Taxaceae – Yew Family
Taxus brevifolia .... Pacific Yew, Western Yew
Torreya californica .... California Nutmeg

Taxodiaceae – Bald Cypress Family
Sequoiadendron giganteum .... Big Tree, Sierra Redwood, Giant Sequoia

Typhaceae – Cattail Family
Sparganium angustifolium .... Narrowleaf Bur Reed
Sparganium emersum ssp. *emersum* .... Emersed Bur Reed
Sparganium natans .... Small Bur Reed
Typha angustifolia .... Narrowleaf Cattail
Typha domingensis .... Southern Cattail
Typha latifolia .... Broadleaf Cattail

Urticaceae – Nettle Family
Hesperocnide tenella .... Western Nettle
Urtica dioica .... Hoary Nettle
Urtica dioica ssp. *holosericea* .... **Hoary Nettle**
Urtica urens .... Dwarf Nettle*

Valerianaceae – Valerian Family
Centranthus ruber .... **Red Valerian, Jupiter's Beard***
Plectritis ciliosa ssp. *ciliosa* .... **Long-tubed Plectritis, Long-spurred Plectritis**
Plectritis macrocera .... White Plectritis
Valeriana californica .... **California Valerian**
Valerianella locusta .... Corn Salad*

Verbenaceae – Vervain Family
Phyla nodiflora .... Lemon Verbena
Verbena hastata .... Blue Vervain
Verbena lasiostachys var. *lasiostachys* .... **Western Verbena**
Verbena litoralis .... Seashore Vervain*

Violaceae – Violet Family
Viola adunca .... **Western Dog Violet**
Viola bakeri .... Baker's Violet
Viola beckwithii .... **Great Basin Violet, Beckwith's Violet**
Viola cuneata .... Wedgeleaf Violet
Viola douglasii .... **Douglas' Violet**
Viola glabella .... **Stream Violet**
Viola lobata ssp. *integrifolia* .... Pine Violet
Viola lobata ssp. *lobata* .... **Pine Violet**
Viola macloskeyi .... **Macloskey's Violet**
Viola odorata .... English Violet
Viola pinetorum ssp. *grisea* .... Greyleaf Goosefoot Violet
Viola pinetorum ssp. *pinetorum* .... Yellow Goosefoot Violet
Viola praemorsa ssp. *linguifolia* .... Astoria Violet
Viola purpurea ssp. *integrifolia* .... Small-leaf Violet
Viola purpurea ssp. *purpurea* .... **Mountain Violet, Oak Violet**
Viola purpurea ssp. *quercetorum* .... Mountain Violet
Viola sheltonii .... **Shelton's Violet, Fan Violet**
Viola sororia ssp. *affinis* .... Leconte Violet
Viola tomentosa .... **Woolly Violet**

Viscaceae – Mistletoe Family

Arceuthobium abietinum .... Fir Dwarf Mistletoe
Arceuthobium americanum .... Lodgepole-pine Dwarf Mistletoe
Arceuthobium californicum .... Sugar-pine Dwarf Mistletoe
Arceuthobium campylopodum .... Dwarf Pine Mistletoe
Arceuthobium cyanocarpum .... Limber-pine Dwarf Mistletoe
Arceuthobium divaricatum .... Pinyon Dwarf Mistletoe
Arceuthobium douglasii .... Douglas-fir Dwarf Mistletoe
Arceuthobium littorum ....Coastal Dwarf Mistletoe
Arceuthobium monticola .... Mountain Dwarf Mistletoe
Arceuthobium occidentale .... Foothill-pine Dwarf Pine Mistletoe
Arceuthobium siskiyouense .... Knobcone-pine Dwarf Mistletoe
Arceuthobium tsugense .... Hemlock Dwarf Mistletoe
Phoradendron densum .... Bigleaf Mistletoe
Phoradendron juniperinum .... Juniper Mistletoe
Phoradendron libocedri .... Incense Cedar Mistletoe
Phoradendron macrophyllum .... Bigleaf Mistletoe
Phoradendron villosum .... Oak Mistletoe

Vitaceae – Grape Family

Parthenocissus quinquefolia .... Virginia Creeper*
Parthenocissus vitacea .... Woodbine
Vitis californica .... California Wild Grape

Zygophyllaceae – Caltrop Family

Tribulus terrestris ....**Puncture Vine, Caltrop***

*B*ibliography and Selected References
Richard Hanes

Abrams, Leroy. 1923. *Illustrated Flora of the Pacific States.* Vol. I–IV. Stanford, California: Stanford University Press.

Balls, Edward K. 1962. *Early Uses of California Plants.* California Natural History Guides: 10. Berkeley and Los Angeles, California: University of California Press.

Beedy, Dr. Edward C. and Dr. Peter Brussard. 2002. *Nevada County Natural Resources Report:A Scientific Assessment of Watersheds and Ecosystems.* Prepared for the Nevada County Planning Department, Nevada City, California.

Beyers, J. L. 2004. *Postfire seeding for erosion control: effectiveness and impact on native plant communities.* Conservation Biology 18: 947–956.

Blackwell, Laird R. 1997. *Wildflowers of the Tahoe Sierra.* Redmond, Washington: Lone Pine Publishing.

———— 1999. *Wildflowers of the Sierra Nevada and the Central Valley.* Redmond, Washington: Lone Pine Publishing.

Bossard, Carla C., John M. Randall and Marc C. Hoshovsky. 2000. *Invasive Plants of California's Wildlands.* Berkeley and Los Angeles, California: University of California Press.

Brewer, William H. 2003. *Up and Down California in 1860-1864: The Journal of William H. Brewer, Fourth Edition, with Maps.* Berkeley and Los Angeles, California: University of California Press.

California Native Plant Society. 2001. *Inventory of Rare and Endangered Plants of California*, sixth edition. Rare Plant Scientific Advisory Committee, David P. Tibor, Convening Editor. California Native Plant Society. Sacramento, California.

Carville, Julie Stauffer. 1997. *Hiking Tahoe's Wildflower Trails* (revised edition of *Lingering in Tahoe's Wild Gardens*). Redmond, Washington: Lone Pine Publishing.

Case, Frederick W. and Roberta B. 1997. *Trilliums.* Portland, Oregon: Timber Press.

Coleman, Ronald A. 1995. *The Wild Orchids of California*. Ithaca, New York: Cornell University Press.

Coon, Nelson. 1974. *The Dictionary of Useful Plants.* Emmaus, Pennsylvania: Rodale Press.

D'Antionio, C. M., and P. M. Vitousek. 1992. *Biological invasions by exotic grasses, the grass/fire cycle, and global change.* Annual Review of Ecology and Systematics 23: 63–87.

Davidson, B. LeRoy. 2000. *Lewisias.* Portland, Oregon: Timber Press.

Elle, E. and R. Carney. 2003. Reproductive assurance varies with flower size in *Collinsia parviflora* (Scrophulariaceae). *American Journal of Botany* 90: 888–896.

Emery, Dara E. 1988. *Seed Propagation of Native California Plants*. Santa Barbara, California: Santa Barbara Botanical Garden.

Fauver, Toni. 1998. *Wildflower Walks and Roads of the Sierra Gold Country.* Grass Valley, California: Comstock Bonanza Press.

Felton, Ernest L. 1965. *California's Many Climates*. Palo Alto, California: Pacific Books.

Ferris, Jim, Michael Lynch, and Sheila Toner. 2006. *American River Canyon Hikes: Practical Guides to Hikes in the Canyons of the North and Middle Forks American River*. Auburn, California: Auburn State Recreation Area Canyon Keepers.

Fuller, Thomas C. and Elizabeth McClintock. 1986. *Poisonous Plants of California.* Berkeley and Los Angeles, California: University of California Press.

Graf, Michael. 1999. *Plants of the Tahoe Basin.* Berkeley and Los Angeles, California: University of California Press.

Harlow, Nora and Kristin Jacob, eds. 2003. *Wild Lilies, Irises and Grasses: Gardening with California Monocots.* Berkeley and Los Angeles, California: University of California Press.

Hickman, James C., ed. 1993. *The Jepson Manual: Higher Plants of California.* Berkeley and Los Angeles, California: University of California Press.

Horn, Elizabeth L. 1998. *Sierra Nevada Wildflowers.* Missoula, Montana: Mountain Press Publishing Company.

Jepson, Willis Linn. 1911. *A Flora of Western Middle California.* San Francisco, California: Cunningham, Curtiss & Welch.

————— 1909-1922. *A Flora of California.* Vol. I, II, III Part I and II. Berkeley, California: University of California.

————— 1925. *A Manual of the Flowering Plants of California.* Berkeley, California: University of California.

Keater, Glenn. 1990. *Complete Garden Guide to the Native Perennials of California.* San Francisco, California: Chronicle Books.

Keeley, Jon E. 2002. *Fire Management of California Shrubland Landscapes.* Environmental Management 29: 395-408.

————— 2006. *Fire Management Impacts on Invasive Plants in the Western United States.* Conservation Biology 20(2): 375-384.

Kozloff, Eugene N. and Linda H. Beidleman. 1994. *Plants of the San Francisco Bay Region: Mendocino to Monterey.* Pacific Grove, California: Sagen Press.

Laughlin, D. C., J. D. Bakker, M. T. Stoddard, M. L. Daniels, J. D. Springer, C. N. Gilar, A. M. Green, and W.W. Covington. 2004. *Toward Reference Conditions: Wildfire Effects on Flora in an Old-Growth Ponderosa Pine Forest.* Forest Ecology and Management 199: 137-152.

Mackey, Samantha and Albin Bills. 2004. *Wildflowers of Table Mountain, Butte County, California.* Chico, California: California State University, Chico publication 13.

Madden, Derek, Ken Carters, and Cathy Snyder. 2005. *Magpies and Mayflies: An Introduction to Plants and Animals of the Central Valley and Sierra Foothills.* Berkeley, California: Great Valley Books, Heyday Books.

Mandel, Stephen, Otis Wallen, Eric Peach, et al. 1998. *The American River: A Recreational Guidebook.* Auburn, California: Protect American River Canyons (PARC).

Mason, Herbert L. 1957. *A Flora of the Marshes of California.* Berkeley and Los Angeles, California: University of California Press.

Meals, Hank. 2001. *Yuba Trails 2: A Selection of Historic Hiking Trails in the Yuba River and Neighboring Watersheds.* Nevada City, California: Hank Meals.

Munz, Philip A. and David D. Keck. 1973. *A California Flora and Supplement.* Berkeley and Los Angeles, California: University of California Press.

Munz, Philip A. 2004. *Introduction to California Spring Wildflowers of the Foothills, Valley and Coast.* Revised edition. Berkeley and Los Angeles, California: University of California Press.

Murphey, Edith Van Allen. 1959. *Indian Uses of Native Plants*. Ukiah, California: Mendocino County Historical Society.

Nakamura, Gary and Julie Kierstead Nelson. 2001. *Illustrated Field Guide to Selected Rare Plants of Northern California*. Oakland, California: University of California Agriculture and Natural Resources publication 3395.

Nevada County Fire Plan Committee. 2004. *Nevada County Fire Plan*. Nevada City, California: Nevada County Planning Department.

Niehaus, Theodore F. 1976. *A Field Guide to Pacific States Wildflowers*. Peterson Field Guide Series. Boston, Massachusetts: Houghton Mifflin.

Oswald, Vernon H. 1994. *Manual of the Vascular Plants of Butte County, California*. Sacramento, California: California Native Plant Society.

Robbins, W.W., Margaret K. Bellue, and Walter S. Ball. 1951. *Weeds of California*. Sacramento, California: California Department of Agriculture.

Sawyer, John O. and Todd Keeler-Wolf. 1995. *A Manual of California Vegetation*. Sacramento, California: California Native Plant Society.

Schaffer, Jeffrey P. 1998. *The Tahoe Sierra: A Natural History Guide to 112 Hikes in the Northern Sierra*. Berkeley, California: Wilderness Press.

Schmidt, Marjorie G. 1980. *Growing California Native Plants*. Berkeley and Los Angeles, California: University of California Press.

Schnell, Donald E. 2002. *Carnivorous Plants of the United States and Canada*. Portland, Oregon: Timber Press.

Shapiro, Dr. Arthur M. 1996. "Status of Butterflies," *Sierra Nevada Ecosystem Project: Final Report to Congress*. Vol. II, Chap. 24. Davis, California: University of California, Centers for Water and Wildland Resources.

————— 2002. "Butterfly Gardening in the Northern California Foothills," *Redbud Chapter Newsletter*. Vol. 11, No. 4. Grass Valley, California: California Native Plant Society.

Skinner, John, Charley Price, et al. 2002. *Sierra Outdoors: A Recreation Guide for the North-Central Sierra Nevada*. Grass Valley, California: Aardvark Publications.

Smith, Gladys L. 1984. *A Flora of the Tahoe Basin and Neighboring Areas and Supplement*. San Francisco, California: The University of San Francisco.

Smith, M. Nevin. 2006. *Native Treasures: Gardening with the Plants of California*. Berkeley, Los Angeles, London: University of California Press.

Storer, Tracey I. and Robert L. Usinger. 1963. *Sierra Nevada History*. Berkeley and Los Angeles, California: University of California Press.

True, Gordon H. 1973. *The Ferns and Seed Plants of Nevada County, California.* San Francisco, California: California Academy of Sciences.

—————— Checklist of the Plants of Nevada County. Unpublished.

Turner, Mark and Phyllis Gustafson. 2006. *Wildflowers of the Pacific Northwest.* Portland, Oregon:Timber Press.

United States Dept. of Agriculture Forest Service. 1988. *Range Plant Handbook.*Toronto, Ontario, Canada: General Publishing Company, Ltd.

Weeden, Norman F. 1986. *A Sierra Nevada Flora.* Berkeley, California: Wilderness Press.

Whitson,Tom D., ed. 1996. *Weeds of the West.* 5th ed. Jackson Hole, Wyoming: Pioneer Press.

Wiese, Karen. 2000. *Sierra Nevada Wildflowers.* Helena, Montana: Falcon Publishing.

Witham, Carol W. 2006. *Vernal Pools of Mather Field, Sacramento County.* Sacramento, California: California Native Plant Society.

Internet Sources

Author unknown. *Cal Photos: Plants.* http://calphotos.berkeley.edu/flora/ (15 Jan. 2007)

Author unknown. *Calflora.* http://www.calflora.org/ (15 Jan. 2007)

Author unknown. *California Climate Summaries.* http:// www.wrcc.dri.edu/summary/climsmca.html (15 Jan. 2007)

Author unknown. *California Native Plant Link Exchange.* http:// www.cnplx.info (14 Jan. 2007)

Author unknown. *Fish and Wildlife Service Fire Management Handbook.* http://www.fws.gov/fire/redbook/index.htm (14 Jan. 2007)

Author unknown. *The Nature Conservancy Global Fire Initiative.* http:// www.tncfire.org (12 Jan. 2007)

Author unknown. *Public Domain Software for the Wildland Fire Community.* http://fire.org (14 Jan. 2007)

Author unknown. *Ready To Use Factoids.* http://www.cnps.org/cnps/ admin/factoids.php (20 Jan. 2007)

Brewer, William H. *Up and Down California in 1860-1864:The Journal of William H. Brewer.* http://www.yosemite.ca.us/library/ up_and_down_california/ (5 Apr. 2007)

California Native Plant Society. http://www.cnps.org (19 Jan. 2007)

Keeley, Jon E. *Jon Keeley's Products.* USGS Western Ecological Reasearch Center. http://www.werc.usgs.gov/seki/jkproducts.asp (17 Jan. 2007)

Randall, John M. and Mandy Tu. *Biological Control.* http://tncweeds.ucdavis.edu/products/handbook/06.BiologicalControl.pdf (14 Jan. 2007)

Rare Plant Scientific Committee. *CNPS Inventory.* http://cnps.web.aplus.net/cgi-bin/inv/inventory.cgi (22 Jan. 2007)

Redbud Chapter, California Native Plant Society. http://www.redbud-cnps.org/index.htm (3 Apr. 2007)

Shapiro, Dr. Arthur M. *Art Shapiro's Butterfly Site: Monitoring butterfly populations across Central California for more than 34 years....* http://butterfly.ucdavis.edu/ (16 Apr. 2007)

Wilson, Burt and Celeste Wilson. *Las Pilitas.* http://www.laspilitas.com/ (15 Jan. 2007)

Glossary

Roger McGehee and Bobbi Wilkes

Achene: The ovary that matures into a small, dry, one-seeded fruit. Sunflower and buttercup seeds are examples.

Acuminate: Quickly tapering to a point.

Acute: Gradually tapering to a point.

Alternate leaves: Only one leaf attaches at each node, and leaves are on alternate sides along the stem.

Annual: Plant that completes its life cycle in one year or less.

Anther: Pollen-producing structure at the tip of a stamen.

Aromatic: Having an odor.

Ascending: A stem that curves gradually upward.

Asymmetrical: Not symmetric in shape, not divisible into halves equal in appearance in any aspect.

Awn: A bristlelike appendage, usually at the end of a structure.

Axil: The upper angle formed between the leaf or petiole and the stem to which it is attached.

Axillary: Within the leaf axil.

Banner: The large upright petal at the top of a flower in the Pea family.

Basal leaves: Leaves located near the base of a stem.

Basal rosette: Several leaves forming a whorl at the base of the plant.

Beaked fruit: One in which the style forms a beaklike structure in the mature fruit.

Berry: A general term that describes a fleshy fruit whose seeds are not enclosed in a hard central "stone," such as blackberries and strawberries.

Biennial: Plant that germinates, produces roots and foliage during its first growing season, and then blooms, produces seed, and dies during its second.

Bilateral symmetry: Usually, irregular corollas have only one plane of symmetry. Although the flower is irregular, the left half is a mirror image of the right half.

Bisexual: A flower is bisexual if it contains both male parts (stamens) and female parts (pistils).

Bract: A leaflike structure that sometimes occurs on the stem at the base of a flower or at the base of an inflorescence of flowers.

Bracteate inflorescence: A flower head composed of both flowers and bracts.

Bractlet: A very small bract or a secondary bract occurring just below or between the sepals (as in a rose).

Bulb: An underground structure containing a short stem and several layers of fleshy modified leaves. An onion is a good example of a bulb.

Bulblet/Bulbil: A small vegetative reproductive structure that, when separated from the parent plant, forms a separate plant. It may occur on roots, stems, or leaves.

Calyx tube: The part of the calyx that is fused.

Calyx: The sepals of a flower considered as a unit, forming the outer floral layer that encloses and supports the developing bud, usually green.

Capsule: A dry fruit whose seeds are (usually) contained in several compartments (carpels).

Caudex: The woody base of an otherwise herbaceous stem.

Cauline leaves: Borne along a stem.

Cespitose: Having a densely clumped, tufted, or cushionlike growth form, with the flowers held above the clump or tuft.

Chaff: Small, paperlike bracts that sometimes occur between disk flowers or ray flowers or both in the Sunflower family.

Circumpolar: A plant that is found around the world in similar habitats.

Clawed petals: Having a long, narrow base.

Cleft leaves: Sharply cut about halfway to the central leaf vein.

Cleistogamous: Budlike, unopened flowers that generally self-pollinate.

Compound leaves: Leaves that are divided to the central leaf vein. Each segment is referred to as a leaflet. Leaves may be divided more than once (once-divided, twice-divided, etc.).

Cordate leaves: Shaped like a heart.

Corm: A fleshy, food-containing, short, underground stem that is attached to roots below and to an aboveground stem above. A Gladiolus "bulb" is a good example of a corm.

Corolla: The petals of a flower considered as a group or unit.

Cyme: A more or less flat-topped cluster of flowers in which the central or terminal flower opens first.

Decumbent: A stem that mostly lies on the ground, except for its tip, which grows up.

Decurrent leaf: A leaf with its base attached to and growing down the plant stem.

Disk flower: The central tubular flowers of a member of the Sunflower family; can occur with or without outer ray flowers.

Dissected leaves: Cut deeply, but not all the way to the central leaf vein. They are considered simple leaves rather than compound leaves.

Drupe: A fleshy fruit whose single seed is enclosed in a hard central "stone." These are sometimes referred to as "stone fruits." A peach is a good example.

Elliptical leaves: Oblong; longer than wide, with widest part of the leaf in the middle.

Entire leaves: Having a smooth margin without notches or indentations.

Epipetalous: Usually applied to stamens, suggesting that they are attached or partly attached to the petals.

Exserted: Usually applied to stamens or pistils, indicating that one or the other or both extend beyond the petals.

Fibrous: 1) Fine root hairs that are highly branched and often matted, as opposed to thick fleshy roots; 2) stem tissue containing tough fibers.

Filament: The stalk (usually threadlike) of a stamen bearing the anther.

Filiform leaves: Long and slender.

Follicle: A dry fruit that opens lengthwise along one side, releasing the seeds.

Fringed: Having ragged or finely cut margins.

Fruit: The ripened ovary, together with its seeds, of a flowering plant.

Funnelform/Funnel-shaped: Usually refers to a fused calyx or corolla which looks like a funnel: narrow at the base and gradually widening toward the top.

Glabrous: A surface that is smooth and contains no hairs.

Glandular: A surface containing glands. A gland is a small, round structure on the end of a hair that exudes a substance.

Glaucous: A surface covered with a whitish, waxy substance.

Globular: An inflorescence shaped like a sphere. A type of umbel that may be simple or compound.

Herb: A plant lacking a permanent woody stem; includes annuals, biennials, and perennials.

Herbaceous: A plant that has leaves and stems that die at the end of the growing season to the soil level and that lacks a permanent woody stem.

Herbage: The nonwoody, aboveground, nonreproductive parts of a plant, especially the leaves, stems, wings, bracts, and other soft parts as a unit.

Hypanthium: A cup-shaped structure (formed by the fusing of the bases of calyx, corolla, and stamen) that surrounds or encloses the pistils. Commonly found in roses.

Inferior ovary: An ovary that appears to be beneath its flower or to have sepals, petals, and stamens at or above the top of it.

Inflorescence: A cluster of flowers on a stem. An inflorescence may be **simple**, a single cluster, or **compound**, several clusters.

Insectivorous: A plant that is designed to capture insects.

Intergrade: To merge gradually from one extreme to another through a more or less continuous series of intermediate forms.

Irregular flower: A flower, like a pansy or a monkeyflower, that is identical on its left and right side if "split in half" on the flower's surface vertically, but not identical if it is split horizontally. Of course this only works if one is looking at the flower right side up!

Keel petals: Two lower petals in a Pea family flower that are fused near their tips, and that envelop the stamens and pistil.

Lanceolate leaves: Shaped like a lance, widest in the basal half, often tapered to an acute tip.

Latex: A milky, often sticky, secretion that coagulates on exposure to air.

Leaf sheath: That part of a leaf that wraps around a stem.

Leaflet: A leaflike segment of a compound leaf.

Legume: The fruit of a member of the Pea family. A pea pod is a good example. When mature, the pod opens along two sides, exposing the seeds.

Ligulate: A strap-shaped part on a flower or membranous appendage on a leaf. Often refers to the lobed single petal of the ray flower in the Sunflower family.

Limb: Refers to the separate or lobed upper parts of a fused corolla or calyx. These upper parts or limbs look like separate petals or sepals as they arise from and spread outward from the fused corolla/calyx tube below. An example would be members of the Phlox family.

Linear leaves: Long and thin and flat, resembling grass leaves.

Lobed corolla or calyx: A segment of the unfused portion of a corolla or calyx.

Lobed leaves: Having deeply indented margins, but the cut does not extend all the way to the central leaf vein.

Locule: A compartment in a compound pistil or anther.

Loculicidal: A fruit that opens by splitting down the center of a locule of a compound ovary.

Matted: A surface containing many intertwined hairs.

-merous: Refers to the number of flower parts. For example, a 3-merous flower has 3 sepals, 3 petals, etc.

Mucilaginous: Slimy.

Mycorrhiza: A symbiotic relationship between a soil fungus and the roots of a plant.

Mycotrophic: A species of plant that maintains a symbiotic relationship with mycorrhizal soil fungi.

Nectar glands: Glands near the base of the petals that secrete nectar. These are also called nectaries or nectary disks.

Needlelike leaves: Very slender; pine and fir needles are good examples.

Node: The place on a stem where leaves, flower stems, or branches originate.

Nutlet: Each segment of a compound ovary, such as in the Borage family.

Oblanceolate leaves: Similar to lanceolate leaves, except they taper at the base rather than at the tip.

Oblong leaves: Look like round leaves that have been stretched at both ends. Their sides are parallel and their ends are rounded.

Obovate leaves: Shaped like an egg and attached to stem at the narrower end.

Obtuse leaves: Leaf tip is rounded.

Opposite leaves: Two leaves attach at each node, and each leaf is located directly across from the other.

Ovary: The part of a pistil in which one or more eggs are produced and fertilization occurs. It matures into a fruit.

Ovate leaves: Shaped like an egg and attached at the broad end.

Palmately compound leaves: A leaf divided into leaflets radiating from a common point, like the fingers on one's hand.

Panicle: Branched inflorescence in which basal or lateral flowers (or some of them) open before the terminal or central flowers on any branch.

Pappus: A modified calyx composed of scales, bristles, and awns occurring on top of the ovaries/achenes of disk and/or ray flowers in the Sunflower family; aids in seed dispersal.

Pedicel: A stem leading to a single flower.

Peduncle: A stem leading to a single flower, as in a tulip, or to an inflorescence.

Pepo: The fleshy fruit of a member of the Cucumber family. It differs from a berry by having a "rind." Gourds and watermelons are good examples.

Perennial: A plant that lives for more than 2 years, sometimes for many years.

Perfect flower: One with both male and female parts; bisexual.

Perianth: A collective term for the sepals and petals as a unit, excluding pistils and stamens.

Personate: A two-lipped flower with a prominent petal that projects outward, "closing off" the flower throat. Pollinators push their way past the projecting petal into the throat to pollinate the flower.

Petal: Flower part inside the sepals, usually brightly colored and usually serving to attract pollinators.

Petiole: A leaf stalk.

Phyllaries: Special bracts that occur on the receptacle of the inflorescence (flower head) of a member of the Sunflower family. The phyllaries, as a group, are often referred to as an involucre.

Pinnately compound leaves: A leaf divided into leaflets along the central leaf vein. If there is a single leaflet at the end of the central leaf vein, that leaflet is called the terminal leaflet.

Pistil: The female part of a flower composed of the ovary, style, and stigma.

Plicate leaves: Having accordion-like folds or pleats.

Prostrate: A stem that lies entirely on the ground.

Pubescent: Hairy.

Raceme: Unbranched inflorescence of flowers with stalks; flowers opening from bottom to top.

Radial symmetry: A flower has radial symmetry if it is symmetrical in many planes. Regular flowers have radial symmetry.

Ray flower: Long outer margin flowers of a flower head in the Sunflower family; can occur with or without central disk flowers.

Receptacle: The base of the flower on which the flower parts are borne.

Recurved: Gradually curved downward or backward.

Regular: A flower that is radially symmetrical, so that no matter where the flower is "split" in half when looking down upon it, each half is identical to the other half, such as in a yellow buttercup or a rose.

Rhizome: A horizontal, underground stem.

Salverform: A slender tube opening and spreading abruptly at the top, typically used to describe a fused corolla flaring open near the petal tips.

Scalloped (Wavy): An edge that undulates in and out.

Scape: A leafless flowering stalk; however, bracts may occur along the stalk that can resemble small leaves.

Scorpioid: An inflorescence that is coiled, like a caterpillar.

Sepal: The outermost structures of a flower, often acting as protectors of the flower when it is in bud; often green.

Serrate (Toothed) leaves: Having small, sawlike teeth along their margins.

Sessile: Stalkless; without a petiole, peduncle, or pedicel.

Sheathing petiole: A petiole of a leaf that envelops a stem.

Silicle: A short silique, in which the fruit is only slightly longer than wide.

Silique: The fruit of a member of the Mustard family. The seeds are borne on a thin central membrane (septum) and are released as the two halves of the fruit move away from each other.

Simple leaf: A single leaf that is not divided into smaller leaflets.

Spatula-shaped leaves: Having a narrow handlelike base and a broad, flat, rounded end.

Spike: An inflorescence in which the flowers are attached to the main stem without stalks; flowers open from bottom to top.

Spur: A hollow projection of a petal or sepal, usually containing nectar glands.

Stamen: The male part of a flower, composed of the filament and the anther.

Staminode: A stamen that lacks an anther, and is therefore sterile.

Stigma: The tip of a pistil. It is usually sticky and functions as a receptor for pollen.

Stipule: A small leaflike appendage found at the leaf node, sometimes a spine.

Stolon: A prostrate, aboveground stem that forms roots and shoots at nodes, a runner.

Stoloniferous: A plant that forms stolons, such as a strawberry plant.

Style: The narrow, stalklike part of a pistil that connects the stigma and the ovary.

Subshrub: Plant with the lower stems woody and the upper stems and twigs not woody. Dies back seasonally.

Subtend: Occurring immediately below.

Succulent: Having fleshy leaves and/or stems designed for storing water.

Superior ovary: An ovary that sits above the petals.

Symmetrical: See bilateral and radial.

Taproot: Main, tapered root that generally grows straight down into soil and has smaller, lateral branches.

Tendril: A modified stem or leaf used for support or climbing.

Terminal leaflet: Leaflet on the end of a pinnately compound leaf. (Not all pinnately compound leaves have terminal leaflets.)

Trailing stem: Prostrate and aboveground; does not form roots.

Triangular leaves: Shaped like broad triangles and attached to stem at the broad end.

Trifoliate (3-foliate) leaves: Compound leaves composed of three leaflets. A clover leaf is a good example.

Truncate: The tip (or the base) of the leaf looks like it has been cut straight across with a pair of scissors.

Tuber: A fleshy, food-containing segment of an underground stem. A potato is a good example of a tuber.

Tubercles: Small, rounded, pimplelike structures on a surface.

Tubular: Shaped like a tube. This term is used for the corolla or calyx or perianth.

Umbel: The pedicels join the stem at a common point, causing the inflorescence to look like an umbrella or a sphere. It may be simple or compound.

Urn-shaped: A constriction occurring at the mouth of a corolla.

Whorled leaves: Several leaves attach at each node and are arranged in a ring.

Widespread species: One that occurs over a large geographic area, but may or may not be abundant.

Wings: The two side petals on a flower in the Pea family.

Woody: Containing supportive or protective dead tissue. This dead tissue does not develop on annual or herbaceous plants.

Xerophytic: Adapted to dry environments.

*I*ndex

666666666

Index

M

Habitat Codes
AQ = Aquatic
CH = Chaparral
FW = Foothill Woodland
GR = Grasslands
LC = Lower Conifer Forest
MM = Mountain Meadows
RO = Rock Outcrops
RP = Riparian
SA = Subalpine/Alpine
SG = Serpentine/Gabbro
SP = Sagebrush/Pine
UC = Upper Conifer Forest
VP = Vernal Pools